DATE DUE

OCT 27 79			
GAYLORD			PRINTED IN U.S.A.

DEFENSE OF THE POOR

IN CRIMINAL CASES

IN AMERICAN STATE COURTS

A FIELD STUDY AND REPORT

LEE SILVERSTEIN

VOLUME 2: STATE REPORTS

76576

AMERICAN BAR FOUNDATION

Board of Directors

William T. Gossett ....President

Ross L. Malone ....Vice-President

Robert K. Bell ....Secretary

Glenn M. Coulter ....Treasurer

Robert M. Benjamin	**Ex officio:**
Harold J. Gallagher	Paul Carrington
Erwin N. Griswold	Joseph H. Gordon
W. Page Keeton	Edward W. Kuhn
Phil C. Neal	Edward E. Murane
Whitney North Seymour	Lewis F. Powell, Jr.
Harold A. Smith	

Special Adviser:
E. Blythe Stason

Executive Committee

Harold J. Gallagher
Ross L. Malone
Phil C. Neal
Whitney North Seymour
William T. Gossett, Ex officio

Administration

Geoffrey C. Hazard, Jr. ....Administrator

John C. Leary ....Deputy Administrator/Librarian

William B. Eldridge ..Deputy Administrator/Project Development

Donald M. McIntyre, Jr. ....Research Supervisor

Noble Stephens ....Controller

iii

INTRODUCTION TO VOLUMES 2 AND 3

These two volumes contain the individual survey reports for the 50 states and the District of Columbia. They were written by the state reporters and approved in each instance by the American Bar Association state committee or the committee chairman. (See volume 1, pages 11 and 174, as to the state committees.) Taken together, the reports are an encyclopedia of criminal procedure in the states as well as a summary of the survey findings. It is hoped that they will amplify and explain the national report in volume 1.

Unfortunately the state reports could not be published as early as originally hoped. Several of the reporters were delayed by illnesses, accidents, and pressing business obligations. The task of editing the reports and inserting the docket studies and other needed information required considerable time. Some of the state reports or articles based on the state surveys have already been published in various legal periodicals with permission of the Bar Foundation. (Most are listed in volume 1, pages 271-275). The present publication, however, is more complete since it includes the docket studies and late questionnaire returns. It also has the advantage of making all the reports available in one publication.

In order to make the state reports as current as possible, I have inserted notes in brackets to indicate recent changes in statutes, creation of new defender offices, and other changes. The longer notes are labeled "Editor's note"; for the shorter ones identification did not seem necessary. These notes reflect all known developments to July 1, 1965.

The reports, with minor exceptions, are written according to a common outline. Thus, the reader who has used one report can readily find the information he requires in any of the others. The fullest and most provocative discussion of assigned counsel systems is in the reports for Alaska, Arizona, California, Colorado, District of Columbia, Georgia, Idaho, Iowa, Maryland, Michigan, Missouri, Montana, New Jersey, New Mexico, Oregon, Utah, Virginia, Washington, West Virginia, Wisconsin, and Wyoming. Defenders are most fully discussed in the reports from California, Connecticut, District of Columbia, Florida, Illinois, Indiana, Louisiana, Massachusetts, Minnesota, Missouri, Nebraska, Oklahoma, Pennsylvania, Rhode Island, and Tennessee. In particular, the section giving conclusions and recommendations that appears at the end of each report may provide ideas useful not only to that state but also to other states beset with similar problems.

Because the reports were written by many different persons, they vary in style and points of emphasis. The Bar Foundation staff has attempted to achieve a measure of uniformity, but minor differences may obtain from one report to another in such details as punctuation, capitalization, and citation form. For these we ask the reader's indulgence. My legal assistants and I are responsible for the docket study sections of the reports and in addition for considerable sections of the reports from Florida, Michigan, Nevada, Pennsylvania, Texas, Vermont, and West Virginia.

INTRODUCTION

Concerning the mail questionnaires, we doubt the reliability of the returns where less than 50% of the addressees responded. Nevertheless, reports of such returns are included as roughly indicative of opinion in the states, even though they may not be representative of the whole group of judges, prosecutors, or assigned counsel. In general, however, the reader will find that responses were very good in most states, especially from judges and prosecutors. In the docket studies the report is usually omitted if data were available for less than 80% of the sample cases. (See volume 1, pages 177-179, as to research methods.)

Again, I would like to thank the state reporters and committee members for their outstanding contributions to the project.

LEE SILVERSTEIN

Chicago, July 15, 1965

ALABAMA

Prof. Sam A. Beatty, Tuscaloosa,
and J. Louis Wilkinson, Associate, Birmingham

A. INTRODUCTION

Alabama, a "deep south" state, in 1960 had a population of 3,266,740. The state is divided into 33 judicial circuits, each having at least one circuit judge and one circuit solicitor (prosecuting attorney). In addition, each of its 67 counties has its own county solicitor (prosecuting attorney). The following counties were selected for survey:

TABLE 1

Sample Counties

County (chief city)	1960 population in thousands	Location in state	Remarks
Jefferson (D) (Birmingham)	634.8	North central	Iron and steel, heavy and light manufacturing, commercial center
Mobile	314.3	Southwest	Maritime and commercial center
Fayette (D)	16.1	West central	Farming, light manufacturing
Madison (D) (Huntsville)	117.3	North	Space engineering, heavy and light manufacturing, farming, George C. Marshall Space Center
Montgomery (D)	169.2	South central	State capitol, commercial center
Russell (D) (Phenix City)	46.3	Southeast	Farming, suburban (near Fort Benning, Georgia)

(D) indicates that a docket study was made.

Table 2 supplies additional information on the counties surveyed.

B. CRIMINAL PROCEDURE AS IT AFFECTS INDIGENT PERSONS

Jurisdiction to return indictments and try felony cases in Alabama is vested exclusively in the circuit court. The majority of felony cases begin with the arrest of the suspect. Alabama law (*Ala. Code, tit.* 15, §160) requires that the defendant be taken forthwith before a magistrate. In most counties, the magistrate is a county judge or a city recorder and is almost without exception a lawyer. In some parts of Mobile County justices of the peace who are not lawyers act as committing magistrates, but in all the other sample counties committing magis-

1

TABLE 2
Additional Data on Sample Counties

County	Felony defendants, 1962	% indigent	% indigent who waived counsel	Lawyers in private practice	No. of appointments of counsel, felony cases, 1962	No. of lawyers who served, 1962	Typical payment for felony guilty plea
Fayette	25	60*	25*	5	ND	ND	$100
Madison	269	75*	60*	70	30	12	50
Mobile	775	20*	0	240	ND	ND	ND
Russell	152	33*	0	13	ND	ND	ND
Jefferson	1829	33*	0	550*	ND	ND	$100
Montgomery	450-500*	7*	ND	198	35	ND	$100

* denotes estimate. ND indicates no data available. Estimates for Fayette and Mobile were based on solicitor's information; for Madison, on judge's information; for Montgomery, on circuit clerk's information.

trates are invariably lawyers. At the appearance before the magistrate, state law requires that the magistrate either formally examine the defendant or set a date for his formal examination not later than 10 days from the date of first appearance, during which period the defendant may be bailed in all but capital felony cases. In practice, the first appearance before the magistrate is the time at which the defendant is formally examined and bail is set, unless the defendant at this time waives his right to preliminary hearing. Bail is usually set by the magistrate independently of the solicitor's office. It follows no set schedule but is determined by the magistrate's evaluation, which varies with such factors as severity of the offense and absence of mitigating factors. In Russell County there is a fixed schedule which is followed by committing magistrates, and in Fayette County the practice is to follow recommendations from the solicitor in setting bail. In three of the sample counties, first appearance before the magistrate usually takes place within 25 to 48 hours following arrest. Appearance is usually within 12 hours after arrest in Madison and Fayette Counties, whereas in Jefferson County, the largest in Alabama, it does not generally take place until between 73 hours and 7 days after arrest. Preliminary hearings are generally held in all felony cases in each of the sample counties and are rarely waived.

Throughout Alabama the formal charge against the defendant in all felony cases is made by grand jury indictment. In Fayette, Jefferson, and Madison Counties, counsel is appointed at arraignment on the indictment. In Montgomery, counsel is provided either between indictment and arraignment or at the time of arraignment. In these four counties, therefore, there is no opportunity as a practical matter to reduce bail. In Russell County, however, counsel is usually appointed at the first appearance of the defendant before the magistrate; and in Mobile there is no fixed procedure, since the defendant is brought into court for appointment of counsel at some time between arrest and arraignment. Consequently it is true that in these two counties there may be an opportunity to seek reduction in bail by virtue of earlier appointment of assigned counsel.

Procedure for appointment of counsel is remarkably consistent throughout the six counties surveyed in Alabama. Counsel is generally provided for the indigent at his first appearance before a magistrate or at arraignment. The defendant is simply brought into the courtroom and the judge asks him if he can afford counsel. Upon receiving a negative reply, the judge then asks the indigent accused if he wants appointed counsel and explains that this service will be provided at no cost to the accused if he requests it. There is no investigation in any of the sample counties to determine indigency. The judge simply takes the defendant's conclusion about his ability to retain counsel as determinative of this question.

In Jefferson and Fayette Counties the judge goes further and urges the defendant to accept appointment of counsel. In Madison, Russell, Montgomery, and Fayette Counties, however, the judge merely explains that counsel will be provided at no cost to the accused and appoints counsel only if the defendant then requests it.

Compensation for attorneys is provided by statute in capital cases only. A minimum of $50 and maximum of $100 is fixed, the amount to be determined by the trial judge. In practice, all attorneys who represent indigents in capital felony cases are given the maximum sum. Since the *Gideon* case, the legislature has set aside a fixed sum for the compensation of counsel for indigents in noncapital cases, but there is no statutory assurance that counsel will be paid in the event the amount is used up prior to his assignment. In Montgomery, the average fee in such cases has been about $35 when funds were available. No provision is made under state law for reimbursement of defense counsel's costs of investigation, preparation, expert witnesses, etc., nor has any county so provided. There is no public defender system in any of the sample counties.

In none of the sample counties is counsel provided for misdemeanants. This is consonant with the practice throughout the whole state. In two of the sample counties, Madison and Fayette, counsel is not usually appointed for a defendant who pleads guilty, although the plea of guilty would not necessarily be a waiver of the right to counsel in a capital felony proceeding. In the other sample counties, counsel is provided even where the plea is guilty, and the appointed counsel is expected to be present at the sentencing. His presence is expected also where a trial is held and the defendant is convicted. In all of the sample counties, counsel is provided for the sentencing of a defendant who has pleaded guilty, and, in all the counties save Jefferson, counsel will be provided for the sentencing of a defendant who has been convicted after a trial. Mobile, Russell, and Montgomery Counties provide counsel on appeal, while Madison and Jefferson do not. There were no data available from Fayette. In habeas corpus, coram nobis, and other postconviction remedies, five of the sample counties provide counsel. Only one of the sample counties, Mobile, provides counsel in cases of probation revocation or sexual psychopath hearings, and two of them provide counsel in cases involving civil commitment of the mentally ill.

Counsel appointed for trial usually continue to serve on appeal. There is no additional compensation for counsel on appeal and no allowance for travel expenses to the state capital.

C. OPINIONS OF THE JUDGES

One judge was interviewed in each of the six sample counties. Questionnaires were mailed to 29 of the remaining circuit judges in the state. Replies were received from 22 judges, a response rate of 76%.

On question 7a of the interview, "Under an ideal system, at what stage in a criminal case do you think the indigent person should first be provided with a lawyer if he wants one?", all of the six judges thought the appointment should be at an earlier stage than the present system requires (viz., arraignment). Two thought the appointment should be made between the arrest and first appearance before a magistrate, and two thought it should take place at the first appearance before a magistrate. One judge favored appointment between the first appearance and preliminary hearing, leaving only one of the six who thought appointment need not take place until the time of the preliminary hearing itself. Of the 22 judges responding to the mailed questionnaire, 17 concurred in the thought that appointment should precede arraignment. Twelve of these favored a time of selection not later than preliminary hearing. (See Table 3.)

Interestingly, none of the 22 suggested a time for appointment later than that presently required under Alabama law. There seems to be little doubt that an overwhelming majority of the judges participating in this study were keenly aware of the value to the indigent of representation in the initial stages of the criminal process. However, on the question of unfairness to the indigent accused if he does not get a lawyer at the stage designated by the judge, the judges in both groups were almost evenly divided in their responses, only 12 of 23 feeling that it was unfair to the indigent if appointment were made at some later stage. Five judges gave equivocal answers or left the question blank. On the problem of financing such a system, 17 of 19 who gave definite answers thought financing was practically possible, but many expressed grave doubts both as to the manner in which this was done (many preferring state to federal handling of the problem) and the severity of the tax burden they felt would necessarily be imposed.

On question 8a of the judge interview, "Under an ideal system do you think a lawyer should be provided for the indigent accused in certain specified types of cases and proceedings?", all of the interviewed judges who gave definite responses (four of six) felt that in habeas corpus, coram nobis, and other postconviction remedies counsel should be provided. The same result was found in response to the same query for both probation revocation and sexual psychopath hearings. Three of the four judges who gave a positive response also agreed that counsel should be provided in civil commitments of the mentally ill (including alcoholics and narcotic addicts), while a majority (three of five) favored counsel for the defendant being sentenced following a plea of guilty. Only in the case where the indigent was charged with a misdemeanor did a majority (three of four) feel that counsel should not be provided for the pauper defendant.

Judges answering mail questionnaires agreed with those interviewed in all

4

cases except in regard to probation revocation hearings, where 13 of 21 (63%) would not require counsel to be offered under the ideal system. It should be noted that only a bare majority (12 of 22) favored appointments where the defendant was being sentenced following a plea of guilty.

On the question "Is it unfair to the indigent person if he does not have a lawyer for the cases and proceedings noted in the preceding question?", a slight majority of the two groups answered affirmatively for cases involving civil commitments of the mentally ill and sexual psychopath hearings. An overwhelming majority of the two groups voted "no" where either a misdemeanor would be charged or a probation revocation hearing would be conducted (17 of 20 and 21 of 24, respectively). Only 14 of the 28 judges responded directly to the question of whether it was feasible to finance a system to provide counsel in the kinds of proceedings already noted, but this group was unanimous in conceding that such a system could be financed, even though many seemed to feel that to do so would perhaps overburden the taxpayer either directly or indirectly.

Asked "What percentage of felony defendants appearing before you are indigent?", the interviewed judges gave estimates which ranged from 10% to 75%, the average estimate being approximately 32% (all six responded). Of the 22 judges answering by mail, 21 gave estimates which ranged from 10% to 99%, with the average approximating 42%. On the question of what percentage of these persons waived appointment of counsel when offered, the average estimate was approximately 30%, ranging from as little as zero to as much as 85%.

To the interview question, "What system do you use for finding lawyers to appoint in ordinary criminal cases?", two of the judges admitted to using any attorney present in the courtroom, while two others used a roster of all the attorneys admitted to practice. Only one judge used his own list of names in making his selections. Of the mail group 9 out of 22 used a roster of all the attorneys admitted to practice, subject to reasonable exceptions (age, infirmity, etc.); lists furnished by the bar association and personal lists were fairly frequently used (5 of 22, and 4 of 22, respectively). Three of these judges used any attorney who was present in court, while one indicated that he used no definite system in this regard. On the question "Do you have a special system for very serious cases, such as crimes punishable by death or a long prison sentence?", 11 of 25 judges (44%) gave an affirmative answer. Some made a special effort to find counsel they felt to be leaders to represent such indigents, while others liked to appoint two defenders rather than the customary one in these instances. Of the six judges interviewed four indicated that they would appoint a lawyer whom the indigent accused requested by name. The interviewed judges also were unanimous in stating that they would appoint separate lawyers in cases where there were two defendants who had interests that might conflict with each other. If the defendant objected to the appointed lawyer, two of the interviewed judges averred that they would appoint someone else. Three, however, would refuse, although two of the three would appoint another attorney if the defendant could show good reason for not wanting to keep the originally assigned defender.

On the question whether lawyers should be compensated for their services to the indigent, an overwhelming majority of both groups (26 of 27) answered in favor of what they felt to be reasonable compensation. The amounts suggested ranged from $25 up to the minimum fee schedule of the bar, depending upon the nature and circumstances of the case involved. On the question "Would you care to comment on whether present compensation to lawyers for services to indigents is adequate?", five of the six judges interviewed gave a definite answer and were unanimous in their feeling that present fees in such cases are inadequate. Out of 28 judges in both groups 26 felt that the lawyer should be reimbursed for his out-of-pocket expenses incurred in the investigation and preparation of the indigent's defense.

To the questions "How do you think appointed lawyers compare with lawyers retained by defendants?", and "How do you think appointed lawyers compare with district attorneys?", response indicated that judges feel that appointed counsel compare favorably to both retained counsel and district attorneys. Four of the six interviewed judges acknowledged that appointed counsel were on a par with retained counsel, two disagreeing, while five of the six felt that appointed counsel compared favorably with the district attorney, one disagreeing. Of 27 judges who answered this question, 24 definitely concurred in the favorable comparison. Almost all those judges who felt the assigned counsel were not on a par with retained counsel or district attorneys cited lack of experience as the chief difference.

On the question, "Do you have a problem in getting lawyers to serve as appointed counsel?", all six of the interviewed judges said they had experienced no appreciable difficulty, and all estimated that less than 1% asked to be excused. Of 20 judges answering this question, 15 unequivocally said they had little or no trouble getting lawyers to serve as appointed counsel. Three of the four judges interviewed who answered the question directly said they would excuse an attorney from serving if he had a valid reason. One judge said he would not excuse any attorney from serving regardless of the circumstances.

In general, as one might expect, the younger judges did favor earlier appointment of counsel than did the older members of the bench. For example, 10 of the younger group favored appointment of counsel at or before the indigent's first appearance before a magistrate; only two of the older judges preferred this early appointment, while three of the five judges who favored the present time of appointment (at arraignment) were in the senior category. There was no significant indication, however, that the groups differed with respect to any general dissatisfaction with the present system, nor did either show any marked difference in willingness to suggest ways in which the system might be improved. In fact, most seemed more interested in defending the process of indigent defense from federal encroachment than in actually defending the indigent in state prosecutions.

D. OPINIONS OF THE CIRCUIT SOLICITORS

Five of the six circuit solicitors from the sample counties were personally interviewed; the remainder were mailed questionnaires, which resulted in 14 replies, or a response rate of 44%.

These judicial officers devote their full time, over 30 hours per week, to their duties. Only five of those responding by mail reported adequate funds to run their offices. The chief complaint concerning lack of funds for investigation, etc., was that, save for automobile travel expenses, no reimbursement was available. Of those personally interviewed, however, four of the five felt they had adequate funds to run their offices. One of these had six full-time lawyers and four full-time secretaries as employees; one had two full-time lawyers, one full-time and two part-time secretaries; one had three part-time lawyers and two part-time secretaries; and one had two part-time lawyers, two full-time secretaries, and one investigator as employees. The one solicitor interviewed who did not feel satisfied with funds available to run his office had as employees four part-time lawyers and one full-time secretary.

The solicitors possessed varied experience. Five had a year or less in the office, while one had between 2 and 4 years, five had from 5 to 9 years, another five had from 10 to 14 years, and two had 15 years or longer. On the other hand, four had practiced criminal law for 15 years or longer, two had 10 to 14 years of such experience, and five had 5 to 9 years of experience. Another five had from two to four years of experience, and three had a year or less.

The solicitors' opinions about the time of appointing counsel are shown in Table 3 below. Considering an ideal system, five solicitors felt that arraignment was the stage at which a lawyer should first be made available to the indigent; five felt that between the filing of the indictment and arraignment was the proper stage; one said that after preliminary hearing but before the indictment is filed would be proper. One solicitor favored availability at the preliminary hearing, and one favored some time between the first appearance before a magistrate and preliminary hearing. Three solicitors chose first appearance before a magistrate as the proper time; two maintained that a lawyer should first be made available between arrest and first appearance, one agreeing with this choice in capital cases only, insisting that in noncapital cases, appointment at the trial would suffice. Nine thought it would not be unfair if counsel were not provided at the stage selected, six felt it would be unfair, and two had no comment. Two felt this depended upon the circumstances. One of these said: "It depends on the circumstances of the case. If he is guilty and has given a statement to that effect, it is not [unfair]."

While there was substantial agreement that a system of counsel appointments should be financed, no general method was proposed. Some believed that more taxes would solve the problem. One suggested a trial tax. Another recommended federal financing, with state control over operations. One solicitor suggested that in the long run a public defender system would be more economical.

When questioned about the kinds of cases and proceedings in which counsel for indigents should be available under an ideal system, 9 solicitors were in favor of counsel at sentencing for the defendant who pleaded guilty and 10 were opposed; 11 favored counsel at sentencing for the defendant convicted by trial, and 8 opposed this. Twelve were in favor of providing counsel in habeas corpus, coram nobis, or other postconviction remedies, and seven were not receptive. One remarked that coram nobis was being "abused."

7

In hearings on probation revocation, the figures were almost reversed, with 12 against providing counsel and 6 in favor. Sexual psychopath hearings were considered serious enough by 12 to justify availability of a lawyer, but 7 did not believe an ideal system required counsel. The responding solicitors were 15 to 2 against providing counsel ideally in misdemeanor cases. Considering civil commitment of the mentally ill, alcoholics, and narcotics addicts, the solicitors were 10 against and 8 for availability of counsel. Although these responses showed much division of opinion, on the question whether it is unfair to the indigent if he does not have a lawyer for such cases, the overwhelming sentiment was definitely "no," except in habeas corpus and coram nobis postconviction remedies, where there were 9 "yes" and 10 "no" answers. Perhaps the prevailing sentiment was expressed by one comment: "Capitalism is not based on the idea of free service to the individual. We pay the prosecutor because the crime is against society as a whole. Society pays—let the individual pay." If this is a prevalent view, it is unfortunate that the concept of justice by adequate representation has been confounded with the profit motive.

In Alabama, the assigned counsel system is the means by which counsel is provided for the indigent defendant. Sixteen solicitors thought that appointed counsel were of the same quality as retained counsel, while only two felt they were better, and one solicitor thought assigned counsel were not as able as those retained. But, of those who commented, seven considered the present system for determining indigency too lenient and seven considered it about right. One interviewee complained that there was in fact no system, because the appointing judge simply took the defendant's word; another commented that the system was inadequate. No actual counts were available on the number of felony defendants who were indigent. Estimates ranged from 90% to as few as 3%. Most put the figure around 65%. Solicitors estimated that 1% to 90% of these indigent felony defendants waive appointment of counsel.

The solicitors were not hesitant about commenting on whether lawyers representing indigents should be compensated. Of the 35 who responded, 19 said that compensation was proper, and 16 felt that present compensation rates are inadequate. Suggestions about compensation were varied. Some proposed pay rates according to type of case, e.g., $25 for plea of guilty, $50 for noncapital case, and $200 to $500 for each capital case. Another suggestion was that the local bar fee schedule should control. Also, 17 felt that the lawyer should be reimbursed for out-of-pocket expenses for investigation and preparation, with only 2 disagreeing.

Only 2 of the 19 solicitors replied that they did not reveal to defense counsel such things as confessions, statements of witnesses, and exhibits; 17 replied affirmatively and 9 stated a practice of disclosing everything. In individual instances, only witnesses' lists were revealed to the adversary, or expert witnesses' statements, or confessions. Some made revelation depend on the circumstances of each case, and one solicitor made this depend on his opponent's ethics. No uniform practice, however, was revealed.

Nor was there uniformity in the comments dealing with improvement of the present system. Indeed, five had no comment at all. Four felt that adequate compensation was the paramount need, and two suggested legislation generally. One solicitor suggested a public defender, one was opposed to a public defender, and one thought the present system all right. Only two raised the question of determining indigency, while one thought the system should be enlarged to cover more types of cases. There was one sparkling reply: "Looks like our country is in the midst of Hades."

E. OPINIONS OF DEFENSE ATTORNEYS

Twenty-seven questionnaires were mailed to attorneys who had at one time or another represented indigent defendants. Fifteen replies established a response rate of 55%, somewhat larger than that of the solicitors queried.

The lawyers so responding had professional experience ranging from 3 years of practice (two responses) to 15 to 29 years of practice (five responses). Two had 5 years of practice, four had 6 to 9 years of practice, and two had 10 to 14 years' experience. The lawyers were evenly divided as to appointments in 1962; eight had been appointed to represent indigent accused in a state trial court of general jurisdiction during that year, while seven had not. Of those so appointed, five represented two persons each, two represented one person each, and one represented six to nine persons. Five of these defendants were charged with crimes punishable by death or life imprisonment. These eight lawyers reported that before they had represented an accused person by appointment in 1962, two had handled 10 to 19 criminal cases, two had handled 20 to 49 criminal cases, and four had experience in 50 cases or more.

In connection with the last case in which they were appointed in 1962, only one was appointed between arrest and first appearance, i.e., arraignment before a magistrate; two were appointed after the indictment was filed but before arraignment; three were appointed at arraignment; one was appointed after arraignment but before trial; and one was appointed at trial. Six of these eight stated that they were appointed in time to represent the accused adequately; of the two answering negatively, one was appointed at trial, the other at arraignment. The last case in which they were appointed concerned auto theft for one of the lawyers, burglary for two, forgery for one, murder for two, and possession of a still for one. Three answered that they received compensation for their services in that case, while five did not; one was repaid in part for out-of-pocket expenses, but seven were not; and six of the eight counsel answered that their fee for this same service to a client who had retained them would range from $100 to $1000.

None of the counsel represented any indigent defendants on appeal in a state court in 1962, and only 2 of the 15 represented indigents in postconviction proceedings. The number of cases and the compensation received were not given.

Only 5 felt that the present system for assignment of lawyers to represent indigent defendants is unfair to indigents, while 10 said it is fair. However, all 15 suggested changes. Seven would appoint a lawyer at an earlier stage (at preliminary hearing or before arraignment), and 10 would pay out-of-pocket expenses of lawyers in investigation and preparation. Indeed, 10 of the 15 counsel who responded said that the system was not fair to lawyers; the remaining 5 thought it fair. All these lawyers thought that appointed counsel should be paid for their services, and four thought counsel should be paid more. One suggested that counsel be provided in additional kinds of cases, such as serious misdemeanors. Two recommended the creation of a public defender office.

F. COMPARISONS AMONG JUDGES, PROSECUTORS, AND DEFENSE ATTORNEYS

The survey revealed several possible differences in the attitudes among judges and prosecutors. For the purpose of comparison, the judges were divided into two groups of approximately equal size according to years of service on their present courts. The half with the longest periods of service are called senior judges, and the remainder are called junior judges. Results are shown in Table 3 below.

An interesting possible difference in the attitude of defense counsel as compared with judges and prosecutors is suggested by the fact that while 23 of 28 judges and 14 of 19 prosecutors were quite definite in feeling that counsel for the indigent should be appointed at a stage earlier than the present law provides (a group response rate of almost 80%), less than 50% (7 of 15) of those persons who had actually defended indigents suggested that appointment be made at an earlier date, a provision which would seemingly benefit their group most significantly.

It is also interesting (and perhaps sad) to note that while two-thirds of the defense group felt the present system was unfair to them, only one-third felt the same system was unfair to the accused.

The three groups concurred overwhelmingly in the feeling that counsel should be paid; but only 4 of 15 in the defense group suggested higher pay, while 31 out of 35 judges and solicitors considered the present pay standards inadequate. Along the same line, only 67% of defense counsel felt that out-of-pocket expenses incurred in the investigation and preparation of an indigent person's case should be paid, while over 90% of the judges and prosecutors favored payment.

Only 1 of 15 in the defense counsel group suggested that counsel be provided in cases of misdemeanors. This is in comparison with an equally large percentage of judges and solicitors who disapprove of such a practice.

In conclusion, the general attitude of the defense counsel group seems to be one of less interest and more apathy than is true of the other groups. Perhaps this is explainable or even to be expected, since under the assigned counsel system the individuals comprising this group have less frequent professional contact with indigent persons and concomitantly reflect less interest in the whole problem, including both the indigent person and their own personal relationship to his possible defense.

G. THE DOCKET STUDY

The docket study affords information about disposition of cases in five counties and sentencing in four counties. Otherwise, the records available were so incomplete that they did not show such information as whether the defendant had counsel, whether he was released on bail, and whether a preliminary hearing was held.

TABLE 3
Comparison Among Judges, Prosecutors, and Defense Attorneys

	Jr. judges	Sr. judges	Prosecutors	Total
Total responding	16	12	19	47
Ideal stage for first appointment of counsel				
1. Between arrest and first appearance before a magistrate	3	2	2	7
2. At first appearance before a magistrate	7	0	3	10
3. Between first appearance and preliminary hearing	1	2	1	4
4. At preliminary hearing	1	2	1	4
5. After preliminary hearing but before filing of indictment or information	0	1	1	2
6. After filing of indictment or information but before arraignment thereon	2	2	5	9
7. At arraignment on indictment or information	2	3	5	10
8. No response	0	0	1	1
Is present compensation of lawyers adequate?				
Yes	1	0	3	4
No	5	10	16	31
No response	10	2	0	12
Should out-of-pocket expenses be paid?				
Yes	15	11	17	43
No	1	1	2	4
No response	0	0	0	0

Table 4 indicates that the proportion of defendants pleading guilty to the principal offense was 55% for the state as a whole, with 9% of the defendants pleading to a lesser offense. The highest rate of guilty pleas was in Jefferson and Montgomery Counties. A relatively small number of cases went to trial, about 6% for the entire state.

Table 5 shows that, for the state as a whole, 42% of the defendants were sentenced to imprisonment, including county jail, while 16% were placed on probation and 9% had a fine only. The extent of use of probation varied widely among the counties, being least used in Russell County and most used in Montgomery.

TABLE 4
Disposition in Felony Cases
Alabama, 1962

County	Total sample	Plea guilty	Plea lesser offense	Dis-missed	Found guilty	Ac-quitted	Pend-ing	Other
Jefferson	150	96	24	18	5	5	1	1
Madison	43	4	1	3	2	1	31	1
Fayette	18	12	0	1	0	0	5	0
Russell	19	11	3	4	0	0	1	0
Montgomery	50	36	2	6	5	1	0	0
Weighted total percentages		55	9	12	4	2	19	0

TABLE 5
Sentencing in Felony Cases
Alabama, 1962

County	Total sample	No sentence No.	%	Prison No.	%	Proba-tion No.	%	Fine No.	%	Misc.	No data No.	%
Jefferson	150	24	16	78	52	30	20	17	11	1	1	1	1
Fayette	18	6	33	7	39	3	17	2	11	0	0	0	0
Russell	19	5	26	11	58	1	5	2	11	0	0	0	0
Montgomery	50	7	14	22	44	16	32	5	10	0	0	0	0
Weighted total percentages		32		42		16		9		1		1

H. CONCLUSIONS AND RECOMMENDATIONS

1. There is uniformity neither in the stage of appointment of counsel nor in the appointment procedure. The practices vary widely between circuits. A uniform system is desirable for its certainty and its equal application. These matters should be studied further by the Alabama Bar Association with the view of proposing a rule of court to the Supreme Court of Alabama under its rule-making power. Act. No. 526, Reg. Sess. (1963) does not cure these objections.

2. Assessments vary as to the manner of determining indigency. Indeed, there does not appear to be a system in the usual sense. Both as an aid to the appointing judge and as a protection against abuse, clear and appropriate guides should be established to determine whether an accused person is entitled to free counsel.

3. Minimum compensation of counsel should be increased. Presently, the amount authorized compensates neither for legal services nor for the costs of investigation, preparation, or the expense of providing expert witnesses. The bar must decide whether in this context the defense of an indigent shall be on par with the quality of the prosecution of the case against him.

4. The present system of keeping records is inadequate, with little or no provision for the indigent situation. More complete data should be kept in one central file in each county.

ALASKA

William H. Jacobs, Anchorage

A. INTRODUCTION

Alaska's population was 226,167 in 1960, and its projected population for July 1, 1963, was 248,000 (U.S. Department of Commerce). The state is divided into four judicial districts, with main population centers as follows: first district, Juneau; second district, Nome; third district, Anchorage; fourth district, Fairbanks. Alaska has no counties. The third and fourth districts were selected for survey. In 1960 the third district population was 111,796, and that of Anchorage was 44,237. The principal economic activities center around civilian and military construction, transportation and shipping, numerous federal agencies, agriculture, salmon fishing and packing, and very extensive oil exploration, with several producing wells and one refinery. Two large military installations are just outside Anchorage.

The fourth district had a population in 1960 of 58,984; that of Fairbanks was 13,311. This district has a small but important agricultural economy, and Fairbanks, which is the northern terminus of the Alaska Railroad, is the commercial and trading center for a large part of Alaska. There are two large military installations near Fairbanks. The following tables give additional information about the districts surveyed:

District	Felony defendants, 1962	% of indigents°	% of indigents who waived counsel°	Lawyers in private practice
Third	153	78	7	85
Fourth	61	43	0	24

° These figures are averages of estimates supplied by the superior court judges and district attorneys.

District	No. of appointments of counsel in felonies, 1962	No. of lawyers who served	Typical payment for felony guilty plea	Total compensation
Third	143	70	$50	$9881
Fourth	61	23	$50	$4650

A docket study was made of 49 representative cases from the third district for 1962. The study revealed that 39 defendants (80%) had counsel and 10 did not. Of those who had counsel, 25 were retained (51% of all defendants) and 14 were assigned (29%). Preliminary hearings were held in 10 of the 49 cases. In the 39 remaining cases 12 defendants waived the hearing, 20 were cases of a type where hearings are not usually held, and in 7 cases there were no data.

Thirty-one of the defendants were released on bail, 12 were not, and data were unavailable for 6.

Of the 49 defendants, 17 pleaded guilty to the principal offense charged and 3 pleaded to lesser offenses, a total of 41%. Thirteen cases went to trial, resulting in four convictions and nine acquittals. Six cases were dismissed, one resulted in commitment to a mental hospital, and nine ended in miscellaneous other dispositions. Seventeen defendants were sentenced to imprisonment, 15 were placed on probation, and 2 had their drivers' licenses suspended. These figures include some defendants who are counted under more than one heading because they had a combination sentence, such as fine and imprisonment. Also 20 defendants were not sentenced, or their cases were pending, and no information was available for one.

B. CRIMINAL PROCEDURE AS IT AFFECTS INDIGENT PERSONS

1. *Jurisdiction of courts.* The Supreme Court of Alaska has final appellate jurisdiction in all actions and proceedings. The court consists of three justices, including the chief justice, and on occasion sits in each of the four judicial districts. There is one superior court for the entire state with original statewide jurisdiction in all criminal matters. However, each judge is assigned to one of the four judicial districts: one superior court judge each in Ketchikan, Juneau, and Nome, two in Fairbanks, and four in Anchorage.

Each of the four districts has a district magistrate court with one to five district magistrates having jurisdiction over misdemeanors and ordinance violations. Although district magistrates need not be licensed to practice law, at present 8 of the 13 magistrates are licensed in at least one United States jurisdiction. The presiding judge of the superior court in each district appoints the district and deputy magistrates for his district, and they serve at his pleasure.

Deputy magistrates are not required to be lawyers. They serve in less populated outlying towns and are permitted to hold other offices or positions, or engage in any other profession or business that does not interfere with their judicial duties, which are usually part time. The four districts have from 7 to 19 deputy magistrates, who may give judgment for the recovery of statutory penalties or forfeitures not exceeding $500; may give judgment of conviction upon plea of guilty in any criminal proceeding within the jurisdiction of the district magistrate's court, i.e., misdemeanors and ordinance violations; may hear, try, and enter judgments in all cases involving ordinance violations; and may hear, try, and enter judgments in all cases involving other misdemeanors if the defendant consents in writing that the deputy magistrate may try him. As a practical matter, all misdemeanors are tried in the magistrate and deputy magistrate courts, and felonies are tried exclusively in the superior court. Exceptions to this rule are made in misdemeanors at the discretion of the district attorney, where difficult questions of public policy or close questions of statutory construction are involved.

2. *Arrest and preliminary proceedings.* Most felony cases begin with the arrest of the accused, although some defendants are arrested only after an indictment has been returned by the grand jury. The person arrested must in all cases be

taken before the nearest available district or deputy magistrate without unneces sary delay, and in any event within 24 hours after his arrest, including Sundays and holidays. This requirement applies to peace officers of every description, and a magistrate must make himself available at all hours to receive bail. The latter duty may, however, be delegated to the person admitting a defendant to jail, or to some other appropriate person. (The Alaska Rules of Criminal Pro- cedure are closely modeled on the Federal Rules.)

Immediately after arrest, any prisoner has the right to telephone or otherwise communicate with an attorney or any relative or friend, and the attorney has the right immediately to visit the accused. State law requires the magistrate to inform the accused of the complaint against him, to deliver a copy of the com- plaint to him, and to inform the defendant of his right to retain counsel and to have a preliminary examination; to inform the defendant that he is not required to make a statement and that any statement he makes may be used against him; to allow the defendant reasonable time and opportunity to consult counsel; and to admit the defendant to bail as provided by law.

In practice, these rules are scrupulously followed by the police and district magistrates. In both districts surveyed, the usual time elapsing between arrest and first appearance is less than 12 hours. When working in outlying areas, the police occasionally have difficulty with the 24-hour rule, because the weather not infrequently makes travel impossible.

State law provides that every defendant has the right to a preliminary exami- nation before a magistrate, and this right may be waived only in writing. In both districts, preliminary examinations are held regularly except when waived. Waivers occur in about 50% of the third district and about 40% of the fourth district cases.

At the preliminary examination, the following proceedings occur: the magis- trate reads the complaint to the defendant together with any supporting state- ments and affidavits, and must subpoena the complainant and any witnesses examined prior to the filing of the complaint without cost to the defendant, if he so requests. At this time, a subpoena for other witnesses may be issued upon the defendant's filing an affidavit showing, among other things, that the evidence of the witness is material to the defense and that the defendant is unable to pay witness fees. The state first presents the evidence in support of its case, and all witnesses must be examined in the defendant's presence and may be cross- examined by him. The magistrate informs the defendant that he has a right to make a statement to answer the charge and explain the facts alleged against him but that he is not required to make a statement and failure to do so may not be used against him at trial. After the defendant's statement is made or waived, he may produce and examine witnesses, and the state may cross- examine them. The defendant's statement is competent testimony before the grand jury and may be offered in evidence at the trial. Either the state or the defendant may have adverse witnesses excluded from the courtroom so that they may not hear the testimony of other witnesses. In the deputy magistrate courts the defendant's statement must be reduced to writing, and in the district magistrate courts the entire proceedings are electronically recorded.

17

Some of the deputy magistrates in outlying areas introduce informalities into the proceedings. These deputy magistrates are, with one exception, not lawyers. At arraignment, the defendant is always informed of his right to have counsel and bail and is always told of his right not to make a statement. There is a tendency, however, on the part of some deputy magistrates, to treat the preliminary examination as an aid to the police and the investigative process, in addition to its normal purposes. Moreover, among deputy magistrates who do not view a preliminary examination in this way, there is a tendency to encourage the accused to waive his right to the examination. Deputy magistrates occasionally forget to tell the defendant of his right to make or not to make a statement at the preliminary examination. Proceedings before deputy magistrates are not conducted by a prosecuting attorney.

In some outlying areas, although the accused is always told of his right to have counsel upon being arraigned, this is of very little practical importance. A significant number of defendants appearing before deputy magistrates actually do not know what a lawyer is and so of course have no idea how a lawyer might be helpful. In addition, it would be difficult and probably impossible for a defendant, even one who could pay an average fee, to obtain counsel to assist him at this stage of the game. This is because the lawyers are located in the centers of population and would not be interested in flying on short notice to some other place, perhaps many hundreds of miles away, to appear in this stage of a criminal proceeding. For all practical purposes, the right to have a lawyer does not mean anything to defendants in outlying areas until they are held to answer to the grand jury and are brought into the larger city where the superior court for that district sits. All these things cause more inconvenience than injustice, because the superior court judges are quite liberal in allowing defendants to withdraw their waiver of a preliminary hearing, where there is any likelihood that the defendant has been disadvantaged by it. A number of appointed counsel did state, however, that their defense had been rendered difficult by damaging statements made at first appearances or preliminary hearings.

3. *Indictment, information, and arraignment.* The formal charge against the defendant is made either by grand jury indictment or by information. In the third district, indictment is waived and an information filed in about 50% of the cases. In the fourth district, indictments are used most of the time, and informations only occasionally. A recent change in the third district is that the grand jury now meets every month. This has substantially reduced the period between arrest and arraignment on the indictment, during which persons who cannot make bail remain in jail. Also, fewer defendants are waiving their right to be indicted. This is probably because many defendants, or their attorneys, recognize that proceeding by indictment does not now take substantially longer than proceeding by information. In the third district, about 80% of the persons held to answer make bond. Of those who make bond, about 80% have professional sureties.

Procedure for appointment of counsel is substantially uniform throughout the state. If the defendant appears for arraignment or trial without counsel, the court must advise him of his right to have counsel and must ask if he desires it. If he states that he desires but is unable to employ counsel, and makes an affidavit to that effect, the court will appoint counsel to represent him. In practice, the judges go further in looking after the best interests of the defendant than would be required by the wording of the statute. The judges usually explain that appointed counsel will be provided at no cost to the defendant, and, where the charge is especially serious or the defendant either youthful or ignorant, some judges will urge the defendant to accept appointment of counsel, explaining to him that he may be seriously disadvantaged without an attorney. Three judges in the first and fourth judicial districts absolutely refuse to permit an indigent defendant to waive the appointment of an attorney. In the third district, with very few exceptions, persons under the age of 21 are not allowed to waive. Although the constitutionality of this practice might be questioned, the point has never been raised in this jurisdiction.

Typically, when the defendant is brought before the court on the date set for arraignment on the indictment or information, he is informed of his right to counsel and that counsel will be appointed for him if he is indigent. After appointment of counsel, the judges uniformly allow from one to several days or even longer before the defendant is required to plead. The judge determines indigency by questioning the defendant as to salary or wages and the ownership of various kinds of property. The fact that a defendant may be out on bail is not taken into consideration in determining indigency. The defendant is required to sign a pauper's oath.

Defenses and objections based on defects in the institution of the prosecution, or in the indictment or information, other than that it fails to show jurisdiction in the court or to charge an offense, may be raised only by motion before trial. Failure to present such defenses or objections constitutes a waiver thereof, but the court for cause shown grants relief from the waiver. A motion based on such defense or objection is to be made before the plea is entered, but the court permits it to be made within a reasonable time thereafter. The defense of insanity need not be asserted at this time.

4. *Selection and compensation of assigned counsel.* The system for selecting attorneys to serve is uniform in the districts surveyed. The judges select from a roster of all attorneys admitted to practice, subject to exceptions for age, infirmity, and the fact that one lawyer may have recently finished an unusually difficult appointment. Of the 85 attorneys in private practice in the third district, 70 served as appointed counsel one or more times in 1962. In the fourth district, where 24 attorneys were available for appointment, 23 served in 1962. In especially complicated cases or on charges that carry severe penalties, the judges without exception take special care to appoint an attorney more experienced and skillful than average in the trial of criminal cases. In such cases, one of the fourth district judges appoints one younger attorney and one older, more experienced man. Although this was sometimes put with extreme tact, each judge interviewed stated or implied that there were some attorneys whom he would not appoint in most criminal cases, either because

they were not considered adequate in criminal trial work or because they do not do any such work.

Compensation for attorneys is fixed by court rule at $50 for a guilty plea and sentencing and $50 per day or part thereof spent in trial. Three judges remarked that they exercise discretion or apply a liberal interpretation to the court rule on fees in compelling cases. In any event, attorneys are never paid much more than the statutory amount. Defendants who can pay a small fee do not create a problem in Alaska. The basic attitude of all judges is that defendants are either able to hire counsel or they are not. In some cases in each district, where the judge feels it is part of the rehabilitation process for a defendant placed on probation, the court may require (1) that the defendant repay the state the amount paid his attorney under the court rule or (2) that as a condition of probation the defendant pay the attorney a reasonable fee within his means or earning power, and in such a case the appointed attorney is not paid by the state. In the third district, a defendant placed on probation is routinely required to pay court costs, based on ability to earn a living and on the nature of the offense. On occasion these costs have been anywhere from $25 to $1,000. This is flexible and is reduced subsequently if something develops making payment difficult. The money goes into the state general fund.

Limited funds are available in the court system budget to reimburse counsel for expenses of investigation, preparation, expert witnesses, and travel, but the court must approve the expenditure in advance. Apparently most attorneys either do not make such expenditures or do not seek reimbursement, because only $130.50 was devoted to this purpose in 1962. One attorney stated that a "blizzard of paper work" is required to have expenditures approved in advance.

The uniform practice is not to provide counsel for misdemeanors, except of course where a defendant is charged with a misdemeanor along with a felony.

Trial counsel makes post-trial motions addressed to the trial court, but, if an appeal is to be taken, and in habeas corpus proceedings, the trial court appoints either the same or different counsel. The superior court may authorize an appeal or petition for review without payment of fees and costs or giving security therefor, by a person who makes an affidavit that he is unable to pay such fees or costs or give security. An appeal or petition for review may not be taken in forma pauperis if the superior court certifies in writing that it is not taken in good faith. Upon the filing of a like affidavit, the superior court may direct that the expense of preparation of the record, furnishing a transcript of the evidence or proceedings, and of the costs of duplicating briefs, be waived. The superior court may appoint an attorney to represent any such person unable to employ counsel. The superior court or the Supreme Court may dismiss an appeal or deny a petition if the allegation of poverty is untrue, or "if satisfied that the appeal or petition for review is frivolous or malicious." Attorneys appointed to represent indigent persons on appeal "shall be paid a fee established by the court, commensurate with the time and legal problems involved." All of the above procedure is established by Rule 15, Rules of Administration, and Supreme Court Rule 43.

C. OPINIONS OF JUDGES

Two superior court judges were interviewed in each of the two districts surveyed. Of the remaining superior court judges, questionnaires were mailed to the two in the first district, and the judge who presided in the second district in 1962 was interviewed, using the mail questionnaire.

When asked at what stage in a criminal case an indigent person, under an ideal system, should first be provided with a lawyer if he wants one, all judges agreed that appointment should be at an earlier stage than the present system provides. Two thought appointment should be at the preliminary hearing, two thought it should be between first appearance and preliminary hearing, one thought it should be at first appearance before a magistrate, and two thought it should be between arrest and first appearance. Four judges stated that it is unfair not to appoint a lawyer at the stage they had designated, and the other three said it was not necessarily unfair, while acknowledging that it is unfair in some cases. Two judges thought that appointment at the preliminary hearing could be financed, and one thought appointment at an earlier stage might be no more expensive. Two judges thought appointment at the ideal stage probably could not be financed, and the remaining two judges stated categorically that it could not be.

The judges were asked if, under an ideal system, a lawyer should be made available to the indigent defendant in the following kinds of proceedings: (1) sentencing of a defendant who pleaded guilty; (2) sentencing of a defendant convicted by trial; (3) habeas corpus; (4) hearing on revocation of probation; (5) sexual psychopath hearing; (6) misdemeanors; and (7) civil commitment.

They were asked also if it is unfair not to make counsel available in these proceedings, and whether counsel is made available in their courts. The following tabulation shows the answers given by the seven judges responding to this question:

Proceeding	Should be made available? Yes	No	Is unfair if not made available?	Counsel is made available
(1)	6	1	6	7
(2)	7	0	5	7
(3)	6	1	6	7
(4)	5	2	4	5
(5)	No such proceedings held			
(6)	4	2	3	0
(7)	7	0	7	7

These results probably show an understandable reluctance to state categorically that a certain proceeding is always unfair if counsel is not made available. Some qualified answers were given. One judge stated that proceedings (4) and (6) would be unfair where the case is presented by a prosecuting attorney, otherwise not. Another judge agreed with respect to misdemeanors prosecuted by an attorney. Another said that counsel is provided on revocation of probation in most cases. Four judges said that counsel should be made available in habeas corpus actions only where the proceeding is meritorious, and one judge had never been presented with a habeas corpus proceeding.

Several judges drew the useful distinction that counsel should be provided in misdemeanors where the prosecution is conducted by an attorney (before district magistrates), but that counsel would be unnecessary where proceedings are before deputy magistrates. There was quite a range of opinion on the feasibility of financing provision for counsel in misdemeanor cases. Two judges categorically said it could be financed, and one was certain it could not. The other comments were in the general vein that the cost would be staggering, that it would be very difficult, or that the state probably could not afford it.

All judges interviewed appoint separate lawyers for defendants having interests that may conflict. Five judges stated that the compensation presently provided for appointed atorneys is inadequate, one said it is adequate, and the remaining judge chose not to comment. Five judges thought appointed counsel compared very favorably or were equal to retained counsel. One stated that standards of performance for appointed counsel were lower, and one had no comment. In comparing appointed counsel with prosecuting attorneys, five judges felt that appointed counsel compared very favorably or were equal to the prosecution, and three felt that appointed counsel were generally better. The superiority of appointed counsel over the prosecution was expressed in terms of experience.

Six judges have no problem in getting appointed attorneys to serve; the remaining judge does have a problem with this. The latter judge stated that 60% of appointed attorneys ask to be excused, and his policy is to excuse attorneys not experienced in criminal work. All other judges excuse appointed attorneys only for conflicting time commitments or other very good or compelling reasons. All of these judges experience a very low frequency of requests to be excused. In all cases but one, such requests are made less than 10% of the time.

The state courts in Alaska began to function in early 1960, so none of the superior court judges have served on their present courts much over four years. No significant pattern of opinion appears to exist among the judges according to their age or their prior legal experience.

There was general agreement that representation of indigents has been adequate and that in only a very small minority of cases has a convicted defendant raised a question about the competency of court-appointed counsel. One judge commented that the present system works better than we have had any right to expect, but added that counsel should be provided in the magistrate's and district magistrate's court. This judge felt there are gross miscarriages of justice in that court in his district when a defendant has no lawyer.

All judges agreed that the appeals and review procedure as set up by the rules is altogether fair and practicable. Because of *Douglas v. California,* the present practice is more liberal than the rules provide: appeals and petitions for review are now routinely granted and counsel routinely appointed.

Two judges believe a public defender system is desirable and that it is now or will ultimately be necessary in Alaska. One judge doubted that satisfactory personnel could be obtained at a salary level the state would be willing to pay. This judge was also quite sure that the present budget level for the court system could not begin to provide for such a program. Six of the judges believe that more realistic compensation should be paid to appointed counsel, and it was noted by several that the volume of cases is becoming burdensome on some lawyers, particularly those in solo practice.

D. OPINIONS OF DEFENSE ATTORNEYS

A questionnaire was mailed to the 70 attorneys in the third district and the 23 in the fourth district who were appointed in 1962. The response rate for the third district was 56% and for the fourth district 39%, giving an average response rate of 52% for the two districts. Some respondents failed to answer all questions asked. [For a copy of the questionnaire, see volume 1, page 223.]

On the question about the stage of appointment for the last case handled in 1962, answers were as follows:

Time of appointment	Third district°	Fourth district
At or before first appearance	0	0
Between first appearance and preliminary hearing	1	2
At preliminary hearing	0	1
After preliminary hearing, before filing of indictment	1	1
After filing of indictment, before arraignment	18	3
At arraignment on indictment	7	0
After arraignment on indictment, before trial	10†	1
At trial	0	0

° According to the docket study an attorney is always appointed, if desired, before acceptance of a plea other than "not guilty."

† The large number of answers in this category must reflect a confusion over the term arraignment, which many attorneys use in referring to the first appearance before a magistrate.

Each attorney was also asked if he was appointed in time to represent the accused person adequately and whether he thought the present system for assignment of lawyers was fair to the indigent persons and to the lawyers.

It was thought that significant differences might appear in the answers given these questions, related to the number of years of practice an attorney had had and also to his prior experience in criminal practice. The respondents were classed in the following groups:

Group A   Less than 5 years' practice, more than 19 criminal cases
Group B   Less than 5 years' practice, less than 19 criminal cases
Group C   6 to 14 years' practice, more than 19 criminal cases
Group D   6 to 14 years' practice, less than 19 criminal cases
Group E   Over 14 years' practice, more than 19 criminal cases
Group F   Over 14 years' practice, less than 19 criminal cases

Respondents were asked what changes, if any, they would recommend in the present system of appointing counsel. The possible responses were as follows:

(1) appoint lawyer at an earlier stage of case;
(2) pay out-of-pocket expenses that lawyers incurred in investigating and preparing case;
(3) pay lawyers more for their services;
(4) provide counsel in additional kinds of cases, such as serious misdemeanors;
(5) improve the system which the judge uses in selecting lawyers to be appointed.

The responses, divided according to groups A to F (see supra) and also totaled for all respondents, are shown in Tables 1 and 2.

TABLE 1
Replies of Assigned Counsel

Group	Question No. 1 Yes	No	Question No. 2 Yes	No	Question No. 3 Yes	No	Public defender
A (1)		1		1	1		
B (11)	8	3	4	7	3	8	3
C (18)	14	2	8	9	3	15	4
D (10)	6	3	5	5	2	8	2
E (6)	3	2	2	4	1	5	
F (2)		1		1		2	
Total (48)	31	11	20	27	10	38	9
	6 no answer		1 no answer				

TABLE 2
Changes Recommended by Assigned Counsel

Group	No. 1	No. 2	Recommended changes No. 3	No. 4	No. 5
A (1)					1
B (11)	6	7	6	3	4
C (18)	7	11	12	6	4
D (10)	5	6	3		4
E (6)	1	4	3	1	1
F (2)			1	1	
Total (48)	19	28	25	11	14

Of the 48 attorneys responding, 42 were compensated for their services and 6 were not. Six attorneys were repaid their out-of-pocket expenses in full, eight were repaid in part, and the rest were repaid nothing.

Of the 48 attorneys, 0 had been appointed in 1962 to serve on appeal and one on habeas corpus. The fees paid the attorneys ranged from $150 to $200, although two received no compensation. Attorneys responding to the questionnaire defended 10 individuals charged with crimes punishable by life imprisonment in 1962 (there is no capital punishment in Alaska). These cases all arose in the third district, and 6 of the 10 defendants were represented by counsel having prior experience in more than 50 criminal cases each.

Table 1 shows that attorneys with 6 to 14 years' practice and prior experience in more than 19 criminal cases (the largest group of respondents) were confident of having been appointed early enough to provide an adequate defense. From three-eighths to two-thirds of the attorneys in the other groups were not, in their opinion, appointed early enough to make an adequate defense. Whether the system of appointment is fair to indigent persons elicited more "no" answers than "yes" answers in five of the six experience groups. The question whether the system is fair to lawyers elicited many more "no" answers than "yes" answers in every group. The total results show that 26% of attorneys thought they were not appointed in time to represent the defendant adequately, 57% believed the system for assignment of attorneys is not fair to indigent defendants, and 79% believed the system is not fair to lawyers. Nine of the respondents (19%) suggested that a public defender system should be established.

That 74% of appointed attorneys felt they were appointed early enough to provide an adequate defense, but 57% believed the present system of assignment is unfair to indigent defendants, suggests that there are important shortcomings in the system other than the stage at which counsel is appointed. The frequency with which certain changes in the system were recommended is shown in Table 2: of responding lawyers, 58% thought the state should repay out-of-pocket expenses incurred in investigation and preparation; 52% said appointed counsel should be paid more for their services; 40% believed counsel should be appointed at an earlier stage; 29% wanted improvement in the system by which the judge selects lawyers to be appointed; and 23% would have counsel provided in additional kinds of cases, such as serious misdemeanors.

The respondents reported the amounts they would have charged clients who retained them for services comparable to those rendered in the last cases to which they were appointed in 1962. In the third district, the average fee would have been $1,415, and in the fourth district the average would have been $585. Since there were 143 appointments in the third district and 61 appointments in the fourth district, a very rough approximation of the total value of legal services rendered by appointed counsel in 1962 is $202,345 for the third district and $35,685 for the fourth district. In 1962, the compensation actually paid appointed counsel was $9,881 in the third district and $4,650 in the fourth district. Perhaps the disparity between the districts in the average fee that would have been charged reflects a greater unwillingness on the part of attorneys in the former to engage in any criminal practice. In any event, it appears that the state of Alaska will never be likely to pay appointed counsel what they themselves would charge for similar services.

One third-district lawyer suggested that every attorney in the district be assessed $200 per year for a "defense fund," which would be distributed on a time-spent basis at the end of each year. This would indeed be a small sum compared to what appointed counsel would charge a solvent client, but it would in fact almost triple the amount of money presently spent in this district. Although an improvement, this would be a small step in alleviating some real hardships.

One attorney reported in a careful cost breakdown that a successful appeal to the Supreme Court of Alaska which he handled cost him $1,210 in actual overhead costs, in addition to $2,400 worth of time spent on the case. Two more extreme examples were reported by the Juneau Bar Association, although not in connection with this study. Recently two solo practitioners in the first district each spent almost one month away from their regular work on unusually difficult cases. The office expenses of each were in excess of $1,000 per month. One of these attorneys was paid $350 for his services, the other $250. The latter attorney found it necessary to make a bank loan to meet his office expenses for that month.

A common spontaneous opinion voiced by many respondents is that "many attorneys" are never appointed, that appointments follow no regular system, and that either young lawyers or good trial lawyers carry the whole burden. This study shows that these opinions are not accurate. Another recurrent opinion was that attorneys specializing in civil work should never be appointed at all, either because this takes too much time from their practice or because they are unable to do an adequate job.

The commonly expressed opinion most relevant to this study is that a much more careful investigation should be made in determining indigency. This comment, from an attorney who has been practicing between six and nine years and has had experience in over 50 criminal cases, is illustrative: "Also, I have been appointed to represent persons who are not 'indigent in fact.' These persons are out on bail in some instances and have sufficient property to pay a defense attorney. Many of the persons whom I have been appointed to defend in the past are hardened or professional criminals who use a good attorney as a shield. In my state, careful screening would eliminate appointments to criminal defendants who are not really indigents. I would estimate that 50% of the cases fall into this category."

E.   OPINIONS OF DISTRICT ATTORNEYS

The district attorneys in the third and fourth districts were interviewed, and mail questionnaires were sent to the others. No reply was received from the second district.

Two of these attorneys were first admitted to practice in 1960, and the other was admitted in 1957. All three have served as district attorney, or as his assistant, for from two to four years. All devote full time to their duties and handle both civil and criminal work. Two of the three district attorneys feel that they have inadequate funds to run their offices, the principal difficulty being that there are no funds for investigations and that travel funds are limited. The latter is important in areas where travel is possible only by airplane or boat. It was also thought that additional personnel are needed.

Two district attorneys thought that under an ideal system counsel should be provided between the first appearance and preliminary hearing. One of these thought it was unfair not to provide a lawyer at this stage, saying that most cases are won or lost at this point. The other district attorney thought it would very seldom be unfair, because the defendant would not be damaged unless the charge were frivolous. The third district attorney thought that appointment should be made after preliminary hearing but before filing of an indictment. He thought it unfair if a lawyer is not appointed at this stage, because thereafter substantive legal decisions must be made which affect the outcome of the trial. Each district attorney thought appointment at this stage could be financed, two of them commenting that this would be every bit as feasible as the present system. More of an attorney's time would be taken up early in the case, but the advantages gained would more than compensate for this later, and a more effective defense could be provided.

Two district attorneys agreed that it is not unfair to omit appointment of counsel in revocation of probation proceedings, and the other, in whose district counsel is provided, said it is unfair. One of the former explained that a lawyer is always provided for this in his district, but that it is unnecessary and tends to complicate and protract the proceedings without benefit to the indigent. He stated that the court should usually accept the decision of the probation office, because the staff is well qualified and conscientious.

Two district attorneys agreed that counsel should be provided in serious misdemeanor cases and that it is unfair not to do so. Both thought this could be financed, and one added that a much more careful determination of indigency should be made if counsel is to be appointed for serious misdemeanors. The third district attorney did not think it unfair not to provide counsel for misdemeanors and believed this could not be financed.

Two district attorneys were satisfied with the present system for determining indigency. The third felt that the present system is too lenient and thought a questionnaire or some other more systematic method should be used.

In the first district, assigned counsel were thought to be as good as lawyers retained by defendants. This district attorney stated that it is easy to feel they are not as diligent but pointed out that indigents are often misfits with poor character and a criminal record, and this makes the case much more difficult for counsel. In the third district, where attorneys are appointed who do not practice criminal law, they are considered not nearly as good as lawyers retained by defendants. The present system of providing counsel for indigent defendants was characterized as completely unsatisfactory. In the fourth district, appointed counsel compares favorably when attorneys are appointed who have made it known that they are interested. The system of appointing attorneys in alphabetical order from a roster of members of the bar was considered unsatisfactory because attorneys frequently are appointed who lack interest and do not put forth much effort. This district attorney felt that the whole indigent case load in his district could be handled by the number of attorneys who are quite willing to be appointed. These interested attorneys were felt to be skillful and able to do an excellent job in all their appointments.

All district attorneys agreed that lawyers should be reimbursed for their out-of-pocket expenses for investigation and preparation and that the present rates of compensation for appointed lawyers are inadequate. One district attorney qualified this by saying that appointed counsel should not be compensated and all should share the burden equally, adding that, if they are to be compensated at all, it should be on a fee schedule equal to private retainers. Another district attorney said that the rate of compensation should be at least triple the present amount in all cases, and, where a life sentence is possible, the minimum compensation should be $2,500.

All of the district attorneys are willing to disclose to defense counsel such things as confessions, statements of witnesses, reports of expert witnesses, and exhibits under certain circumstances. This is especially true where the issue is sanity or mental state, rather than whether the defendant committed the act charged. Disclosure also depends on whether the information appears to be flowing in free exchange, or whether the defense is "only fishing for alibi information." All three district attorneys said that disclosure depends mostly on the character of the defendant and defense counsel and it makes no difference whether the defendant is indigent.

Concerning persons who can pay a moderate fee, one district attorney said that a person placed on probation is sometimes required to repay the state the fee paid his appointed attorney. Another solution was proposed, that is to have the court appoint an attorney and have the state pay the difference between a reasonable fee and what the defendant can pay. Both district attorneys who were interviewed were very strongly opposed to trying a case where the defendant does not have counsel.

When asked to comment on how the present system for providing counsel might be improved, both district attorneys who were interviewed suggested a public defender system. In the fourth district it was thought "this might be useful," and that one full-time attorney would be required. This district attorney suggested a novel drawback to the public defender system. He was concerned that juries might come to think that the proceedings are perfunctory if all defenses were conducted by one man. In the third district, it was thought a minimum of four attorneys would be required. This district attorney added that the public defender's office should be a separate department from the state court system, perhaps an independent branch of the Department of Law (Attorney General's Office). It was thought this arrangement would have a better chance of obtaining adequate finances.

On February 15, 1963, a bill authorizing the establishment of a public defender system was introduced in the House of Representatives. A copy of this bill is attached as an appendix. It is not expected that anything will be done with the bill until the publication of the National Report and recommendations arising out of this project.

F. CONCLUSIONS AND RECOMMENDATIONS

On the basis of the foregoing report, the following conclusions and recommendations are submitted:

1. Serious consideration should be given to establishing a public defender's office in Juneau, Ketchikan, Anchorage, and Fairbanks. This is particularly true for Anchorage. It is expected that considerable time would be required for the drafting and passage of adequate legislation on this matter. In addition, there may be considerable debate over financing a public defender system in the immediate future. The state is involved in many expanding programs, and whether this system would be given high priority is subject to serious doubt.

2. Since a public defender system may not be instituted for some time, the assigned counsel system should be changed to eliminate the shortcomings revealed by this study. The following changes are recommended:

a. Compensation for appointed attorneys should be increased. The amount presently paid for a plea or trial should be at least tripled. A minimum fee of $1,000 plus the usual compensation established by rule should be paid in cases where life imprisonment is possible.

b. The budget of the state court system should be increased to allow much more money than is presently available for investigations and expert witnesses. Court approval in advance should be required for such expenditures, but, with more money available, the judges could be more liberal in allowing such expenditures.

c. Appointed counsel should be made available at the preliminary hearing, because unrepresented defendants frequently make damaging statements at this stage of the proceeding. This would cost the state very little more money, but great advantages would be gained by appointed counsel and the indigent defendant.

d. Counsel should be appointed for serious misdemeanors. It is obvious that serving a sentence of just under one year is a much greater punishment to many defendants than receiving a felony conviction followed by several years of probation.

e. A more systematic method should be used in determining indigency. Defending indigent persons is already a burden on members of the bar, and their efforts should not be expended on persons who are able, albeit with some effort, to pay for a privately retained attorney. This will become increasingly important if Recommendation d is followed.

f. For the more difficult and/or serious felony defenses, there should be appointed one older attorney with much experience in criminal trial work, and one younger attorney. The younger man would be of assistance to the attorney primarily responsible for the defense, and in turn he would learn the skills necessary for taking on such responsibilities later in his career.

3. Some arrangements should be made for reimbursement by the federal government where attorneys are appointed to represent indigent military personnel.

APPENDIX

House Bill No. 72, Introduced in Alaska Legislature Feb. 15, 1963, by Messrs. Gravel and Rader.

A BILL

For an Act entitled: "An Act providing for the appointment of public defenders for indigent persons charged with felonies, misdemeanors, or violations of ordinances."

BE IT ENACTED BY THE LEGISLATURE OF THE STATE OF ALASKA:

Section 1. AS 22.20 is amended by adding new sections to read:

ARTICLE 4. PUBLIC DEFENDERS.

Sec. 22.20.170. PUBLIC DEFENDER SYSTEM. There is created a public defender system to be administered by the supreme court.

Sec. 22.20.180. APPOINTMENTS. (a) The presiding judge of the superior court in each judicial court in each judicial district may appoint one or more attorneys admitted to practice in the state to serve as public defenders to represent indigent persons charged with committing felonies, misdemeanors, or with violating ordinances.

(b) A public defender serves at the pleasure of the presiding judge.

Sec. 22.20.190. COMPENSATION. An attorney appointed a public defender receives compensation as determined by the administrative director with the approval of the chief justice and the supreme court.

Sec. 22.20.200. PRIVATE PRACTICE BY PUBLIC DEFENDER. An attorney appointed a public defender may not engage in the private practice of law without the permission of the presiding judge and administrative director.

Sec. 2. This Act takes effect on the day after its passage and approval or on the day it becomes law without such approval.

ARIZONA

David L. Grounds, Phoenix

The members of the A.B.A. Associate State Committee were of great assistance in gathering data for this report. They consisted of W. Edward Morgan of Tucson, chairman, Robert J. Welliever, and Jerry Sullivan, both of Phoenix.

[Editor's note: since this report was written Mr. Grounds advises that two important developments have occurred in Arizona. One is enactment in 1964 of legislation authorizing a public defender to be established by local option in counties with 100,000 persons (Maricopa and Pima are the only two that are eligible). (Ariz. Rev. Stat. §§11-581 to 11-586.) The defender is to be appointed by the county board of supervisors, and his salary is to be not less than 70% of that paid to the county attorney. The public defender is to serve in felonies from preliminary hearing through trial and appeal. He also is to represent patients in sanity hearings. The defender is not authorized to engage in private practice. Part-time deputies are authorized. The other new development is that the practice now being established in justice of the peace courts is that the justice offers to provide counsel at the stage of the preliminary hearing.]

A. INTRODUCTION

For a number of years Arizona has been experiencing a phenomenal population explosion. In 1960 the state had a population of 1,302,161. In 1963, as of the first of the year the Chamber of Commerce estimated that the population was 1,580,000. From 1960 to midyear, 1963, the population of Maricopa County, the most populous county, jumped from 663,510 to an estimated 810,000. Phoenix, the capital and largest city, had a midyear population of 503,576, compared to 439,170 in 1960. The state has only 14 counties. Each has a county attorney and one or more superior court judges. Personal interviews with the county attorneys and the superior court judges were made in the following counties:

County (city)	Location in state	Remarks	1960 population in thousands	No. of practicing attorneys
Maricopa (Phoenix)	South central	Manufacturing, agriculture, Indian reservations, tourist trade	663	1013
Coconino (Flagstaff)	North central	Lumber and wood industry, mining, livestock, tourist trade	42	22
Pima (Tucson)	South	Manufacturing, farming, mining, tourist trade, Indian reservations	266	403
Cochise (Douglas)	Southeast	Agriculture, copper, mining, electronic research, tourist trade	55	27

In addition to personal interviews in the above counties, docket studies were made in Maricopa and Coconino Counties.

The following tabulation gives information concerning indigent defendants accused of felonies. It includes the four counties covered by personal interviews, and nine other counties from which the information was received by mail questionnaire.

County	Criminal cases filed in superior court in 1962*	Felony cases, % of indigents†	% of indigent defendants who waived counsel†
Maricopa	1973	50 plus	less than 5
Coconino	162	50	75
Pima	568	60	5
Cochise	125	75	50
Gila	68	60 to 75	100
Santa Cruz	40	80	60
Greenlee	8	no response	75
Yuma	131	90	3
Yavapai	87	40	70
Apache	11	50	65
Pinal	168	60	90
Navajo	97	90	60
Graham	36	90	75

* Report of Administrative Director of Supreme Court, 1962, Table K.
† These figures were supplied as estimates by the judges and county attorneys in these counties.

B. CRIMINAL PROCEDURE AS IT AFFECTS INDIGENT PERSONS

In Arizona, jurisdiction to return indictments and try felony cases is vested exclusively in the superior courts. They also have exclusive jurisdiction to try high misdemeanors, which are prosecuted by direct information. Examples of high misdemeanors are (1) leaving the scene of an accident in which there was an injury and (2) contributing to the delinquency or dependency of a minor.

The great majority of felony cases begin with the arrest of the suspect. The law requires that he be taken immediately before a magistrate. Felony proceedings are instituted by filing a complaint with the justice of the peace in the precinct wherein the crime was alleged to have occurred. The justice need not be a lawyer, although in a few counties, such as Pima, he may very well be. At the first appearance before the justice of the peace the accused should be informed of the nature of the charge, have his bail set unless it is a capital offense, and be informed of his right to counsel and to a preliminary hearing. Also at this stage of the proceeding the defendant should be given a copy of the complaint. After the defendant has had or waived a preliminary hearing, he is bound over to the superior court, whereupon an information is filed against him. In all but a few exceptional cases, counsel for the indigent accused is not appointed until arraignment upon the information or indictment in the superior court.

Quite a number of justices are sincere and extremely conscientious to see that all the rights of the accused are protected at the first appearance. In a few counties, however, lay justices do omit to tell the accused of his right to counsel and certainly do not adequately explain the nature and purpose of a preliminary hearing. For this reason it is not uncommon, after the case has reached the superior court, to have it remanded to the justice court for a preliminary hearing. It is suspected that occasionally a canny and sympathetic justice of the peace, who knows that the defendant ought to have counsel at the preliminary hearing and regrets his inability to appoint someone, deliberately faults the record by failing adequately to explain the nature and purpose of the preliminary hearing. He knows that if he does not make a good record it will be remanded, and on the next go-around, the indigent defendant will have counsel.

At the first appearance before the magistrate, bail is usually set according to some prescribed schedule. This schedule may vary from county to county or from time to time in the same county, and some counties have no schedule. The state affords some protection for the indigent accused of crime who cannot make bail in the short time allowed for initial proceedings. The appearance before a magistrate is in the main immediately following his arrest. The information must be filed against him within 30 days after the preliminary hearing or its waiver. Trial must be within a 60-day period after the indictment has been found or the information filed, unless the accused waives this right.

Even with these safeguards, however, it is not unusual for an indigent person who cannot make bail to remain in jail for longer periods. As indicated above, bail is set at the first appearance before a justice of the peace. Since counsel for the indigent is not appointed until arraignment on the information in the superior court, the opportunity to seek a reduction of bail is usually not available until that time. There are a number of conscientious justices of the peace, however, who will reduce the bail themselves where the defendant has been incarcerated for an unusually long period through no fault of his own.

All counties in Arizona utilize the assigned counsel system. With the exception of Maricopa County, the procedure of appointment of counsel under this system is fairly uniform. In counties of smaller population, it is a simple matter for the judge to keep a roster of attorneys who are admitted to practice in that county and to select one from this roster to represent the accused. Acceptance of the assignment is not mandatory, but it is usually honored. If it is known that a particular lawyer does not wish to represent an indigent person, then he simply is not called. In other thinly populated counties the judge refers to the active bar list of that county.

In Maricopa County attorneys who wish to represent indigent accused place their names on a list of "available attorneys" from which the selection is made. Obviously attorneys who never wish to represent an accused or appear in a criminal case do not have their names placed on this list. Those on the list make up less than 10% of the county bar. The Maricopa county attorney is a staunch critic of this system. He feels that most of the attorneys who place their names on the list, with few exceptions, are the more newly admitted members of the bar, and because of inexperience this may result in inequities to an accused. He therefore advocates the public defender system.

Many attorneys throughout Maricopa County have also voiced their opposition to the existing system, but for other reasons. Under this system, counsel who have placed their names on the "available list" must be present in court on the morning of arraignments and wait until their names are called, which may not occur at all on a given day. This results in a tremendous waste of time.

At the time of arraignment upon the indictment or information the defendant appears before the bench, the judge asks a series of questions concerning the defendant's financial status, and if satisfied that he is indigent, appoints an attorney to represent him. The defendant is required by law to take a pauper's oath to the effect that he does not have money or property with which to provide himself with counsel. The attorney assigned to represent the accused may, if he wishes, arraign the defendant at that time, or he may request that the arraignment be set over to a future date to allow him an opportunity to investigate further before entering a plea. The reason for a continuance is that certain motions directed to the sufficiency of the indictment or the information may be deemed waived unless asserted at the time of the arraignment. Because of this, it has become fairly common for attorneys at the time of arraignment to reserve a certain number of days, usually 10, within which to plead further to the sufficiency of the information or the indictment. The method of determining indigency is commented upon below, in Section C.

At the time of the arraignment, most judges are extremely careful to make sure that the accused clearly understands that counsel will be provided at no cost to him if he is found to be indigent. In many counties, for example, Coconino, the judge is extremely hesitant to allow the defendant to go to trial without counsel, even though the defendant has waived his right. An example of this occurred in Maricopa during 1962, when an accused appeared before the bench on a capital case and would not let the court appoint an attorney for him. Nevertheless, counsel was appointed for the defendant, and he was told that if he did desire consultation or aid from counsel, all he had to do was ask. A waiver of counsel in open court on a lesser felony, however, may preclude the defendant from having counsel assigned to him later. Most of the judges set no hard and fast rule on this matter, and it varies according to the circumstances. The varying practices of the individual judges may help account for the wide variation in the proportion of indigent defendants who waive counsel, as shown in the second tabulation in Section A.

Compensation for attorneys in cases of indigent defendants is provided by statute (A.R.S. §13-1673) and "shall be such amount as the court in its discretion deems reasonable, considering the services performed." However, the Supreme Court, in a formal letter to the presiding judge of Maricopa County superior court, has authorized the presiding judge to allow fees in capital cases up to $500, and in noncapital cases up to $150. On consultation and pleas of guilty, the rate is $5 per hour, up to a limit of $50 in noncapital cases and $100 in capital cases. In some counties counsel are reimbursed for their out-of-pocket expenses, in others they are not. Arizona law requires that, when counsel is appointed, he shall be paid by the county in which the court presides.

As indicated earlier, none of the counties provide counsel in misdemeanors, except where the defendant may be charged with a misdemeanor along with a felony. It should be noted that Rule 163 of the Arizona Rules of Criminal Procedure refers to appointment of counsel only "on a charge of felony." This rule further provides that the assignment of counsel shall not deprive the defendant of the right to engage other counsel at any stage of the proceedings, as a substitute for counsel assigned to him by the court. The usual accepted practice, where a defendant pleads guilty, is not to appoint counsel for him. However, it is the opinion of this reporter that if an indigent defendant chooses to plead guilty and requests counsel, the court would in all probability appoint one for him. If the accused has counsel assigned for trial and is found guilty, the counsel also appears with him at the time of sentencing.

In respect to appeals, Arizona law (A.R.S. §13-1721) requires that appointed counsel be paid by the county in which the court from which the appeal is taken presides. Compensation for services rendered on appeal is such amount as the Supreme Court deems reasonable. It is not unusual for the counsel appointed in the trial court to continue on appeal. It is also not unusual, however, for trial counsel to make post-trial motions addressed to the trial court, but for the court to appoint different counsel for purposes of appeal. A full transcript and record on appeal is provided at public expense.

The state prison is located in Pinal County. As a consequence the postconviction remedy of habeas corpus is prosecuted in that county. This has created quite a problem for Pinal, especially since counsel is not appointed for a petitioner in a habeas corpus proceeding. The judges' opinions for the necessity of appointing counsel in postconviction remedies is reflected in the tabulation in Section C.

C. THE JUDICIAL VIEW

Personal interviews were conducted with at least one judge in each of the counties of Maricopa, Coconino, Pima, and Cochise. Questionnaires were mailed to judges of the 10 other counties, and 9 of them responded. The experience of the judges ranged from slightly over a year on the bench to more than 20 years. It was found, however, that experience on the bench is not a major factor in the opinions expressed.

What should an "ideal system" afford to the indigent? This was asked of all judges, both in the personal interview and mail questionnaires. Their replies were quite interesting when compared to the present practice. One judge indicated that counsel should first be made available to the indigent person between arrest and first appearance before the magistrate; three said it should be at the first appearance before a magistrate; two felt it should be at the preliminary hearing; and four thought it should be after the filing of an indictment or information, but before the arraignment date. Three judges said that the present system should be followed under the "ideal system," that is, appointment at the time of arraignment on the indictment or information.

Numerous other questions were asked of the judges concerning their thoughts on the availability of counsel to the indigent defendant in particular kinds of cases and proceedings. The following tabulation expresses the composite thoughts of the judges under the "ideal system."

Should counsel be made available to the indigent defendant on:			Would it be unfair to the indigent defendant if not offered counsel at this stage?			Would it be possible to finance a system to provide counsel in these cases and proceedings?		
	Yes	No	Yes	No	No comment	Yes	No	No comment
Sentencing of defendant who pleaded guilty	4	9	2	7	4	4	5	4
Sentencing of defendant convicted by trial	7	6	4	5	4	5	4	4
Habeas corpus, coram nobis, or postconviction remedy	10	3	8	2	3	5	4	4
Hearing on revocation of probation	5	8	4	6	3	5	4	4
Misdemeanors	2	11	3	7	3	5	4	4
Civil commitment, etc.	11	2	9	1	3	5	4	4

Only two judges thought that counsel should be made available to the indigent defendant for misdemeanors, although some would draw the line between "misdemeanors" and "high misdemeanors." No explanation was given for this distinction other than that upon a low misdemeanor, the maximum sentence to jail is six months, whereas on a high misdemeanor it is a year. The judges were fairly evenly divided about the possibility of financing a system to provide counsel in the various cases and proceedings. Some judges felt that the tax consequences of such a program would be overwhelming, while others thought that the financing of such a program was of secondary importance, i.e., the rights of the accused are paramount.

The relationship of indigency to crime is illustrated in the second tabulation in Section A. As indicated, of all felony defendants brought before the court, the percentage of those who were indigent ranged from 90% in three counties down to 40% in the lowest one.

The judges were unanimous in reporting that they encountered no problems in getting lawyers to serve as assigned counsel. With the exception of one county, the percentage of lawyers who asked to be excused was extremely low. Eight judges answered that none asked to be excused, three said that only 1% to 9% asked to be excused, and one judge had no comment. Only the judge from

Coconino County reported that 30% to 40% of the attorneys asked to be excused; but the bar in this county is so small (see first tabulation, Section A) that a very few persons could distort the statistical picture.

When asked to comment on whether, in their judgment, the compensation paid lawyers for services to indigent accused persons was adequate, eight responded that they thought it was, three answered in the negative, and two had no comment. This should be contrasted with the attorneys' viewpoint as indicated below in Section E, "The Defense View."

How does assigned counsel compare to the county attorney? The judges were almost unanimous in indicating that assigned counsel was not a "pushover." Of the 13 judges responding to this question, 11 indicated that court-appointed attorneys were equal or better in experience and ability. Only one judge rated appointed counsel at a lower level.

The judge determines whether the defendant is eligible for free legal counsel. In the great majority of counties, this is done by questioning in open court, the indigent defendant being required to take a pauper's oath at the conclusion thereof. A few judges, if they feel that it is warranted, have members of their staff make a further investigation outside the courtroom. Four of the judges indicated they took many factors into consideration in determining indigency: salary or wages of the accused; ownership of car and other personal property; ownership of real property; stocks, bonds, bank accounts; pensions, social security and unemployment compensation; whether the defendant is out on bail; financial resources of the parents or spouse; and financial resources of other relatives. The remaining judges' determinations were not quite so extensive. A few of the judges simply ask the defendant whether he is employed and whether he has any real or personal property, and warn him that if he is not telling the truth he may be prosecuted for perjury. The judges differed somewhat as to what factor, standing alone, would preclude a finding of indigency. Some of the factors were financial resources of the spouse or parents; ownership of an automobile; and, in cases where the defendant is out on bail, whether he has a cash bond. If the defendant is found ineligible for provision of counsel as an indigent, the great majority of judges simply tell the defendant that he should retain his own lawyer if he wishes to have one.

The extremely divergent views of the judges on providing counsel for the indigent are expressed by some thought-provoking statements. Said one judge, "Many criminal cases are routine, and probation is often imposed on guilty pleas; so frequently a needless expense to society is imposed if a lawyer is appointed in every instance. Much depends, of course, on whether or not a judge is reasonable and fair minded, as I believe most judges are." Another judge said, "The financing is of secondary importance to the problem of presenting adequate representation. The rights of the defendant are paramount to the question of costs involved."

D. THE PROSECUTION VIEW

Personal interviews were held with the county attorneys of Maricopa, Coconino, Pima, and Cochise Counties. Questionnaires were returned from six of the other ten county attorneys. (The territorial jurisdiction of the county attorney is limited to one county.)

The experience in office of these county attorneys ranged from a year or less up to 14 years. All but two were recent members of the bar. The majority of those responding held the position of county attorney on a part-time basis. Of course in the larger counties, such as Maricopa and Pima, this office is a full-time job. Fifty per cent of the respondents felt that funds available were inadequate to run their offices.

The county attorneys were asked when, under an ideal system, counsel should first be made available to the indigent defendant. Every county attorney who responded to this question felt that the present system of affording the defendant counsel at the time of arraignment on the indictment or information was not adequate. Two thought it should be at the preliminary hearing; one stated it should be at the first appearance before a magistrate; one said it should be between the first appearance and the preliminary hearing; and two thought it should be between the arrest and the first appearance before a magistrate. All of the county attorneys except one believed that providing counsel at these particular stages could be financed, but that it would present problems. Some suggested that such a system might be abused, in which case it would be necessary to become much stricter in determining indigency.

The county attorneys were also asked about the availability of counsel in various cases and proceedings under an "ideal system." The views of those responding are expressed by the following tabulation:

Should counsel be made available to the indigent defendant on:			Would it be unfair to the indigent defendant if not offered counsel at this stage?				Would it be possible to finance a system to provide counsel in these cases and proceedings?		
	Yes	No	Yes	No	Could be	No comment	Yes	No	No comment
Sentencing of defendant who pleaded guilty	3	3		3	2	1	2	2	2
Sentencing of defendant convicted by trial	3	3		4	1	1	2	2	2
Habeas corpus, coram nobis, other postconviction remedy	4	2	3	2		1	2	2	2
Hearing on revocation of probation	3	3	2	2	2	0	2	2	2
Misdemeanors	2	4		4	2	0	2	2	2
Civil commitment, etc.	5	1	1	3	2	0	2	2	2

The majority of the county attorneys felt that assigned counsel compared equally in experience and ability with lawyers retained by defendants. Only one county attorney felt that assigned counsel did not compare as well.

The county attorneys were also asked their thoughts on the present system for determining eligibility for free counsel. Of 10 responding, 4 felt that it was too lenient, and the remainder that it was "about right."

As to whether the present rates of compensation for lawyers' services to indigent persons are adequate, seven felt that they were not, only two indicating that they were, and one had no comment.

Many of the county attorneys differed in their policy on making available to defense counsel such things as confessions, statements of witnesses, reports of expert witnesses, and exhibits. Every county attorney responding indicated that there was some disclosure, even though it might be limited. Coconino County, for example, indicated that disclosures were made in approximately 9 out of 10 cases, the possible exception being where a defense of insanity is raised. In these situations, statements or other evidence would be withheld to rebut the defense of insanity. In Maricopa County, the county attorney feels that there is liberal disclosure, but that primarily it depends upon the case and the integrity of the opposing counsel. In Pima County, disclosure is made of statements and confessions made by the defendant, and of exhibits. However, reports of expert witnesses and statements of other witnesses are withheld. On the other hand, all of these items are made available to the defense counsel in Cochise County.

E. THE DEFENSE VIEW

This part of the study was made entirely by questionnaires, of which 110 were mailed to attorneys in 11 counties, and 64 (58%) were returned from attorneys distributed over 8 counties: 29 from Maricopa, 8 from Pinal, 6 from Yuma, 5 each from Yavapai, Cochise, and Navajo, 4 from Coconino, and 2 from Gila.

The experience of the attorneys interviewed ranged from 1 to over 55 years in practice. Of the 64 attorneys who returned the questionnaires, 53 had been appointed as counsel for indigent persons during 1962. The number of cases handled by these attorneys varied from 1 to over 30 during that year. Twenty-nine attorneys had cases where the crime charged was punishable by death or life imprisonment.

In expressing their dissatisfaction with the present assigned counsel system, many of the attorneys indicated that for the most part the court appoints young attorneys. The returns, however, showed that the average lawyer had served in at least 25 to 30 criminal cases prior to being appointed in 1962.

The time of appointment, as indicated earlier in this report, is provided by Rule 163 of the Arizona Rules of Criminal Procedure, which reads in part:

> [B]efore the defendant is arraigned on a charge of felony, if he is without counsel, the court shall ask him if he desires the aid of counsel and if he answers in the affirmative, and declares under oath, that he has no means to employ counsel, the court shall assign counsel to represent him.

Almost without exception counsel who represented indigents in 1962 were appointed at the time of arraignment on the indictment or information. On some occasions, however, as in capital cases, counsel may be appointed at an earlier stage if requested by the magistrate. But this is the exception rather than the rule.

The lawyers were not unanimous on whether they were appointed in time to represent the accused adequately. Approximately two-thirds said in effect that appointment at the time of arraignment was early enough, but many of them qualified their answers. Some said they were lucky (because of the result in their favor), but others were of the opinion that it is absolutely essential that counsel be appointed at an earlier stage in order to protect all of the defendant's rights.

Although all the attorneys had been paid some compensation, there was dissatisfaction because the compensation afforded was inadequate, and in many instances out-of-pocket expenses were paid only partially or not at all. One attorney cited an example where he was appointed on a first-degree murder case. Immeasurable time was spent on preparation, one full day was consumed at the preliminary hearing, and the trial lasted seven and one-half days. The fee was $400.

Of the 64 attorneys responding, only 10 had undertaken an appeal during 1962.

A dual question was next posed to the attorneys. First, is the present system for assignment of lawyers to represent indigent persons accused of crime fair to the defendant, and, second, is it fair to the attorney? Of the 64 attorneys reporting on this question, 34 said the present system was fair to the indigent, 26 said that it was not, and 4 made no comment. On the other hand, as to whether the present system was fair to the attorney, 50 said that it was not, 11 said that it was, and 3 had no comment. The chief feeling of unfairness to attorneys was due to inadequate compensation. Another fact previously mentioned was that lawyers were required to waste time waiting in court to be appointed. This abuse occurs largely in Maricopa County.

F. THE DOCKET STUDY

The docket study revealed that 15% of the defendants in Maricopa and 62% in Coconino had no counsel (see Table 1). In Maricopa 53% of the defendants had retained counsel and 32% had assigned counsel. The data as to release on bail for Coconino County, available for 44 cases, showed that only 17 defendants (39%) were released. Insufficient information was available for Maricopa. In Coconino preliminary hearings were held for only 3 defendants out of 43 for whom information was available; 32 defendants waived the hearing. Insufficient information was available for Maricopa.

As shown in Table 2, the proportion of defendants who pleaded guilty to the principal offense was 37% in Maricopa and 68% in Coconino, for a weighted average of 48% for the two counties. An additional 6% pleaded to lesser offenses. In the cases that went to trial, most of the defendants were convicted. Maricopa had a high proportion of dismissals.

Table 3 shows the sentence, if any, imposed in each case. Because of the combined effect of dismissals and acquittals, 52% of the defendants in Maricopa were not sentenced at all, while 21% were sentenced to prison, including the county jail, and 22% were placed on probation. In Coconino County, where only 24% of the defendants were not sentenced, 42% had prison sentences and 32% were placed on probation. The table indicates a somewhat more frequent use of probation, suspended sentence (without probation), and fines in Maricopa County than in Coconino.

TABLE 1
Retained and Assigned Counsel in Felonies
Arizona, 1962

County	Total sample	Did defendant have counsel? Yes No.	%	No No.	%	Retained No.	%	Assigned No.	%	No data[*] No.	%
Maricopa	148	117	85	21	15	73	53	44	32	10	7
Coconino	50	19	38	31	62	13	26	6	12	0	0
Weighted total percentages		60		40		39		21		3	

[*] % in this column refers to the total sample; % in the other columns refers to the total cases for which data are available.

TABLE 2
Disposition in Felony Cases
Arizona, 1962

County	Total sample	Plea guilty	Plea lesser offense	Dismissed	Found guilty	Ac-quitted	Pend-ing	Other
Maricopa	148	40	8	50	23	10	5	12
Coconino	50	34	3	7	1	2	3	0
Weighted total percentages		48	6	24	9	6	5	3

TABLE 3
Sentencing in Felony Cases
Arizona, 1962

County	Total sample	No sentence No.	%	Prison No.	%	Pro-bation No.	%	Suspended sentence No.	%	Fine No.	%	Misc. No.	%	No data[*] No.	%
Maricopa	148	75	52	31	21	32	22	1	1	5	3	2	2	2	1
Coconino	50	12	24	21	42	16	32	0	0	1	2	0	0	0	0
Weighted total percentages		27		32		27		0		3		0		1	

[*] % in this column refers to the total sample; % in the other columns refers to the total cases for which data are available.

41

G. CONCLUSIONS AND RECOMMENDATIONS

The state bar committee on criminal law and procedure, at the request of the Supreme Court, has undertaken a comprehensive review of the rules of criminal procedure for the superior courts. It is recommended that the committee include as a part of their review the following:

1. *Should Arizona continue with the assigned counsel system?* Many attorneys have voiced criticism of this system for numerous reasons, i.e., that the method of selection of attorneys is unfair; that many attorneys are newer members of the bar; that many feel the bar as a whole should contribute their time and effort; that the system as applied to Maricopa County results in a waste of time; and that the coordinate items of compensation and reimbursement of attorneys are inadequate. There is no question that the institution of a public defender system would cure all of these complaints. The present system is being supported only by those attorneys who desire to serve as assigned counsel.

2. *Appointment of counsel.* Counsel for the indigent defendant should be assigned prior to the preliminary hearing. Without question, the great majority of those who were interviewed indicated that the present system of appointment of counsel at the time of arraignment was inadequate. The subject was discussed at the 1963 judicial conference of Arizona superior court judges in Tucson, and serious consideration is presently being given to the appointment of counsel at the preliminary hearing stage. If this bears fruit, many of the inequities now existing at the lower court level will be cured. Appointment of counsel at the preliminary hearing stage would doubtless result in greater expenditures by the county for attorneys' fees; however, this may be offset in some degree by the fact that if counsel is appointed at the time of the preliminary hearing, many "weak" cases can be washed out at this stage, instead of waiting until the time of trial, when the costs incident thereto are far greater.

3. *Complete explanation of defendant's rights at first appearance.* Justices of the peace should be continually reminded of the importance of explaining to the accused all of his rights at the first appearance. In particular a detailed explanation should be given the accused of the nature and purpose of a preliminary hearing and its importance to him. Under the present system a preliminary hearing that is held for a defendant not represented by counsel is almost meaningless. Furthermore, without counsel at this critical stage, he is almost certain to be bound over to superior court.

4. *Disclosures to defense counsel.* There should be a uniform policy of disclosure among county attorneys to defense counsel regarding confessions, statements of witnesses, exhibits, etc., except in cases where nondisclosure is absolutely necessary, i.e., to rebut a defense of insanity.

5. *Appointment of counsel in other proceedings.* Serious consideration should be given to the question of making counsel available to indigent defendants accused of high misdemeanors. Many feel that it would be impossible to finance such a system. On the other hand, if confined to high misdemeanors, the plan may very well be workable. High misdemeanors are prosecuted by direct information in the superior court. There is no preliminary hearing as in a felony.

Therefore counsel would need to be appointed only at the trial. As to appointment of counsel at a habeas corpus proceeding, there can be no doubt that this remedy is extremely technical and should be handled by an attorney. On the other hand, many feel that this would be abused. Counsel is not presently afforded in cases of this nature.

6. *Compensation.* A detailed study should be made as to the feasibility of increasing compensation for attorneys. Many lawyers feel that they should give freely of their time and effort, yet only 10% of the Maricopa County Bar is contributing anything by way of defense for the indigent. It is felt that attorneys should certainly be reimbursed fully for reasonable expenses incurred in investigation, preparation, and trial. A uniform system should be incorporated throughout the state on payment to attorneys for reasonable expenses incurred. Immediate steps should be taken to provide means of compensating counsel when he has represented an indigent defendant at the preliminary hearing stage.

7. *Docket records.* The system of keeping docket records should be more uniform throughout the state. More complete data about each case should be kept in one central file in each county.

ARKANSAS

Thomas E. Downie, Little Rock

The A.B.A. Associate State Committee consisted of Jack L. Lessenberry, Little Rock, chairman; Charles M. Mooney, Jonesboro; Elton A. Rieves III, West Memphis; and Charles B. Trumbo, Fayetteville.

A. INTRODUCTION

Arkansas had a population of 1,786,272 in 1960. The state is divided into 75 counties, which are organized into 18 judicial districts. Each judicial district has one or more elected circuit judges and one elected prosecuting attorney. Each county usually has at least one resident deputy prosecuting attorney, who is appointed by the prosecuting attorney. The counties selected for the survey are as follows:

County (City)	1960 population in thousands	Location in state	Remarks
Pulaski (D) (Little Rock)	242	Central	State capital, commercial and industrial center of state
Lonoke	24	East central	Agriculture: cotton, rice, soybeans
Saline (Benton)	28	West central	Light manufacturing, bauxite mining
Crittenden (D) (West Memphis)	47	Eastern	Agriculture. Across Mississippi River from Memphis, Tennessee
Union (D) (El Dorado)	49	Southern	Oil production and refining
Washington (D) (Fayetteville)	55	Northwest	Truck farming, poultry, state university, tourist industry

(D) indicates that a docket study was made.

The following table gives additional information about the counties surveyed.

County	Felony defendants, 1962	% Indigent	% who waived counsel*	Lawyers in private practice	No. of appointments of counsel in felonies, 1962†	No. of lawyers who served†	Typical payment for felony guilty plea
Pulaski	409	20	7	651	80	22	None
Lonoke	No data	60	50	18	No data	No data	None
Saline	45	45	25	16	5	5	$25
Crittenden	194	85	35	26	70	15	$25
Union	96	30	60	64	20	No data	None
Washington	66	10	None	80	No data	No data	None

* Average of estimates supplied by judge and prosecuting attorney for each survey county.
† Based on estimates supplied by judge and/or prosecuting attorney for survey county.

B. CRIMINAL PROCEDURE AS IT AFFECTS INDIGENT PERSONS

Justices of the peace have original jurisdiction, except as set forth below, over all misdemeanors committed within their townships. Most municipal courts have original jurisdiction of misdemeanors coextensive with the county boundaries, and all municipal courts have original jurisdiction (1) exclusive of justices of the peace and of the circuit courts over violations of all ordinances of the municipality wherein the court is situated; and (2) exclusive of the justice of the peace and concurrent with the circuit court over misdemeanors committed within the municipality.

Municipal courts and justices of the peace have jurisdiction to sit as examining courts and commit, discharge, or recognize offenders to the court having jurisdiction of the trial, and to bind persons to keep the peace. Usually municipal judges are licensed attorneys, but justices of the peace are not.

Circuit courts in Arkansas have original jurisdiction, derived in criminal matters from the criminal code and the common law. Circuit courts also have appellate jurisdiction over municipal, justice of the peace, and police courts. Appellate jurisdiction is vested in the Supreme Court of Arkansas, which is composed of a chief justice and six associate justices elected by the people for eight-year terms.

Arkansas law provides for both indictment by the grand jury and charge by information filed by the prosecuting attorney or his deputy directly in the circuit court. The great majority of felony cases in Arkansas are brought by the filing of the information. After the information is filed, the defendant is arrested, usually on a bench warrant issued by the circuit judge. In some instances a preliminary hearing is held either in municipal court or in justice of the peace court, and the defendant is bound over to circuit court if there is probable cause to believe he committed the offense charged.

In most cases, the first appearance is at the time of arraignment, wherein the defendant is informed of his rights and the charges against him, asked if he has or wants counsel, and is then asked to plead. The arraignment is conducted by the circuit judge, who is an experienced lawyer. Where the preliminary hearing before a committing magistrate is used, the justice of the peace is usually not a lawyer, but, if the magistrate is the municipal judge, he will be a licensed attorney.

Normally bail is set at the time the bench warrant is issued on the information, and the defendant may be admitted to bail between the time of his arrest and his arraignment. There are no set schedules for bail in any of the counties. Bail is set usually upon recommendation of the prosecuting attorney and will vary according to the circumstances of each particular case.

Preliminary hearings other than the arraignment are rarely asked for in any of the counties. The survey reflects that the first appearance varies greatly in length of time after arrest: Crittenden and Union Counties usually take only 13 to 24 hours; Washington, Saline, and Pulaski, 25 to 48; and Lonoke, 49 to 72.

In many counties, after the information is filed and the defendant is arrested, it is not unusual, if he is unable to make bond, for him to remain in jail for three to six months before arraignment. The first opportunity for the defendant to express his wishes concerning the appointment of counsel is usually at arraignment, when the judge asks the defendant's wishes after telling him of his rights and the significance of the charges against him. The defendant may then make his wishes known, at which time the court will appoint an attorney for him if he wishes one appointed. The arraignment is the first contact between the judge and the accused, so it is really the first chance for the appointment of an attorney, unless a defendant specifically requests one earlier and is able to communicate this to the judge. In a few instances, especially in capital offenses, counsel is appointed earlier.

If, after the appointment of counsel at the time of arraignment, counsel feels he needs time to prepare a defense, the judge will grant the time, and usually will pass the case until the next criminal term of court, which may be six months away. If defendant is unable to make bond, he will have to remain in jail for this period. The judge sets the bond in all counties. In most counties, the prosecuting attorney makes a strong recommendation concerning the amount of the bond, which the judge usually follows. There is usually no chance of a reduction of the bail, so the absence of an attorney at this stage is no real handicap. Most prosecuting attorneys and judges set the bond realistically in the first instance, taking into consideration the seriousness of the charge, the likelihood that the defendant may skip bond, and his ability to make the bond.

The procedure for appointment of counsel varies little in the counties surveyed. Arkansas has no public defender system. The assigned counsel on a case-by-case method is used exclusively for indigents accused of crime. When the defendant appears at the arraignment, he is called before the bench, advised of his rights, advised of the charge, and asked if he has counsel or wants counsel. If he wants counsel, he is asked if he is able to employ counsel of his own choosing, and if he wishes to do so time is granted for this. If the defendant says he is unable to retain counsel because of indigency, the trial judge asks a series of questions of the defendant concerning his resources, employment, and other pertinent information. Actually, the judge usually knows before arraignment whether a defendant is able to employ counsel, since the arresting officers and prosecuting attorney have investigated the case and reported to the judge about the financial status of the defendant.

Most defendants are capable of raising funds with which to employ an attorney, and most of them do. Some defendants feel that the state should take care of them and claim to be indigent, when in reality they are not. The Arkansas judges seem to do an admirable job in their determination of just who is really indigent and deserving of the appointment of counsel. There are no fixed standards for determining indigency. It is a personal thing with each trial judge, but each seems to take about the same factors into consideration. All the judges interviewed expressed the feeling that those persons capable of paying any kind of a fee should do so, and, if they are capable of paying only a small fee, counsel should be appointed and should be allowed the fee.

The two methods used by trial judges to determine whom to appoint are the traditional methods of appointment: any attorney present in court, or the judge's own list of members of the local bar. The judge takes into consideration the ability, experience, health, time available, and age of the attorney to be appointed. The judges appoint more than one attorney in serious cases and make sure that experienced counsel is provided. They attempt to apportion the appointments in an equitable manner among the members of the bar. Attorneys accept the responsibility of representing indigent defendants even though they receive no compensation. Most of them feel that this is an obligation the bar owes to society.

A defendant after being found indigent may wish to waive his right to counsel. After being advised of the charges and his rights, the defendant is asked if he wishes counsel and is apprised that counsel will be appointed to represent him at no cost to him. He may at this time decline the appointment of counsel. Most judges do not want to force counsel upon a defendant. However, in Washington County, counsel is appointed in all felony cases whether or not defendant wants counsel. The prosecuting attorneys, as well as judges, prefer that a defendant accept appointment of counsel rather than represent himself in a trial, and, unless a defendant is to plead guilty, he is encouraged to accept it. At present, counsel is appointed before a guilty plea is taken in almost all instances in Arkansas. Many defendants prefer to plead guilty and try to convince the judge to suspend the sentence, or to let them begin the serving of their sentence in order to expedite their return to freedom.

The legislature in Arkansas has provided the following method by which appointed attorneys may be compensated for their services:

> Ark. Stats. (Supp. 1961) §43-2415, *Attorney Appointed to Defend Persons—Fees:* Hereafter the Quorum Court of any county of the State of Arkansas whose population did not exceed 100,000 by the most recent federal census may make an appropriation to pay for the services of attorneys appointed by the Circuit Court to defend persons accused of crime. In all counties where said appropriation has been made, any attorney at law appointed by the Circuit Court to defend a person charged in said court with the commission of a crime, whether misdemeanor or felony, shall receive for his services in representing said accused a fee of not less than Twenty-Five Dollars ($25) and not more than Two Hundred Fifty Dollars ($250), the amount of which shall be fixed by the Circuit Court. Said fee shall be paid in all cases, notwithstanding the entry of a plea of guilty or a *nolle prosequi* or dismissal.
>
> Ark. Stats. (Supp. 1961) §43-2416, *Court to Certify the Amount of Fee:* The judge of the court appointing the attorney to defend the accused, as provided in Section 1 hereof, shall certify to the county court the amount of the fee fixed by the court and mandamus will lie to enforce payment by the county of the sum so certified out of the funds appropriated by the Quorum Court for said purpose.

Of the six counties wherein the survey was conducted, only three have used these provisions. Union County in the past has provided funds with which to pay appointed attorneys, but presently no funds are available for this purpose. Crittenden and Saline are the only counties surveyed now paying appointed counsel. In the other counties, if appointed counsel can work out a fee arrangement with the defendant after appointment, the arrangement is sanctioned by the trial court. In the two counties where fees are allowed, they range from $25 to $100, depending on the work done and the seriousness of the offense. No provision is made in any county for the reimbursement of defense counsel's out-of-pocket expenses or costs of investigation. In the two counties where fees are allowed, the expenses incurred are considerd by the trial court in setting the fee allowed.

In none of the sample counties is counsel provided for misdemeanors. This seems to be the accepted practice throughout the state. In only one county is counsel appointed in all felony cases where a defendant pleads guilty. In the others, counsel will be appointed if requested and if the defendant meets the requirements of indigency. The defendant's counsel, whether retained or assigned, will be present at the sentencing whether a trial is held or a plea of guilty is entered.

The supreme court appoints appellate counsel, but usually chooses counsel who served in the circuit court. There have been no changes in method since *Douglas v. California* (372 U.S. 353 [1963]), and *Draper v. Washington* (id. 487). A complete transcript and record of the trial are provided at public expense for the indigent appellant. Fees of counsel are allowed on appeal. In capital cases they range from $150 to $200. Travel expenses to the state capital are assumed to be included in the fee allowed.

C. OPINIONS OF THE JUDGES

The circuit judge was interviewed in each of the 6 survey counties and questionnaires were mailed to all 12 judges for the other 12 districts. Nine judges replied. Thus 15 out of 18 districts are represented in the study. In Pulaski County, one circuit judge is responsible for all the criminal cases on the docket, and he hears nothing but criminal cases. Crittenden and Union Counties each have two circuit judges. These two judges alternate hearing criminal and civil cases. Each judge will have one criminal and one civil term of court each year in each county in the district. In the other three counties, there is only one circuit judge for the district.

To the question "Under an ideal system at what stage in a criminal case do you think the indigent person should first be provided with a lawyer if he wants one?", four of the six judges interviewed responded that counsel should be provided at an earlier stage than is being done at present, and two of these thought counsel should first be provided at first appearance before a magistrate. Of the remaining two judges, one said that counsel should first be provided at arraignment on the indictment or information, as is presently the case, and the other thought it should be done after arraignment on the indictment or information. Four of the judges thought it unfair to the indigent if he did not get counsel at the stage recommended; one hedged, replying that the circumstances of each case should control; and only one thought it unfair. Three of the judges thought that such a program could be financed, while the other three had no comment on this problem.

On the same question in the mail questionnaire only eight of the nine judges answered all or substantially all of the questions. The answers were as follows: seven of the eight felt that under an ideal system counsel should be provided at a stage earlier than it is at present, i.e., at arraignment. Four thought counsel should be provided after the return of an indictment or filing of an information, but before arraignment thereon. One judge replied that the defendant should be provided counsel at first appearance before a magistrate; one felt counsel should be provided between first appearance and preliminary hearing; and one thought the defendant should be provided with counsel at arraignment on indictment or information. Five of the judges answering the question thought it unfair if counsel was not appointed at the stage they prescribed, and two did not. By the same margin they believed that a program of paying assigned counsel could be financed.

On the basis of the opinions expressed, there appears to be no correlation between the age, number of years on the bench, and general experience of the judge and his answers to these questions.

D. OPINIONS OF PROSECUTING ATTORNEYS

The prosecuting attorney was interviewed in each of the 6 sample counties, and a questionnaire was mailed to the prosecuting attorneys for each of the other 12 districts; 7 replied.

Prosecuting attorneys are elected in Arkansas, one from each judicial district. The prosecuting attorney may appoint a deputy in each county. In Lonoke, a survey county, the prosecuting attorney has no deputy in any of the four counties which make up his district. In Pulaski, another survey county, the prosecuting attorney has a staff of five full-time lawyers and one part-time lawyer for his two-county district. Prosecuting attorneys also represent the counties in civil matters. As a group they felt that the present system of providing counsel for indigent defendants was adequate to protect the rights of defendants, but inadequate as to compensation for appointed attorneys.

1. *Results of interviews.* Five of the six interviewed prosecuting attorneys felt that appointed counsel were just as able and did as good a job as retained counsel, while one felt that appointed counsel did not work as hard because he would not receive compensation. Three of the six thought that the judge's present system for determining indigency was "about right"; two, that it was too lenient; and one, that there was no system at all. All six prosecuting attorneys said that appointed attorneys should be compensated for their efforts and should be reimbursed for their out-of-pocket expenses. Four of the six made their complete file available to the defendant's counsel, whether appointed or retained. The other two prosecuting attorneys vary their practice, depending upon the case. Five of them felt that a defendant who could pay a moderate fee should pay. One had no comment on this matter. All six object to trying cases where the defendant is not represented by counsel.

Two prosecuting attorneys said that counsel under an ideal system should be provided as at present, i.e., at arraignment on the indictment or information. One thought that after arraignment on the indictment or information would be ideal; one, at time of the trial; and one, after filing of an indictment or information but before arraignment thereon. One other said that between arrest and first appearance before a magistrate, if defendant requested counsel at that stage, would be ideal, but if not provided at that stage it would not be unfair to the indigent defendant. Four of the prosecuting attorneys felt that if counsel were not provided at the ideal time it would be unfair to the defendant. The other prosecutor did not think it unfair that defendant not receive counsel after filing of the indictment but before arraignment.

2. *Results of mail questionnaires.* Five of the seven prosecuting attorneys questioned by mail found appointed attorneys just as able and experienced as retained counsel. Two thought that appointed counsel tended to be less experienced and less able. Four felt that the judge's present system of determining indigency is about right, while three considered the judge too lenient. All prosecuting attorneys responding by mail felt that attorneys should be compensated for their services. Four favored payment of out-of-pocket expenses, while two had no comment. Four thought that present compensation is adequate, and two, that it is inadequate.

Four of the prosecuting attorneys make at least a part of their file available to all defendants, including three who make the complete file available. Of the other three prosecutors, one makes nothing available in any case until the court orders him to do so, one makes his file available to appointed but not retained counsel, and one answered that the circumstances of the case would determine his policy. Prosecuting attorneys responding by mail, by a margin of six to one, agreed that the present stage at which counsel is provided is not ideal. One recommended that under an ideal system counsel should be provided between arrest and first appearance before a magistrate; three, at first appearance before a magistrate; and one each at the stages of (a) after preliminary hearing but before the filing of an indictment or information, (b) after the filing of an indictment or information but before arraignment thereon, and (c) at arraignment on indictment or information (the present practice). Three said it would be unfair to the defendant if the stage they suggested were not used; two did not feel that it would be unfair; and two thought that the circumstances of each case would dictate what was fair.

E. OPINIONS OF DEFENSE ATTORNEYS

Questionnaires were mailed to 33 attorneys in the sample counties who were appointed to represent indigent defendants, and 24 responded. The responses indicate that the courts almost invariably appoint lawyers with some experience in criminal practice. Of 20 defense lawyers appointed in 1962, 12 indicated that they had previously handled more than 50 criminal cases, and 13 had been in private law practice for 10 years or more. These lawyers were appointed on an average of five times per year to defend indigent persons.

Over half of the lawyers received no compensation for the last case assigned to them in 1962. None of them, however, undervalued their services, and to the question "How much would you have charged a client who retained you for your services in this case?", the answers gave an average fee of $901.25. The sample included six cases punishable by death or life imprisonment, for which the average fee would have been $2100.

Of the 20 lawyers, 8 were appointed to defend at the arraignment on the indictment or information, 5 were appointed after arraignment but before trial, and 4 were appointed at or before the defendant's first appearance before a magistrate. Three of the lawyers were appointed after bringing of the indictment or filing of the information, but before arraignment. Fifteen of the 20, howevei felt that they were assigned in time to present an adequate defense. One gave qualified answer of yes, "because no out-of-pocket expenses were provided t make an investigation of the case." This raises some question as to whether th indigent person in fact received an adequate defense under these circumstances Only one lawyer stated that he had been repaid for óut-of-pocket expenses, anc this only in part. One lawyer had represented an indigent defendant on appea in 1962, and none were appointed in habeas corpus, coram nobis, or other post conviction remedies.

The sampling was approximately evenly divided on whether the present system for assignment of lawyers to represent indigent persons was fair to the indigent person, but they voted 15 to 7 that the system was not fair to the lawyers. Those who did not feel the system fair to the defendant qualified their answers with such remarks as "as fair as possible" and "maybe not a good system but at least a system." The underlying reason for the negative answer to the question "Is the system fair to lawyers?" was apparently based on the lack of adequate compensation and the lack of any method of reimbursing for out-of-pocket expenses. Of 22 responding, 4 felt that lawyers should be appointed at earlier stages of the case than they are at present, and 2 thought that the judges should improve the systems they use in selecting lawyers to be appointed. The lawyer appointed for appeal complained that he spent six weeks working on the case, used two secretaries for a week to type the brief, and had other expenses, but received nothing. The same thing had happened to him the previous year.

The consensus of these defense attorneys is that the representation of indigent persons accused of crime is a responsibility of the bar, recognized by each lawyer when he is admitted to practice, and that he is, in effect, functioning as an arm of the court in performing this duty.

F. COMPARISONS AMONG JUDGES AND PROSECUTING ATTORNEYS

For purposes of comparison, the judges were divided into two groups according to years of service on the bench and are designated below as senior judges or junior judges. The same procedure was followed in dividing prosecuting attorneys into two categories. Results are shown in the tabulation below.

G. DOCKET STUDIES

Results for the docket studies of actual cases in 1962 in four of the sample counties are shown in Tables 1 through 6. The weighted total at the bottom of each table is an estimate for the state as a whole, obtained by multiplying the county samples by appropriate weighting factors.

Table 1 shows that the proportion of defendants not released on bail ranged from 50% in Union County to 71% in Pulaski, with a state estimate of 63%. Table 3 shows that an even higher proportion of defendants were found indigent, namely, 79% as a state estimate. This indicates that some defendants who make bail are nevertheless indigent. Table 4 shows considerable variation among the

Comparisons Among Judges and Prosecuting Attorneys

	Senior judges*	Junior judges	Senior prosecutors	Junior prosecutors	Total
Total responding†	9	5	5	8	27
Ideal stage for first appointment of counsel					
Between arrest and first appearance	1	2	1	1	5
At first appearance before a magistrate	3	0	0	3	6
Between first appearance and preliminary hearing	1	0	0	0	1
After preliminary hearing but before indictment	0	0	0	1	1
After filing the indictment but before arraignment	2	2	0	2	6
At arraignment on information	1	1	3	0	5
After arraignment on information	0	1	0	1	2
At trial	0	0	0	1	1
Is present compensation adequate to appointed counsel?					
Yes	2	0	0	4	6
No	4	3	2	2	11
No comment	4	1	3	2	10
Should out-of-pocket expenses be paid?					
Yes	5	2	5	5	17
No	1	0	0	1	2
No comment	4	3	0	2	9

* One judge returned his questionnaire unanswered.
† Judges and prosecuting attorneys replying by mail are included.

four counties as to whether defendants have counsel and if so whether retained or assigned counsel. The proportion of defendants without counsel ranged from 5% in Washington County to 75% in Union County, with a state estimate of 36%. Changes in local practice have no doubt occurred since the *Gideon* decision in 1963.

Table 2 shows the extent to which preliminary hearings are held. They appear to be common in Union, Crittenden, and Pulaski Counties but rare in Washington County.

Table 5 shows the disposition of the cases. For the state as a whole an estimated 64% of the defendants pleaded guilty to the principal offense, and 5% pleaded to lesser offenses. Of the 12% of the cases that went to trial, 9% resulted in verdicts of guilty, including 1% guilty of lesser offenses, while 3% of the cases resulted in acquittals. As shown in Table 7, sentences were imposed on an estimated 78% of all the defendants; the remaining cases were dismissals, acquittals, and the like. Of the 78%, 43% were sentenced to terms in prison or jail, while only 29% were placed on probation. The extent of use of probation varied among the counties, the greatest use being made in Washington County, followed by Crittenden, Washington, and Pulaski in that order.

H. CONCLUSIONS AND RECOMMENDATIONS

There seems to be no marked change in the system of providing counsel to represent indigent persons accused of crime in Arkansas since the case of *Gideon v. Wainright* and other recent decisions of the United States Supreme Court touching on this matter. The fact, however, that this survey is being conducted

TABLE 1
Frequency of Release on Bail of Felony Defendants
Arkansas, 1962

County	Total sample	Yes No.	%	No No.	%	No data[*] No.	%
Union	20	9	50	9	50	2	10
Washington	18	6	33	12	67	0	0
Crittenden	40	13	35	24	65	3	8
Pulaski	49	14	29	34	71	1	2
Weighted total percentages			37		63		5

[*] % in this column refers to the total sample; % in the other columns refers to the total cases for which data were available.

TABLE 2
Frequency of Preliminary Hearings in Felonies
Arkansas, 1962

County	Total sample	Yes No.	%	No, waiver No.	%	No, not used in this kind of case No.	%	No data[*] No.	%
Union	20	18	100	0	0	0	0	2	10
Washington	20	0	0	0	0	20	100	0	0
Crittenden	40	33	100	0	0	0	0	7	18
Pulaski	49	33	87	5	13	0	0	11	22
Weighted total percentages			70		3		28		13

[*] % in this column refers to the total sample; % in the other columns refers to the total cases for which data were available.

TABLE 3
Was Felony Defendant Determined Indigent?
Arkansas, 1962

County	Total sample	Yes No.	%	No No.	%	No data* No.	%
Union	20	1	5	18	95	1	5
Washington	20	4	20	16	80	0	0
Crittenden	40	11	28	28	72	1	3
Pulaski	49	16	33	32	67	1	2
Weighted total percentages			21		79		3

* % in this column refers to the total sample; % in the other columns refers to the total cases for which data were available.

TABLE 4
Retained and Assigned Counsel in Felonies
Arkansas, 1962

County	Total sample	Did defendant have counsel? Yes No.	%	No No.	%	Retained No.	%	Assigned No.	%	Combination or type unknown No.	%
Union	20	5	25	15	75	4	20	1	5	0	0
Washington	18	19	95	1	5	15	75	4	20	0	0
Crittenden	40	23	58	17	43	10	25	11	28	2	5
Pulaski	49	42	86	7	14	26	53	16	33	0	0
Weighted total percentages			65		36		43		21		1

TABLE 5
Disposition in Felony Cases
Arkansas, 1962

County	Total sample	Plea guilty	Plea lesser offense	Dis- missed	Found guilty	Found guilty lesser degree	Ac- quitted	Mental commit- ment	Pend- ing	Other
Union	20	13	2	5	0	0	0	0	0	0
Washington	18	11	0	2	1	0	1	1	2	0
Crittenden	40	24	1	6	4	0	2	0	2	1*
Pulaski	49	34	4	2	5	1	1	1	0	1
Weighted total percentages		64	5	14	8	1	3	2	4	0

* No data.

TABLE 6
Sentencing in Felony Cases
Arkansas, 1962

County	Total sample	No sentence No.	%	Prison* No.	%	Probation No.	%	Suspended sentence No.	%	Fine No.	%
Union	20	5	25	10	50	4	20	0	0	1	5
Washington	18	6	33	4	22	7	39	0	0	3	17
Crittenden	40	9	22	16	40	17	42	2	5	0	0
Pulaski	49	5	10	30	61	10	20	3	6	3	6
Weighted total percentages		22		43		29		3		9	

If a sentence was for any combination of prison, probation, suspended sentence (without probation), and fine, it is recorded under each of these columns.
* Includes county jail.

will probably make the judiciary and the bar more aware of the need for a closer examination of the system in this state.

Methods of determining indigency are at present unstandardized and in some instances haphazard. One result of the instant survey might be a recommended standard for determining indigency.

The consensus among the sampling of judges, prosecutors, and defense counsel in Arkansas seems to be that indigent defendants are presently represented adequately, and that their rights are being protected. The chief difficulty at present is that appointed attorneys are in most cases serving without any, and in all cases without adequate, compensation. The answer to this problem is not an easy one. The Arkansas legislature recently recognized this problem by passing what amounted to an enabling act, authorizing counties to appropriate funds for the purpose of paying appointed counsel, but making no mandatory provision to insure that the county does so appropriate. Therefore, most counties have failed to use this legislation at all, and those which have, have used it sparingly with token appropriations. Either the state should provide funds or a mandatory provision should be enacted to insure that all counties make adequate appropriations for compensating assigned counsel and reimbursing his out-of-pocket expenses.

This is a continuing problem, and the cost of providing counsel for indigent defendants should be recognized as an ordinary expense of operating the courts.

CALIFORNIA

Prof. Norman Abrams, Los Angeles, and Bernard
Petrie, San Francisco

The members of the A.B.A. State Committee provided valuable counsel in connection with the preparation of this report. The chairman of the committee was Arthur B. Dunne of San Francisco and the vice-chairman was Philip F. Westbrook, Jr., of Los Angeles.

A. INTRODUCTION

According to statistics prepared by the California State Department of Finance, California had an estimated total population of 16,455,000 in 1961 and 17,094,000 in 1962. The state is divided into 58 counties, and the California constitution provides that there shall be in each county a superior court, "for each of which at least one judge shall be elected by the qualified electors of the county. . . ." In the 1961-1962 fiscal year there were 332 authorized superior court judgeships in the state, with more than one-third assigned to Los Angeles County. The original jurisdiction of the superior courts includes "all criminal cases amounting to felony, and cases of misdemeanor not otherwise provided for." Superior courts also have appellate jurisdiction in such cases arising in municipal and in justices' courts "as may be prescribed by law." Each county is divided into judicial districts, and, as of the end of the 1960-1962 biennial period, there were 370 judicial districts in the state, in which were located 72 municipal courts and 298 justice courts. Municipal courts have jurisdiction over misdemeanors, and justice courts, with limited exceptions, have jurisdiction over misdemeanors punishable by a maximum fine of $1,000 or imprisonment of six months.

A number of general provisions in the Government Code (§§27700-27711) provide for the establishment of local public defender systems. These provisions empower the board of supervisors of a county to set up a public defender's office, either appointive or elective, and to fix his salary and expense allowance. A defender is required to have practiced for one year and, in counties of more than 850,000 population, must devote full time to the duties of his office. In all counties, public defenders, even those who are part-time, are banned from private criminal defense work. Where a county opts for an elected public defender, a four-year term of office is required. In the absence of special local provisions, an appointed public defender serves at the will of the county board of supervisors. A general statutory provision also describes in some detail the duties which a public defender is required to perform. Of the 58 counties in California, 23 have established a public defender office.

In a county, or city and county, in which there is no public defender, or in a case where the court finds that the public defender has properly refused to represent the person accused, a provision of the Penal Code (987a) requires that reasonable compensation, to be determined by the court, is to be made to counsel who is appointed in the superior court or in the municipal or

TABLE 1
The Sample Counties

County	1960 population in thou-sands	Remarks	Type of system	Felony defendants, 1962
Contra Costa	409	Rural and transition	Assigned counsel	470
Los Angeles (D)	6038	Third largest metropolitan area in U.S.; business and industrial center; large minorities population	Public defender	16,473
Riverside	306	Agricultural and light industry; citrus fruit center	Public defender	603
Sacramento	503	State capital; farming and commercial	Public defender	1047
San Francisco (D)	740	Metropolitan; financial center and seaport	Public defender	1800
San Diego (D)	1033	Metropolitan; second largest population in state; aircraft industry; naval base; close to Mexican border	Assigned counsel	1339
Santa Clara (D)	642	Rural and metropolitan; burgeoning population; electronics and aircraft	·Assigned counsel	951
Shasta (D)	59	Rural; farming, timber; tourist; numerous Indians from Trinity County	Assigned counsel	130
Tulare (D)	168	Rural; agriculture; large farm labor population	Public defender	348

(D) indicates that a docket study was made.

justice court. Sums so paid are to be taken out of the general fund of the county. In addition to these general statutory provisions, which in effect give each county the option between a public defender and assigned counsel system, a county may "either by passage of ordinances not inconsistent with the general law or by adoption of charters" enact additional provisions governing the particular system it adopts. In Los Angeles, for example, the county charter describes the duties of the public defender, and in addition provides that any duties added by state law shall become the duties of the public defender.

Five of the nine sample counties in California have adopted public defender systems: Los Angeles, Riverside, San Francisco, Sacramento, and Tulare. Moreover, the City of Los Angeles operates a public defender's office for misdemeanors, and the City of Long Beach, with a population of over 300,000, operates a similar office. San Diego, the second most populous county in the state, has an assigned counsel system. The issue of whether to adopt a public defender has been the subject of some debate in that county in recent years: on October 2, 1963, the San Diego County Board of Supervisors issued a report again rejecting a proposal to adopt a public defender system. Similarly, Contra Costa County still operates under an assigned counsel system, but proposals not yet acted upon have been made there to adopt a public defender. The two remaining counties in the sample, Santa Clara and Shasta, have assigned counsel systems. [Santa Clara established a public defender in February, 1965. See Chapman, "Setting Up a Public Defender Office," 23 Legal Aid Brief Case 293 (1965).]

Tables 1, 2, and 3 contain pertinent information regarding the sample counties and the system each has adopted to provide counsel for indigent accused persons.

B. CRIMINAL PROCEDURE AS IT AFFECTS INDIGENT PERSONS

In the counties surveyed, most felony cases are prosecuted by information, although indictments may also be used. Prosecution by information is commenced by the filing of a written complaint under oath with a magistrate, usually either a municipal or a justice court judge. If the person complained against is not in custody, the magistrate issues a warrant for the arrest of the defendant, endorsing thereon the amount of bail to be required for his appearance. If prior to the filing of a complaint a person is arrested without a warrant, a complaint must thereupon be filed before the magistrate "without unnecessary delay." By statute, an arrested defendant "must in all cases be taken before the magistrate without unnecessary delay, and, in any event, within two days after his arrest. . . ." Also by statute, after arrest, any attorney may at the request of the prisoner visit him, and the arrested person also has, "immediately after he is booked, and except where physically impossible, no later than three hours after his arrest, the right to make, at his own expense . . . at least two telephone calls . . . completed to the person called," one to his attorney, employer, or a relative, and the other to a bail bondsman. "Wilful delay" in taking an arrested person before a magistrate or refusal to allow the attorney visit or deprivation of the right to make the two telephone calls constitutes

TABLE 2

Public Defender Systems

County	Los Angeles	Riverside	Sacramento	San Francisco	Tulare
Selection of public defender	Appointed[1]	Appointed	Appointed	Elected[14]	Elected[14]
Civil service	Yes	No	Yes	No	No
Total staff[2]	93	5	11[3]	13	3
Full-time lawyers	0	2	7	8	0
Part-time lawyers	66	2	0	0	2
Investigators	10	0	1	1	0
Budget (current fiscal year)	Approx. $1,000,000	$36,300	$128,000	$164,338	$13,600
Salary range (per month)	$ 608-1540[4] 1816-2142[5]	$417-516[4a] 575-715[4] 842-1048[5]	$ 905-1100[4] 1450-1550[5]	$ 764-1337[4] 1707[5]	$375[4a] 500[5a]
Felony defendants	10,563[6]	––	1104[7]	3545[8]	468[9]
All cases (involving possible restriction on liberty of the individual)	30,382[10]	1030[11]	2355[12]	10,668[13]	––

[1] Based on competitive examination.

[2] Includes secretarial and clerical personnel.

[3] Does not include investigative and administrative assistance volunteered by students in the law enforcement program at Sacramento State College.

[4] Applicable to full-time deputy.

[4a] Applicable to part-time deputy.

[5] Applicable to full-time chief.

[5a] Applicable to part-time chief.

[6] Represents new felony defendants received 1960-61.

[7] Defendants represented in the superior court.

[8] Includes felony hearings in the municipal court, juvenile court hearings, and defendants in the superior court.

[9] Defendants represented, 1961-62, as reported orally by the public defender. Compare Table 1, Felony defendants, 1962.

[10] Includes separate listing of preliminary hearings amounting to 12,745 cases (1960-61).

[11] Listed as "total number of persons represented" (1962-63).

[12] Total number of defendants represented in the municipal and superior courts.

[13] Includes 7123 misdemeanor defendants in the municipal court (1962).

[14] Deputy defender(s) appointed by the public defender.

TABLE 3
Assigned Counsel Systems

County	San Diego	Los Angeles (limited to conflict of interest cases)	Contra Costa	Santa Clara	Shasta
Number of lawyers in county	880[1]	9549[1]	202	717	32[1a]
Number of lawyers on appointment list	Several hundred (est.)	Several hundred (est.)	202	164	14
Total number appointments, 1962-63	813[2] 2286[2a]	446[3]	No record	No record	94[4]
Number of lawyers who served	158[2]	266[5]	76	No record	No record
Composition, appointment list	Volunteer, names removed upon request	Volunteer, publicized through legal newspaper	All lawyers in county	Volunteer	Volunteer[6]
Method of selection	Rotation; telephone call by clerk	Loose rotation; personal choice of appointing judge	Rotation; telephone call by clerk	Rotation	Rotation
Typical or average fee	$ 15[7] 75[7a] 100[7b] 50[7c]	$427 per case[8]	$50 first appearance	$50 pre-trial[9] $65 trial day[9a]	$25[10]
Total fees, 1962-63	$88,697	$190,692[11]	$61,800[12]	$59,000.95[13]	$11,978.83

(Footnotes on following page.)

[1] Includes active members of the bar employed by the government.

[1a] Actual count.

[2] Felony appointments at the municipal court level as reported by the presiding judge of the municipal court.

[2a] Total number of court appointments reported by the chief administrative officer of the San Diego courts. Probably reflects as a separate appointment the reappointment of the same counsel in the same case at the superior court level.

[3] Estimated projection based upon 186 appointments during a five-month period in 1962-63.

[4] Projection based on count of 36 assignments in 50 cases (total, 130 cases).

[5] Estimated projection based upon appointment of 111 attorneys in a five-month period during 1962-63.

[6] List of volunteers kept by a private lawyer paid $60 per month by the county; his office is liaison between the court and the lawyers appointed.

[7] Fee according to schedule for handling an arraignment.

[7a] Fee according to schedule for more than one half day of trial up to one full day.

[7b] Fee according to schedule for more than one half day of trial up to one full day, capital case.

[7c] Fee according to schedule for one half day or less of trial.

[8] Estimated average fee based upon expenditure of $79,455 for 186 cases during a five-month period, 1962-63.

[9] For all work short of trial.

[9a] For each of the first three trial days with no fee thereafter. Fees covered in footnotes 9 and 9a are used by one judge; others award higher fees.

[10] Fee set by the board of supervisors for each appearance and for each trial day.

[11] Estimated projection for one year, based upon expenditure of $79,455 for a five-month period.

[12] Fiscal year 1961-1962 for municipal and superior courts. Budget for the fiscal year 1962-1963 is $70,000.

[13] Municipal court, $23,785; superior court, $35,215.

a misdemeanor. Refusal by an officer to allow the attorney visit also subjects that officer to a forfeiture of $500, recoverable by civil action.

According to the individuals interviewed, arrested persons in the counties surveyed are customarily brought before a magistrate within the 48-hour maximum, and often within a shorter period. There was, however, an indication in San Diego County that in some misdemeanor cases it is 70 to 80 hours before the prisoner is brought before a magistrate. Under California law, failure to bring the prisoner before a court within the specified period does not have the effect of excluding as evidence admissions or confessions obtained during that period. [Editor's note: This was written before the decision in *Escobedo v. Illinois,* 378 U.S. 478 (1964), and *People v. Dorado,* 40 Cal. Rep. 264, 394 P. 2d 952 (1964), aff'd on rehearing, 42 Cal. Rep. 169, 398 P. 2d 361 (1965)]. There was no indication in any of the counties surveyed that violations of the attorney visit requirement occur with any frequency. The suggestion has been made, however, that prisoners are sometimes barred from making their phone calls by excuses such as that the lines are busy or that no change is available. Both civil actions and criminal prosecutions against police officers for violating any of these statutory requirements are practically nonexistent.

There is no indication that in the public defender counties surveyed the required phone call is used to call the public defender's office. Typically in those counties the public defender only comes into contact with a defendant after the first appearance before a magistrate. Public defenders from the Los Angeles County office may on rare occasions interview a prisoner before his first appearance if specially requested to do so by a friend or relative. An earlier study indicated that in Los Angeles the defender would not do so unless circumstances suggested that early action was imperative. By statute, a public defender has authority to accept a case at the request of a defendant even without court appointment.

The first appearance and the preliminary hearing before a magistrate normally occur in a municipal or justice court. Municipal court judges in the state must have been admitted to practice for at least five years prior to appointment. There is no such practice requirement for justice court judges, and in the counties surveyed they are often not lawyers. In Shasta County, for example, only two of eight justice court judges are lawyers.

If an accused person was arrested without a warrant, bail is normally fixed by the magistrate at the first appearance. The amount of bail for felonies is customarily fixed by the judge in his discretion. In Riverside, for example, three basic bails ($1000, $2500, or $5000) are used in felony cases, depending on the type of crime charged. By statute, the inferior court judges in each county are required to adopt a bail schedule for misdemeanors.

Where the charge is one over which the superior court has original jurisdiction, the magistrate is required by statute to deliver to the accused a copy of the complaint, inform the accused of his right to counsel, ask him if he desires counsel, allow him a reasonable time to send for counsel, and even provide a messenger to take a message to counsel named by the accused within the judicial district. If the "defendant desires and is unable to employ counsel, the court must assign counsel to defend him."

Most initial appointments of counsel are made at the first appearance before the magistrate. There is some minor variation among the counties surveyed, and even among magistrates within the same county, regarding the determination of indigency. But for the most part, the standard applied is whether private counsel would be interested in handling the case for the type of fee which the defendant can afford. In the southern California counties surveyed the nature of the inquiry into indigency at the first appearance is typically cursory. In most courts the defendant is simply asked if he can afford counsel, often in a rapid-fire, mechanical tone. If he replies "no," the court appoints the public defender or assigns private counsel, as the case may be. In Tulare County, the number of questions asked may vary with the type of defendant. The county has a large, economically depressed farm labor population. When a defendant from this group comes before the court, as one judge put it, "You just know without any inquiry that he cannot afford counsel." In San Diego County, the magistrate may ask the defendant whether he is employed and owns a car. At least one municipal court judge there indicated that he applied a bail test of indigency; if the defendant were out on bail, counsel would not be assigned unless it appeared, for example, that the accused's family had put up the bail money. In most courts, the fact that the defendant is out on bail is not a determining factor, though it is taken into consideration. In Los Angeles, if the defendant is in custody the appointment is practically automatic; where the defendant is on bail some inquiry is made, but it is cursory. On the other hand, a Riverside municipal judge indicated that the nature of his inquiry, which usually consists of a single question, does not hinge on whether the defendant is on bail.

The public defender in some cases supplements the magistrate's determination of indigency by further inquiry. In Los Angeles, for example, a defendant for whom counsel has been appointed but who is out on bail is asked to fill out a form asking detailed questions regarding his financial status and is interviewed by an investigator from the public defender's office. In Riverside, the public defender uses oral questions regarding the availability of bail money to determine a defendant's general financial condition, because theoretically the defendant is more likely to respond truthfully to such questions. In San Diego, some judges assume that assigned private counsel will make further inquiry as to the accused's financial condition. The local rules of the municipal court, San Diego judicial district, provide that if assigned counsel, who is compensated according to a fixed fee schedule, ascertains that the defendant can pay a reasonable attorney fee in excess of that set by the court, he is to report this fact to the judge; and if the defendant so desires, the previously assigned attorney may represent him pursuant to a fee arrangement to be privately made between attorney and client. One judge suggested that the possibility of making such a private fee arrangement provides some incentive to assigned counsel to inquire further into the financial condition of the accused.

In northern California, judges in Shasta County orally question the defendants, but written financial statements or affidavits are used in the other four counties, Contra Costa, Sacramento, Santa Clara, and San Francisco. The public defender administers the matter in the public defender counties, and the court clerk handles it in the other counties. If a defendant makes bail in San Francisco County, or if there is any other indication that he might be able to pay counsel, the public defender refers him to a panel of three lawyers from the San Francisco Bar Association, which considers the defendant's ability to retain private counsel. This follows a similar procedure used in Alameda County for many years. According to statistics compiled by the secretary of the San Francisco Bar Association, about one-third of the cases considered by the panel are referred to the private bar, and two-thirds are sent back to the public defender.

In Contra Costa County, indigents for whom counsel are appointed and who are placed on probation are required, as a condition of probation, to make a payment to the probation office to cover the cost, or a portion thereof, of the legal services provided.

In all of the counties surveyed, waiver of counsel by indigent defendants rarely occurs. Estimates of the number of defendants who in fact waived counsel ranged from zero to 2% of the total number of indigents. At least one of the judges interviewed said that he never permitted waiver of counsel by an indigent. One judge in Riverside indicated that he would not force counsel on a resisting defendant, but in the same county the public defender stated that the practice was to appoint him as advisory counsel if the defendant insisted on waiver. All of the municipal court judges indicated that they made strenuous efforts to dissuade an indigent accused from waiving counsel.

The time interval between the first appearance and the preliminary hearing varies somewhat in the counties surveyed. The penal code provides that the preliminary examination may be postponed for not less than two nor more than five days to allow the defendant time to obtain counsel. In Los Angeles, the preliminary is usually held within four or five days after the first appearance. Although the public defender who is assigned to that branch of the municipal court on a continuing basis is notified by the clerk of his appointment immediately after the first appearance, he ordinarily does not see the defendant until the day before or the morning of the preliminary. At that time he interviews the defendant, usually for 10 to 20 minutes or more, depending on the gravity and complexity of the case and how heavy his calendar is. In Riverside, the public defender normally interviews the defendant within 24 hours after the first appearance, which is usually continued to the following day. In San Diego, preliminaries are held about three weeks after the first appearance. The clerk of the municipal court, on the afternoon of a first appearance, telephones attorneys from a list of those who have indicated they are available and arranges for counsel to represent each felony defendant. The assigned attorney is required by rule of court to interview the defendant within 48 hours after assignment.

When a defendant in a noncapital felony appears at the preliminary with counsel, the complaint is read to the defendant, and he is asked to plead guilty or not guilty. No guilty plea is permitted from a defendant not represented by counsel. The defendant must be present while witnesses are examined, and he has the right to cross-examine them. He also has the right to produce and examine his own witnesses. The defendant himself may not be examined unless represented by counsel, or unless he expressly waives his right to counsel. In homicide cases, a transcript of the testimony of the witnesses must be kept; in other cases, a written transcript is to be made upon the demand of either the prosecution or defense. If the defendant is held to answer he can, on demand, obtain a copy of the transcript, the costs of which are paid for by the county. A noncapital felony defendant who pleads guilty is certified to the superior court, where proceedings are had as if the defendant had pleaded guilty in that court; in such cases, no indictment or information need be filed. In capital felony cases, a defendant may waive his right to a preliminary examination, but an order must be issued holding him to answer, and an information must be filed in the superior court within 15 days. Similarly, in all other cases where a preliminary examination is conducted and the defendant is held to answer, the district attorney must file an information within 15 days.

In Tulare County, approximately one-half of all felony defendants waive the preliminary. Waivers in appropriate cases are expedited by a unique procedure in this county: involving the use of a written appearance-waiver form which the defendant, public defender, and district attorney sign and which is then presented to the magistrate in the proper judicial district. A "gentlemen's agreement" exists, however, between the district attorney and the public defender that the case will be sent back to the magistrate for preliminary examination if any reason therefor appears at the superior court proceedings. Use of this procedure in cases where the defendant admits the charge, it is claimed, tends to save unnecessary "dead time," and permits two part-time defenders to handle what would otherwise be a very heavy case load. Waiver of the preliminary also occurs in more than half the cases in Shasta County. In contrast, very few waivers of the preliminary occur in Los Angeles or San Francisco Counties. In Los Angeles the prevalent practice is to hold the examination but then to submit the case to the superior court on the transcript of the preliminary proceedings. Waiver of the preliminary is discouraged in Los Angeles on the theory that a defendant's admission of guilt may not always be reliable, and the prosecution should be required to prove its case.

The California rules regarding criminal discovery permit a relatively broad discovery by the defendant. Indications in the counties surveyed were that the district attorney almost universally cooperates in permitting defense counsel to inspect the material in his files, even without a formal discovery order, but that in some counties the district attorney's office may require certain private attorneys to use formal discovery procedures to obtain the desired information.

In most cases, the judge of the superior court before whom an indigent is arraigned will reappoint the office of the public defender or the same private attorney who represented the defendant at the preliminary examination. The questioning of the defendant as to indigency was a little less cursory when an original appointment was being made in the superior court, but at least one judge (Tulare County) indicated that the nature of the inquiry was the same whether or not there had been a prior appointment at the preliminary hearing stage. On original appointments in the Superior Court of San Diego County, the nature of the inquiry differs from that made at the municipal court level in that at least some of the judges require the defendant to fill out, under oath, a fairly detailed "affidavit of financial inability to employ counsel." In general, however, the superior court judges interviewed indicate, with the same limited range of variations, that they applied a standard and made an inquiry similar to that relied upon by the magistrate's court.

All felony defendants in Los Angeles County are arraigned in the Criminal Master Calendar Department of the superior court. If the defendant pleads guilty, sentence will be imposed later by the master calendar judge; if he pleads not guilty, the master calendar judge assigns the case for trial to one of the 17 criminal trial departments. If the defendant appears at his arraignment in custody without counsel, the master calendar judge, with practically no inquiry, appoints the public defender. If the defendant is out on bail, however, the judge asks the defendant a series of brief questions concerning his financial condition. In general, a very liberal test of indigency is applied. Appointment of the public defender in Los Angeles means, in effect, appointment of the office of the public defender. One or two staff attorneys are regularly assigned to each criminal department of the superior court, including Master Calendar, for periods up to a year. Assignment of an indigent's case to a particular department for trial thus has the effect of appointing the defenders in that department, who allocate between them the cases thus assigned. By far the largest number of appointments of counsel for indigents is made in the Master Calendar department. Occasionally, however, the issue of appointment, particularly appointment of private counsel because a conflict of interest has appeared, will not arise until the case is in a trial department.

Despite the existence of the public defender system in Los Angeles, many appointments of private counsel are still made at the superior court level, mostly but not exclusively in the Master Calendar department in cases involving a conflict of interest for the public defender. The determination of the conflict rests solely with the public defender, and the court never inquires beyond the defender's statement that there is such a conflict. The court appoints private counsel from a list of attorneys who have indicated that they are available. Compensation paid to such attorneys is fixed by the court in its discretion, usually on the basis of an affidavit submitted by the attorney indicating the nature and estimated value of his services. Money for investigation is often included in the amounts allotted. Though a proposal to adopt a fee schedule for such cases in Los Angeles was made last year, it was rejected. During a five month period in 1963 (the only period for which detailed information was available), 111 private attorneys were appointed by the Superior Court of Los Angeles County in 136 different criminal cases, involving an outlay of $79,455 in fees.

In Riverside County, which also has a public defender, appointments of private counsel have been made, on occasion, not only in cases involving a conflict of interest but also in some that were expected to involve a protracted trial. In such cases, the fees for private counsel were set by the court in its discretion, and the amount was charged against the public defender's budget. The public defender's office has indicated, however, that, as a result of a recent change of office policy, appointments of private counsel are now limited to conflict of interest cases or to cases prosecuted in an outlying court.

The following statement described the current practice regarding appointment of counsel on appeal in the Third District Court of Appeal, which receives cases from both Shasta and Sacramento Counties:

> Before *Douglas v. California* the court declined to appoint counsel for indigents only in cases of guilty pleas. Thus, this district did not pursue the practice of screening the record and sometimes declining appointment, as did the Second District. Now, after the *Douglas* case, the Third District appoints counsel in cases of guilty pleas as well. A full transcript is provided free of charge. In a significant portion of the cases in which counsel are appointed, such counsel write a so-called no-merit letter and do not bother to write a brief, enabling a swifter disposition. Even in such cases a research attorney and the judge assigned to write the opinion go over the case and examine the transcript. Counsel are appointed from a panel of young attorneys who volunteer. Sometimes, through inexperience, these attorneys

overlook points, but they are backed up by the court's research attorney. Compensation varies from $50 to $300.

As a result of the decision in *Douglas,* the Riverside County Public Defender's Office has recently undertaken, at the request of the Fourth District Court of Appeal, to handle all indigent appeals arising from Riverside. No final arrangements for compensation have been made yet, but 'the hope of the public defender is that the district court of appeal will be able to make payments for his services by transferring money to the county out of the fund from which it ordinarily pays private appointed attorneys. In several such appeals the defender has filed a statement in lieu of brief, in which he indicates that he has reviewed the transcript and has found no grounds for appeal. Apparently court-appointed counsel in appeals arising from Los Angeles are being required to file a similar statement setting forth the facts of the case, the issues potentially involved on appeal, and the conclusion, if appropriate, that the appeal is without merit. The Los Angeles County Public Defender, even prior to *Douglas,* took an appeal in a limited number of cases handled by its office at the trial level, but there is no indication that *Douglas* has affected the number of appeals handled by this office.

In cases in which the death penalty is imposed, an automatic appeal is taken by the defendant even without any action by him or his counsel. In such cases, where counsel has been appointed by the court, by statute the cost of preparing the defendant's brief, not to exceed $100, is paid by the state. By statute also, where the Supreme Court or district court of appeal appoint counsel, the court is to fix a reasonable fee for such counsel. In cases arising from Los Angeles County there was a marked increase in the number of appointments of private counsel on appeal immediately after March 18, 1963, the date of the *Douglas* decision. Thus, from August 14, 1962, to March 18, 1963, about 33 appointments of counsel were made by the district court of appeal, whereas from March 18 to July 2, 1963, there were 112 such appointments.

There have been California decisions holding that a person charged with a misdemeanor has a right to be represented by counsel and also, though this is not so clear, to have counsel appointed by the court. In general, however, attorneys have not been appointed to represent indigent persons charged with misdemeanors in a municipal or justice court. In San Francisco, however, misdemeanors constitute the bulk of the public defender's practice. He considers the initiation of such representation a major accomplishment of his administration. Also, within the city limits of Los Angeles, the office of the city public defender represents persons charged with misdemeanors in the municipal court, but the Los Angeles County public defender does not handle such cases.

On rare occasions, municipal court judges in Riverside, Sacramento, and San Diego Counties appoint counsel in serious misdemeanor cases. In the past in San Diego, when a private attorney has been appointed to represent a defendant in a misdemeanor case, he may subsequently be compensated, in a sense, by appointment out of order in a felony case, for which he receives a fee. In Sacramento, the public defender is sometimes asked by a judge to defend a person charged with a serious misdemeanor. In Riverside, a municipal court judge indicated that if a misdemeanor defendant asked for counsel he appointed a private attorney to serve without fee, chosen from the bar lists of newer practitioners. Moreover, the public defender there also sometimes talks to misdemeanor defendants and advises them of their legal rights, though he does not defend them at trial.

A 1963 amendment to Penal Code (§987a) provides for payment of reasonable compensation to counsel assigned in misdemeanor cases "in a county, or city and county, in which there is no public defender, or in a case in which the court finds that because of conflict of interest or other reasons the public defender has properly refused to represent the person accused. . . ." (Another bill which would have required public defenders also to represent persons charged with misdemeanors was enacted by the legislature, but was pocket vetoed by the governor.) The effect of the statutory amendment is to authorize for the first time compensation for private counsel appointed in misdemeanor cases in California. At first there was some doubt whether the provision would apply in public defender counties where the public defender, as a matter of policy or authority, does not handle misdemeanor cases. This doubt was resolved in Los Angeles County in *In re Hollinger* (77 L.A. Daily J. no. 18 [Jan. 24, 1964] p. 1), where the court ruled that the words "or other reasons" in the statute should be construed to allow compensation for court-appointed counsel in a public defender county. Also, in 1965 the legislature enacted a statute providing for representation by public defenders in misdemeanor cases.

C. OPINIONS OF THE JUDGES

1. *Interviews.* Interviews were conducted with 10 superior court judges and 6 municipal court judges in four southern California counties. Four superior court judges and one municipal court judge were interviewed in five northern counties. The consensus of the judges who indicated their views on the ideal stage at which an indigent person should be provided with counsel favored the first appearance before a magistrate. Thus, 7 of 12 replying superior court judges unequivocally chose the first appearance. Two of the remaining five judges thought that the stage between arrest and first appearance was the ideal, but that it was not practicable to provide an attorney this early; and a third judge indicated similar doubts. Only one judge unequivocally took the position that appointment after arrest was the ideal: only in that way, he said, would matters be equalized between rich and poor. Of five municipal court judges responding, four selected the first appearance as the ideal stage, and only one chose the time between arrest and first appearance; but he did suggest that it was financially feasible to provide counsel at that early a point.

Only 3 of the 21 judges, 1 from superior court and 2 from municipal courts, indicated that it is not necessary, under an ideal system, to provide an attorney for all hearings on revocation of probation. Eight judges in all, six in the superior court and two in the municipal court, took the position that it is also unnecessary to provide a lawyer for a person charged with a non-serious misdemeanor.

The five San Diego judges who were questioned were divided on the adequacy of the compensation schedule for assigned counsel. One superior court and two municipal court judges concluded that the newly revised fee schedule (see Table 3) provided adequate compensation. One superior court judge thought that, even with the recent increase in fees, the compensation provided was not adequate to obtain attorneys with proper qualifications; and the remaining superior court judge stated that for the young attorney the compensation was adequate whereas for the experienced practitioner it was not, but that "it was all that the taxpayers could afford to pay." The judges from the other assigned counsel counties also felt that the compensation was adequate. Indeed, one judge believed that the bar should represent indigents without fee and that, if the bar did not do so, fees should be low. The judge, however, allows $50 for all work before trial and $65 for each of the first three days of trial without any compensation thereafter.

In the one southern California assigned counsel county, appointed lawyers were compared unfavorably with both retained lawyers and the district attorney's staff. Thus, four out of five San Diego judges thought that retained attorneys generally were more experienced than those appointed, while the fifth judge stated that appointed attorneys were frequently better. Similarly, the same four judges evaluated the district attorney's staff as superior to appointed lawyers, while the same single judge considered appointees and the district attorney's deputies more or less equal in ability.

By contrast, in the three southern California public defender's counties, six out of seven judges favored the public defender, if only by a very slight margin, over the average retained attorney; and only one judge, from Tulare County, thought them equals. Five out of eight judges, in comparing the public defender and the district attorney's staff, rated them equals. Two judges, both from Riverside County, thought the public defender was better, and a third judge from Tulare County favored the public defender himself over the ordinary deputy in the district attorney's office. Again by way of contrast, all of the northern California judges stated that both public defenders and assigned counsel compared favorably with retained counsel.

Some of the remarks of the judges interviewed merit mention. The judge in Shasta County stated that the assigned counsel system worked well. His view was that a volunteer panel was better than a rotation system among all lawyers because an unwanted job would not be performed well, and that some compensation was necessary to induce those with experience to volunteer. He also thought that when the county's population passed 100,000 (it was 70,000 in 1963) the appointment of a public defender would be timely. To be compared with this is the view of a judge from Santa Clara County, with a population in 1960 of nearly 650,000, who has opposed a public defender before the board of supervisors for two reasons: (1) he estimates the initial cost of setting up the public defender's office at $120,000, and (2) he believes that as a matter of principle a public defender will undermine the people's confidence in government. He reasons' that one of the purposes of the criminal law is to show the citizen-taxpayer that his government protects him; if the government pays for the defense also, that will undercut the feeling of confidence. He also fears that the public defender may pull his punches because of a continuing relationship with the district attorney. Similarly one judge in San Diego County strongly took the position that an assigned counsel system provides representation as good as that provided by a public defender system and that it is much cheaper. He described the public defender system as one of those "New Deal" ideas. Another San Diego judge noted that 55% of the land in San Diego County is not on the local tax rolls because it is controlled by the federal government. Moreover, a substantial number of military personnel, most of whom are indigent, are charged with crime in San Diego. Although he is generally opposed to federal aid programs, he believes that the federal government has a special responsibility to provide assistance for a program of indigent representation in a county like San Diego. A Los Angeles judge described the average public defender as more able than 70% of those attorneys who practice criminal law. He noted that defenders are highly competitive about winning cases and, because in the nature of things they are doomed to "lose" a large number of cases, they sometimes develop a defeatist attitude.

2. *Mail questionnaires.* A total of 55 mail questionnaires were sent to superior court judges in the 49 nonsample counties, two judges being contacted in counties with more than four judges. Returns were received from 35 judges representing 34 counties on the list. Sixteen of these counties have a population under 50,000, and eight have a population of 50,000 but less than 100,000. Of the judges polled, 17 had served for more than 5 years on their present court, and 5 had served for more than 10 years.

Almost one-half of the 35 replies (17) indicated that the first appearance before a magistrate is the ideal stage at which a lawyer should first be made available to an indigent. Almost as many judges (14) chose the stage between arrest and first appearance as the ideal. Only 2 judges out of 35 thought that appointment should be as late as the preliminary hearing stage.

Eleven of 14 (78%) of the judges who chose "between arrest and first appearance" as the ideal stage of appointment concluded that such a system could be financed, and only one categorically stated that it could not be. Eight of these 14 judges, and 6 of the 11 who thought such a system could be financed, came from counties with a population under 50,000.

In reply to the question whether under an ideal system a lawyer should be made available to the indigent in the specified types of proceedings (question 7a, Form VIII), 19 judges (54%) took the position that a lawyer should be provided in each of the listed proceedings. Ten judges (28%) would not provide counsel in misdemeanor cases under an ideal system. Three of these judges had ten years or more of experience on the superior court bench, and all but two had at least 5 years of such experience.

Estimates of the percentage of indigent felony defendants who appeared before the judges replying ranged from a low of 35% to a high of 95% with the largest concentration in the 70% to 80% bracket. Only three judges provided figures representing an actual count, and these figures were 80%, 76%, and 69%. Most of the estimates of percentages of waivers of counsel by indigents ranged from zero to 10%. Two judges, however, estimated that 50% of the indigents waived counsel, and one estimated a seemingly incredible 75%. Finally, one judge indicated that by actual count, 41% of a total of 29 felony defendants had waived.

Thirteen of the judges selected the private lawyers appointed in ordinary felony cases either from a bar association list of names or from the roster of all attorneys admitted to practice, and 5 used a list of their own. Only one judge indicated that he would appoint any attorney present in court, and he combined this method with the use of a bar association list. Seventeen indicated that they used a special system of appointment for serious crimes, and eight of this group noted that their special system involved the appointment of two attorneys to represent a single defendant.

The judges divided more or less evenly on whether the present rates of compensation for lawyers for services to indigent accused persons are adequate. A total of 13 (52%) of those responding, including a few from public defender counties, said "yes," and 12 said "no." It is noteworthy that a similar percentage of appointed lawyers from the sample counties thought the system of assignment is fair to lawyers (see infra).

In the assigned counsel counties, 12 out of 19 (63%) of the judges replying thought that appointed lawyers and retained lawyers were comparable in ability and experience. Five thought that the retained lawyer on the average was a little better, while two favored the appointed attorney. Similarly, 15 out of 23 (65%) concluded that appointed lawyers and the district attorney are comparable in experience and ability. Five thought that the district attorney is somewhat superior, while three preferred appointed counsel.

In the public defender counties, 9 out of 15 (60%) thought that the defender and retained lawyers were comparable in ability and experience, 4 favored the defender and 2 preferred retained lawyers. Of this same 15, 13 thought that the district attorney and the public defender were equal in ability and experience.

In determining indigency, 24 out of 32 judges said they rely only on a series of questions in open court. Practically all of the judges indicated that in determining eligibility for appointment they take into account at least four and in some cases as many as seven or eight of the listed factors (question 18b, Form VIII), but one judge indicated that he simply takes the defendant's unsworn statement that he has no funds or property to employ counsel. Moreover, the same judge stated that in 11 years on the bench he had never found an accused person ineligible to have counsel appointed for him as an indigent, and he estimated that 80% of the persons accused of felonies who appeared before him were indigent. Only four judges indicated that the fact that the accused person was out on bail would preclude a finding of indigency. Similarly, four judges would refuse to appoint where there was ownership of an automobile, and five, where the financial resources of the accused's spouse were adequate.

Several of the judges appended to their mail questionnaire brief remarks which reveal a wide range of attitudes and merit quotation:

(1) If the defendant understands the charge, knows he is guilty thereof, and admits his guilt, there does not appear to be any more reason for an indigent defendant to have a lawyer, than one who is not indigent. The court will see that he is fully advised of his rights and that the same are protected. . . .

(2) Counsel should be provided to all who wish it, or seem to require it (without, of course, forcing counsel on them). . . .

(3) One of the big problems in California is that by reason of volume the Public Defenders become specialists; hence, people prefer them to other lawyers and try to cover assets—or other capabilities of retaining private counsel.

(4) It is my impression, gained from assignments to more populous counties, that a salaried public defender system is more satisfactory than selection of counsel from local bar associations.

(5) The number of indigent persons charged with crimes seems to be increasing. I think our local practice of appointing counsel has many advantages over the public defender system. Our appointed lawyers, almost without exception, defend their clients vigorously. Any indifferent lawyers, who do it for the fee, aren't appointed.

D. OPINIONS OF DISTRICT ATTORNEYS

1. *Interviews.* Ten prosecutors were interviewed in the nine sample counties. The district attorney himself was interviewed in eight of the counties; in one the district attorney was unavailable because of illness, and a high ranking deputy was interviewed; and in one county both the district attorney and a deputy were interviewed.

Only 2 of 10 prosecutors thought that appointment of counsel for the indigent immediately after arrest was the ideal, but they had doubts as to the feasibility of such a system. The other eight thought that appointment at the first appearance before a magistrate or between the time of the first appearance and the preliminary hearing was the ideal and that delay of the appointment beyond that time would be unfair to defendants.

Eight of the 10 prosecutors thought that the system used to determine indigency was too lenient, while the remaining 2 approved the system as "about right." Several suggested that a person who had some means, but for whom counsel was appointed, should be required to pay a small fee.

All eight district attorneys interviewed stated that they had adequate funds to run their offices. By contrast, the two deputies thought the funds provided were inadequate.

In comparing retained attorneys and counsel appointed by the court, all of the prosecutors from public defender counties indicated that the defenders and their deputies on the average did a better job of defending the accused than retained counsel. In fact, two of these prosecutors went so far as to denigrate most retained counsel as hacks. Also two of the four prosecutors from assigned counsel counties favored assigned counsel slightly over retained counsel but suggested that, in some instances, notably the more serious cases, assigned counsel lacked necessary experience. The two remaining prosecutors saw no particular difference between the capabilities of assigned and retained counsel, but one of these emphasized that both classes of attorneys were usually drawn from the same group.

All six district attorneys who were in the five counties using a public defender agreed that the defender is completely independent. One district attorney said the statement to the contrary (question 24) was "crazy" and another called it "sheer nonsense." Those interviewed made a number of recommendations for improving the system of providing counsel for the indigent accused, including: (1) improvement of standards for determining indigency, (2) elimination of the inexperienced or incompetent from assigned counsel panels, and (3) more careful selection of counsel to be assigned in serious cases.

2. *Mail questionnaires.* Mail questionnaires were sent to the district attorneys of the 49 nonsample counties, and replies were received from 25, a response rate of just over 50%. All of them believed that counsel under an ideal system should be furnished by or before the preliminary. Six prosecutors, or almost 25%, believed representation after arrest would be ideal. Only one of the six, however, considered it unfair if counsel were not furnished then, and he had had lengthy prior experience on the defense. Only one prosecutor believed appointment of counsel at the preliminary hearing itself to be timely enough, but he also thought that appointment was not needed at all unless the defendant was innocent! Most (17) of the prosecutors felt appointment would be ideal either at the first appearance (opinion of 8) or between then and the preliminary hearing (opinion of 9).*

The prosecutors opposed furnishing counsel for indigents charged with misdemeanors even under an ideal system, but by the narrow margin of 13 to 11, and two of those who were negative would at least provide counsel in serious misdemeanor cases. One prosecutor stated vehemently that furnishing counsel in misdemeanor cases was a luxury we could not afford.

More than half (14) of the prosecutors replying by mail thought the system for determining indigency was too lenient. One of these suggested that the defendant give a lien to the county for fees. The rest thought the system about right.

Eleven of the 12 answering by mail thought that the public defender could be independent and zealous. One prosecutor foresaw the risk of loss of independence unless the defender were elected by an understanding electorate, but it is noteworthy that his county did not itself have a public defender.

Only two prosecutors of those replying by mail stated that available funds

* It may be worthwhile here to note an ambiguity in the ideal stage question which it was not possible to clarify in connection with the mail responses to this question. There may be as many as four separate steps involved in the appointment of counsel for an indigent: (1) determining that he is an indigent and that counsel is to be furnished by the court, (2) actual designation of the particular attorney, (3) actual notification of the particular attorney, and (4) contact of the attorney with the accused. When a mail response indicates that appointment between the first appearance and the preliminary hearing is the ideal, it may mean that the occurrence of (1) at that time is the ideal, although this seems unlikely, or that (2) or (3) or (4) [or (2) and (3) and (4)], or any feasible combination of these steps occurring between the first appearance and the preliminary, is the ideal. Thus there may be no practical difference between a response which chooses appointment at the first appearance as the ideal, having in mind only the formal determination of indigency and that counsel should be provided, and a response that the stage between the first appearance and the preliminary is the ideal, having in mind actual designation and notification of the attorney.

were not sufficient. One of these desired funds to buy equipment, increase salaries, and hire an investigator. Several, while indicating enough funds for present staff, would have liked to increase their personnel, and also to increase staff compensation in order to retain competent men.

Almost all of the mail replies indicated that assigned counsel and the public defender were comparable to retained counsel. Again some, particularly in rural counties, noted that assigned and retained counsel were drawn from the same group.

Only a few of the mail replies contained suggestions for improvements. These were varied, including (1) to furnish better investigative facilities, (2) to make procedure for appointments uniform, (3) to appoint all lawyers in the county instead of just a few idle ones, and (4) to require one attorney to represent joint defendants unless a real conflict exists.

E. OPINIONS OF DEFENSE ATTORNEYS

1. *Interviews.* Five public defenders and one deputy defender were interviewed in five counties, Los Angeles, Riverside, San Francisco, Sacramento, and Tulare. In Los Angeles, the public defender indicated that though in general he had adequate funds to run his office, he could use several additional deputies and more administrative personnel. There was no indication in Los Angeles that the defender's investigative staff, which consists of 10 full-time persons, is undermanned.

In Riverside, where there is a full-time public defender, a full-time assistant, two part-time deputies, and no investigators, the public defender indicated that he has adequate funds to run his office. He anticipates the need for at least one additional part-time deputy for the next fiscal year and perhaps more, depending on the impact on his office workload of the increased number of appeals cases. On the other hand, his office is not yet large enough to require the services of a full-time investigator. He believes, however, that it might be useful to have a fund to pay for special investigation costs. At present he or one of his assistants investigates matters where possible or obtains assistance from the district attorney or sheriff's investigative staff.

The public defender of Sacramento County also indicated that his staff of six full-time lawyers was adequate. He has some funds available for investigation and, like the Riverside defender, sometimes uses the investigative facilities of the district attorney's office.

The public defender of San Francisco County, who has seven full-time lawyers in his office, has made formal application for two more full-time deputies. He stated that the size of his present staff does not allow the deputies to devote adequate time to the cases to be tried. (The Bar Association of San Francisco, in a report dated August 30, 1962, concluded that the "quality of representation of indigents has not been sufficiently maintained," primarily because of inadequate staff.) The San Francisco defender, who is an elected official, believes that the fact that he is elected enables him to retain his independence.

Tulare has a part-time public defender, also elected, and a part-time deputy. Though the defender there has adequate funds to run the office with the present staff, he believes that the workload justifies at least one full-time defender, plus perhaps a part-time man, and that some provision should be made for investigation. He also noted the inevitable conflict for the part-time defender between the demands of defender work and the pressures of private practice.

2. *Mail questionnaires.* Mail questionnaires were sent to lawyers who were appointed to represent indigents in 1962 in three assigned counsel counties in northern California, Contra Costa, Shasta, and Santa Clara, and in one southern California county, San Diego. Questionnaires were also sent to private attorneys in three public defender counties, Los Angeles, Riverside, and Tulare, who were appointed in conflict of interest or other cases. [See volume 1, page 223.]

a. Contra Costa. Questionnaires were sent to 73 counsel in Contra Costa County, and 44 replied. Seven were appointed between the arrest and first appearance, and one of these thought that such appointment was not timely. All of the 13 who were appointed at the first appearance considered such appointment timely. Seventeen were appointed between the first appearance and the preliminary hearing, and only one of these thought his appointment not timely. Two were appointed at the preliminary hearing and thought that appointment timely. One was appointed after the preliminary hearing but before the indictment, and he thought that appointment not timely. There were three other appointments at later stages varying from after arraignment on the indictment or information to after conviction (for a defendant not theretofore represented).

All 42 answering the question regarding compensation received compensation. Of those answering the question regarding repayment for out-of-pocket expenses, 26 said that they were repaid, while 9 were not.

The following recommendations were made: earlier appointment, by 12; repayment of out-of-pocket expenses, by 18; payment of a fee, by 5; payment of a greater fee, by 18; payment of a fee for defending misdemeanors, by 2; representation of accused misdemeanants, by 13; and a public defender, by 12, even though this choice required writing in on the form rather than merely circling a printed option.

The remarks were illuminating. One lawyer with experience in handling 600 criminal cases criticized the system of using a panel of all lawyers; he suggested that too many lawyers advised clients to plead guilty, when the clients could be acquitted or convicted of a lesser degree. Another suggested that the present system tends to induce guilty pleas, since counsel are more adequately compensated for pretrial appearances than for trial time. Another observed that apparently there was not a true rotation because some lawyers served more times than others, while one criticized the judges for blindly rotating, even in serious cases. One lawyer suggested a yardstick of $20 per hour for fees, with a committee of lawyers to review the hours spent, to guard against abuse. Another observed that assigned counsel were less costly to the county than a public defender because the lawyers are willing to take appointments at low fees and subsidize the county. Finally, 1 of the 12 lawyers opting for a public defender stated that the system of assigned counsel works a hardship on the conscientious.

b. Santa Clara. Questionnaires were sent to 59 counsel in Santa Clara County, and 29 replied. Several of those had not had any criminal experience before appointment to their first case in 1962. Frequency of appointment varied from many lawyers with just a few appointments to some with appointments ranging from 20 to 29 cases. The timing of appointments varied throughout the categories in question 5, and in only a few instances did counsel consider the appointment not timely enough. One said, "Several times I have been appointed only after law enforcement agencies have interrogated the accused and obtained damaging but often inaccurate statements."

Counsel in Santa Clara County uniformly received compensation for their services, but some were repaid for out-of-pocket expenses, while others were not. Most of the attorneys felt that the system was fair to the indigents, but they split about evenly as to fairness to lawyers. A few stated that the system was not fair to lawyers in serious cases because of added expenses for investigation and expert witnesses. One lawyer observed that the inadequate compensation to lawyers and the lack of funds for expert witnesses amounted to a lack of due process. Another particularly criticized the system for determining indigency, noting that a financial statement was required but that little attention was paid to it. Another lawyer observed that the system was fair only to the guilty indigents because counsel had experience enough to seek a mitigation of punishment in such cases.

c. Shasta. Questionnaires were sent to 17 counsel in Shasta County; and 11 were returned, while one lawyer responded by saying that he had not represented indigents for years. Two lawyers had not had any criminal experience prior to appointment. The number of appointments in 1962 varied from 5 to 19 cases. Appointments had been made at various stages, though most (seven) had been made between the first appearance and the preliminary hearing. Of the seven, five thought their appointments had not been timely, in four instances because interrogation had produced a confession, and in one case because of what was deemed insufficient time before the preliminary hearing.

All of the lawyers received fees, but the pattern of reimbursement for expenses was irregular. Eight stated that the system was fair to indigents, while one said it was not. Six replied that the system was fair to lawyers and five, that it was not. Three attorneys preferred a public defender. The president of the Shasta County Bar Association recommended that all experienced lawyers should serve on the panel, and not merely the younger ones.

d. San Diego. Questionnaires were sent to 127 assigned counsel in San Diego, and 48 were returned. Nine attorneys indicated they had represented 10 or more defendants in 1962. Included among these were three attorneys each of whom had been appointed to represent more than 20 indigents during this period. Most of the San Diego attorneys replying, however, had only represented between four and nine indigents in 1962.

Of the 48 San Diego lawyers who responded, 16 had, in 1962, represented defendants charged with crimes punishable by life imprisonment or death. One lawyer from San Diego indicated that during this one year period he had represented five such defendants. With few exceptions, most of those lawyers appointed in life-death cases had had extensive criminal practice experience prior to appointment in such cases in 1962. Most had experience in at least 50 prior criminal cases, and very few had previously been involved in less than 20 criminal matters. Two attorneys from San Diego, however, who had each represented a single defendant charged with a life-death crime, were without experience in a criminal case prior to their first appointment in 1962.

Most San Diego appointments take place at the first appearance in the municipal or justice court, and the appointed attorney is notified that same day. Only three of the attorneys appointed in San Diego indicated that they had not been appointed in time to represent the accused adequately. But a number of those who indicated that they had been appointed in time qualified their responses by statements such as the following:

> [B]ut law enforcement officers usually have obtained written or recorded statements from indigent clients prior to arraignment, whereas clients of means usually obtain [a] lawyer immediately upon arrest before statements are obtained and have [the] benefit of being advised not to discuss [the] case or give any statement, which is often crucial.

A total of 39 replied to the question whether the system of assignment of lawyers was fair to the indigent, and 28 (71%) replied affirmatively. Twenty-three out of 44 (52%) gave affirmative replies to the question whether the system was fair to lawyers. (A somewhat similar query was put to all of the members of the San Diego Bar by the Public Defender Committee of the San Diego Bar Association prior to the recent instituting of changes in the fee schedule; and it is interesting to compare the results. In reply to the question, "Is the present system of representation of indigent felony defendants adequate?" 116 out of 232 (50%) answered "yes," and 94 replied in the negative.)

Thirty-three of the 48 returns from San Diego suggested that lawyers should be paid for out-of-pocket expenses incurred in investigation and preparation; 26 recommended that lawyers should be paid more for their services; and 20 included both of these recommendations. One attorney proposed that the services of a tax-supported investigative bureau should be made available to appointed attorneys. Other recurring recommendations, in descending order of frequency, were that counsel should be provided in cases such as serious misdemeanors, that appointments should be made at an earlier stage, and that the system of selection should be improved. Several specific proposals were also made in connection with these recommendations; for example, one attorney suggested "a panel of lawyers which the police must contact when an arrestee in a capital offense [case] expresses a desire to consult counsel." Another, similar suggestion was that "a panel of young lawyers should be set up to counsel *all* persons booked into jail as to their rights." Finally, it was suggested that young attorneys should be appointed as associate counsel in capital cases, to provide them with experience in handling such matters.

e. Los Angeles, Riverside, and Tulare. A total of 36 questionnaires were sent to private counsel appointed in conflict of interest and other cases in Los Angeles, Riverside, and Tulare, and of 30 returns received in reply, 25 were from Los Angeles County.

Nine of the Los Angeles attorneys and three from Tulare had in 1962 represented defendants charged with crimes punishable by life imprisonment or death. All of the attorneys appointed in such cases in these counties had had extensive prior criminal practice experience.

Of 29 who replied to the question whether the present system for assignment is fair to the indigent, 21 thought it was. Fourteen of 26 also thought the system was fair to lawyers.

One Los Angeles attorney suggested that lawyers should not be appointed by the judge who will try the case so that "the lawyer can be free of obligation to the appointing judge."

F. COMPARISONS AMONG JUDGES, PUBLIC DEFENDERS, AND ASSIGNED COUNSEL

Some tentative conclusions regarding comparative attitudes of those who participate in the process of providing counsel for indigents can be drawn from the foregoing data (see Table 4). Thus, public defenders seem uniformly to favor appointment between arrest and first appearance whereas judges and prosecutors are divided on the question whether appointment should be at that stage or later. Moreover, the largest number of prosecutors favor appointment between the first appearance and the preliminary hearing, while the largest number of judges favor appointment at the first appearance. Though this discrepancy in attitude may be illusory (see footnote, section D, subsection 2 supra), it could reflect the fact that the judges are predisposed to emphasize their own role in the appointment process, while prosecutors prefer appointments at a later stage.

Both prosecutors and public defenders seem equally satisfied with the adequacy of the funds to run their offices. A larger proportion of judges than assigned counsel seem to think, however, that lawyers are adequately compensated. It should be noted that the lawyers' responses were cast in terms of "fairness" rather than adequacy of compensation and thus may take account of non-financial factors also.

A more interesting comparison can be made of responses to this question by lawyers appointed in assigned counsel counties with those appointed in conflict of interest cases in public defender counties. The gross statistics indicate that 55% of the former thought the system is not fair to lawyers, whereas 54% of the latter (Los Angeles, Tulare, and Riverside) took a contrary position. Similarities between the two groups of assigned counsel are even more striking if one compares the 54% figure from a single assigned counsel county, San Diego, with the data from the Los Angeles–Riverside–Tulare responses, which were also 54%. It would appear fair to conclude from such data that the attitude of appointed attorneys working in an assigned counsel county regarding fairness to lawyers does not differ significantly from that of attorneys practicing in public defender counties who are appointed principally in conflict of interest cases. Moreover, there is no indication that the attitudes on fairness to the attorney depend on whether a fairly liberal fixed fee schedule is used, as in San Diego, or a judicial discretion compensation system, as in Los Angeles in conflict of interest cases. Under either system, those private attorneys who actively participate in the system, and on a voluntary basis, are about evenly divided on

TABLE 4
Comparisons Among Judges, Prosecutors, Public Defenders, and Assigned Counsel

	Superior court judges	Municipal court judges	Prose-cutors	Public defenders	Assigned counsel (assigned counsel counties)	Assigned counsel (conflict of interest appointments in public defender counties)
Total responding						
(interview)	14	7	10	6	0	0
(mail questionnaire)	35	0	25	0	133	30
Ideal stage for first appointment of counsel:						
Between arrest and first appearance	16	1	8	4	—	—
At first appearance	25	4	11	—	—	—
Between first appearance and preliminary hearing	—	—	14	—	—	—
At preliminary	2	—	1	—	—	—
No response	4	—	—	—	—	—
Is present compensation to lawyers adequate?						
Yes	19	3	26[1]	4[1]	55[2]	14[2]
No	13	—	7	1	67	12
No response	—	—	2	—	6	—
How do assigned counsel compare with retained?						
Assigned counsel favored	4	2	2	—	—	—
Retained lawyers favored	6	—	4	—	—	—
Considered equals	15	—	15	—	—	—
No response	—	—	—	—	—	—
How does the public defender compare with retained counsel?						
Public defender favored	11	—	10	—	—	—
Retained lawyers favored	2	—	—	—	—	—
Considered equals	10	1	7	—	—	—
No response	—	—	—	—	—	—

[1] For prosecutors and defenders, these figures represent responses to the question: "Do you have adequate funds to run your office?"

[2] These figures refer to the assigned counsel question, "Is the system fair to the lawyers?"

whether the system is fair to lawyers. This conclusion is supported by the fact that 55% of the San Diego lawyers recommended that lawyers should be paid more for their services, and 46% of the Los Angeles group made a similar recommendation. It should also be noted that 70% of the lawyers in both the San Diego and the Los Angeles group recommended that lawyers should be paid for out-of-pocket expenses, and that 42% of the San Diego replies and 40% of the Los Angeles group included both recommendations. Such statistics should be compared with the following comment, which one lawyer appended to his reply:

> Lawyer gets some cash, an opportunity to exercise and improve his skill; the indigent may send in other work; I don't see how paying lawyers more will improve anything except their living standard.

No significant differences are discernible between the attitudes of judges and prosecutors comparing the merits of assigned and retained counsel or public defenders and retained counsel. It is noteworthy, however, that both judges and prosecutors heavily favored the public defender over retained counsel, while giving a slight edge to retained counsel over assigned lawyers.

Table 4 compares views expressed on selected issues by judges, prosecutors, public defenders, and assigned counsel. The total responses for each category include the replies of both those interviewed and those who responded to a mail questionnaire.

G. THE DOCKET STUDY

The docket study covered representative felony prosecutions in six of the nine sample counties for the year 1962. (For details as to the method of conducting the docket study, see volume 1, Appendix B, pages 171-181.) Results appear in Tables 5 to 10.

Table 5 shows that virtually all defendants in the sample cases had counsel and that most of the others waived representation by counsel. The proportion of defendants who retained their own counsel ranged from a low of 10% in Tulare County to a high of 36% in Los Angeles and San Francisco Counties, with a projected statewide average of 30%.

Table 6 shows whether the defendant was found indigent and therefore eligible for representation by assigned counsel or public defender. The percentage varied from a low of 61% in San Francisco to a high of 90% in Tulare County, with a statewide figure of 69%. The latest annual report of the Administrative Office of the California Courts shows 35,614 criminal filings in 1963-1964. Therefore, assuming that each filing represents one defendant, approximately 24,600 individual felony defendants must be offered counsel each year in California.

Table 7 shows the percentage of defendants who are released on bail in each county. The lowest rate of release was in Shasta County, where only 24% of the defendants made bail, and the highest rate was in Contra Costa County, where 46% of the defendants made bail. The projected statewide average was 39%.

Table 8 indicates that although preliminary hearings are held in 75% of the cases in the state as a whole, the percentages in the counties vary widely, from

28% in Shasta to 93% in Los Angeles. Why do so many defendants waive the hearings in certain counties while so few do so in other counties? Dispositions of cases are shown in Table 9. For the state as a whole, 68% of the defendants pleaded guilty, including 10% who pleaded to lesser offenses. The highest rates of guilty pleas were in Shasta and Tulare Counties. The highest proportion of trials was in Los Angeles County, where 36% of the cases went to trial.

Table 10 shows the kinds of sentences, if any, imposed on the defendants. If a defendant had a combination sentence, such as fine and imprisonment, he was counted separately under both columns. Imposition of prison sentences, including county jail, varied from 57% in San Diego to 92% in Tulare, with a statewide figure of 64%. The most frequent use of probation was in Shasta County. Contra Costa led in the use of fines.

TABLE 5
Representation by Retained Counsel,
Assigned Counsel, and Defenders in
Felonies,
California, 1962

County	Total sample	Did defendant have counsel? Yes No.	%	No No.	%	Re-tained No.	%	As-signed No.	%	De-fender No.	%	Combination or type un-known No.	%	No data† No.	%
Shasta	50	47	92	3*	6	9	18	36	73	0	0	4	8	1	2
Los Angeles	252	248	100	0	0	90	36	1	0	145	58	12	5	4	1
San Diego	110	107	97	3	3	35	32	71	65	0	0	1	1	0	0
Tulare	50	50	100	0	0	5	10	1	2	43	86	1	2	0	0
Contra Costa	50	45	90	5*	10	8	16	36	72	0	0	1	2	0	0
San Francisco	150	141	99	2	1	52	36	0	0	89	62	0	0	7	5
Weighted total percentage		98		2		30		21		44		1		1	

* Those persons waived representation by counsel.
† % of no data refers to total sample; % in other columns refers to cases for which data were available.

H. CONCLUSIONS AND RECOMMENDATIONS

On the basis of their investigation and the materials contained in the fore-going report, the reporters have reached the following conclusions:

1. Whether to adopt a public defender or assigned counsel system should remain a matter of local option on the county level. Though, on balance, the public defender systems observed seem to provide somewhat better repre-

TABLE 6

Was Felony Defendant Determined Indigent?
California, 1962

County	Total sample	Yes No.	%	No No.	%	No data* No.	%
Shasta	50	36	78	10	22	4	8
Los Angeles	252	156	63	91	37	5	2
San Diego	110	72	67	35	33	3	3
Tulare	50	45	90	5	10	0	0
Contra Costa	50	41	84	8	16	1	2
San Francisco	150	87	61	55	39	8	5
Weighted total percentages			69		31		3

* % of no data refers to the total sample; % in other columns refers to cases for which data were available.

TABLE 7

Frequency of Release on Bail of Felony Defendants,
California, 1962

County	Total sample	Yes No.	%	No No.	%	No data* No.	%
Shasta	50	12	24	37	74	1	2
Los Angeles	252	103	41	146	58	3	1
San Diego	110	38	35	71	65	1	1
Tulare	50	15	30	35	70	0	0
Contra Costa	50	23	46	27	54	0	0
San Francisco	148	64	43	85	57	1	0
Weighted total percentages			39		61		1

* % of no data refers to total sample; % in other columns refers to cases for which data were available.

sentation, there may be local factors which make an assigned counsel system more adaptable to the needs of a particular county. The decision as to which system to adopt should not, however, turn on the issue of cost alone but should also be based upon a careful assessment of the adequacy of the representation provided.

2. Though a state statute permits a public defender to be part-time in counties with a population of less than 850,000, every public defender county without a full-time defender should consider carefully whether its indigent defense needs are being adequately met, particularly in view of the inevitable conflict between the demands of defender work and the pressures of private practice.

TABLE 8
Frequency of Preliminary Hearings in Felonies, California, 1962

County	Total sample	Yes No.	%	No, waiver No.	%	No, not used in this kind of case No.	%	No data* No.	%
Shasta	50	14	28	36	72	0	0	0	0
Los Angeles	252	227	93	12	5	5	2	8	3
San Diego	110	17	58	35	36	6	6	12	11
Tulare	50	20	41	29	59	0	0	1	2
Contra Costa	50	31	62	19	38	0	0	0	0
San Francisco	150	117	82	8	6	17	12	8	5
Weighted total percentages			75		23		3		3

* % of no data refers to total sample; % in other columns refers to total cases for which data were available.

TABLE 9
Dispositions in Felony Cases, California, 1962

County	Total sample	Plea guilty	Plea lesser offense	Dis- missed	Found guilty	Found guilty, lesser degree	Ac- quitted	Mental commit- ment	Other
Shasta	50	41	5	3	1	0	0	0	0
Los Angeles	252	116	29	11	63	16	12	2	3*
San Diego	110	80	3	0	14	0	7	0	6
Tulare	50	38	4	1	7	0	0	0	0
Contra Costa	50	33	6	2	4	0	5	0	0
San Francisco	150	85	17	10	21	5	4	2	6
Weighted total percentages		58	10	4	18	4	4	1	0

* one is "no data."

TABLE 10

Sentencing in Felony Cases,
California, 1962*

County	Total sample	No sentence No.	No sentence %	Death No.	Death %	Prison No.	Prison %	Probation No.	Probation %	Suspended sentence No.	Suspended sentence %	Fine No.	Fine %	No data† No.	No data† %	Misc. No.	Misc. %
Shasta	50	3	6	0	0	35	70	25	50	1	2	4	8	0	0	1	2
Los Angeles	252	28	11	1	0	146	58	95	38	0	0	37	15	0	0	2	1
San Diego	110	12	11	0	0	62	57	47	43	0	0	11	10	1	1	1	1
Tulare‡	50	2	4	0	0	46	92	13	26	0	0	0	0	0	0	4	8
Contra Costa	50	7	14	0	0	31	62	23	46	0	0	16	32	0	0	0	0
San Francisco	150	19	13	0	0	103	69	52	36	2	1	16	11	0	0	7	5
Weighted total percentages			10		0		64		39		0		14		0		3

* If a defendant had a combination of prison and probation, or other combination, he is counted under each column; hence the total is more than 100%.

† % of no data refers to total sample; % in other columns refers to total cases for which data were available.

‡ Tulare County had one case in which the sentence was pending.

3. Further studies should be made in public defender counties of the extent to which appointments of private counsel occur in conflict of interest and other cases with a view to determining whether such appointments are and should be utilized as a means of generally supplementing the public defender system.

4. Inquiry should be made in each county as to whether adequate investigation facilities are being provided to counsel representing the indigent. In public defender counties, wherever the need can be justified, at least one full-time investigator should be provided. Where the caseload of the defender's office does not require this much, special funds, adequate in amount, should be provided to permit the defender to employ investigative assistance on an ad hoc basis. In assigned counsel counties, the problem of providing such assistance is more difficult but not insoluble. Various avenues should be explored including, for example: (a) permitting assigned counsel to employ investigators without prior court approval, limited only by some maximum dollar amount and the court's subsequent determination of reasonableness, liberally applied; or (b) requiring prior court approval for employment of investigators, but with an announced judicial policy that applications for investigation funds will be looked upon with favor; or (c) establishment, on an experimental basis, of a county-supported investigative bureau with appropriate administrative controls, to which assigned counsel can turn for assistance.

5. Efforts should be made in assigned counsel counties, particularly in San Diego County, to insure the competency and experience of appointed attorneys in all cases. Appointment of associate counsel should not be limited to life-death cases, but should be regularly utilized as a means of giving junior bar members necessary trial experience. Studies should also be made to determine whether further increases in the applicable fee schedule will tend to encourage additional, experienced practitioners to put their names on the court's appointment list. Compensation of assigned counsel throughout the state should be made more uniform, possibly by the establishment of a statewide minimum fee schedule.

6. The prevailing approach in determining eligibility for appointment of counsel is to apply a very liberal test of indigency, relying mainly on the accused's oral statement and possible further inquiry by appointed counsel or the public defender. A uniform approach to and test for indigency should be applied throughout the state. To this end, it may be desirable to revise the statutory definition to indicate the exact nature of the inquiry to be made, and perhaps supplement this with an affidavit form to be used throughout the state. Moreover, judges, prosecutors, and defenders should be encouraged to make this a frequent topic for discussion at statewide and local professional meetings. Consideration should also be given to possible methods for tightening the test for indigency. In this connection studies should be made of the impact of such a change on the quality of representation provided to the marginal indigent and the additional administrative costs created thereby.

7. A pilot study should be conducted to determine the cost and feasibility

of providing counsel, or at least minimal legal advice, immediately following arrest under both assigned counsel and public defender systems.

8. A follow-up survey should be undertaken after some lapse of time to determine how the new legislation providing for compensation to counsel appointed in misdemeanor cases is being implemented.

9. Where a county public defender undertakes, as in Riverside County, to handle all appeals by indigents, provision should be made, by statutory amendment if required, to transfer state funds to the county commensurate with the services performed.

10. A uniform system of keeping statistics for public defender offices and for assigned counsel systems should be devised, and these statistics should be made generally available through publication in the Judicial Council Reports or in a separate, regularly published pamphlet. Such statistics will permit quick evaluation and comparison of effectiveness, costs, and other significant aspects of indigent defense systems used in different counties.

11. Any differences between statistical record-keeping on the county and state level in the field of criminal law administration should be eliminated. For example, in Los Angeles, felony filings are numbered on a case-by-case basis; on the state level, in the Judicial Council Reports, felony filings refer to the number of individual defendants. It may be useful also to add items to the statistics already kept, particularly in the field of misdemeanor prosecutions.

12. Consistent with the bar's special responsibilities in this area, standing indigent defense system committees should be established by every local bar association, which should have the responsibility for periodically reviewing the operations of the local system of providing counsel for indigent accused persons.

COLORADO

Prof. Jim R. Carrigan, Boulder

This report is the product of work by many people. Among the contributors were Hardin Holmes, chairman of the A.B.A. Associate State Committee and Paul Hicks, Jr., an associate in Mr. Holmes' Denver law firm. Special acknowledgments should go to the district judges and the clerks of their courts who gave freely of their time and energy to assist in gathering the necessary facts. District court clerks especially deserving of mention include Robert W. Awenius of Jefferson County, Mrs. Ruth Burns and Mrs. Mary Henderson of El Paso County, Frank Conry of Denver, Mrs. Marie Horne of Pueblo County, and Mrs. Dorothy Silvernale of Adams County.

Several University of Colorado Law School seniors provided very valuable aid in gathering statistical information. They are Robert Brown, Anne McGill, and Robert Showalter.

A. INTRODUCTION

Colorado had a population of 1,753,947 according to the 1960 census. The relatively low gross population figure fails to reflect, however, the extremely high rate of population growth, particularly in Denver and its suburbs, since World War II.

Colorado has 63 counties varying in population from 208 persons to about half a million. There are 18 judicial districts, each having 1 district attorney and anywhere from 1 to 10 district judges.

The counties selected for the survey were the following:

County	1960 population in thousands	Location in state	Remarks
Adams	120	Immediately north of Denver	Fastest growing county in state from 1950 to 1960, commercial and industrial center
Delta	16	Western slope	Ranching, farming, tourism
Denver	494	Central - just east of mountains	State capital, regional commercial, shopping, industrial, transportation, medical and educational center
El Paso	144	South central	Very light industry, shopping center, small college, extensive tourism, and 2 military operations in addition to U.S. Air Force Academy
Jefferson	128	Suburban county immediately west of Denver	High percentage of commuters, some light industry, and commercial
Pueblo	119	South central	Heavy steel, shopping, and commercial

The six counties selected for the sample include the five most populous counties in the state. Only one county in the sample is in the western half of the state. Three of the six sample counties are part of the Denver metropolitan area which, except for artificial historical boundaries, is really a single population center or city. The following table has additional information about the counties surveyed:

County	Felony defendants, 1962	% of indigents°	% of indigents who waived counsel°	Lawyers in private practice	No. of appointments of counsel in felonies, 1962	No. of lawyers appointed	County funds spent for attorney fees, 1962
Adams	149	48	2½	23	64	26	$ 12,425
Delta	35	92½	32	10	16§	8	900°°
Denver	1679†	55½	11	1526	631	500¶	172,472
El Paso	222	58	11	114	90	33	11,258
Jefferson	146	42	3	98	50	28	13,835
Pueblo	222‡	76½	54	70	55	22	7260

° Average of estimates supplied by judges and district attorney.

† Estimate based on actual figure for the number of informations filed in Denver District Court during 1962.

‡ 1961 figure used because 1962 figure not available.

§ Estimate based on docket study.

¶ Estimate supplied by the clerk's office.

°° Estimate.

B. CRIMINAL PROCEDURE AFFECTING INDIGENT DEFENDANTS

The district courts in Colorado have exclusive original jurisdiction in felony cases. District court grand juries have authority to indict, but the indictment procedure is very rarely used.

New rules of criminal procedure modeled on the federal rules were adopted by the Colorado Supreme Court effective November 1, 1961. These rules require that an officer making an arrest "with warrant" take the arrested person "without unnecessary delay before the nearest available justice of the peace, where a copy of the warrant shall be given to him." (Colo. Sup. Ct. R. Crim. P. 5 [a]). A person arrested without a warrant must be taken "within a reasonable time" before the nearest available justice of the peace. There is no explanation available for the difference in language in these two situations, and probably no difference in the time involved was intended.

As a practical matter, most felony arrests in Colorado are made on warrants issued by justices of the peace on the sworn complaints of law enforcement officers or aggrieved citizens. Only in Denver are all the justices who issue these warrants attorneys. (As of January 1, 1965, the Colorado justice of the peace system will be abolished and the magistrate function will be served by county judges who will be lawyers in all but the smaller counties.)

The rules of criminal procedure require the justice of the peace to tell the defendant the nature of the complaint against him, the amount of bail, of his right to retain counsel, and of his right in felony cases to have a preliminary examination. In addition, the rules require the justice to inform the defendant that he is not required to make a statement and that any statement he makes may be used against him. In addition the justice is required to allow the defendant a reasonable time and opportunity to consult counsel. Finally, the justice must admit the defendant to bail. All offenses are bailable except "capital offenses when the evidence of guilt is strong." (Id. R. 46 [a] [1].)

Practically speaking, the right of preliminary examination is an illusory one, for the new rules have followed the prior statutes by authorizing the district attorney, with the consent of the district court, to file a direct information, thus cutting off the defendant's right to a preliminary examination. The direct information procedure is employed almost everywhere in the state, and in nearly all cases. One exception is the judicial district which includes Delta County, one of the sample counties. As a matter of policy the district attorney whose district includes Delta County holds preliminary examinations in nearly all felony cases.

The initial setting of bail is done by the justice of the peace in most cases. The amount is recommended by the district attorney's office and the recommendation is usually followed.

Where the case is first started by the justice of the peace complaint and arrest warrant procedure, the arrested defendant is jailed and the district attorney then must file in district court an information charging the felony. At this stage there may be and often is some delay, particularly in the more populous areas where the volume of cases creates administrative problems in their processing between police departments, sheriffs' offices, and district attorneys. The district attorney of Adams County enforces a self-imposed restriction that an information against a man must be filed in district court within 48 hours after his arrest.

The time lapse between arrest and the filing of the information in district court is vital to the indigent defendant, for it is not until he is brought into district court for arraignment on the information that he has an opportunity to obtain the aid of counsel. Even though the justice of the peace may have set bail, he may need counsel to assist him in getting the bail reduced to a reasonable figure and to aid in obtaining the help of friends or relatives to raise bail.

In Denver County, students of the University of Denver Law Center provide counsel in misdemeanor cases brought in the Denver municipal courts. A similar service is provided misdemeanor defendants in the Boulder County court and the Boulder municipal court by student counsel of the University of Colorado Legal Aid Clinic.

The Colorado Rules of Criminal Procedure provide:
> If the defendant appears in court without counsel, the court shall advise him of his right to counsel. In any felony case, if upon the defendant's affidavit or sworn testimony and other investigation the court finds that the defendant is financially unable to obtain counsel, an attorney shall be assigned to represent him at every stage of the trial court proceedings. (Id. R. 44.)

91

A long-standing statute provides:

> In all indictments or informations for crimes or misdemeanors in any of the district courts of this state where by reason of the inability of the defendant to employ counsel, the court may assign him counsel for his defense, it shall be the duty of the court so assigning counsel to allow him a fee, to be fixed by the judge of the court, to be paid out of the county treasury. . . . (Colo. Rev. Stat. §39-7-29 [1953].)

Although the authority to appoint counsel in misdemeanor cases seems clear, most Colorado district judges do not have occasion to exercise this authority, for nearly all misdemeanor cases are filed in justice of the peace or county courts. Several district judges indicated, however, that they would not hesitate to appoint counsel in misdemeanor cases, particularly in those involving the more serious charges.

There is no great variation in procedure for appointment of counsel in felony cases. The sample counties reflect the statewide practice of first acquainting the defendant with his right to appointed counsel when he appears for arraignment. If it then appears that he is indigent and eligible for appointed counsel, an attorney is appointed for him and the arraignment is continued, usually until about a week later, to allow time for the appointed attorney to confer with the defendant and conduct some investigation prior to entry of a plea.

There is some variation in the methods used by district judges to select attorneys for appointments. Most prepare a roster of attorneys available for service from a list of the local bar, deleting the names of those who by reason of age, infirmity, or expressed preference choose not to handle criminal appointments. A more selective process is used in choosing appointees in capital cases, the goal being to assure that the best qualified and most experienced trial attorneys available are appointed. The usual procedure is to appoint two attorneys in capital cases. Separate attorneys are appointed as a matter of course where codefendants have a conflict of interest.

The usual procedure for determining indigency which qualifies a defendant for appointed counsel begins with an oral interrogation of the defendant by the district judge in open court. In several of the sample counties this is followed by having the defendant sign and swear to an affidavit of indigency. Where it appears from the judge's interrogation that the defendant has sufficient funds to pay a small fee or a portion of a fair fee, but not enough to retain counsel privately, most Colorado judges would appoint counsel, requiring the defendant to pay what funds he has to the court toward the appointed attorney's fee.

Several district judges refuse to allow indigent felony defendants to waive counsel under any circumstances. These judges go so far as to require that a defendant who insists on trying his own case have appointed counsel sit with him during the trial to answer questions regarding procedure.

The Colorado practice regarding appointment of counsel for appeals and postconviction remedies requires that the trial court appoint counsel for these proceedings. Counsel appointed at these stages are selected and compensated on the same basis as trial counsel. The recent United States Supreme Court right-to-counsel cases have had slight effect in Colorado, except perhaps to increase the number of appeals and requests for counsel at the appellate and postconviction stages.

All funds for compensating appointed counsel come from the county revenues. There is some feeling that since the district courts are state, not county, courts, they should be financed by the state, and that this statewide financing should include the payment of fees for appointed counsel.

[Editor's note: since the foregoing section was written, Adams County established a public defender, in January, 1965, under permissive legislation enacted in 1963. A public defender office has also been established at Durango for three counties in the 6th Judicial Circuit.]

C. OPINIONS OF THE JUDGES

The Colorado study began with a telephone interview with the then chief justice of the Supreme Court, Honorable Albert T. Frantz. There were personal interviews with 3 of the 10 district judges in Denver, and with 2 of the judges in each of the other five counties except Delta and Jefferson. In each of the last-named counties only one judge was available for interview when the survey was made. Thus 11 judges were interviewed in the six sample counties. The remaining 30 Colorado district judges were contacted by mail questionnaire, and 18 of them responded. (For a copy of the interview and mail questionnaires used, see vol. 1, pp. 227, 237.)

Question 7 of the judge interview asked: "Under an ideal system, at what stage in a criminal case do you think the indigent person should first be provided with a lawyer if he wants one?" Of the 11 judges interviewed 9, representing five of the six counties surveyed, thought that appointment of counsel should be at an earlier stage in the proceedings than presently provided. Six of them, representing four of the six counties, thought that counsel should be appointed between arrest and the first appearance before a magistrate. One judge who preferred this system indicated that counsel should be available at that stage of the proceedings to perform a purely advisory function, with a different attorney to be appointed later as the trial defense attorney if an information is filed. Another judge noted that having counsel available at this initial stage of criminal proceedings probably would require keeping an attorney on duty at the county jail or on call for jail interviews.

Only two judges, one of whom had very recently been elevated to the bench from a position as district attorney, were satisfied with the present time of appointment (after filing of the information at or before the arraignment and plea).

Of the 18 judges who returned mail questionnaires, 7 would prefer to have counsel appointed, in the words of the questionnaire, "Between arrest and first appearance before a magistrate." One judge voted for appointment "at first appearance before a magistrate." The other 10 apparently approve the present system, for they all elected "after the filing of an indictment or information but before arraignment thereon," which describes the system now generally employed in Colorado. Of the latter 10 judges, however, one volunteered that he wanted counsel appointed "at the first appearance in my court," and another indicated that he felt a defendant should be given counsel as soon after his arrest as he requested an attorney.

Because of the clear division of choices between the first and sixth alternatives among the 18 judges who answered question 6 on the mail questionnaire (same as question 7 on personal interview), parts (b) and (c) of this question are particularly interesting. Of the seven judges who would prefer to appoint counsel at the earliest opportunity listed (response "1"), four felt it is unfair not to provide counsel at that stage, and three thought it is not unfair. The judge who voted for counsel at the second earliest stage noted that it was "not necessarily" unfair not to provide an attorney then. Of the 10 judges who checked response "6" on this question (the present Colorado system), 7 indicated that it is unfair not to provide counsel at this stage, 2 felt that it is not unfair, and 1 was ambivalent.

On the question whether the "ideal" system could be financed, 6 of the 10 "mail questionnaire" judges who preferred the present system indicated it can be financed (which seems obvious since it *has been* financed for many years). Of the seven who favored appointment of counsel at the first or second stage indicated, three thought that such a system could be financed, one more felt it probably could not be financed by the small counties without state aid, and two felt it could not be financed at all. The remainder expressed no opinion regarding financing.

Responding to question 8(a) of the judge interview questionnaire, all but 3 of the 11 district judges personally interviewed already provided appointed counsel for the sentencing of a defendant who had pleaded guilty or had been convicted after trial and for the postconviction remedies listed. In Colorado there is some doubt whether the trial judge may appoint counsel for indigents in habeas corpus proceedings because the state Supreme Court has characterized these as civil rather than criminal in nature.

Three judges interviewed did not think counsel should be provided for the sentencing of a defendant who has pleaded guilty. One of those three did not think counsel should be provided for the sentencing stage even for one convicted after a trial. But counsel is generally provided in both of these situations in most Colorado courts as shown by the other judges interviewed and the mail questionnaires. Three of the 11 judges interviewed did not think that counsel should be provided for postconviction remedies, but the general practice and accepted rule in Colorado, subject to the above stated qualification regarding habeas corpus, is contrary. The same three judges did not think counsel should be furnished for the hearing on revocation of probation. One of those 3 did not think counsel should be appointed for "sexual psychopath" hearings, but he was the only judge of the 11 interviewed who held that view.

Four of the 11 judges personally interviewed thought it unnecessary to appoint counsel in misdemeanor cases. Several of the others, however, mentioned that although few misdemeanor prosecutions are filed in their district courts, since misdemeanors are handled in lower courts, they do occasionally appoint counsel in such cases.

Civil commitments of the mentally ill are handled in county court rather than district court, and the usual practice is to see that the person to be committed has representation.

Of the 18 district judges who responded by mail, 3 clearly demonstrated by their responses to question 7(a) the feeling that the pendulum has swung too far in favor of defendants. Of those three, two preferred to deny appointed counsel in all the situations listed under this question. One of these volunteered: "It seems to me all of our attention is to the welfare of prisoners and not the taxpayers." This negative position, however, is highly atypical among Colorado district judges, as demonstrated by the other 15 mail questionnaires. Most of these favored broad use of appointed counsel except in misdemeanor cases, although several would prefer appointing counsel even in misdemeanor cases. Two of the majority group did not think counsel should be appointed for postconviction remedy hearings and sexual psychopath hearings.

The judges gave the following responses to the question, "Do you think it is unfair to the indigent person if he does not have a lawyer for such cases and proceedings?"

Case or proceeding	Personal interview Yes	No	Mail questionnaire Yes	No
1. Sentencing of defendant who pleaded guilty	3	6	9	7
2. Sentencing of defendant convicted by trial	8	1	9	6
3. Postconviction remedies	6	3	6	8
4. Revocation of probation	3	6	5	10
5. Sexual psychopath hearing	7	2	10	4
6. Misdemeanors	4	5	5	8
7. Commitment—mentally ill	2	0	7	7

There were several comments to the effect that only in "serious" misdemeanors would it be unfair *not* to provide indigents with counsel. Some judges who acknowledged the need for counsel in passing on sexual psychopaths were influenced by the seriousness of the possible prison term involved—one year to life. Most of the judges did not comment on commitment of the mentally ill because this procedure is handled in the county court.

One judge, after indicating "no" after all seven of these options, added the comment, "Of course, in any case it is better for defendant to have a lawyer." Frequently, the judges qualified a "yes" to the question on postconviction remedy proceedings by stating that counsel should be available only if the proceeding was not entirely frivolous. Many judges seem to feel that postconviction remedy procedures are being abused and over-used. One judge avoided a direct answer by stating that the circumstances of each case should be examined. Another avoided "yes" or "no" answers (by mail) by stating that at *any* stage of *any* criminal case a defendant should have counsel if requested. These responses were not counted as "yes."

Regarding the problem of financing a broader system of providing counsel to indigents, 6 of the 11 interviewed judges said that this would present no serious problem. A judge from Denver felt that the public defender system would be the most economical mode of financing. Three judges suggested that the cost should be shifted from county taxpayers to the state. One judge was pessimistic about receiving adequate financing from the present conservatively oriented state legislature.

On the question of financing, the judges returning mail questionnaires had diverse opinions. Five felt that the present system could be expanded without serious financial strain. Three suggested a public defender system, one on a statewide and state-supported basis. Four flatly stated that a system to provide defense in all the situations listed could not be financed, and two more expressed doubt whether it could be paid for. One judge suggested that it was time for the state to take over financing the defense of indigents. The others declined to state an opinion.

With respect to what percentage of felony defendants are indigent, the estimates of judges interviewed ran from a low of 33⅓% to a high of 95%, averaging 61⅔%. The only judge who made an actual count found that 40% in his court were indigent in 1962. Of the indigents in felony cases, the judges interviewed estimated that 26% (average of all estimates) waived the right to counsel after being fully informed.

Three of the judges replying by mail made actual counts of the percentage of felony defendants who were indigent. One found 96% indigent, one 43%, and one 25%. The 12 judges who estimated the per cent indigent gave figures from 25% to 90%, the average estimate being 60%. Of 15 mail questionnaire judges who estimated the per cent of indigent felony defendants who waive counsel, 4 indicated that none waive representation, and 3 of those 4 indicated that they do not permit an indigent defendant charged with a felony to waive counsel. The average estimate for the group of 15 ran 23% waiver. (This average was computed by taking into account the four indicating that none waive counsel).

Considerable variety was apparent in the systems employed to select lawyers for appointment. Responding to Question 10(a), four judges interviewed stated that they used their own lists of lawyers, and only one used a bar association list. Two indicated they used as a starting point a list of all attorneys admitted to practice, and two, employment of some combination of options 3, 4, and 5. Two judges volunteered disavowal of any political influence in the appointment process, but one judge frankly admitted that politics does enter into the formulation of his list of prospective appointees. All the judges indicated that special efforts are made to obtain well-qualified, experienced trial counsel in the more serious cases, especially capital cases.

Most of the judges would not, in any circumstance, appoint a lawyer for whom the defendant asks by name. Several stated that this policy is based on a knowledge or opinion that some lawyers "hang around the jail" or otherwise solicit. Four judges of those interviewed indicated that in some exceptional circumstances they might accede to a defendant's request for a particular lawyer.

Colorado judges are not overly sympathetic to the indigent defendant who requests a change of attorneys. Most of those contacted, however, would hold a hearing to allow the defendant to state his grievance against the attorney initially appointed, and if there appeared to be legitimate grounds for complaint, would appoint another attorney.

All judges would appoint separate lawyers for defendants in the same case who had conflicting interests.

On the subject of compensation for appointed attorneys, there was little uniformity. Of all the 11 judges personally contacted, 6 paid appointees at a flat $15 per hour for most work. This coincided with the then current bar association minimum fee rate for hourly work, which in Denver has since been increased to $20 per hour. Three of the remaining judges used the fee schedule as a general guide, two paid at the rate of $10 per hour for preparatory work plus $100 to $200 per day for time spent in trial, and one paid $75 per day for both preparation and actual trial time. Several judges commented that attorneys owe the public a responsibility to donate some services for indigents, and therefore they cannot expect to be compensated at the same rates they would charge a client who might retain them privately. Six of the 11 judges personally interviewed require assigned counsel to submit an itemized statement showing the services rendered.

Only one of the 11 judges personally interviewed felt that the rates of compensation paid appointed attorneys are inadequate. Another preferred not to comment. All the others agreed that the compensation is adequate and several noted the substantial improvement in compensation achieved over the past few years.

All Colorado district courts contacted reimburse appointed counsel for out-of-pocket expenses for investigation and preparation so long as the court feels the amounts involved are necessary expenditures and not excessive in amount.

All but two of the judges personally interviewed ranked appointed counsel equal in quality of representation to privately retained counsel. One judge ranked appointed counsel better than those privately retained, and one thought the appointees were inferior to retained counsel. A similar but not identical result appeared in comparison of appointed counsel and members of the district attorneys' staffs. One judge thought appointed counsel were of better quality, generally speaking, than the district attorney's staff, two thought the appointees were inferior to the prosecutors and the rest thought they were about equal. One judge distinguished between appointed lawyers who take their cases to trial and those who enter pleas of guilty, stating that those who go to trial "are on a par with" prosecutors, but "not all lawyers who enter pleas of guilty are."

Judges queried personally indicated that a very low percentage of lawyers ask to be excused from court appointments. No judge estimated this number at over the lowest option provided on the form (1% to 9%). One judge estimated it at 1% and four judges estimated it at 0, stating that their appointment lists are so made up that the problem simply does not occur. One judge noted that some attorneys are reluctant to represent sex offenders.

In response to the question regarding "the problem of the person who can pay a moderate fee" but not enough to retain a good defense attorney, two judges flatly stated that such a person is not indigent and it is his own responsibility to obtain counsel. All the others personally queried follow the practice of determining if his assets are insufficient to obtain competent counsel. If so, these judges would appoint an attorney for him and apply whatever assets he did have to the fee paid the court-appointed attorney. This seems to be the general Colorado practice. In these circumstances judges will not appoint an attorney chosen by the defendant. One judge commented that he feels "the out-and-out indigent" is better off than the man with moderate means.

In answer to the request for "other comments" on the problem, one judge said: "Some lawyers 'pad' their bills, but we know who they are. On the other hand, some are too modest and don't bill for their full services."

In response to this final question, one judge felt that attorney's fees for appeals should not be paid by the public unless, after examining the record, the appointed attorney felt that there was real, substantial error and so advised the trial court.

Five of the 11 judges interviewed personally took advantage of this question to promote a public defender system in the more populated areas. One of these felt that there should be a combination of the assigned counsel and public defender systems for Denver. The public defender's function would be to "enter the case immediately when a prisoner is booked. He would speak to the prisoner merely to *advise* him of his rights. The public and law officers have rights too, but they know their rights." Under this judge's suggested system, the public defender would remain as counsel in the case until the pleading stage. If the defendant pleaded not guilty, the court would then appoint a trial attorney for him. If he pleaded guilty, the public defender would continue as his counsel to assist in bringing all mitigating circumstances to the court's attention prior to sentencing. This judge felt that such a system would give a defendant "great help at early periods, yet at the trial he will have a personal attorney who can be a true advocate giving the case individual attention." The same judge felt that the public defender should have a budget *greater* than that of the prosecutor, because the latter has available all the investigating resources of the police department.

D. OPINIONS OF THE DISTRICT ATTORNEYS

All six of the district attorneys whose districts include the six Colorado sample counties were personally interviewed. In addition, mail questionnaires were returned representing all of the remaining 12 districts.

Of the six prosecutors personally interviewed, one had 10 to 14 years of prosecution experience, three had 5 to 9 years of such experience, and two had 2 to 4 years. However, two of these six had practiced criminal law for 5 to 9 years, two had practiced in this field for 10 to 14 years, and two, for over 15 years.

Only in Denver is the office of district attorney considered by law to be a full-time job. Nevertheless, five of the six district attorneys personally interviewed indicated that they put in over 30 hours per week on duties of the office. The sixth stated that he spent between 20 and 29 hours per week. Of those answering this question on the mail questionnaire, two thirds stated that they put in over 30 hours a week, and all the rest stated that they spent between 20 and 29 hours a week. Colorado district attorneys perform only very minimal civil duties. Most of such work devolves upon a separate officer, the county attorney.

Of the six district attorneys personally interviewed, three said that they presently have adequate funds to run their offices and three said that they do not. Similarly, half of those responding by mail thought their funds were adequate and half did not. Of those who said their funds are adequate, two asserted, however, that there is not sufficient financing for investigation. All the district attorneys queried in person stated that funds for investigation were available, and some had regular, full-time staff investigators in addition to personnel of the police department and sheriff's office.

Sixteen district attorneys expressed opinions about the ideal stage for appointment of counsel. This included 4 district attorneys who were interviewed and 12 who responded by mail. Of the 16, 10 said the ideal stage was after the filing of an information but before arraignment. Seven recommended an earlier stage, including three who said "between arrest and first appearance before a magistrate." One recommended appointment at arraignment on the information. Nine of the 16 thought it would be unfair if counsel were not provided at the stage recommended. On the matter of financing the majority (12 of 16) clearly thought their ideal system presented no problem, but the others either suggested that the state rather than the county should assume the burden, or mentioned a public defender system. One said: "Cost already is prohibitive. Too much [is] done now to protect criminals."

On the question of providing a lawyer in miscellaneous cases and proceedings, responses were as follows:

	Case or proceeding	Provide counsel? Yes	Provide counsel? No	Unfair if not provided? Yes	Unfair if not provided? No
1	Sentencing of defendant who pleaded guilty	8	8	7	7
2	Sentencing of defendant convicted by trial	11	5	10	5
3	Postconviction remedies	11	5	8	6
4	Revocation of probation	8*	7	7	7
5	Sexual psychopath hearing	12	3	7	7
6	Misdemeanors	5	11	6	7
7	Commitment—mentally ill	10	4	7	5

* Also an additional one said "yes and no."

As to financing representation for these cases and proceedings, 12 thought it could be done and 3 saw a problem or said it could not be done. One of the latter commented, "For misdemeanors it would bankrupt the county." Three persons specifically mentioned a public defender.

Four of the six district attorneys personally interviewed thought that the present court appointment system of providing counsel for indigents is satisfactory and works well. The Denver district attorney declined to respond to this question because he is a member of the bar association committee on the public defender program and did not want to comment until that committee's report is published. District attorneys in Pueblo and Colorado Springs, the cities ranking second and third in size, did not think that a public defender system in their respective cities would cost less than the present system. Moreover, they did not seem to think the need for a public defender has yet been shown. One suburban district attorney said of the present system: "It's lacking in certain respects. Assigned counsel don't get into the case soon enough. The police have very little restraint on them in their decision to arrest. They make too many unfounded arrests."

In comparing the quality of court appointed attorneys with those privately retained by the defendant, there was little variation among the six district attorneys interviewed. Two felt the appointed attorneys compared "fairly well" but lacked experience. One of these stressed the extra enthusiasm of appointed lawyers. Of the remaining four, three felt that appointed attorneys were about equal to those privately retained. One, however, pointed out that in murder cases and the more serious crimes, the court appoints an experienced attorney whose ability and experience are likely to be on a par with the retained attorney and the prosecutor, whereas for lesser felonies this prosecutor thought retained counsel are superior to appointed attorneys.

Regarding the present system of determining indigency, three of the six district attorneys characterized the present system as too lenient, one thought it too strict, and two described it as about right. One of those who feel the system is too lenient asserted that too often defendants have money for a bond but claim they cannot afford an attorney. He felt there should be more thorough investigation of a defendant's assets and ability to pay. The one district attorney who described the system as too strict explained that he felt there was too great a tendency toward "reliance on resources of friends and relatives" in applying the standard. Two thirds of those replying by mail felt that the present system of determining indigency is "about right," and the remaining third all thought it is "too lenient."

Estimates of district attorneys personally interviewed on the percentage of felony defendants who are indigent ranged from 50% to 90%. The average estimate was 66%%. The district attorneys polled by mail estimated that an average of 61% of felony defendants are indigent.

An average of 18% of indigent defendants waive appointment of counsel, according to estimates of the prosecutors personally interviewed. Those polled by mail gave estimates that averaged 26% in this category.

There was unanimous agreement among the district attorneys interviewed regarding compensation of assigned counsel. All six felt that assigned counsel should be paid at the bar association minimum fee schedule rates. The consensus is that present compensation is adequate. Out-of-pocket expenses for investigation are now paid by the public in all six sample counties.

Replies by mail questionnaire showed that 10 district attorneys believe counsel should be compensated for services on behalf of indigents and only 1 that they should not. One left the answer blank. Eight who replied by mail thought the present compensation rates are adequate and four that they are inadequate. Here too consensus seemed to be that counsel should be paid at bar association minimum fee standard rates. All who answered the question regarding expenses of investigation felt that these should be paid by the public. The prosecution's discretion in the matter of what evidence will be disclosed to defense counsel prior to trial is somewhat limited by Rule 16(a) of the Colorado Rules of Criminal Procedure, which in pertinent part provides:

> Upon the motion of a defendant at any time after the filing of the indictment or information, the court may order the prosecuting attorney to permit the defendant to inspect and copy or photograph designated books, papers, documents, photographs or tangible objects, obtained from or belonging to the defendant or obtained from others by seizure or by process, upon a showing that the items sought may be material to the preparation of his defense and that the request is reasonable.

Replies of the district attorneys personally interviewed revealed widely varying practices regarding disclosure to defense counsel of "such things as confessions, statements of witnesses, reports of expert witnesses, exhibits, etc." One of the six interviewed stated a flat policy of disclosing none of these items. Another said his office normally did not disclose confessions or witnesses' statements "except in unusual cases." Nevertheless, he said, "We do more often than not disclose reports of expert witnesses and exhibits." A third stated that he revealed to opposing counsel only "confessions in writing" but none of the other items listed. Two (one from the least populated district and the other from the most heavily populated district) follow a policy of full disclosure with slight qualifications. Such disclosure will not be made in favor of a defense attorney suspected of merely conducting a "fishing expedition" to "set up" a defense. One of the six personally interviewed stated that as a general rule his office would not disclose the listed items. But, he stated, in some cases and with certain lawyers "we will disclose our entire file." As an example he said disclosure would be made when a defense attorney is trying in good faith to determine whether his client is lying to him.

More than half of the district attorneys queried by mail expressed, in varying language, a liberal, if not a full, disclosure policy. One of these stated the single exception of confessions. Three follow a policy of disclosing as little as possible, one of these indicating that disclosure might be made only to obtain a guilty plea, but no disclosure would be made if the case was likely to go to trial. One prosecutor said that his practice in these matters varies from case to case. Three others indicated by their answers a policy of disclosing only what the quoted rule requires.

On the problem of the defendant who can pay a moderate fee, one of the six district attorneys personally interviewed declined any comment, and another stated simply, "If he can get a lawyer, he should get one himself." A third said: "He should not be provided a lawyer at public expense. In most cases a lawyer will accept, on a retainer basis, a note or some form of security for future payment of the part of the fee he can't pay immediately." Three of the six interviewed showed somewhat more concern for the defendant in this situation. These three agreed that the court can handle the situation by taking whatever funds the defendant has and applying them toward paying the fee of a court-appointed attorney, with the balance of the attorney's fee to be paid by public funds. The six district attorneys personally interviewed expressed, in only slightly varying degrees, strong distaste for going to trial against a defendant who chooses to conduct his own defense without an attorney. One said: "The prosecution has an unfair advantage." Another protested that the "defendant in this situation may get into the record many things an attorney couldn't get in." A third felt that counsel should be required, and added: "We can't (in case where defendant acts as his own lawyer) put on our best case because we have to lean over backward to make sure he gets a fair trial." One district attorney noted the local practice of requiring at least that an appointed attorney sit at the counsel table with the defendant who insists on trying his own case. Such an attorney would act in an advisory capacity.

Of the six district attorneys personally interviewed, only one declined to make any suggestions for improving the present system, asserting that it works well. One thought there is need to improve the "general quality of the trial bar," and three cited a need to improve the system for determining indigency, their language indicating that "improve" was used to connote a need to tighten procedures on the ground that too many persons are now obtaining counsel at public expense who can afford to pay for an attorney.

One district attorney personally interviewed suggested that more specific standards be set by the courts so that assigned counsel will know just what is expected of them. The same attorney commented that "counsel should be provided at an earlier stage of the proceedings."

Only one of those interviewed recommended a public defender system. He reasoned that with that system, "there would be fewer trials, and more pleas of guilty." He stated his view that the average "public defender would not be as capable as an assigned attorney in major cases or capital cases." But he added that the public defender would probably "be a lot more ethical than some big city defense attorneys."

Only three of the district attorneys questioned by mail responded to the request for comments on how the present system could be improved. One of these favored "establishment of a full-time public defender system." Another suggested adoption by the state courts of the present federal system, in which counsel serve without compensation as a public duty. The third favored expansion of provision for counsel on appeal.

Generally speaking the district attorneys were not quite as concerned about the defense of indigents as were the district judges. Nevertheless, it must be said that all of the district attorneys interviewed evinced sincere concern with the plight of indigent defendants and a most commendable attitude of fairness toward them.

E. OPINIONS OF DEFENSE ATTORNEYS

The experience and opinions of defense attorneys were tested by questionnaires sent to 81 attorneys selected from the docket study in the six sample counties. Responses were received from 61 attorneys, 5 in Adams, 6 in Delta, 28 in Denver, 6 in El Paso, 6 in Jefferson, and 10 in Pueblo. The sample of attorneys in each of those counties represents a cross-section of the profession and includes both younger and older attorneys, many with experience in more than 50 criminal cases and some with experience in less than 5 criminal cases.

Of the 61 attorneys replying, 56 indicated they had served as appointed counsel in 1962 in at least one case. Their experience in criminal practice before the first case in which they were appointed in 1962 was as follows:

No. of attorneys	No. of criminal cases
2 (both in El Paso)	0
11	1-4
6	5-9
7	10-19
11	20-49
19	50 or more

The attorneys listed in their answers more than 25 different crimes of which indigent persons had been accused. However, there appeared to be no correlation possible between the attorney's experience and the nature of the crime involved in the case he was assigned to defend. Burglary and breaking and entering were reported much more frequently than any other crimes (20 cases). The next most frequent crime was "manslaughter, voluntary, first degree or unspecified" (10). There also appeared to be no correlation between the nature of the crime and the attorney's opinion as to whether he had been appointed in time to represent the accused person adequately, and no relation to the stage at which he was appointed.

The defense attorneys were asked at which stage in the proceedings they had been appointed in their last case in 1962 that had been concluded. Responses were as follows:

(1) between arrest and first appearance (arraignment on the warrant) before a magistrate, 7;

(2) at first appearance (arraignment on the warrant) before a magistrate, 4;

(3) between first appearance (arraignment on the warrant) and preliminary hearing, 4;

(4) at preliminary hearing, 2;

(5) after preliminary hearing but before the filing of an indictment, information, etc., 0;

(6) after the filing of an indictment, information, etc., but before arraignment thereon, 29;

(7) at arraignment on indictment, information, etc., 7;

(8) after arraignment on indictment, information, etc., but before trial, 5;

(9) at trial, 0.

In Section B above, it was pointed out that the criminal procedure of Colorado provides for appointment of counsel at the time the defendant is brought before the court for arraignment on the information, etc., but before the actual arraignment, i.e., requiring him to plead. Thus in the typical case in Colorado, counsel is appointed at a point somewhere between stage 6 and 7 on the above list, but an answer of 6 or 7 properly reflects the general practice. Twenty-nine of the attorneys replied they had been appointed at stage 6, and seven at stage 7, so that more than 50% of those answering the question had been appointed in accordance with the usual procedure. In El Paso County five out of six said they had been appointed at stage 6, and in Pueblo County four out of seven said they had been appointed at stage 8, while one attorney from Pueblo said that it was customary in that county to be appointed at stage 8. Of the 50 attorneys who expressed an opinion as to whether they had been appointed in time to represent the accused person adequately, 43 said "yes" and 7 said "no." In Delta, El Paso, and Jefferson Counties all who replied said "yes," as did 22 of 24 in Denver. In all of those counties, except for one instance in Denver, the attorneys had been appointed at least as early as the arraignment on the information, etc. However, in Adams County, where similar procedures prevail, three out of four felt that they had not been appointed in time to represent the accused person adequately. In Pueblo two out of five attorneys felt they had not been appointed early enough, which may well coincide with the procedure apparently followed there. However, out of five attorneys appointed at stage 8, three felt they had been appointed early enough, which, together with comments from other attorneys, may indicate that the facts of each case will be decisive. For instance, in a case where a defendant gives a confession at the time of arrest an attorney appointed at stage 1 (arraignment on the warrant) will feel he has not been appointed early enough.

The attorneys were asked to state whether in their opinion the present system for assignment of lawyers to represent indigent persons accused of crime was fair to the indigent persons as well as fair to the lawyers. Since all of the questionnaires and answers were handled by mail, it is difficult to judge whether all of the attorneys interpreted the word "fair" in the same manner. Forty said the system was fair and 17 said it was unfair to indigent persons; 31 said the system was fair and 25 said it was unfair to the lawyers. The only significant variation in responses from the various counties was that the majority of replies from Adams, El Paso, Jefferson, and Pueblo Counties were that it was unfair to lawyers.

The questionnaire set forth six specific changes that the attorneys might recommend, in addition to others that they might write in. Replies were as follows:

(1) appoint lawyer at earlier stage of case, viz. _____, 11;

(2) pay out-of-pocket expenses of lawyers incurred in investigation and preparing case, 17;

(3) pay lawyers for their services, 7;

(4) pay lawyers more for their services, 22;

(5) provide counsel in additional kinds of cases, such as serious misdemeanors, 16;

(6) improve the system which the judge uses in selecting lawyers to be appointed (explain below), 14.

Since more of the attorneys felt that the present system was not fair to lawyers than felt it was not fair to indigent persons, it is interesting to analyze the list of suggested changes shown above in terms of whether the recommended change would benefit primarily lawyers or indigent persons. Numbers 2, 3 and 4 would appear to be of primary benefit to lawyers, whereas 1 and 5 would benefit indigent persons. Number 6 would depend upon the type of change. Under this number some lawyers indicated they felt compelled to serve as appointed counsel and recommended that appointments go first to attorneys desiring appointment. Such a change would be of benefit primarily to lawyers. Another suggested change was to appoint more experienced counsel rather than young lawyers, which would be of benefit primarily to indigent persons.

In addition to the replies noted above, seven of the attorneys indicated that no changes at all were necessary.

Relatively few of the attorneys added remarks or suggested changes that were not listed on the questionnaire. Several suggested as an alternative to number 2 of the recommended changes, that investigators be provided for defense counsel. Since all of the attorneys questioned had been paid for their services, at least in part, recommended change number 3 was generally inapplicable. However, 19 of the 50 reporting on repayment for out-of-pocket expense answered no repayment or payment only in part, and therefore several attorneys recommended changes in that area. Only two attorneys suggested making the test of indigency stricter. Numerous attorneys mentioned the need to have appointments made without regard to the political ties between judges and the attorneys whom they select.

The public defender system was the exclusive change recommended by seven attorneys, and others recommended it in addition to other changes, although no question referred to a public defender system. Only one attorney was critical of it: he said that the heavy schedule of a public defender would make him too willing to enter guilty pleas. The principal advantages of a public defender system that were mentioned were establishing contact with the defendant at an earlier time and obtaining better investigative services. There was a difference of opinion whether the public defender system would avoid politics.

This report on what the defense attorneys said is directed primarily at their experience in criminal trials of indigent persons, since 59 out of 60 handled no appeals for indigent persons, and 55 out of 59 said they had handled no habeas corpus or other postconviction proceedings. Generally speaking, the defense attorneys evidenced a real concern about the defense of indigents, and the answers of only a few indicated concern primarily for their own welfare.

F. DOCKET STUDY

A study was made of representative cases from the court dockets in all six sample counties for the year 1962. (For details of study methods see volume 1, pages 178-179.) Results are shown in Tables 1 to 5.

Table 1 indicates that for the state as a whole, based on a projection from the six counties, 88% of the felony defendants had counsel. The proportion varied in different counties, however, being as low as 70% in Pueblo. When the number of defendants who had counsel are divided according to type of counsel, it appears that Denver had by far the largest proportion of assigned counsel. For the state as a whole, 48% of all defendants had assigned counsel.

As shown in Table 2, the proportion of felony defendants determined to be indigent was 73% in Denver County, 58% in El Paso, and 41% in Jefferson. Information from the other counties was insufficient to report a figure.

Table 3 indicates the extent to which felony defendants were released on bail in the sample counties. The percentage ranged from 11% in Delta County to 70% in Jefferson, with a weighted statewide figure of 53%. In Denver 55% were released.

Table 4 shows how the cases were terminated. For the state as a whole 51% of the defendants pleaded guilty, including 10% who pleaded to lesser offenses. Another 21% of the cases were dismissed, while 20% reached trial, resulting in 13% convictions and 7% acquittals. Pueblo County had a high proportion of guilty pleas compared with the other counties, and Jefferson had an unusual number of dismissals. El Paso had a high proportion of pleas to lesser offenses.

Sentences rendered, if any, are shown in Table 5. For the state as a whole, 37% of the defendants were sentenced to prison, including county jails, while 24% were placed on probation and 2% had suspended sentences without probation. The most frequent use of probation was in Adams County, and the least frequent use was in Pueblo.

G. CONCLUSIONS AND RECOMMENDATIONS

On the basis of the information studied the following conclusions and recommendations are submitted:

1. The present assigned counsel system seems to be functioning satisfactorily in most areas of the state.

TABLE 1
Retained and Assigned Counsel in Felonies
Colorado, 1962

County	Total sample	Did defendant have counsel? Yes No.	%	No No.	%	Retained No.	%	Assigned No.	%	Combination or type unknown No.	%	No data* No.	%
Denver	50	48	96	2	4	13	26	35	70	0	0	0	0
Jefferson	20	17	85	3	15	10	50	7	35	0	0	0	0
Adams	47	42	96	2	5	18	41	16	36	8	18	3	6
Pueblo	20	14	70	6	30	8	40	5	25	1	5	0	0
Delta	19	15	79	4	21	6	32	9	47	0	0	0	0
El Paso	20	19	95	1	5	9	45	10	50	0	0	0	0
Weighted total percentages		88		12		36		48		2		1	

* % of no data refers to total sample; % in other columns refers to cases for which data were available.

106

COLORADO

TABLE 2
Was Felony Defendant Determined Indigent?
Colorado, 1962

	Total sample	Yes No.	%	No No.	%	No data[°] No.	%
Denver	50	35	73	13	27	2	4
Jefferson	20	7	41	10	59	3	15
El Paso	20	11	58	8	42	1	5
Weighted total percentages			55		46		16

[°] % of no data refers to total sample; % in other columns refers to cases for which data were available.

TABLE 3
Frequency of Release on Bail of Felony Defendants
Colorado, 1962

	Total sample	Yes No.	%	No No.	%	No data[°] No.	%
Denver	50	27	55	22	45	1	2
Jefferson	20	14	70	6	30	0	0
Pueblo	20	9	45	11	55	0	0
Delta	19	2	11	16	89	1	5
El Paso	20	9	45	11	55	0	0
Weighted total percentages			53		47		5

[°] % of no data refers to total sample; % in other columns refers to cases where data were available.

TABLE 4
Disposition in Felony Cases
Colorado, 1962

County	Total sample	Plea guilty	Plea lesser offense	Dis- missed	Found guilty	Found guilty lesser degree	Ac- quitted	Mental commit- ment	Pend- ing	Other
Denver	50	20	7	7	6	0	1	1	7	1
Jefferson	20	3	1	14	0	0	0	0	2	0
Adams	47	19	0	10	12	0	3	0	1	2
Pueblo	20	14	1	0	2	0	2	1	0	0
Delta	19	11	0	3	2	0	3	0	0	0
El Paso	20	3	6	5	3	1	2	0	0	0
Weighted total percentages		41	10	21	12	1	7	1	6	1

TABLE 5
Sentencing in Felony Cases
Colorado, 1962

County	Total sample	No sentence No.	%	Prison No.	%	Probation No.	%	Suspended sentence No.	%	Pending No.	%
Denver	50	17	34	19	38	9	18	2	4	2	4
Jefferson	20	11	55	3	15	5	25	1	5	0	0
Adams	47	18	38	11	23	16	34	0	0	0	0
Pueblo	20	3	15	13	65	4	20	0	0	0	0
Delta	19	5	26	6	32	7	37	0	0	0	0
El Paso	20	7	35	8	40	4	20	0	0	0	0
Weighted total percentages			33		37		24		2		2

2. There is too great a diversity in the standards for compensating counsel from one county to another; there is need for establishment of a minimum fee schedule statewide to expressly cover services rendered by court appointed attorneys.

3. In Denver County, at least, there should be immediate consideration of establishment of some form of private or public defender office to either replace or supplement the present assigned counsel system there.

4. The possibilities of further involving law students at the University of Colorado and the University of Denver in the defense of indigents accused of crime should be explored.

CONNECTICUT

Richard C. Sanger, Avon

The reporter wishes to thank the people who have been a particular help in gathering data and making suggestions regarding the report. Arthur M. Lewis of Hartford, chairman of the state committee, has been extremely helpful in reviewing the report, as were other members of the committee, L. Stewart Boham, Richard A. Kelley, James J. Shea, and Jacob D. Zeldes. Several state officials devoted time and effort in providing statistics on the court system. John J. Nachyly, acting secretary of the Judicial Council, made available resources of his office and the many reports that are submitted to him. Mr. John F. Halloran, executive secretary of the Judicial Department, provided budgetary statistics. The persons interviewed were gracious in their manner and frank in their discussions of the public defender system, making this survey a thoroughly pleasurable experience for the reporter.

A. INTRODUCTION

Connecticut had a population of 2,535,234 in the 1960 census, ranking 25th among the states. The estimated 1962 population was 2,663,000. It ranks 48th among the states in area. Most of the population is concentrated in the central portion of the state along the Connecticut River Valley, along the coastal towns which bound Long Island Sound, and in the southwestern portion of the state within commuting radius of New York. These densely populated regions fall within five counties: Hartford, New Haven, New London, Fairfield, and Middlesex. The remaining three counties, covering generally the northeastern and northwestern portions of the state, are rural and less densely populated. Since abolition of county government in 1959, the counties are significant for purposes of venue only. The court system at all levels is statewide.

The counties selected for survey were as follows:

TABLE 1

Counties Included in Indigent Persons Survey

County	1960 population in thousands	Felony defendants, 1962-63	Remarks
Hartford (D)	690	528	Industry, insurance, state capital
New Haven (D)	660	389	Industry
New London	186	511	Shipyards
Fairfield	654	306	Industry, commuters for New York employment

(D) indicates that a docket study was made.

Judges, state's attorneys, and public defenders were interviewed in each of the sample counties. Mail questionnaires were sent to state's attorneys in the other counties.

B. CRIMINAL PROCEDURE AS IT AFFECTS INDIGENT PERSONS

The Superior Court is the court of general civil and criminal jurisdiction. It sits in at least one location in each county. In 1959 the municipal and minor court system was abolished and a circuit court established, effective January 1, 1961. The state was divided into 18 circuits without reference to county lines. There are 44 circuit court judges, all lawyers and all on a full-time basis. The circuit court has jurisdiction over misdemeanors and over felonies for which the maximum penalty does not exceed five years. The court is limited, however, in the sentence which it can impose, to one year's imprisonment or $1,000 fine, or both. Except in the rare case of a Superior Court bench warrant issued for a suspect's arrest and presentment to the Superior Court, all criminal defendants are presented in the circuit court promptly after arrest. Prompt presentment and advice concerning right to counsel is required by recent legislation (Pub. Act 126 [1963], reprinted in the Appendix to this report).

TABLE 2
*Schedule of Public Defender Salaries and Case Load**

County	Defender's salary	Total criminal cases in superior court, including serious misdemeanors	Number of public defender cases
Fairfield†	$6000	317	131
Hartford†	7500	646	441
Litchfield	3250	80	42
Middlesex	3250	56	19
New Haven†	6000	406	179
New London	4000	572	354
Tolland	3250	87	29
Windham	3250	107	53
Waterbury	3500	114	62
Total		2385	1310

* Source: Conn. Judicial Council, court year July 1, 1962–June 30, 1963.
† Assistant public defender's salary is $4500.

Connecticut adopted the public defender system in 1923 and presently has one public defender in each county and in the city of Waterbury. The three larger counties have assistant public defenders. (see Table 2 for case load). The public defenders and their assistants are appointed annually by the judges of the Superior Court. To qualify for appointment, a public defender must have been in practice for five years and an assistant, for three years (see statutes set forth in Appendix).

The circuit court judge may appoint a special public defender to represent the accused and generally selects a lawyer who is present in the courtroom. During the court year from July 1, 1962, to June 30, 1963, the circuit court made 880 such appointments for cases involving felonies and misdemeanors. The fees for these special public defenders totaled $48,662.69 (see Table 3). The court allows an average of $35 per day or major portion thereof. In most capital

TABLE 3
*Statewide Expenses of Defender Office**

	Public defender	State's attorney
Salaries	$ 53,230.82	$247,159.40
Clerical	682.80	1320.20
Professional services	1034.50	13,481.09
Transcripts	2377.60	13,877.85
Service of process	727.90	2719.50
Witness fees	218.60	34,823.70
Special public defenders	3993.88	
Special prosecutors		8162.50
Investigation	574.00	
Printing, travel, and telephone	1003.97	
Contract service, vehicles, transport of prisoners		47,461.68
Supplies	103.38	6481.84
Other		112.00
Total	$63,947.45	$375,599.76
Circuit court defense 880 special public defenders	48,662.69	
Circuit court prosecution costs		363,002.94
Grand Total	$112,610.14	$738,602.70

* Source: Conn. Judicial Department. Average cost of counsel per defendant, superior court, $43.72; circuit court, $55.30.

offenses the regular public defender of the Superior Court will represent an indigent defendant at his first appearance in circuit court. In New London County the regular public defender appears in circuit court on many serious felony cases, and the judge automatically appoints him a special public defender.

At the preliminary hearing, if the matter is within the jurisdiction of the circuit court for final disposition, the defendant is put to plea; but if counsel desires additional time, a continuance is granted. In matters for which the circuit court cannot make final disposition, the first appearance consists of a probable-cause hearing, in which the defendant or his attorney may examine both prosecution and defense witnesses. The defendant is permitted to take the stand to refute the charges of the state. In practice, most defendants waive their right to a hearing on probable cause, and are thereupon bound over to the next term of the Superior Court, which is the first Tuesday of the following month. If a binding over is ordered, the court fixes bond.

Determination of indigence in circuit court varies from judge to judge. A few examine the defendant under oath at the preliminary hearing and if indigence is shown, they appoint a special public defender. Other judges take an oral unsworn statement from the defendant.

In the Superior Court the state's attorney for the county where the alleged offense has occurred files an information on or before the first day of the next term. The defendant is put to plea on this information or on a substitute information that may be filed. If he pleads not guilty, he elects his type of trial and the matter is put down on the appropriate calendar. If he pleads guilty or is later found guilty, the court orders presentence investigation by the probation department and, upon receipt of this report, sentences him.

In all counties the regular public defender represents indigent defendants from the time of their first appearance in Superior Court. The public defender in Hartford County interviews all prisoners in the county jail between the time they have been bound over and the time of their appearance in Superior Court. Prisoners desiring his services receive them. If the defendant is able to post bond, however, the public defender does not represent him unless the court makes a determination of indigence and directs him to do so. In some instances, particularly in companion cases, the Superior Court will appoint a special public defender to represent each of the defendants. A reasonable sum, fixed by the judge, is paid to the special public defender (see Table 3).

C. THE PUBLIC DEFENDER'S OFFICE

The regular public defenders maintain austere offices in the several county courthouses. These offices are used primarily for interviewing defendants. All of the public defenders maintain private practice, including criminal practice, and therefore have their own offices where they prepare their cases. Office expenses are not reimbursable, but expenses of printing are paid along with some other expenses (see Table 3).

In all counties the public defender experiences good cooperation from the office of the state's attorney, although the degree of cooperation varies from county to county. In Hartford and New London Counties the state's attorneys' files are usually available to the public defender, including confessions, statements of witnesses, and other evidentiary matters. Usually this information is supplemented by his personal investigation. In New Haven and Fairfield Counties, however, the public defender has access to the state's attorneys' files only in rare instances when the state's attorney will show the defender a confession made by the defendant. In New Haven County part of the investigative load is carried by the Public Defender Association at Yale Law School. This is a student-operated project working directly under the public defender and in conjunction with a faculty adviser. No course credit is given, and students participating vary from year to year. In Fairfield County the public defender himself investigates most of the cases by means of weekend and evening interviews with witnesses. In some instances the public defender will apply to the court for permission to employ a professional investigator. Usually such motions are granted. The costs for special investigations during the recent court year were $574, as shown in Table 3.

Except for capital cases, the work of the public defender begins after the bind over from circuit court, although often he is called for advice concerning the bind over hearing by a special public defender appointed by the circuit court. No formal records are kept by the public defenders' offices other than the case files. The public defender is appointed by the Superior Court to represent every defendant who does not have private counsel. In the memory of all persons interviewed, not a single defendant has been unrepresented when appearing before the Superior Court. Even where defendants specifically waive counsel, the public defender is appointed. In these situations, he advises the defendant appearing pro se when to object to the introduction of evidence and testimony, when motions must be filed, etc. The defendant then chooses whether to follow the advice. In all cases, once appointed, the public defender carries the matter through to its conclusion unless replaced by private counsel. About half of all appeals from criminal convictions taken to the Supreme Court of Errors have been handled by the public defender. Several cases involving indigents have gone to the United States Supreme Court on appeals taken by the public defender, or, in one instance, by the state's attorney.

All persons interviewed expressed satisfaction with the present public defender system. All believed that the earliest point at which it is practical to supply a defender is at the first appearance before the circuit court. To delay appointment of counsel beyond that point, however, would be unfair to the defendant. Nevertheless, some said that if the defendant is properly advised of his rights by the circuit court, including his right to remain silent, it might be fair to the defendant not to have counsel until the time for plea. All agreed that an ideal system would provide the defendant with counsel from the time of his arrest. A form to be provided at the police station advising the accused of his rights to counsel and to remain silent is presently under consideration, but this procedure has not been initiated as yet.

D. OPINIONS OF THE JUDGES

Three judges were interviewed: two members of the Superior Court and the chief judge of the circuit court. All three agreed that under an ideal system counsel should first be provided at the time of first appearance before the committing magistrate, although one added that ideally, counsel should be provided at the time of the crime, but that administratively the first appearance is the earliest when counsel can be appointed. Only one of the three judges thought it unfair if counsel is not provided at this stage, however, the others saying "no" and "not necessarily," depending upon what occurs at first appearance, the type of crime, and the intelligence of the defendant. If he is advised of his right to remain silent at a first appearance, then he is adequately protected. All three judges thought the financing of such a system presented no problem.

All three judges agreed that under an ideal system counsel should be provided for sentencing of a defendant who pleaded guilty, or who was convicted by trial, and for misdemeanors. Only one would provide counsel, however, for habeas corpus or other postconviction remedy, or for a hearing on revocation of probation, and none of the judges thought counsel was necessary in civil commitment of a mentally ill person. Comments about unfairness if counsel were not provided generally followed the opinion about providing counsel. Only one judge gave an opinion about financing. He said, "The cost of our system is not prohibitive and goes beyond the point of the minimum 'fair trial' standards."

Two of the judges gave estimates of the proportion of felony defendants who are indigent. Each said it depended on the county. One estimated the range at 50% to 90%, while the other said 30% to 80%.

The judges were enthusiastic in their praise of the regular public defenders throughout the state. Stressed most often were the qualifications of the defenders, most of whom have served for many years. The phrase "experience and ability to evaluate cases" was used to characterize the public defender by the three persons interviewed. All felt that defendants represented by the public defenders were represented at least as well as defendants represented by private counsel. The judges stated that their own duties were made easier by the fact that all defendants are represented by qualified counsel, so that the court need not be cast in the dual role of defending and judging.

E. OPINIONS OF THE STATE'S ATTORNEYS

Three of the eight state's attorneys were interviewed in person, and a fourth responded to a mail questionnaire. All had considerable experience either in the state's attorney's office or in comparable practice, the youngest having been admitted to the bar in 1946. One of the four devoted full-time to the office, while the part-time men devoted from over 30 hours a week to 10 to 19 hours.

All four of the state's attorneys said they had adequate funds to operate their offices, which are staffed with investigators, county detectives, and permanent secretaries. Assistant state's attorneys are appointed in the larger offices.

Asked how they felt about the present system for determining eligibility for free counsel, three of the state's attorneys said it was about right, while one said it was too lenient.

The answers about the proportion of defendants who were indigent showed wide variation. At the extremes were estimates of 10% and 90%, while the other figures were 68%, based on an actual count in Hartford County, and 50%, based on an actual count in Litchfield County. All four state's attorneys agreed that none of those who are indigent waive appointment of counsel.

The state's attorneys were uniformly in favor of the public defender system. They cooperate with the defender neither more nor less than with private counsel. They respect the public defender for his ability and experience, and there is no question in their minds that trying a case when they are opposed by the public defender is as difficult as any. State's attorneys in all counties believe that the investigative facilities for the public defender are adequate.

Each state's attorney was asked the following question:

"Some lawyers say that the public defender cannot be completely independent and zealous in representing indigents because he is just another public official paid from the same source as the judge and yourself. What do you think about this?" All of the state's attorneys agreed that the proposition was false.

F. OPINIONS OF THE PUBLIC DEFENDERS

The four public defenders interviewed believe the public defender system provides the best possible defense for the accused. One felt that it should be expanded to include regularly appointed public defenders, on salary, in the circuit court system. All believed that their relations with the state's attorney were good, but the public defenders in New Haven and Fairfield Counties felt that they greatly needed investigative assistance. There was some feeling that the special public defender appointed in the circuit court should work more closely with the regular public defender in order to provide continuity of defense. The same case was cited by two persons interviewed, where the special defender appointed in the circuit court advised the defendant in a serious felony that the state would be unable to prove its case. The defendant was bound over. After a review of the facts the regular public defender was certain the accused could not possibly avoid conviction. The defendant refused to plead guilty to a lesser charge and insisted on a jury trial. He was found guilty of the original charge and received a heavy sentence.

All public defenders stressed the need to get to the accused as soon after the crime or as soon after the arrest as possible. To this end, they visit the jails often and make special efforts to see defendants in capital cases as soon as they read in the newspaper that an arrest has been made.

Each defender was asked the same question about independence as that asked the state's attorneys. In response, all said the statement was not true. One of them said: "The public defender is first a lawyer, dedicated to his client's causes. That he is paid by public funds is immaterial. There are no pressures, no fears of losing a job. Financially to lose such a job would be a favor. The whole system is as it should be—based upon the people who operate it and their personal dedication."

G. THE DOCKET STUDY

A study was made of representative cases from the court dockets in 1962 in New Haven and Hartford counties. Results are shown in Tables 4 to 9. According to Table 4, all defendants in the sample had counsel. In New Haven 56% of the defendants had the public defender or assigned counsel, while the comparable figure in Hartford was 44%. Similarly, as shown in Table 5, 55% of the defendants in New Haven and 43% of the defendants in Hartford were found indigent.

Table 6 shows that 48% of the defendants in New Haven and 39% of the defendants in Hartford were not released on bail, which is usually another indication of indigency. In each county a few persons who were able to make bail were nonetheless determined indigent so that they were eligible for free counsel.

Table 7 indicates a wide difference in the frequency of preliminary hearings between the two counties, with Hartford showing 65% frequency and New Haven only 17%. Waivers of the hearings in New Haven account for most of the difference.

There was little difference between the two counties in dispositions of cases, as shown in Table 8. Pleas of guilty, including pleas to lesser offenses, accounted for 80% of the defendants in New Haven and 74% in Hartford· Table 9 shows the sentences, if any, that were imposed. For the two counties together, 56% of the defendants were given sentences to prison, including county jails, 33% were placed on probation, and 3% drew suspended sentences without probation. Probation appears to have been much more common in Hartford County than in New Haven.

TABLE 4
Retained and Assigned Counsel in Felonies
Connecticut, 1962

County	Total sample	Did defendant have counsel? Yes No.	%	No No.	%	Retained No.	%	Public Defender No.	%	Assigned No.	%	Combination or type unknown No.	%	No data° No.	%
New Haven	50	48	100	0	0	21	44	26	54	1	2	0	0	2	4
Hartford	50	50	100	0	0	27	54	21	42	1	2	1	2	0	0
Weighted total percentages		100		0		49		48		1		2		2	

° % of no data refers to total sample; % in other columns refers to cases for which data were available.

TABLE 5
Was Felony Defendant Determined Indigent?
Connecticut, 1962

County	Total sample	Yes No.	%	No No.	%	No data° No.	%
New Haven	50	27	55	22	45	1	2
Hartford	50	21	43	28	57	1	2
Weighted total percentages		49		51		2	

° % of no data refers to total sample; % in other columns refers to the cases for which data were available.

TABLE 6
Frequency of Release on Bail of Felony Defendants
Connecticut, 1962

County	Total sample	Yes No.	%	No No.	%	No data° No.	%
New Haven	50	26	52	24	48	0	0
Hartford	50	28	61	18	39	4	8
Weighted total percentages		56		44		4	

° % of no data refers to total sample; % in other columns refers to cases for which data were available.

TABLE 7
Frequency of Preliminary Hearings in Felonies
Connecticut, 1962

County	Total sample	Yes No.	%	No, waiver No.	%	No, reason unknown No.	%	No data[*] No.	%
New Haven	50	7	17	25	60	10	24	8	16
Hartford	50	32	65	11	22	6	12	1	2
Weighted total percentages			43		40		18		9

[*] % of no data refers to total sample; % in other columns refers to cases for which data were available.

TABLE 8
Disposition in Felony Cases
Connecticut, 1962

County	Total sample	Plea guilty	Plea lesser offense	Dis-missed	Found guilty	Found guilty lesser degree	Ac-quitted	Mental commit-ment	Pend-ing
New Haven	50	32	8	3	6	0	1	0	0
Hartford	50	30	7	7	4	0	0	1	1
Weighted total percentages		62	15	10	10	0	1	1	1

H. CONCLUSIONS AND RECOMMENDATIONS

The major point of disagreement in the views of the judges, state's attorneys, and public defenders was the adequacy of investigative facilities available. The state's attorneys indicated it was not a problem and the judges were not dissatisfied, but the public defenders generally stated that more extensive facilities are needed. The problem is reduced where the state's attorneys open their files; elsewhere, investigation is sorely needed.

The majority of persons interviewed favor extending the regular public defender system to include the lower courts so as to provide better defense. The change could be made with no additional cost to the state and might result in a savings. This reporter, therefore, recommends extension of the public defender system to the circuit court.

Few persons interviewed considered the determination of indigence a problem. The prevailing view was that a person would hire private counsel if he could afford it. All stated that payment of a moderate fee, even if paid to the state, would be improper. It was suggested, however, that if fees of private counsel were reduced somewhat, there would be more defendants with private counsel. Since this flexible system seems to be working, there is no reason for a more formal investigation of finances.

TABLE 9

Sentencing in Felony Cases
Connecticut, 1962*

	Total sample	No sentence No.	%	Prison No.	%	Probation No.	%	Suspended sentence No.	%	Fine No.	%	Misc. No.	%	No data No.	%
New Haven	50	4	8	31	62	11	22	3	6	3	6	0	0	0	0
Hartford	50	9	18	25	50	22	44	0	0	4	8	2	4	0	0
Weighted total percentages			13		56		33		3		7		2		

* If a defendant had a combination sentence, such as fine and probation, he is counted under both columns. Hence the totals may be more than 100%.

118

In interviewing the various people and observing the defenders themselves, it was clear that the system is based upon the people who operate it, and depends upon their dedication. There was no question that each of the public defenders is dedicated to providing the best possible defense for every accused. The public defenders are among the most qualified criminal lawyers in the state. Their experience and ability to evaluate cases enables them to handle the tremendous workload of cases assigned to their offices. The existing system provides counsel at an early stage in the proceedings and continues until the final resolution and disposition of each case.

[Editor's note: since this report was written, the legislature has enacted a law providing for 22 regular public defenders for the circuit courts, the defenders to be appointed by the circuit court judges. The law also defines the relationship between circuit court defenders and Superior Court defenders.]

APPENDIX
Table of Statutes

Public Defender: present statute, mode of appointment, experience . . . . § 54-80 (Conn. Gen. Stat.)

The judges of the superior court shall, at each annual meeting in June, appoint an attorney at law, of at least five years' practice and residence, in each county in the state, except New Haven county, in which they shall appoint one such attorney for the New Haven district and one for the Waterbury district, to be public defenders thereof for the ensuing year and shall from time to time, make rules and regulations necessary for the conduct of such office. Each such public defender shall act as attorney in the defense of any person, charged with crime in either the superior court or the court of common pleas for the county for which he has been appointed, when such person is without funds sufficient to employ counsel for such defense. Each such public defender shall receive a salary which shall not be less than one-half the salary paid to the state's attorney in the same county. The public defender may, in accordance with the rules and regulations adopted by the judges of the superior court, act, within the county or district for which he has been appointed, as attorney for the defense of any such person upon any preliminary hearing before any court in the state or before any committing magistrate. Any vacancy in the office of public defender shall be filed by the chief justice until the next annual meeting of the judges of the superior court (Pub. Act 564, §1 [1961]).

Assistant in Hartford, New Haven and Fairfield counties . . . . §54-80a

The judges of the superior court shall, at each annual meeting in June, appoint an assistant public defender for each of the counties of Hartford, New Haven and Fairfield, who shall be an attorney at law of at least three years' active practice at the bar. The judges of the superior court shall provide the public defender with such office space, investigative and clerical assistance as may be necessary for the adequate discharge of his duties, and the reasonable expense therefor shall be allowed as court expense (Pub. Act 564, §2 [1961]).

Expenses. Appointment of Special Defender . . . . §54-81

At the close of each criminal term or session of the superior court or court of common pleas, the public defender shall file with the clerk an itemized statement of expenses necessarily incurred by him during such term and any such preliminary hearing as provided in section 54-80, and the court shall allow a reasonable sum for such expenses, which shall be taxed and paid as other expenses in criminal cases in either said superior court or court of common pleas. The judge presiding at any term or session of the superior court or court of common pleas, may upon his own motion or upon application of the public defender for such county, appoint an attorney other than the public defender to represent any person charged with crime in any criminal court in such county, if, in the opinion of such judge, such appointment should be made, and in such case the judge of the court in which such representation was made shall allow a reasonable sum for such services, with due regard for time spent in preparation for trial, in trying such case and in taking an appeal, and necessary disbursements in connection therewith, such amount to be paid as are other court expenses (Pub. Act 564, §3 [1961]).

Special public defender for circuit court ....§54-81a

In any criminal action in the circuit court, the judge before whom the matter is pending shall, if he determines that the interests of justice so require, appoint an attorney to act as special public defender and represent the defendant. The judge shall allow a reasonable sum for such services and necessary disbursements, and such amount shall be paid by the state in the same manner as other court expenses (Pub. Act 28, §13 [1959]).

Right to Counsel-confessions ....Pub. Act 126 (1963)

Section 1. When any person is arrested without a warrant or under a warrant, except under a warrant issued under section 2 of this act, section 54-163 of the general statutes or 54-169 of the 1961 supplement thereto, such person shall be presented before the circuit court session next held in the circuit where the offense is alleged to have been committed. Before any person so arrested is put to plea, he shall be advised that he has a right to retain counsel, that he has a right to refuse to make any statement and that any statement he makes may be introduced in evidence against him. Each such person shall be allowed a reasonable opportunity to consult counsel and shall be admitted to bail if the offense is bailable.

Sec. 2. Section 54-43 of the general statutes is repealed and the following is substituted in lieu thereof:

Upon the representation of any state's attorney that he has reasonable ground to believe that a crime has been committed within his jurisdiction, the superior court or, when said court is not in session, any judge thereof, may issue a bench warrant for the arrest of the person or persons complained against, and in such case shall, except in cases punishable by death or life imprisonment, fix a bond for the appearance of such person or persons in such amount as to said court or to such judge appears reasonable. When any person is arrested on a bench warrant issued by order of the superior court or, when said court is not in session, by a judge thereof, the officer or indifferent person making such arrest shall forthwith bring such person before the clerk or assistant clerk of the superior court for the county where such warrant was issued, which clerk or assistant clerk shall thereupon advise such person that he has a right to retain counsel, that he has a right to refuse to make any statement, and that any statement he makes may be introduced in evidence against him, and shall order such person to enter into a recognizance with surety to the state in such sum as said court or such judge has fixed conditioned that such accused person shall appear before the superior court having criminal jurisdiction then in session or next to be held in and for the county where such bond is required, to answer to the bench warrant and information filed in such case; and on his failure to enter into such recognizance or if the offense charged in such bench warrant and information is not bailable, such clerk or assistant clerk shall issue a mittimus committing such person to jail until he is discharged by due course of law.

Sec. 3. Any admission, confession or statement, written or oral, obtained from an accused person who has not been so presented to the first session of the court, or who has not been informed of his rights as provided by this act, shall be inadmissible.

DELAWARE

Richard Allen Paul, Wilmington

Members of the Delaware A.B.A. Associate State Committee were Warren B. Burt, Wilmington, chairman; James A. Walsh, Wilmington; and Nicholas H. Rodriguez, Dover.

A. INTRODUCTION

Delaware had a population of 446,292 according to the 1960 census. Of this number 307,446 were concentrated in New Castle County, the largest of the three counties which compose this state.

New Castle County is largely urban (86.6%) and affluent (average family income is $6800); the population is young (median age 29.5 years) and growing (40.5% increase in population between 1950 and 1960). The principal industries are manufacturing, chemicals, and research.

The county had 492 felony defendants in 1962. (This does not include felony charges where the grand jury did not return a true bill nor charges where at the preliminary hearing the magistrates did not bind the defendant over. In the case of multiple offenses the defendant was counted once.) There were 271 lawyers in private practice, of whom 99 were on the list for appointment of counsel to represent indigents. According to the docket study, as explained in Section H below, 45% of the felony defendants were indigent. None of this group waived appointment of counsel.

B. CRIMINAL PROCEDURE AS IT AFFECTS INDIGENT PERSONS

Jurisdiction to try criminal felonies is vested in the superior court. It is a state-wide court of civil and criminal jurisdiction and is composed of one president judge and six associate judges.

The attorney general in Delaware is an elected official holding office for four years. He appoints a chief deputy and other assistants. The office prosecutes criminal cases in the superior court in all three counties. There is no county prosecuting attorney. The chief deputy noted that he devoted over thirty hours weekly to his duties and that these duties include some civil representation for the state. His staff, state-wide, consists of 12 attorneys, 10 secretaries, and 3 investigators.

The great majority of felony cases begin with the arrest of the suspect. An arrested person is required to be brought before a committing magistrate "without unreasonable delay." The magistrates are justices of the peace who are not required to be lawyers except that in the municipal court of Wilmington the judges are lawyers. The superior court criminal rules, which are based for the most part on the Federal Rules of Criminal Procedure, require that the arrested person, upon being brought before the committing magistrate, be informed of the complaint against him, of his right to retain counsel, and of his right to a preliminary hearing. The defendant is admitted to bail at this

121

time. The amount of bail is within the discretion of the committing magistrate. Experience indicates that the superior court is liberal in reducing bail upon counsel's application when the committing magistrate has set it, as is sometimes the case, at an arbitrarily high figure.

Throughout Delaware the formal charge against the defendant in felony cases is made by a grand jury indictment. Under the rules, however, the defendant may in open court waive his right to an indictment, thereby allowing the state to proceed by information. An arrested person is usually arraigned on the indictment or information in the next term of court following his arrest. Since there are four terms of court per year, the minimum delay between arrest and trial is three months unless counsel raises preliminary legal questions that must be disposed of by briefing and argument. If that happens the delay can be considerably longer.

Upon a determination of indigency, counsel is appointed in any case where the individual is charged with a felony. Furthermore, counsel is appointed when the individual is charged with a serious misdemeanor in the superior court. Whether an individual receives counsel when charged with a misdemeanor is within the sole discretion of the court. However, in every case where the individual is charged with a violation of the narcotics laws, assault and battery, or any other crime that may result in imprisonment for more than three months, it is generally the practice to appoint counsel.

When a person is incarcerated pending trial because he cannot obtain bond, the presumption arises that he is unable to obtain counsel. A person is contacted almost immediately upon his admission to prison and is asked to fill out a form which contains a request for counsel. In the form he sets forth his assets and signs an affidavit stating that the facts supplied are true and correct. These forms are immediately sent to superior court where counsel is appointed.

Counsel for indigents are appointed from two lists. The first is the murder and rape list. When an individual is charged with these crimes two counsel are normally selected to represent him. One of them has substantial trial experience, while the other has special qualifications in research. The other list of lawyers is for other crimes. The survey indicates that over one-third of the lawyers admitted to practice are on this list. It also includes a substantial number of attorneys not in active practice but who are employed by local business firms.

When a case is tried in the superior court, the trial judge sets the fee for counsel, which is paid by the county governing body, the Levy Court of New Castle County. If the individual pleads guilty in the superior court, the sentencing judge sets the fee. When a case is nolle prossed after appointment of counsel, or when a case is dismissed by the court before trial, any judge is authorized to set the fee.

In each case, the fee is set by the court on a letter application from the attorney, who sets forth the time spent on the case and the work that has been done. Counsel further states that he has received no other compensation. The minimum fee is $35, but the average is higher. When the attorney is engaged in trial, he normally receives no less than $100.

Waiver of counsel is in open court. At arraignment a defendant who does not then have an attorney is advised of his right to employ one and is questioned as to whether he can afford it. If he declines to hire counsel or does not want one appointed, he is informed by the court of the nature of the charge against him. If he still wishes to waive counsel, this is noted by the clerk and taken down stenographically.

With respect to appeals, counsel is appointed by the trial court in most cases. The usual practice is to have the trial attorney continue. Counsel is compensated and a full transcript and record are provided at public expense.

Counsel is appointed for writs of habeas corpus. The rate of compensation is similar to that employed for the trial attorney.

Counsel is rarely appointed in magistrates' courts.

C. OPINIONS OF THE JUDGES

Two judges of the superior court were interviewed, the president judge and the judge who, to a large extent, administered the appointment system for a number of years. The questions asked of the judges were directed toward New Castle County since this was the only county directly surveyed, but the answers will reflect state-wide experience since all judges, with the exception of the president judge, sit in all three counties at one time or another.

On question 7 of the interview both judges expressed the view that the appointment of counsel should be at least as early as the time of the first appearance before the committing magistrate. One of the judges felt that it should be before the first appearance, while the other felt that at this point it was a police matter and would remain so until the first appearance.

Both judges confirmed that attorneys are provided at the sentencing of persons who plead guilty and also at the sentencing of persons found guilty after a formal trial. Both noted that attorneys are provided at habeas corpus hearings and other post-conviction remedies. The president judge indicated that an attorney need not be provided for a hearing on revocation of probation, and his colleague agreed with him. The judges diverged on the question of providing counsel for misdemeanors: one judge felt that the appointment should only be for serious misdemeanors, while the other felt that all misdemeanors should be included. One judge noted that the mentally ill and alcoholics were not committed by the superior court, but that narcotic addicts were and were given counsel upon request. The other judge felt that counsel should be provided in all such cases.

Both judges were of the opinion that court-appointed counsel were at least equal in ability to those retained by non-indigent defendants. Both stated that they had no difficulty in getting attorneys to serve as court-appointed counsel and noted that such counsel rarely if ever sought to be excused.

Both judges indicated that a person who can pay a moderate fee should be allotted court-appointed counsel, and the county should provide the balance. They said that this problem has rarely arisen.

Both felt that the lower courts should be covered by court-appointed counsel at least at preliminary hearings. One, however, noted the practical difficulty of having lawyers attend such hearings in magisterial courts which are spread the length and breadth of the county.

Although both judges felt in general that the system worked well, they did see a need to increase compensation for attorneys and 'to appoint counsel in misdemeanor cases.

D. OPINIONS OF DEPUTY ATTORNEYS GENERAL

Mail questionnaires were directed to the two deputy attorneys general in Sussex County, the entire staff in that largely rural county. In addition, the chief deputy attorney general, who is in charge of the New Castle office, was interviewed.

It should be noted that the prosecuting attorney does not always know whether, in a particular case, the attorney opposing him is appointed or retained. While all deputies are part-time, all of them devote at least half of their working hours to their office. It is not unusual to find the deputies spending between 20 and 30 hours weekly in the attorney general's office.

The previous experience of the deputies in Sussex County was varied. One deputy had had one year's prior criminal experience, while the other had been a member of the bar since 1944. Both had been deputies for less than one year at the time of the survey. The chief deputy had had four years' prior criminal experience and had been chief deputy for less than one year.

In Sussex County, one deputy felt that an attorney should be appointed between arrest and first appearance before a magistrate, while the other felt that appointment after the preliminary hearing, but before arraignment was satisfactory.

In answering questions relating to whether under an ideal system an attorney should be appointed at sentencing to represent a defendant who had pleaded guilty, both felt that an attorney should be present. However, only one believed that it would be unfair if one were not appointed. So too, while both believed that, under an ideal system, a defendant who had been found guilty after a trial should be represented at sentencing, only one believed that the absence of counsel would be basically unfair. The same split of opinion existed with respect to representation for misdemeanors, i.e., both believed it should be provided under an ideal system, but only one thought the lack of it basically unfair.

All the attorneys general interviewed felt that they had no advantage over defense counsel with respect to experience and ability; and their opinion confirms what the judges and defense counsel reported.

One of the Sussex County attorneys general estimated the percentage of indigent defendants to be 33-1/3%, and the other estimated 90%. They all agreed that the percentage of indigents who waive counsel is nil.

They all noted that the confessions and other statements of defendants and co-defendants are regularly made available to defense counsel.

The chief defender recommended the adoption of a public defender system to replace either totally, or in part, the present system of court-appointed counsel, although he expressed the opinion that the present system, with some reforms, was at least workable. His suggested reforms were better compensation for time spent and allowances for investigation. In assessing their own function, the deputies felt that they could use help in investigations. Judging from the number of investigators attached to the attorney general's office, this stands as something of an understatement.

E. OPINIONS OF DEFENSE ATTORNEYS

Mail questionnaires were dispatched to 94 of the 99 attorneys in New Castle County whose names appeared on the superior court list of appointed counsel. Responses were received from 40%.

The range of experience of appointed counsel was great, from 1 year's experience (8%) to 15 to 29 years' experience (13%). The median falls within the 6 to 9 years' category (38%). Eighty-four percent of those on the list had served as counsel in one or more cases in 1962, the statistical year. The average case load was six cases per person.

The survey indicates that prior experience was fairly high. No attorney reported that his first criminal case was as court appointed counsel. Twenty-six percent of those responding reported that they had had at least 10 to 19 criminal cases before being appointed in 1962. Only 11% indicated that they had had as few as 1 prior case, and 16% indicated at least 50 prior cases. These figures seem to indicate a fairly high level of experience in the representation of indigents.

Although the response reported appointments at almost every conceivable stage of a criminal proceeding, the greatest percentage (47%) were appointed after the filing of the indictment or information, but before arraignment. This statistic is consistent with the information received in the judge interviews. Even more significant is the fact that 84% were appointed no later than prior to arraignment. Most of the balance of 16% represented attorneys appointed for sentencing purposes only.

The attorneys seemed satisfied with the stage of the proceeding at which they were appointed. A majority, 81%, felt that they had been appointed early enough in the proceeding to represent the accused person adequately. The "No" answers seemed to reflect a desire, in serious felony cases, to use the preliminary hearing as a method of pre-trial discovery.

Of the lawyers surveyed, 91% reported that they had received compensation for their services rendered to indigents. A few of those reporting no compensation explained that it was the policy of their office not to bill the county for such representation.

Over 75% of the lawyers believed that the system was fair to the indigents. However, with respect to fairness to lawyers, the answers were nearly evenly split: 48% thought the system unfair to the attorneys. The chief complaints were the low rate of compensation, the rather heavy case load, and the failure to appoint at an early stage of the proceeding. Almost all lawyers contacted suggested remedies within the present system such as an improved rate of pay, appointment as soon as possible after arrest, and a better distribution of the case load. Only 18% of those responding suggested that the present system be scrapped in favor of a public defender system, in spite of the fact that a defender bill was before the Delaware General Assembly at the time of this survey.

In conclusion, it seems that the lawyers who work in the system of court-appointed counsel regard it as doing an adequate job for indigents. It would, of course, have been remarkable if they had expressed any other opinion, since they were to a certain extent commenting on their own work. While many felt that it was unfair to attorneys, most suggested reforms within the framework of the present system.

F. THE PUBLIC DEFENDER

[Editor's note: the following description of the defender office supplements the outline provided in the defender statute appended to the Delaware report. This description is based on a questionnaire submitted to the National Legal Aid and Defender Association in May, 1965.

The Delaware public defender office, located in Wilmington, is staffed by four part-time attorneys, one full-time investigator, and two full-time secretaries. They are assisted by three law students who do legal research and investigation and conduct interviews. Each student works about 30 hours a week. The attorneys are permitted to have private civil practice at their own offices. For the 1964-1965 fiscal year the budget is $73,000.

According to the report, the territorial jurisdiction of the office is limited to New Castle County. Within that county the defenders represent indigent persons in magistrates' courts, the Wilmington municipal court, the family court, and the superior court. Cases are also taken to the Supreme Court of Delaware. Virtually all kinds of criminal matters are handled, including habeas corpus, probation violations, and sexual psychopath hearings. The defenders also appear in juvenile delinquency and neglect cases. (See *State v. Naylor*, 207 A.2d 1 [Del. 1965].) In felonies they are usually appointed after the first appearance before a magistrate but before the preliminary hearing. Occasionally they are appointed at the first appearance, and, on rare occasions, immediately after arrest.]

G. COMPARISONS AMONG JUDGES, ATTORNEYS, AND PROSECUTORS

For the purpose of placing some of the statistical information in proper juxtaposition, the table below, which compares the attitudes of judges, prosecutors and defense attorneys, has been arranged.

There seems to be a fairly consistent opinion among judges, prosecutors, and defense counsel that attorneys should be appointed prior to arraignment. In actual practice most attorneys representing indigents are appointed at this stage of the proceeding. However, a significant minority of defense counsel, both judges, and one of the prosecutors, under an ideal system, would favor a much earlier appointment. A good percentage, including both judges, would like to see the appointment at least as early as the preliminary hearing. It is, therefore, not very surprising that the present trend is toward much earlier

	Judges	Prosecutors	Defense counsel	Total
Total responding	2	3	38	43
Ideal stage for appointment of counsel				
Between arrest and first appearance	2	1	3	6
At preliminary hearing	0	0	5	5
After preliminary hearing but before indictment	0	1	4	5
After indictment but before arraignment	0	0	15	15
No answer	0	1	7	8
Is present compensation adequate?				
Yes	0	0	18	18
No	2	2	19	23
No answer	0	1	1	2

appointments, and, since both judges holding this view are exceptionally well placed to implement their opinions, the present trend should continue at least until the public defender system is completely operational.

H. THE DOCKET STUDY

A study was made of 50 representative cases from the superior court docket in 1962. (For method of study see vol. 1, pp. 178-179.) The study showed that of 48 defendants for whom information was available, 26 had retained counsel (54%), 21 had assigned counsel (44%), and 1 had no counsel. Of 49 defendants for whom data were available, 22 were found to be indigent (45%). Information about preliminary hearings, available for only 31 cases, showed that hearings were held in 30 of the cases and that the other one was a kind of case in which hearings were not usually held.

Of the 50 cases, 18 resulted in guilty pleas including 1 plea to a lesser offense, 14 were dismissed, and 14 went to trial. The trials ended in nine convictions including one conviction of a lesser offense, and five acquittals. There were two miscellaneous dispositions and two cases still pending.

Information about sentencing was available for 47 defendants. Of these, 23 were not sentenced. Nine of the remainder were sentenced to prison, 10 were placed on probation, 4 were fined, and 1 was given a sentence of fine or imprisonment. (Imprisonment includes state prison or county jail.)

I. CONCLUSIONS AND RECOMMENDATIONS

In general the survey indicated a system of court-appointed counsel which, in the opinion of many observers, was doing an adequate job in the representation of criminal indigents. The most severe critics of the system were the defense counsel themselves, but their criticisms were not, in all cases, directed to the system itself, but towards the administration of it. Most of the suggested changes could be made within the existing framework. The over-all impression, then, is a system in need of reforms, but a system which, if reforms were made, would be viable.

This reporter can suggest no specific recommendations. The legislature has already enacted a public defender law, which, when implemented, presumably will replace that which was the subject of this survey.

However, until the defender bill is implemented or if the public defender bill will require supplemental assistance from court-appointed counsel, this survey does indicate that such counsel should be aided by an improved rate of compensation, additional allowance for investigation, and continuation of the present trend toward early appointment of attorneys.

APPENDIX

An Act to Create a Public Defender and Making a Supplemental Appropriation Therefor.
Be it enacted by the general assembly of the State of Delaware:
Section 1. Title 29, Delaware Code, is amended by adding thereto a new Chapter to read:
Chapter 26. Public Defender
§2601. Office of Public Defender
There is created the office of public defender.
§2602. Appointment; representation of defendants
(a) The public defender shall be a qualified attorney licensed to practice in this state selected by the Governor. He shall represent, without charge, each indigent person who is under arrest or charged with a crime, if:
(1) The defendant requests it; or
(2) The court, on its own motion or otherwise, so orders and the defendant does not affirmatively reject or record the opportunity to be so represented.
(b) Before arraignment the determination of indigency may be made by the public defender. At or after arraignment the determination shall be made by the court.
§2603. Term of office; compensation; assistants
(a) The public defender shall serve for a term of six years from the date of appointment. He shall receive $10,000 per year as compensation.
(b) The public defender may appoint as many assistant attorneys, clerks, investigators, stenographers, and other employees as he considers necessary to enable him to carry out his responsibilities. An assistant attorney must be a qualified attorney licensed to practice in this State.
(c) The compensation of persons appointed under subsection (b) shall be fixed by the public defender.
§2604. Representation of indigent persons
When representing an indigent person, the public defender shall (1) counsel and defend him, whether he is held in custody without commitment or charged with a criminal offense, at every stage of the proceedings following arrest; and (2) prosecute any appeals or other remedies before or after conviction that he considers to be in the interest of justice.
§2605. Appointment of additional counsel
For cause, the court may, on its own motion or upon the application of the public defender or the indigent person, appoint an attorney other than the public defender to represent him at any stage of the proceedings or on appeal. The attorney shall be awarded reasonable compensation and reimbursement for expenses necessarily incurred, to be fixed by the court and paid by the county.
§2606. Annual reports

The public defender shall make an annual report to the Governor and the General Assembly covering all cases handled by his office during the preceding year.

§2607. Short Title

This act may be cited as the Model Defender Act.

Section 2. The provisions of this Act shall not become effective until July 1, 1964.

Section 3. The budget report, as prepared by the Governor, for the fiscal year next after this act becomes law, shall contain a recommended appropriation to defray the costs of administering this act.

DISTRICT OF COLUMBIA

Henry J. Price*

The members of the A.B.A. Associate State Committee for the District of Columbia were of great assistance in gathering data for this report. The committee consisted of S. White Rhyne, Jr., chairman, John Bodner, Jr., Peter R. Cella, Jr., George W. Shadoan, and Darryl L. Wyland. The assistance and counsel of Gary Bellow, a staff attorney of the Legal Aid Agency for the District of Columbia, is also greatly appreciated.

A. INTRODUCTION

The District of Columbia had a population of 763,956 in 1960. The most recent estimate by the Department of Public Health of the District indicates that the population in 1962 was 791,900. The court of general criminal jurisdiction is the United States District Court for the District of Columbia. This court has 15 judges, 4 or 5 of whom are normally assigned to handle criminal matters during each term of court, a period of three months. However, during the summer recess this number is substantially reduced. There is one vacancy on the bench, but two or more retired judges sit part time, usually handling criminal matters.

The District of Columbia Court of General Sessions has criminal jurisdiction limited to misdemeanors, which are crimes punishable by fine or imprisonment for one year or less. This court has 16 judges of whom 4 are assigned to criminal matters at any one time: one in traffic court, one in drunk and disorderly court, one in jury court, and one "United States Branch," handling court trials, initial misdemeanors and felony appearances, and preliminary hearings.

The United States Attorney for the District of Columbia has 51 full-time lawyers on his staff. This office handles matters in the Court of General Sessions as well as in the district court. Investigative services are performed by federal law enforcement agencies or by the Metropolitan Police Department. The department has an authorized force of 2900 men and is currently operating at virtually full strength.

B. CRIMINAL PROCEDURE AS IT AFFECTS INDIGENT PERSONS

The District of Columbia utilizes three methods for providing representation for indigent defendants: a "public" defender, a private defender, and assigned counsel. The public defender is the Legal Aid Agency for the District of Columbia, which was created in 1960 by an act of Congress.[1] Its operating funds come from the federal government, although it is directly controlled by and responsible to a private board of trustees, which is chosen by a panel of five judges and the president of the Board of Commissioners of the District. It consists of a director, six full-time attorneys, four investigators, and clerical help. [As of March, 1965, the legal staff has grown from 7 to 13 attorneys.] The primary function of the agency is to provide representation for felony defend-

* Prettyman Fellow, Georgetown University, 1962-1963, now in Indianapolis.

ants in the district court at the trial level, at the initial arraignment before the United States Commissioner, and at the coroner's inquest in death cases. It may also handle proceedings before the juvenile court and the Commission on Mental Health.

The private defender is the Georgetown University. Prettyman Fellowship Program or Legal Internship Program, which operates with funds from a private grant. This program combines representation of indigent defendants with academic work for an LL.M. degree. The staff consists of one full-time director, who also teaches at the Georgetown Law Center, and six full-time attorneys, who are recent law school graduates selected on a competitive basis from throughout the country. They begin with an intensive orientation in criminal law, criminal procedure, trial tactics and strategy, ethics, and evidence. Upon notification of passing the District of Columbia bar examination, they begin representing indigents accused of misdemeanors in the Court of General Sessions. After about two months, they begin representing felony defendants in the district court.[2]

In felony cases in district court three kinds of counsel are appointed: staff attorneys from the Legal Aid Agency, Georgetown Fellows, and individual practitioners. The last named are drawn from a list of volunteer attorneys compiled by the Legal Aid Agency. For the year ending May 31, 1963, assignment of counsel was made in 695 cases of 1060 that were docketed; the Legal Aid Agency had 241 cases, the Georgetown Fellows had about 80, and individual lawyers had the rest. A court rule forbids a defendant or his family from making any payment to his assigned counsel, although the Legal Aid Agency will reimburse the attorney for minor investigation expenses such as taxi fare, mileage for use of his car, and phone calls. The staff of investigators of the agency is available to assigned counsel, but, because of the volume of cases, this staff is insufficient to handle all the investigations required.

The Court of General Sessions assigns counsel to indigents at their initial appearance in felonies or in misdemeanor cases. Such assignments are made from a group of attorneys who regularly sit in the courtroom awaiting appointment. The attorney receives whatever fee he can secure from the defendant, but if the defendant is indigent he handles the case on a volunteer, unpaid basis. The District provides no funds for payment of assigned counsel.

There are three stages at which indigent defendants accused of felonies may receive appointment of counsel. The procedure varies for each of these stages. The first stage is the initial appearance before a magistrate for arraignment on the warrant; the second is between filing of the indictment and arraignment thereon; and the third is appeal. These will now be examined in detail.

Since the District of Columbia is a federal jurisdiction, all criminal proceedings are governed by the Federal Rules of Criminal Procedure or by the virtually identical rules of the Court of General Sessions. Jurisdiction to try felonies is vested exclusively in the district court. The great majority of these cases begin with arrest of the suspect, which occurs prior to indictment. The arrested individual is required by Federal Rule 5(a) to be taken "without unnecessary delay" before a committing magistrate. In the District such a magistrate may be either a United States Commissioner, who need not be a lawyer but usually is, or a judge of the Court of General Sessions, who must be a lawyer. At the first appearance before the magistrate, Rule 5(b) requires the magistrate to inform the arrestee of the crime with which he is charged, of his right to remain silent, of the fact that anything he says may be used against him, of his right to a preliminary hearing, and of his right to retain counsel. The magistrates normally give the required information, but they vary significantly in the precision and clarity with which they give it and in their degree of concern that the defendant understands it.

Bail is also normally set at this initial appearance. The most important factor in determining the amount of bail is the recommendation of the assistant United States attorney, which usually follows an approved schedule of bail for various offenses. The nature of the crime charged is more important than the factual and family situation of the individual defendant. Recently a Junior Bar committee made a comprehensive study of the bail system in the District.[3] The committee recommended that selected defendants be released on their personal recognizance, as under the Manhattan Bail Project.[4] [Such a plan was put into effect in 1964.]

Because of the pressure of the "Mallory Rule,"[5] the first appearance before a magistrate usually occurs within several hours after arrest. A committing magistrate is available 24 hours a day, 7 days a week. Instances of unnecessary delay do occur with some regularity, however, and these result in rendering inadmissible any statements made by or information obtained from the defendant during the period of unnecessary delay. If the defendant can make bond and has not yet secured an attorney, usually he will request a continuance of the preliminary hearing so that he may obtain counsel. This continuance must be granted. Retained counsel will normally demand that a preliminary hearing be held. If the arrestee is indigent and cannot afford bond or counsel and is appearing before the United States commissioner, he will be represented by a staff attorney of the Legal Aid Agency. (Indigency is determined by use of a questionnaire and an affidavit.) Such attorneys, with few exceptions, demand that a preliminary hearing be held. If the indigent defendant is appearing before a judge of the Court of General Sessions, he will be appointed counsel as described above. If the arrestee has any funds on his person or can secure any within a short period, he will pay the appointed attorney. In such case, a hearing will probably be demanded. If the arrestee has no funds, the appointed attorney will not usually demand a hearing unless the arrestee is aware of his rights and insists that one be demanded. If the counsel appointed is one of the Georgetown Fellows, he will, with few exceptions, demand a hearing. The court asks no questions to determine indigency. Rather, this is determined by individually assigned counsel. The Georgetown Fellows use the rough standard of ability to make bond as the determining factor.

If the committing magistrate finds probable cause to believe that the arrestee committed the offense charged, he is held for the action of the grand jury. The vast majority of formal charges are made by indictment. This may, however, be waived in writing by the defendant, in which event he will be charged by information. This is normally done only if the defendant desires to plead guilty to the information.

If indictments are filed against persons in jail, a staff investigator for the Legal Aid Agency is notified, and he interviews them there. He determines their eligibility for appointment of counsel by use of a questionnaire which they must complete and swear to. After this determination of indigency has been made, three names of counsel are submitted to the assignment judge in district court, who appoints one of them. If the defendant has been represented at the preliminary hearing by an attorney from the Legal Aid Agency or the Prettyman Fellowship Program, this attorney's name is one of those submitted, and he is usually the one appointed.

If a bonded defendant appears for arraignment on the indictment without counsel and indicates that he had no funds with which to retain counsel, a plea of not guilty will be entered and he will be interviewed by an investigator for the Legal Aid Agency and required to complete and swear to a more detailed application form. If the investigator determines that he qualifies as an indigent, he will receive appointment of counsel. However, a substantial number of such defendants still manage to retain counsel after this interview.

The third stage at which indigent felony defendants receive appointment of counsel is upon appeal where the trial counsel does not wish to continue with the case. Although the Legal Aid Agency does not handle cases on appeal, the Prettyman Fellows frequently do so for defendants whom they represented at the trial level. Assignment of counsel is made by the Court of Appeals for the District of Columbia Circuit from a list of private attorneys who have previously appeared as counsel before that court.

Indigents also receive appointment of counsel in the following cases: habeas corpus, revocation of parole hearings, sexual psychopath hearings, and civil commitment of the mentally ill, including alcoholics and narcotics addicts. Counsel is required at the imposition of sentence in all cases, whether the defendant has pleaded guilty or has been found guilty by the court or jury. The burden upon assigned counsel (except for the relatively few cases handled by the Prettyman Fellows) in habeas corpus cases is rather heavy, as over 500 petitions are filed per year. Most of these petitions come from patients at St. Elizabeths Hospital, the local federal mental institution, with over 8000 patients. Counsel appointed in all of these types of cases are also uncompensated.

C. OPINIONS OF THE JUDGES

The chief judge of the Court of General Sessions and three judges who regularly sit on the criminal trial bench of the district court were interviewed. On question 7 of the judge interview, "Under an ideal system, at what stage in a criminal case do you think the indigent person should first be provided with a lawyer if he wants one?", all four judges indicated that the lawyer should be provided at the preliminary hearing or before. This is not a surprising result, since the indigent is currently provided with a lawyer at his first appearance before a magistrate. One judge did indicate, however, that he felt the ideal system would provide a lawyer between arrest and the first appearance before a magistrate and that it was unfair to the indigent person if he did not get a lawyer at this stage. Two judges had no comment on the problem of financing such representation, and two thought that it should be financed by the government.

A count made by the Legal Aid Agency indicated that 65% of the defendants appearing in district court are indigent. According to the docket study made in district court for this report, 63% of the felony defendants in 1962 were found to be indigent, a figure that corresponds closely to the Legal Aid Agency count. (The judges estimated a higher percentage.) Also the proportion of felony defendants not released on bail was 63%. The judges unanimously indicated that virtually none of these indigents waived appointment of counsel and that such waiver should be discouraged even to the extent of appointing counsel to sit at counsel table and be available to assist the defendant even when he wishes to defend himself.

There was also a unanimous feeling that appointed counsel should be compensated by a reasonable fee based upon the time required and the difficulty of the case. One judge elaborated that this fee could be based upon a rate of $10 an hour, with a maximum of $250 in a capital case and $100 in a noncapital case. He felt that this was a realistic upper limit to present when requesting a legislature to allocate such funds, although the ideal upper limit would be two or three times this figure. The four judges also agreed that counsel should be reimbursed for his out-of-pocket expenses for investigation and preparation.

In response to question 11, all of the judges indicated that appointed counsel gave at least as good a defense as retained counsel, with two judges indicating that the quality of representation was possibly superior in many cases. The four judges likewise noted an equality in ability between appointed lawyers and the assistant United States attorney. However, one noted a distinct advantage to the government because of certain assistant United States attorneys' long experience, and another noted an advantage because of better investigative facilities and the availability of funds for expert witnesses. All the judges agreed that they had no problem in securing lawyers to serve as appointed counsel. Of the two judges who made an estimate of the number of assigned counsel who asked to withdraw, one said this figure is less than 1%, and the other said from 1% to 9%. These estimates, however, do not take into account the lawyers who decline to put their names on the appointment list maintained by the Legal Aid Agency.

The four judges varied in their reaction to the Legal Aid Agency for the District of Columbia. Two judges were enthusiastic about the agency, indicating that the quality of representation by this office was extremely high and that sometimes it was more vigorous and expert than that rendered by private, retained counsel because of the specialization and greater experience of the staff attorneys. The third judge indicated that the quality of representation varied widely due to differences in ability, experience, and trial tactics. The fourth judge thought the Legal Aid Agency should be strictly administrative in nature and stated that he favored the use of private, compensated counsel in all cases. In comparing the representation provided by the Legal Aid Agency with retained lawyers, three of the judges said that it was as good and one said it was usually as good. The same result was reached when they compared the Legal Aid Agency with the United States attorney's office, even though, as three judges noted, the agency did not have adequate financial support. One indicated that the support was probably adequate but that it could use more funds to good advantage.

The judges agreed unanimously as to the invalidity of the objection noted in question 13 of the judge's interview: "Some lawyers say that the public defender cannot be completely independent and zealous in representing indigents because he is just another public official paid from the same sources as the district attorney and the judges." One judge added that the defense is likely to be even more vigorous and expert because of the extensive experience of the staff attorneys and the spirit of competition that has developed between them and the prosecutor's office. Another commented that the representation is never underzealous and in his opinion it is sometimes overzealous to the extent that staff attorneys press meritless technical legal points.

Finally, there was unanimity among the three judges who responded to question 14 on the problem of providing a lawyer for the person who can pay a moderate fee. The judges favored a change in the local court rule that prohibits assigned counsel from accepting a moderate fee from a defendant or his family. One elaborated that such fee arrangements should be made through the court to prevent any possibility of undue pressure being placed upon the defendant or his family.

For comparison of responses of judges with those of others, see Table 1, infra.

[Editor's note: since this report was written Congress adopted the Criminal Justice Act of 1964.[6] This act provides, among other things, for compensation of assigned counsel or payment to the Legal Aid Agency for providing counsel. Funds are also authorized for investigative services and expert witnesses.[7] According to the act, it is to take effect in August, 1965, one year after passage.]

D. OPINIONS OF THE UNITED STATES ATTORNEY

In comparing assigned counsel with retained counsel, the United States attorney indicated that in the district court, they are of approximately equal quality, but on appeal assigned counsel are usually better. In evaluating attorneys for the Legal Aid Agency, he indicated that they are less experienced but likely to fight harder than either retained counsel or assigned counsel.

On the question of standards of indigency, the United States attorney indicated that the standards in the district were very loose and that no meaningful inquiry or examination as to indigency was being made. He estimated that 60% of felony defendants are indigent. On the problem of appointing counsel for the defendant who can pay a moderate fee, he indicated that he would not oppose court appointment in such a case, but that the government should be required to pay only the difference between what the defendant or his family can pay and the standard rate of compensation for court-appointed counsel. The attorney thought that assigned counsel should be compensated for their services at a maximum of $15 per hour and that their expenses should also be paid, subject to court control.

In indicating the office policy on disclosure to defense counsel, the attorney said, "Confessions, yes; statements of witnesses, sometimes; reports of experts, sometimes; exhibits, usually." He indicated that his office cooperated equally with the Legal Aid Agency, retained counsel, and assigned counsel.

On the question of independence of the public defender, the attorney agreed with the judges that the assertion of lack of independence is completely without foundation. He remarked that this certainly has not been true of the Legal Aid Agency. Indeed, he recommended that the agency be enlarged.

For comparison with responses of judges and defense attorneys see Table 1, infra.

E. OPINIONS OF DEFENSE ATTORNEYS

The information contained in this section was compiled from 77 replies received to questionnaire Form V mailed to 111 attorneys in the District of Columbia. (A copy of the questionnaire appears in volume 1, pages 223-225.) The response rate was 69%. The attorneys who received Form V had served as assigned counsel in the district court from October through December, 1962. The answers show that, although the great majority of those responding had been in practice for a considerable period (16 with 6 to 9 years; 19 with 10 to 14 years; 19 with 15 years or longer) a total of 54 out of the 76, or over one-half, indicated that they had rather limited experience in trying criminal cases (12 had no prior criminal cases; 20 had 1 to 4 prior cases; and 8 had 5 to 9 prior cases). In response to a question asking the lawyer how many indigent defendants he represented during 1962, 61% (47 out of 77) said they handled only one case. However, 22% (17 out of 77) indicated that they had been assigned to two cases during the year. One attorney even indicated appointment to the rather startling number of 10 to 14 cases during the year.

Most counsel indicated that they were appointed immediately before or at arraignment on the indictment as is the practice in district court appointments and stated that they were appointed in time to represent the accused person adequately. However, approximately one-fifth of those answering this question (14 out of 71) indicated that they were not appointed in time to give adequate representation. This figure becomes more significant when considered in connection with a later question where 35 out of 77 respondents (45%) suggested the appointment of counsel at an earlier stage of the case.

On the matter of repayment for out-of-pocket expenses, only 2 of the 77 indicated that they were repaid in full, only 8 indicated that they were repaid in part, and 67 indicated that they had received nothing. Although a few of these 67 did indicate that they knew that repayment was available, it appears that at least 38 of them were unaware of it. This was despite the fact that information about the availability of the investigating staff of the Legal Aid Agency and reimbursement for investigative expenses was contained in the same envelope as counsel's notification of appointment.

The responses to question 5(f), "How much would you have charged a client who retained you for your services in this case?", indicate that counsel would have charged a total of at least $95,610 for the services rendered in the 77 cases. This averages $1241 per case, based on charges ranging from $35 to $10,000.

Question 7 inquired about counsel's opinion of the fairness of the assigned counsel system to the indigent and to the attorney, and what changes, if any, counsel would recommend. Of those responding, 44 said the system was fair to the indigent person, while 26 said it was not. On the other hand, only 19 felt that the system was fair to the lawyer involved (7 of these indicated fairness only with qualifications) and 52 (68%) felt that the system was not fair to the lawyer. The recommended change which received the most attention (46 votes) was to pay lawyers for their services. Next in popularity (38 votes) was to pay out-of-pocket expenses. Third (35 votes) was to appoint lawyers at an earlier stage of the case. Only 19 felt that the system by which the judges select lawyers to be appointed needed improvement, and only 10 felt that the system should be improved by providing counsel in additional kinds of cases such as serious misdemeanors. Other recommendations offered were many and varied. Most often appearing was a recommendation to expand the Legal Aid Agency. Twelve respondents made this recommendation. Eight persons suggested that the assigned counsel system, which resulted in excessive appointment of a few lawyers, should be changed to insure that all members of the bar share the load equally. Other comments are contained in an appendix to this report.

F. DOCKET STUDY

A study was made of 110 representative felony defendants from the court docket for the year 1962. [For details as to method of study see volume 1, pages 178-179.] Of the 110 defendants, 107 had counsel, and of these, 35% had privately retained counsel, 38% had assigned counsel, 14% were represented by the Legal Aid Agency, and 6% by the Prettyman Fellows. (For the remaining defendants, either no information was available, or they were represented by a combination of the other kinds of counsel, such as retained counsel during part of the case, then assigned counsel for the rest.) Thus at least 58% of the defendants had counsel provided at no cost to them. The study also revealed that of 105 defendants for whom data were available, 66 (63%) were found to be indigent. Similarly, 67 out of 107 defendants (63%) were not released on bail, which is another indication of inability to retain counsel.

Of the 110 defendants, 42 pleaded guilty to the principal offense charged and 9 pleaded to lesser offenses, a total of 46%. Of 44 cases that went to trial (40%), 32 resulted in convictions of the principal offense and 5 in convictions of lesser offenses, 6 were acquittals, one was a mistrial, nine cases were dismissed, and those remaining were still pending or disposed of in other ways.

As to final disposition, 58% of all defendants were sentenced to various terms of imprisonment, while 15% were placed on probation and 4% were required to pay fines only. The other defendants were not sentenced, by reason of acquittal, dismissal, or pending status.

G. CONCLUSIONS AND RECOMMENDATIONS

On the basis of the material summarized in the foregoing report, the following conclusions and recommendations are submitted:

TABLE 1

Comparisons Among Judges, Prosecutors, and Defense Attorneys
(Including Public Defender and Private Defender)

	Judges	United States Attorney	Legal Aid Agency	Director, Prettyman Fellowship
Should assigned counsel be paid?	4–Yes	Yes	Yes	Yes
Should their out-of-pocket expenses be paid?	4–Yes	Yes	Yes (are paid now)	Yes
Public Defender may not be zealous, etc.	Invalid	Invalid	Invalid	Invalid
Do you think that a lawyer should be provided for a person who can pay a moderate fee?	3–Yes 1–No comment	Yes	Should get own lawyer	No comment
Ideal stage for appointment of counsel: Between arrest and first appearance	1		1	1
At first appearance (currently stage of appointment in D.C.)	2			
Between first appearance and preliminary hearing		1		
At preliminary hearing	1			

139

1. There was unanimous agreement among all the judges, the United States attorney, the director of the Legal Aid Agency and the director of the Georgetown program that assigned counsel should be compensated for their time in representing indigent defendants. Likewise, 60% of the responding assigned counsel indicated that such payment should be made. Therefore, it is submitted that a reasonable system of compensation should be devised and the necessary funds allocated by Congress.

2. Evaluations by the judges, the United States attorney, the director of the Legal Aid Agency, and the director of the Prettyman program indicate that the view suggesting lack of zealousness of a public defender paid out of the same funds as the prosecutor was invalid. Further, evaluations of the performance of the staff attorneys of the Legal Aid Agency were uniformly high, with one or two qualifications. Therefore it is recommended that the Legal Aid Agency be expanded so that, with the assistance of the Prettyman Fellows, it will have a sufficient staff to handle the vast majority, if not the entire caseload, of indigent defendants. A further argument for this expansion as opposed to a system of compensated private counsel is found in comparison of the cost per case of each program. The average charge which would have been made to a regular client by assigned counsel was at least $1241. The cost per case to the Legal Aid Agency was $396. This figure was arrived at by dividing the total number of cases handled by the agency into the total appropriation. Moreover, this figure would be somewhat lower if the following factors could have been taken into consideration: 106 man-hours spent before the United States Commissioner, 139 man-hours spent before the coroner, 14 man-hours spent on mental health cases, 61% of the total investigators' time spent on requests for investigation by assigned counsel, and over $1300 reimbursement for out-of-pocket expenses incurred by assigned counsel. Even if assigned counsel were paid only one-third of what they would charge a private client, the amount would be more than the Legal Aid Agency figure.

NOTES—District of Columbia

[1] 74 Stat. 229, D.C. Code §2-2201-2210 (1960).

[2] See Pye, "Legal Internships at Georgetown," 49 A.B.A.J. 554 (1963). The Fellows have developed a useful trial manual, *Law & Tactics in Federal Criminal Cases* (1964).

[3] Committee on Administration of Bail of the Junior Bar Section, Bar Association of the District of Columbia, *The Bail System of the District of Columbia* (1963).

[4] Ares, Rankin, and Sturz, "Manhattan Bail Project: an Interim Report on the Use of Pre-Trial Parole," 38 N.Y.U. L. Rev. 67 (1963).

[5] Mallory v. United States, 354 U.S. 449 (1957).

[6] 78 Stat. 552, U.S.C. tit. 18, §3006A.

[7] See Shafroth, "The New Criminal Justice Act," 50 A.B.A.J. 1049 (1964); National Legal Aid and Defender Association and A.B.A. Standing Committee on Legal Aid and Indigent Defendants, *Guidelines for Adequate Defense Systems* (1964).

APPENDIX

MISCELLANEOUS COMMENTS BY ASSIGNED COUNSEL

1. Provide or, better, pay for independent investigation work (more than half of my time was spent chasing down witnesses, measuring premises, timing distances, etc.).

DISTRICT OF COLUMBIA

Free the bail rules from rigidity. A $1,000 bail per-felony rule is preposterous when applied to an indigent.

Impress on the bar and on judges that these cases should not be treated perfunctorily. I went to a lot of effort to get my defendant a job offer so that he might be given probation, but the judge seemed to be satisfied that this was the "type of case" in which Youth Correction was appropriate. A wealthy man gets individualized consideration; so should an indigent, and this is what structural reforms should aim for.

2. All members of the bar should be available to be appointed. Lack of criminal experience should justify vacating the appointment in serious crimes only.

Some nominal scale of fees should be provided (fines, etc., could be a source of funds), and lawyers could volunteer for these cases at arraignment. A similar system is used in Great Britain with some success—young lawyers go to court at arraignment and are awarded "Dock Briefs" on appointment. This provides experience for the young, newly admitted lawyers in cases involving lesser crimes and is a source of income for struggling advocates and obviates appointment of senior and experienced lawyers to such cases.

3. My conception of what a lawyer is, or should be (a professional invested with the three characteristics of a professional: a technical and unique knowledge, a direct interest in serving the public without regard to compensation, and a responsibility for the preservation of public safety and order), forbids the placing of a lawyer's talents in the commercial marketplace to be priced when the duty to be performed is a public one. I think compensating lawyers would lead to the creation of a public-supported group of lawyers who did nothing else but collect fees from the government for representing indigents; and, I think, would lead to a lower standard of competency and a shifting of emphasis away from the role of a professional and to the role of a businessman.

A better solution to the situation we have here in the District, when about 1 lawyer out of 10 appointed is either incompetent or indigent himself, would be to bring more lawyers into the program and have a rule that no lawyer shall be appointed to more than 10 or 8 or 6 cases a year. Helping our fellow man have his day in court is the job of all lawyers, not just those that are primarily trial lawyers. To meet the problem of green or inexperienced lawyers, or even incompetent lawyers serving, the Bar itself should continue its professional training programs, or designate a special group of experienced lawyers that could be on call by telephone to informally advise those appointed.

Also, concern should be given to the problem of screening out those able to pay. There is abuse here in the District, where the municipal government is not directly controlled by tax-payers who would save their money if the various welfare programs were closely controlled and supervised.

4. Under certain circumstances it is unfair to the indigent person because attorneys with little or no criminal experience are at a disadvantage as to trial procedure and having a well-seasoned prosecutor oppose them (answer to question 7(a)).

Administrative, corporate, etc., practitioners should not be appointed. There should be either a legal defender system instituted or payment to attorneys for the many hours they are required to donate. The information contained in this questionnaire relates only to the year 1962. In 1963 to date I have been appointed to two more criminal cases and one appeal case, as well as one habeas corpus action. In 1963 to date (June 14, 1963) my two partners and myself have handled 10 court-appointed criminal cases (trials, appeals, habeas corpus). We are predominantly administrative and general law practitioners. This has been a tremendous burden and a great loss of money to us. One Court of Appeals case in 1961 took 240 hours and $50 in out-of-pocket expenses. We average eight years in practice, and at this stage of our careers these appointments represent a great sacrifice. Anything the Bar Association can do about this matter will redound to the benefit of the Bar and to indigents, who deserve adequate representation. . . .

5. My views are based on limited experience . . . . I opened an office in late 1961 and had time on my hands in 1962. I welcomed the appointment to get trial experience, and I devoted more than 100 hours to research. Now that my time is absorbed by other civil work, I wonder what I would do about the research [that would be required]. I like the principle that each

attorney must do a criminal case—it makes for a better bar. But it is a lot to ask of an attorney to work this extensively without any pay. The District of Columbia system permits us to call on professional investigators and on law students for research. The effectiveness of these tools depends on how early in the case the attorney is called in. To get the use of these facilities takes advance notice. When an attorney wants a case, he should have it. So much is said about the need for assistance, but, when I wanted a case, it literally took weeks to get it. Even though I expressed an interest in handling an appellate case nine months ago, none has been assigned. This leads me to think there is no great need, or that the interesting cases are saved for an exclusive club.

6. I believe that the panel of lawyers to handle criminal cases should provide the court with a statement showing both their criminal and civil experience and their preferences as to the types of cases. I believe service should be entirely voluntary and that there should be no difficulty in withdrawing from the panel. If a lawyer does not satisfy the indigent, it should be possible for the lawyer to withdraw and for successor counsel to be appointed. This should be limited to a maximum of one successor. It is my belief that the court is not as well informed as it should be on the experience and preferences of lawyers in making appointments.

If the present system of no compensation is to continue, which produces unsatisfactory results in many cases, the burden of handling criminal cases should fall on all lawyers who hold themselves out as such in the District of Columbia.

FLORIDA

Ernest E. Means, Tallahassee

Members of the A.B.A. Associate State Committee provided invaluable assistance to the reporter in such ways as contacting judges and prosecutors to help arrange interviews and providing constructive criticism of the first draft of this report. This committee consisted of Chester Bedell, Jacksonville, chairman; Paul B. Johnson, state attorney, Tampa; Kingswood Sprott, Jr., Lake Wales; Bruce E. Clary, DeLand; Joel T. Daves, county solicitor, West Palm Beach; William Fisher, Jr., Pensacola; and James Lawrence King, Jr., Miami Beach. Judges, prosecutors, and other officials of the seven counties surveyed cooperated wholeheartedly; and officials of the Florida Probation and Parole Commission, the Florida Division of Corrections, and the Florida Bar, all in Tallahassee, responded promptly to all requests for assistance.

A. INTRODUCTION

Florida is one of the fastest growing states of the union. Population has increased from 1,897,000 in 1940 to an estimated 5,704,000 in 1964. In 1960 it ranked 10th in size, up from 27th in 1940. Agriculture has always loomed large in the state's economy, and manufacturing and commerce are on the increase; but it is the huge tourist industry that probably has the greatest impact on the problem of defending indigents. The courts must deal not only with the large number of transients but also with those who seek to serve or exploit them. The influx of approximately 300,000 Cuban refugees in the Miami area has aggravated the problem there.

Florida has 67 counties. From these, seven were selected at random, according to the number of commitments from the counties to state prisons in 1961-1962: Madison, Pinellas, Hillsborough, Martin, Polk, Palm Beach, and Dade. The committee made four substitutions so that the sample would be more representative of the state in terms of geographical location, economic and cultural activity, and population characteristics. The specific substitutions were as follows: Alachua for Madison (both are agricultural counties in north Florida); Duval for Pinellas (both are about the same size, and Pinellas somewhat duplicated the adjoining county of Hillsborough); Escambia for Palm Beach (important county in northwest Florida instead of "gold coast" county duplicated by Dade); Jackson for Martin (small farm county in northwest Florida instead of small "gold coast" county). The final selection of counties is shown in the table on page 144.

B. CRIMINAL PROCEDURES AFFECTING INDIGENT DEFENDANTS

The basic trial court of general jurisdiction in Florida is the circuit court, the state consisting of 16 circuits. In the nine most populous counties, the legislature has added the "court of record," with jurisdiction of noncapital cases. In these counties the circuit court hears capital cases only. The state attorney, who is a state official serving the entire circuit, prosecutes in circuit court, and the county

143

County (chief city)	1960 population in thousands	No. of lawyers in private practice	Location in state	Remarks
Alachua (Gainesville)	74	84	Central	Agricultural, state university
Dade (Miami)	935	2670	Southeast	Tourism, commerce, large transient population, most populous county, large Spanish-speaking population, vegetable farming
Duval (Jacksonville)	455	646	Northeast	Port city, commerce, light manufacture, naval installations, second largest county
Escambia (Pensacola)	174	113	Northwest	Port city, commercial fishing, naval and air force installations, light industry
Hillsborough (Tampa)	398	516	Eastern	Third largest county, port city, large Spanish-speaking population, light industry, commerce
Jackson	36	13	Northwest	Rural, tobacco, pecans, stable population, minimum security penal institution, state mental hospital
Polk (Lakeland)	195	177	Central	Citrus fruits, truck farming, phosphate mining, minimum security penal institution, light industry

solicitor prosecutes in the court of record, except in two counties where the state attorney handles this court as well as the circuit court.

The system of lower criminal courts varies in different counties. Most counties have justices of the peace, who act as committing magistrates and have jurisdiction over lesser misdemeanors. All counties have the county judge's court, basically a probate court, but also having limited criminal jurisdiction, including the power to act as a committing magistrate. Most justices of the peace are laymen, and most county judges are lawyers. Additional courts have been created in some counties.

The Florida Probation and Parole Commission has a statewide network of

TABLE 1
Organization of Courts and Court-connected Facilities
Florida, 1962

Survey counties	Circuit Court Jurisdiction			Criminal court of record	State attorney		Committing magistrate (also preliminary hearing)		Probation services	
	Docket study made	Capital only	All felonies		Prosecutes all felonies	Prosecutes capital only*	County judge	Justice of peace†	District Office Parole Commission‡	County Probation Office‡
Alachua	X		X		X		X		X(5)	
Dade	X	X		X	X			X(5)	X(8)	X(11)
Duval	X	X		X		X		X(9)	X(8)	X(2)
Escambia		X		X		X	X	X(5)	X(6)	
Hillsborough		X		X	X			X(2)	X(16)	
Jackson	X		X		X		X		X(2)	
Polk		X		X		X	X	X(5)	X(8)	

* In counties in which the state attorney prosecutes only capital felonies, prosecution of non-capital felonies in the criminal court of record is by the county solicitor.

† Figure in parentheses is the number of justices of the peace in the county.

‡ Number in parentheses is the number of supervisors in that office.

145

probation officers who prepare pre-sentence investigations and supervise those placed on probation. In two of the counties surveyed, Dade and Duval, county probation offices have been established by local legislation. Hence in these counties the commission confines itself to supervising parolees and probationers from other counties.

Table 1 sets out the organization of courts, etc., for the counties surveyed for the present study.

1. General procedures. Most felony cases begin with the arrest of a suspect. It is required by statute that the arrested person be taken, "without unnecessary delay," before a committing magistrate. Whether the arrest is with or without a warrant, the magistrate is required by statute to inform the defendant of the charge against him, of his right to the aid of counsel during the preliminary hearing, of his right to waive such hearing, and of his right to refuse to testify. If the defendant waives the hearing, the magistrate either admits him to bail or commits him to custody.

The frequency of preliminary hearings in felonies varies rather widely among the counties surveyed. It ranges from a very high frequency in Duval, where waivers are rare, to a medium frequency in Hillsborough and Escambia, to a low frequency in Polk, Alachua, and Jackson, where the hearing is deemed waived unless demanded by the defendant. Dade is a special case: if the defendant is brought before a magistrate a hearing is usually held, but in a substantial pro-portion of the cases the initial complaint is made before the state attorney, who files an information, thus obviating a preliminary hearing. In all seven counties it was reported that the defendant was more likely to demand a preliminary hearing if he had counsel than if he did not.

Practice in setting bond appeared to be fairly uniform in the seven counties surveyed. When arrest is on a warrant the committing magistrate endorses the amount of bail on the warrant. When the defendant is held for action by the grand jury or the equivalent, application for change of bail may be made to the court having jurisdiction. If the prosecution is initiated by information the judge of the trial court endorses the amount of bail on the capias.

2. Appointment of counsel. The system for providing counsel was greatly modified, effective July 1, 1963. Before that date 63 counties used the assigned counsel system exclusively. Four used assigned counsel for capital cases and a public defender for noncapital cases. Since July 1, 1963, all counties use a public defender for noncapital cases, but counsel are still appointed for capital cases. The public defender system is described in the next section.

For capital cases under both the old regime and the new, attorney's fees of up to $500 are allowed for trial, with an additional $500 if an appeal is taken from a death sentence. The study revealed widespread satisfaction with the operation of this program.

For noncapital cases, under the former system, of the seven counties surveyed, only Duval and the two public defender counties provided counsel for a rela-tively high proportion of defendants. In Duval, by local legislation, a sum of $25,000 a year was appropriated to the criminal court of record for payment of counsel in amounts not exceeding $250 a case. In the other four counties no funds were available for noncapital cases.

The tabulation below shows the situation in 1962. It should be borne in mind that not all felony defendants were indigent and that not all indigents needed or wanted counsel.

County	No. of felony defendants in 1962	No. of defendants represented by public defender, 1962	No. of appointments of counsel in felonies, 1962	No. of lawyers who served	Maximum number of appointments per lawyer
Alachua	153*		15	8	7
Dade	4149	1348	22†	17	2
Duval	900*		146	37	20
Escambia	474		15	13	2
Hillsborough	1117	620	11†	9	3
Jackson	68		11	5	6
Polk	1080*		19‡	8‡	no data

* Estimated.
† Public defender represented defendants charged with noncapital felonies. Therefore, these appointments were for capital cases only.
‡ Figures based on judge's recollection.

In capital cases counsel was appointed after indictment in most counties, although in at least one circuit the appointment was regularly made in time for the preliminary hearing, and in at least eight other circuits this was sometimes done. In noncapital cases counsel was appointed at arraignment on the indictment or sufficiently in advance of arraignment to permit consultation. Only in the two public defender counties was counsel provided as early as the preliminary hearing, and even that was unofficial and sporadic.

The two public defender counties also provided counsel for the more serious and complicated misdemeanors.

Although the statute (§ 909.21) does not specifically authorize reimbursement of appointed counsel for out-of-pocket expenditures, some judges have construed it in this way and others have simply ordered certain expenses to be paid from public funds. The statutes do authorize payment for costs on appeal (§ 924.17), a stenographic transcript (§ 924.23), witnesses (§ 923.36-37), and other costs allowed by law (§ 939.15).

3. *Determination of indigency*. This is uniformly considered a matter for judicial discretion and is expressly made such in the new public defender act. Accordingly, questions on financial status are almost invariably addressed to the defendant in open court. However, in Jackson, Alachua, and Duval Counties, at least, preliminary information is gathered by means of a questionnaire filled out at the jail by the defendant. These questionnaires also provide a permanent record of the defendant's waiver of counsel. In the four remaining counties such waiver is, since the *Gideon* decision, entered in the official minutes of the court. The most striking difference of practice concerning the test of indigency was for de-

fendants who were able to make bond. In Dade and Hillsborough this factor is conclusive and services of the public defender are denied. In Jackson, Escambia, and Duval, on the other hand, this factor is merely considered along with others. With the exception of Duval, however, the three latter counties have had rather limited programs for providing representation, whereas Dade and Hillsborough have had more extensive programs. Perhaps it can be inferred that some such rule of thumb is needed to prevent the abuse of an otherwise liberal system.

4. *Postconviction remedies.* According to a Supreme Court rule adopted April 1, 1963, at the suggestion of the Judicial Council, and in anticipation of the *Gideon* decision, any prisoner may at any time move the court that sentenced him to vacate the sentence on the ground that it was imposed in violation of the constitution or laws of the United States or Florida. The rule potentially applied to some 4500 prisoners. In *State v. Weeks* (166 So. 2d 892 [Fla. 1964]), the Supreme Court considered the right of an indigent prisoner to have counsel appointed in such a proceeding. All three district courts of appeal had ruled that counsel was to be appointed for an appeal from denial of the motion, thus greatly increasing the work load of public defenders. The Supreme Court declared (p. 897):

> There is no absolute organic right to the assistance of counsel at a hearing on a Rule 1 motion or on appeal from an adverse ruling thereon. Each case must be decided in the light of Fifth Amendment due process requirements which generally would involve a decision as to whether under the circumstances the assistance of counsel is essential to accomplish a fair and thorough presentation of the prisoner's claims. To this end, the court may find that the issues in the post-conviction proceedings have been simplified and are clearly drawn so that a fair hearing could be achieved without counsel. In all of these considerations, however, the proper course would be to resolve doubts in favor of the indigent prisoner when a question of the need for counsel is presented.

C. THE PUBLIC DEFENDER SYSTEM

Florida's new state-wide defender system is clearly a result of the *Gideon* ruling. Anticipating that decision, the Judicial Council submitted a public defender bill to the 1963 legislature. The bill, with far-reaching amendments, emerged as Chapter 63-409, effective July 1, 1963. It provided a public defender for each judicial circuit. The governor was to appoint the defenders to serve till the next general election, with the existing defenders in four counties to be preferred in the initial appointments. Thereafter all defenders are to be popularly elected by the electors of their circuits for four-year terms. The defender is to represent any insolvent person "who is under arrest for, or is charged with, a non-capital felony if such person requests it or if the court, on its own motion, so orders and such person does not knowingly, understandingly, and intelligently waive the opportunity to be so represented." The act does not say at what stage the defender is to take the case, but it does say that the court is to determine insolvency, which may be done at any stage of the proceedings.

Even at this early stage it appears that the critical issue in the future of the public defender system will be the degree of financial support by the counties. The state contribution is limited to salaries and travel expenses of the public defender and, in a few circuits, his assistants. (The total available for salaries is $186,250 a year.) Thus the defenders must look to the counties for funds for investigators, secretarial expense, office supplies, law books, etc., as well as for the special assistant public defenders who may volunteer for service in individual cases. With a few exceptions the first response of the counties has been disappointing.

[Editor's note: the 1965 session of the legislature enacted a substantial increase in the appropriations for the public defender offices for the next biennium (1965-1967). The bill includes moderate salary increases for defenders, provisions for assistant defenders in every circuit, and funds for secretaries, office supplies and expense, and travel. The total appropriation is $466,390 for 1965-1966 and $468,775 for 1966-1967.]

The public defender legislation includes two provisions that would require defendants to help pay for the service if they are able: (1) if the trial court adjudges and determines, within a year after the determination of insolvency, that the defendant was not insolvent, the state attorney may proceed against him for the reasonable value of the services rendered and all costs paid in his behalf; and (2) a section in the appropriations act (Ch. 63-410) creates a lien on all real and personal property of the defendant and requires the public defender to file for record a statement of claim for the reasonable value of the services rendered, as determined by the court. The defender is directed to enforce such liens. They are not subject to any statute of limitations. Because of a conflict between these two provisions the attorney general has ruled that the first provision is superseded by the second because it was subsequently enacted. Several of the persons interviewed for the present study thought the lien provision might cause confusion in land titles, usually through similarity of names. An abstract company official was concerned about the perpetual lien, which he pointed out was in conflict with the Marketable Title Act passed by the same session of the legislature, the purpose of which was to obviate the need for tracing any title back for more than 30 years.

D. OPINIONS OF THE JUDGES

In the seven sample counties 12 judges were interviewed, 7 from circuit courts and 5 from criminal courts of record (see Table 1 above). Seven of the judges had served 5 years or longer on their present courts, and four had served 20 years or longer. In the remaining 60 counties questionnaires were mailed to 47 judges. Of these 31 replied (66%). A questionnaire was returned from at least one judge in each circuit. Of the 31 judges, 23 had served on their present courts for 5 years or longer, and 8 had served for 10 years or longer.

The interviewed judges uniformly approved the statutory arrangement for providing counsel in capital cases. For noncapital felonies, however, they favored a more liberal program than is now provided. Ten of the 12 thought that assistance of counsel should ideally be made available at the stage of the preliminary hearing or earlier. Seven of the 10 thought that counsel was needed as soon after arrest as feasible, and 2 of the 7 went on to say that the truly ideal system would provide counsel from the time the defendant first learned that he was under investigation, since he could make damaging statements even before arrest.

149

On the mail questionnaire the judges were similarly asked, "Under an ideal system, at what stage in a criminal case do you think a lawyer should first be made available to the indigent person?" Of the 31 judges replying, 24 would provide a lawyer at or before the preliminary hearing; of the 24, 9 would provide a lawyer between arrest and first appearance before a magistrate, 4 would provide one at first appearance, and 9 would provide one between first appearance and preliminary hearing. Asked next if they thought it unfair to the indigent person if he does not get a lawyer at the stage indicated, 12 of the judges said yes, 6 said no, 2 said it depends on the circumstances, and 4 did not answer.

In both the interviews and the questionnaires the judges were asked if they thought that under an ideal system a lawyer should be made available in certain kinds of cases and proceedings. Results were as follows:

Kind of case or proceeding	Interviews		Questionnaires		
	Yes	No	Yes	No	Sometimes*
Sentencing of a defendant who pleaded guilty	7†	5	14	11	4
Sentencing of a defendant convicted by trial	7†	5	19	9	2
Habeas corpus, coram nobis, or other postconviction remedy	6	6	18	9	2
Hearing on revocation of probation	9	3	13	14	3
Sexual psychopath hearing	9	3	22	6	2
Misdemeanors	9	3	3	23	3
Civil commitment of the mentally ill, including alcoholics and narcotics addicts	7	5	18	8	3

*This column includes such limitations as "only for serious crimes," "only if trial judge thinks so," and "no, if defendant is fully informed and waives his right."

†Counsel is already provided in four counties; judges who so answered are included in this figure.

Of the 31 judges who returned the questionnaires, 26 answered questions about the number of felony defendants appearing before them in 1962 and the proportion who were indigent. Of a total of approximately 4800 defendants, 3000 were estimated to be indigent (65%). The median estimate was 75%. (For the seven survey counties the comparable figures are 8000 defendants, with 3600 estimated to be indigent (45%) and a median estimate of 71%.)

E.   OPINIONS OF STATE ATTORNEYS

Two categories of prosecuting officers were surveyed: state attorneys, who prosecute before the circuit court, and county solicitors, who prosecute noncapital crimes before the criminal courts of record that have been established in certain of the larger counties. In all, seven prosecutors were interviewed (four state attorneys and three county solicitors). In the remaining nine circuits, questionnaires were sent to nine state attorneys and five county solicitors. Nine of these 14, or 64%, returned their questionnaires.

Three of the seven prosecutors interviewed thought that under an ideal system counsel should first be provided for indigents between arrest and the first appearance before a magistrate. One thought counsel should be provided between first appearance and preliminary hearing, two thought that counsel should be provided at arraignment, and one thought that no more was required than that the defendant have counsel at his trial. Seven of the nine prosecutors who responded by mail felt that counsel should be provided before the preliminary hearing: two said "between arrest and the first appearance," three said "at first appearance," and two said "between first appearance and preliminary hearing." The two remaining prosecutors said that counsel should be provided after the filing of an indictment or information but before arraignment.

All seven of the prosecutors interviewed thought that ideally counsel should be appointed in misdemeanor cases, assuming that practical obstacles could be estimated. However, only two of the nine prosecutors who returned questionnaires agreed. Six felt that indigents accused of misdemeanors should not be provided with an attorney and one felt that an attorney should be provided, but with certain limitations.

Each prosecutor was also asked whether, under an ideal system, a lawyer should be provided for the kinds of cases and proceedings listed above in Section D. Five of the seven prosecutors interviewed felt that counsel should be made available in all these proceedings. A majority of the mail respondents also favored making counsel available to indigents for each of these proceedings, except for a hearing on revocation of probation (only two favored this). Eight of the nine mail respondents felt that counsel should be provided for the sentencing of a defendant convicted by trial.

The prosecutors who were interviewed unanimously said they would much prefer that the indigent criminal defendant have counsel at trial, since the defendant without counsel benefits from the sympathy that is aroused in both jury and judge.

F. OPINIONS OF DEFENSE ATTORNEYS

1. *Assigned Counsel.* Questionnaires were sent out to 97 lawyers who had been assigned to represent indigents accused of crime in the seven sample counties. Answers were received from 47 attorneys in 6[1] of the counties, a response rate of 48%.

Of the 47, 40 represented indigents during 1962. Of the 40, 33 had practiced for five years or more and only 1 had practiced for less than a year. Twenty-three had had experience in at least 50 criminal cases prior to their first appointment in 1962. Only seven had experience in less than 10 cases; and of the seven, only four had no previous experience.

Of the 40, 6 lawyers handled 10 or more cases of indigent defendants during 1962; 25 handled less than 4 cases, including 11 who handled only 1 case. A high proportion of the defendants were charged with crimes punishable by death or life imprisonment. Of 35 lawyers answering, 11 had 1 such case, 5 had

2 cases, 4 had 3 cases, 3 had 4 cases, 1 had 5 cases, and 1 had 10 or more cases. When the lawyers were asked what offense the last indigent they defended in 1962 was charged with, 16 answered either "murder" or "rape," which are both capital crimes in Florida. It will be recalled that counsel are compensated for such cases.

The following question was included in the questionnaire: "[In the last case in which you were appointed in 1962,] were you appointed in time to represent the accused person adequately?" Of 34 lawyers answering, 27 said "yes" and 7 said "no." All who answered in the negative were appointed at some stage after the filing of the indictment, and two were appointed after arraignment. The stages of appointment are shown in the following table:

Stage at which counsel was appointed	No. of lawyers appointed at that stage	%
Between arrest and first appearance (arraignment on the warrant) before a magistrate	4	10.0
At first appearance (arraignment on the warrant) before a magistrate	2	5.0
Between first appearance and preliminary hearing	1	2.5
At preliminary hearing	1	2.5
After preliminary hearing but before the filing of an indictment, information, etc.	0	0.0
After the filing of an indictment, information, etc., but before arraignment thereon	17	42.5
At arraignment on indictment, information, etc.	6	15.0
After arraignment on indictment, information, etc., but before trial	9	22.5
Totals	40	100.0

For the last case in which they were assigned in 1962, 25 lawyers received compensation for their services and 15 did not. Of 39 lawyers who incurred out-of-pocket expenses, 9 were paid in full, 5 were paid in part, and 25 were not paid. When asked how much they would have charged for their services in the cases, the 39 lawyers gave sums totalling $71,680[2]; an average of $1843 per case.

Of the 47 lawyers responding to the questionnaire, 2 represented indigents on appeal in 1962. They were compensated $500 and $200 respectively. One represented indigents in a postconviction remedy and was not compensated.

When asked what changes in the present system, if any, they would recommend, 17 of 41 said that lawyers should be appointed at an earlier stage of the case, and 17 said lawyers should be paid for their out-of-pocket expenses. These answers are significant even though Florida now has the public defender system, since assigned counsel are still used for capital cases.

2. *Public Defenders.* Interviews in the sample counties were held with 6 public defenders who serve a total of 19 counties. Two of the defenders had

been admitted to the bar for a year or less; 2 had been admitted for from 4 to 5 years; and 2 had been admitted for 10 years. Three of the defenders had practiced criminal law for a year or less, and only one had over nine years of experience. All six reported that they were part-time rather than full-time defenders, but all spent at least 30 hours a week on the job. When asked what career opportunities were available to defenders, one said "greater public acceptance," but three stated that public acceptance is not yet sufficient to bring about many opportunities. Information concerning the defender offices is presented in Table 2.

The state contribution to the defender offices is only for the salary of the defender and, in some circuits, for assistant defenders. The remaining budget of all six defender offices, which may include salary for additional assistants, investigators[3], office expense, etc., is determined by county commissioners. Of the six defenders, two said the funds allotted to run their offices are adequate, but four complained of inadequacy. Only three of the six have funds for investigation. Three of the defenders said they needed additional staff, and the other three said they had enough.

Four of the six defenders believed the present system for deciding whether a person is eligible for the defender service is "about right." One felt it was too strict and one that it was too lenient. A person who is able to make bail is not eligible for defender services in three of the defender offices. He is "usually not" eligible in the fourth. In the other two counties, this factor was merely considered along with others.

The defender offices enter a case at various stages: one enters between the first appearance (arraignment on the warrant) and the preliminary hearing; one enters at the preliminary hearing, three[4] enter after the filing of an indictment or information but before arraignment thereon; and one enters at the arraignment on the indictment or information. Like the judges and prosecutors, the defenders were asked the following question: "Under an ideal system, at what stage in a criminal case do you think the indigent person should first be provided with a lawyer if he wants one?" All six answered "between arrest and the first appearance before a magistrate," which is a stage earlier than counsel is provided in any county. Further, five of the six believed it was unfair to the indigent person if he did not get a lawyer at this stage.

Responses to questions concerning different types of proceedings are presented in Table 3.

The defenders were asked how the present system for providing counsel to indigents might be improved. Among their suggestions were the following: find a way to stimulate greater public acceptance of the defender, make the defender office appointive, and consolidate the justice of peace districts to facilitate contact with indigents at the preliminary hearing stage.

G. DOCKET STUDY

A study was made of a representative sample of all felony cases commenced in 1962 in four of the sample counties. On the question whether the defendant had counsel, Table 4 shows that the proportion ranged from 31% in Jackson County

TABLE 2

Defender Offices, Florida, 1962

Jurisdiction of public defender	No. of defendants represented	Staff employees						Salary of defender	Total budget of defender office
		Full-time lawyers	Part-time lawyers	Full-time secretaries	Part-time secretaries	Investi-gators	Others		
Hillsborough County	620*	0	3	1	0	1	0	$12,500	$63,500†
Dade County	1500*	0	4	2	0	1	0	9750	50,000‡
Escambia Okaloosa, Santa Rosa, and Walton Counties	—§	0	1	1	0	0	0	8000	25,000¶
Alachua, Baker, Bradford, Gilchrist, Levy, and Union Counties		0	1	0	0	0	0	8000	Uncertain**
Polk, Hardee, and Highland Counties	—§	0	1	0	1	0	0	9750	22,330††
Duval, Clay, and Nassau Counties	—§	0	7	3	0	2	1	13,500	82,940‡‡

*Estimate made by public defender.

†The state contributes $16,250 and the county $46,750.

‡This figure includes the following salaries: senior assistants, $15,000; junior assistant, $6200; investigator, $5500; secretaries, $6800. The state contributes $22,750 and the county $27,250.

§No figures are available because these defender offices were organized during 1963.

¶The state contributes $8000 for the defender's salary, plus travel expenses. Escambia County appropriated $17,000. $15,000 has been requested from the other three counties.

**The state contributes $8000 for the defender's salary. In addition, the county commissioners were requested to make contributions totaling $14,200 per year, including $6000 for an investigator and $3000 for clerical help. Bradford County voted $1562, Alachua refused outright, and the remaining three counties, at the time of writing this report, had taken no action.

††The state contributes $9750 for the defender's salary and $6500 for an assistant's salary. Polk County contributes $6080. The other three counties make no contribution.

‡‡This figure is the budget for 1963-64. It is broken down as follows: salaries, $43,500; equipment, $6500; office supplies, $3500; investigator, $11,000; auto allowance, $1800. The state contributes $16,250 and the counties, $66,690.

154

TABLE 3
Defenders, Miscellaneous Proceedings
Florida, 1962

Kind of proceeding	Does defender office handle such proceedings?		Under ideal system should counsel be provided for such proceedings?		Is it unfair if indigent does not have a lawyer for such proceedings?	
	Yes	No	Yes	No	Yes	No
Misdemeanors	4*	2	5	0	2	1
Habeas corpus, coram nobis, or other post-conviction remedy	3	3	5	0	3	1
Hearings on revocation of probation	2	4	6	0	2	1
Sexual psychopath hearings	3	3	4	1	2	1
Civil commitment of the mentally ill, including alcoholics and narcotics addicts	1	5	4	2	1	1
Parole hearings	1	5				

* One defender office handles serious misdemeanors only.

to 83% in Dade. The public defender of Dade County represented 41% of the defendants. The docket study also revealed that only 29% of the defendants in Dade County and 49% in Duval County were released on bail. (Figures from the other counties were unavailable because the records did not disclose this information.) The outcome of the cases studied is shown in Table 5. Projecting the figures for the four counties to the state as a whole, one finds that 48% of the defendants pleaded guilty, including 8% who pleaded to a lesser offense. Of the 15% of the cases that went to trial, 11% resulted in convictions including 4% lesser offenses. Table 6 shows the sentences or other final results of the cases. For the state as a whole 32% of the defendants received prison sentences, while 18% had probation or suspended sentence.

H. CONCLUSIONS AND RECOMMENDATIONS

On the basis of the foregoing report, and also of the informed knowledge of the members of the associate committee, the following conclusions and recommendations are respectfully submitted:

1. The present study has served to point up the potential value of the statistical reporting program of the Judicial Council of Florida. The committee urges the council to continue this program and recommends that it examine the feasibility of incorporating in its reporting forms new items designed to provide essential information concerning the future operation of Florida's appointed counsel program for indigent defendants accused of capital felonies, and the

TABLE 4
Retained and Assigned Counsel in Felonies
Florida, 1962

County	Total sample	Did defendant have counsel? Yes No.	%	No No.	%	Re-tained No.	%	As-signed No.	%	De-fender No.	%	Combi-nation or type unknown No.	%	No data No.	%*
Escambia	43	19	43	24	57	15	36	2	5	0	0	1	2	1	2
Jackson	49	13	31	29	69	6	14	6	14	0	0	1	2	7	14
Dade	225	166	83	34	17	81	41	1	1	82	41	2	1	25	11

* % of no data refers to total sample; % in other columns refers to the number of cases where data were available.

TABLE 5
Disposition in Felony Cases
Florida, 1962

County	Total sample	Plea guilty	Plea lesser offense	Dis-missed	Found guilty	Found guilty lesser degree	Ac-quitted	Mental commit-ment	Pend-ing	Stet*	Other
Escambia	43	21	1	5	4	1	2	2	1	4	2
Jackson	49	22	1	9	3	2	2	0	6	4	0
Duval	66	21	8	11	2	4	0	0	1	19	0
Dade	225	65	32	32	29	7	21	1	33	5	0
Weighted total percentages		40	8	16	7	4	4	1	7	13	1

* Held on inactive docket.

TABLE 6*
Sentencing in Felony Cases
Florida, 1962

County	Total sample	No sentence No.	%	Prison No.	%	Pro-bation No.	%	Sus-pended sentence No.	%	Fine No.	%	Pend-ing No.	%
Escambia	43	14	33	15	35	5	12	0	0	6	14	4	9
Jackson	49	22	45	17	35	10	20	0	0	1	2	0	0
Dade	225	93	41	67	30	58	26	3	1	3	1	1	0
Duval†	64	37	58	19	30	9	14	1	2	2	3	6	9
Weighted total percentages			41		33		17		1		6		5

* If a defendant had a combination sentence, such as fine and imprisonment, he is counted under both columns; hence totals may be more than 100%.
†Two no data cases are omitted.

new public defender system for the representation of indigent defendants accused of noncapital offenses.

2. The committee observes that Florida's statutory scheme for providing counsel for indigent defendants accused of capital felonies appears to be operating satisfactorily and to have the approval of all who have contact with it. It is true that there is some sentiment among those who operate this program that counsel should perhaps be appointed at an earlier stage than arraignment. Nevertheless, the committee feels that it should refrain from making any recommendations concerning this program, at least until there is time to observe the interactions that must occur between this program and the new public defender system.

3. The committee believes that the lien and recovery provision of Section 3 of Chapter 63-410 is not only a likely source of confusion as to land titles, but that it is also of doubtful constitutionality. More specifically, the committee questions whether the legislature may attach such a condition as is contained in Section 3 to what has been held to be a constitutional right of the indigent defendant accused of a felony. Consequently, the committee recommends the repeal of Section 3 of Chapter 63-410.

On the other hand, the committee approves of the principle that underlies Section 3(2) of Chapter 63-409, which would again become operative upon the repeal of Section 3 of Chapter 63-410. However, the committee recommends that this section be amended in these three respects: (1) to clarify the purpose of the section by limiting its application to cases in which the original adjudication of insolvency had been induced by misrepresentation on the part of the defendant; (2) to increase to two years the period within which a finding of insolvency can be reopened; and (3) to provide that the new proceeding and resulting judgment, if any, shall be in the trial court which made the initial determination of insolvency, rather than in a civil court.

NOTES—Florida

1 Unfortunately, no responses were received from Jackson County.

2 If answers included two figures, such as "between $250 and $500," the average ($375) was used in making this computation.

3 Presumably, since Ch. 63-409 specifies that travel shall be paid for the defenders, the travel expense for assistants and investigators will also come from county funds.

4 One of the three enters capital cases at the justice of the peace level, and withdraws in favor of assigned counsel at a time prior to arraignment.

GEORGIA

Fred S. Clark, Savannah, and Prof. Robert S. Stubbs II, Atlanta

The A.B.A. Associate State Committee, through its chairman, Edwin A. Friedman of Savannah, actively assisted and provided guidance in the course of the project in this state. The subcommittee also included Leah F. Chanin, Macon; Reid W. Harris, Brunswick; John L. Moore, Jr., Atlanta; Marion T. Pope, Jr., Canton; Raymond F. Schuder, Gainesville; Sidney B. Shepherd, Swainsboro; and James C. Whelchel, Moultrie. A committee of the Younger Lawyers Section of the Columbus bar, under the chairmanship of William B. Hardegree, conducted interviews and compiled data in Muscogee County. Invaluable aid was rendered in the docket studies by law students Frank P. Brannen and Alan E. Serby, both of Savannah.

A. INTRODUCTION

The population of Georgia in 1960 was 3,943,116; the estimated population in 1963, based on a preliminary study by the Georgia Health Department is 4,097,500. The State has 159 counties divided into 39 judicial circuits, each circuit containing a superior court for each county therein. Each circuit has one or more superior court judges, there being 57 such judges in 1963, and its own solicitor-general, the prosecuting attorney.

The counties selected for survey are shown in the following tabulations:

County (chief city)	1960 population in thousands	Location in state	Remarks
Catoosa (D)	21	Northwest	Agricultural, becoming suburban, part of metropolitan Chattanooga
Chatham (D)* (Savannah)	188	East	Industrial, commercial, seaport, second largest city, has state port
Cobb (D) (Marietta)	114	North central	Industrial, part of Atlanta metropolitan area
DeKalb* (Decatur)	257	North central	Suburban, part of Atlanta metropolitan area
Emanuel (D)	18	Central	Agricultural
Fulton (D) (Atlanta)	556	North central	State capital and largest city, federal penitentiary, business, transportation and commercial center
Muscogee (Columbus)	259	West	Industrial, has large military reservation
Peach	14	Central	Agricultural
Thomas (D)	34	South	Agricultural
Walton (D)	20	North central	Agricultural
Ware (D) (Waycross)	34	Southeast	Agricultural, small industry

(D) indicates that a docket study was made.
* Chatham and DeKalb Counties were added to the original group of sample counties.

County	Felony defendants, 1962	% indigent*	% of indigents waiving counsel*
Catoosa	16	25.0	3.5
Chatham	420	90.0	0.0
Cobb	119	19.4	25.0
DeKalb	220	3.5	0.0
Emanuel	54	40.0	50.0
Fulton	1704	65.6	0.0
Muscogee	780	50.0	75.0
Peach	ND	20.0	20.0
Thomas	62	75.0	50.0
Walton	77	42.5	50.0
Ware	63	90.0	0.0

ND means no data.
* Average of estimates by judges and solicitors.

County	Lawyers in private practice	No. appointments for indigent felons, 1962	No. lawyers appointed	Total amount paid for services of appointed lawyers	Estimated worth of uncompensated appointed lawyers' services
Catoosa	4	9	7	$ 150	$ 5000
Chatham	175	11*	5*	ND	ND
Cobb	71	ND	45	630	26,500
DeKalb	115	115-120*	ND	912	22,500
Emanuel	17	2*	1*	ND	ND
Fulton	1148	ND	15*	19,135	345,000
Muscogee	118	60*	25*	1670	15,000
Peach	7	ND	ND	ND	ND
Thomas	18	ND	ND	ND	ND
Walton	10	ND	5	424	5100
Ware	35	ND	ND	ND	ND

ND means no data.
* Estimated.

B. CRIMINAL PROCEDURE AS IT AFFECTS INDIGENT PERSONS

Jurisdiction to return indictments and try felony cases is vested exclusively in the superior court.

The great majority of felony cases begin with the arrest of the suspect, who must be taken promptly before a magistrate. In most rural or small counties the magistrate is a justice of the peace or a city official, neither of whom need be lawyers. In the larger counties, which have a county court, usually located in the county's largest city, the judge or judges thereof conduct most of the courts of inquiry or committal hearings. These judges are lawyers. At the court of inquiry, the defendant is advised of the complaint against him and his right to be represented by counsel, and bail is set if the offense is bailable. While there is a right under Georgia law for the defendant to hear the evidence against him, to call witnesses in his own behalf, and to make a statement, these rights appear to be seldom claimed except in serious or capital felonies, where the defendant is represented by counsel of his own selection. In short, it appears that the committal hearing is generally waived, which occurs simply upon the failure of the defendant to demand the same. It appears further to be the general practice to make no determination of indigency or appointment of counsel in felony cases, which are beyond the trial jurisdiction of all committing magistrates except judges of the superior court, and few of these were found who conducted courts of inquiry or committal hearings. One notable exception to this general practice was found in Catoosa County, where upon the arrest of the defendant in a publicized homicide case, the superior court judge from another county in the same circuit immediately appointed two attorneys who represented the indigent accused at the committal hearing and thereafter. Although no precise statement to this effect was obtained, it appears that superior court judges generally refrain from any action in the usual felony case until an indictment or accusation (information) has been returned or drawn, and the defendant is then, in fact, within the court's trial jurisdiction. Further, there seems to be tacit recognition by committing magistrates and attorneys alike that the only officer with capacity to appoint an attorney at a pre-indictment stage in a felony case is the judge of the superior court, although there is no precise statutory authority for this assumption.

Bail is allowable by the committing magistrate for all but capital offenses, and there such may be granted, upon petition of the accused, by the judge of the superior court. In no county surveyed was there found a set schedule for bail bonds. While it was generally stated that the magistrate who conducted the hearing set the amount of bail, upon further inquiry a variety of answers were forthcoming: in Catoosa County the sheriff sets the amount; in DeKalb, the solicitor-general, unless there be a committal hearing, in which case the magistrate would; in Fulton, the solicitor-general after indictment; and in other counties, the sheriff or solicitor-general may recommend or advise as to the amount. All counties surveyed reported that defendants were brought before a magistrate within 48 hours after arrest and that, if allowable, bail was set at that first appearance. Preliminary hearings, as a formal procedural step between the committal inquiry and indictment, are rarely held in any sample county except in a few capital cases, or where demanded by retained counsel.

Throughout Georgia the formal charge of felony against a defendant is made by indictment, although the use of an accusation (information) appears to be widespread in noncapital felony cases. This occurs where the solicitor-general is informed by the accused of his intent to plead guilty and waive indictment, or where such intention is expressed before the judge of the superior court in a preliminary appearance between terms of court or when the criminal calendar is being prepared. A defendant who is denied bail or who cannot make the same may remain in confinement as much as three months awaiting trial, depending upon the time cycle of the convening of the grand jury, or the opening of the criminal term in the county. The same delay appears to obtain, irrespective of the size of the county. The large counties are plagued by crowded dockets, and the small ones by infrequent terms of court, the county usually being but one of several in a judicial circuit. Interviews with judges and solicitors in all parts of the state reflected an awareness of these delays, which are ameliorated somewhat by a greater resort to accusations in lieu of indictments, between-term hearings to accept pleas of guilty, and more liberality in setting bail. Only in Fulton County among the counties surveyed, does it appear that there is a defined system for review of bail as a matter of course, and this does not necessarily mean a reduction thereof: after indictment, the solicitor-general may modify the amount previously set by the committing magistrate.

The procedure for determining indigency varies somewhat in the counties surveyed. In all sample counties the ultimate decision was that of the superior court judge, finally reached after at least a perfunctory questioning as to the accused's financial ability to retain counsel. The questioning usually takes place during an informal hearing after indictment but before a trial calendar is set. In Cobb County the solicitor-general often conducts a cursory inquiry of his own prior to this hearing, and may resist a finding of indigency and, with leave of court, cross-examine the defendant as to his representation of financial inability. In DeKalb and Muscogee Counties, too, the solicitor-general makes an independent inquiry, but there the results of the inquiry, coupled with a recommendation, are submitted to the judge before he undertakes his own questioning. In several counties the judges used the circuit probation officer as an investigator to make a preliminary report. In other counties the judge alone makes the inquiry. In two counties (Chatham and Ware) the defendant is provided counsel in all felony cases, whether he is indigent or not. In no county was indigency determined on the basis of any factor alone, although it was generally reported that the accused's own claim of inability to retain counsel was perhaps controlling, and usually resulted in appointment on that representation, with little more. Assumedly, judges are satisfied with their determinations. Of 26 solicitors questioned, 4 thought judges were too lenient in finding indigency; none thought they were too strict. One solicitor-general (DeKalb County) noted, however, that the effort of judges to be completely fair in this respect had been abused on occasion by defendants who treated the inquiry as a device for delaying trial.

In no county was the question of the defendant's being on bail anything more than a factor to be considered in determining indigency. The response, more often than not, was that indigency through loss of employment might well be assured if the defendant did not manage bail. In Cobb County, an industrial area, it was estimated by the solicitor-general that as many as 50% of the defendants admitted to bail were later able to show indigency and receive counsel by appointment. Other counties reported that from 5% to 10% only were later found indigent.

In all counties in Georgia, a determination that one accused of felony is indigent results in appointment of counsel for the accused by the court. If there be two or more defendants, jointly accused, whose interests may conflict, every judge interviewed indicated that he did, or would, appoint separate counsel for each individual defendant. Most judges represented that they made appointments from those whom they considered best qualified for the particular case. The usual source of appointees was the attorney then in court, although recourse was also made to other attorneys in the county or circuit known to the judge, or to a list of attorneys supplied by the local bar association. In all but Fulton and DeKalb Counties, appointments were spread as uniformly as possible among all attorneys in active practice; in those two counties selections were from those whose practice was primarily criminal law. Another exception is Muscogee County, where appointments are made from a list of attorneys under 35 years of age and of those who have been active in criminal practice. All judges considered whether the appointed lawyers were qualified as criminal law practitioners. One Fulton County judge makes an independent selection of counsel for each case, notifying the attorney, the defendant, and the solicitor-general of the appointment by letter. The defendant's letter informs him of the manner in which he can contact his counsel; the attorney's, of the time for trial, the offense, and other related matters then known by the court. If the indigent defendant be on bail, the bondsman is notified as well and informed of the time of trial. In Chatham County one judge has devised a unique system whereby a list of inmates in the jail who desire counsel is presented to the judge. The judge then appoints counsel from a list of voluntary defenders. The judge has expressed the opinion that this program works well in view of the large number of voluntary defenders on his list (over 50% of the active practitioners).

If the defendant can pay only a moderate fee, he generally is afforded an opportunity to select counsel; that failing, an appointment usually is made. One result of appointments is that the assigned counsel may receive from his client at least a nominal fee. If it be discovered after appointment that the defendant is not in fact indigent, counsel will be relieved in some jurisdictions. In two counties (Cobb and Peach), it was reported that payment of an attorney's fee in such a situation has been made a condition of probation. One judge (Chatham County) particularly felt that it was the duty of the lawyer to provide a defense, and that he never considered the matter of fees. Without exception, all judges indicated they would not appoint an attorney asked for by name by the indigent defendant.

It appears certain that no defendant is brought to trial on a felony charge without first having been afforded an opportunity to be represented by counsel. Indeed, this is a requirement of the state constitution. In every county surveyed it was found that the question of indigency was inquired into well before the defendant is called upon to plead. In Fulton and DeKalb Counties, no plea will be accepted by the court without the defendant's having first consulted with counsel, retained or appointed by the court. In other counties surveyed waiver of counsel is allowed, but only after the judge has at least informed the defendant that, if he be unable to afford counsel and desires one, the court will appoint an attorney for consultation or representation.

Compensation for appointed counsel is allowable in capital felony cases only, the maximum being $150. The judge determines compensation in each case, the payment being made from county funds. Expenses, as approved by the court after application by counsel, may be allowed in capital felony cases up to $500. It appears, however, that in lieu of such action the court usually directs that appearance of witnesses for the defendant, medical examinations, and the like, be procured at public expense. Normal costs of defense investigation and case preparation do not appear to be within the scope of expenses for which reimbursement is allowed. With respect to those cases in which compensation of counsel is authorized, it appears to be the general practice of judges to allow the maximum amount, irrespective of the extent of representation. This was repeatedly justified as ˙a sort of balancing of accounts for the uncompensated services in other cases.

The same court that tries felony cases in Catoosa, Cobb, and Walton counties also tries misdemeanors. In each of these counties indigent misdemeanants may have appointed counsel if desired. In Fulton, DeKalb, Chatham, and Muscogee counties, misdemeanors are tried in the county court. Except in Chatham County, it appears to be the general practice in county court to appoint counsel for indigents, although there is some variation depending upon the trial judge and the nature of the offense. As noted earlier, felony defendants in Chatham, Fulton, DeKalb, and Ware counties do not waive counsel by a plea of guilty but must consult with counsel, retained or appointed, before the plea is accepted by the court. In other counties surveyed, the plea of guilty is suggestive of waiver of counsel, but an opportunity therefor is nevertheless reportedly afforded in each case. In any case where counsel is appointed, for consultation or otherwise, that counsel is present for sentencing.

The counsel appointed for the trial continues into the appellate stage. However, if no appointed counsel served during the trial and an appeal is to be taken, the trial court may appoint counsel for the indigent appellant. Although statutory authority exists for compensation and reimbursement for expenses in capital felony appeals, no funds have been made available by the legislature for such purposes. Thus the court of appeals and the supreme court may certify counsel as eligible for compensation or reimbursement, but those bodies have considered their own operating funds insufficient to permit them to pay attorneys. A solution to this impasse has been suggested by a Fulton County judge: to charge such expenses back to the county wherein the trial itself was held. An indigent appellant, however, is provided with a transcript of the trial record at no expense.

An appeal is the almost exclusive postconviction remedy. No uniform practice exists for appointment of counsel in cases of habeas corpus, but it appears generally that such are not normally made.

C. OPINIONS OF THE JUDGES

The study began with an interview with Chief Justice Duckworth of the supreme court and included interviews with the presiding judge of the criminal division of the court of appeals and with superior court judges in all the sample counties. In Fulton County three judges were interviewed; in Cobb and Muscogee, two; and in each of the other sample counties, one. Additionally, the 31 judges in the other circuits were mailed questionnaires containing substantially the same questions as those raised in personal interviews, and 18 responded (58%).

In the questionnaires and interviews with the judges, each was asked at what stage in a criminal case, under an ideal system, he thought that an indigent person should first be provided with an attorney if he desired one. Of the 35 who answered, 11 specified a time after the filing of the indictment or accusation but before arraignment; 2 preferred the arraignment itself; 3 considered the preliminary hearing or soon thereafter, the proper time; 8, at first appearance before a magistrate or immediately thereafter; and 10, after arrest but before initial appearance. One judge "hedged" and expressed a preference for one time in capital cases and another in the noncapital felonies: for capital cases he preferred appointment at first opportunity after arrest; for other cases, at completion of the preliminary hearing. Eleven of those favoring appointment prior to indictment found a system unfair if counsel were not then provided, and all considered it unfair if counsel were not provided before the accused is called upon to plead. The opinions thus favor, two to one, under an ideal system, an initial appointment at an earlier stage than the prevailing practice, that is, appointment after a formal charge but before arraignment. None of the judges favoring a much earlier appointment than is presently the case considered that any significant financial problem would attach to a system involving such early appointments, one noting wryly that with more taxes anything could be done.

The judges also were asked, again under an ideal system, if they thought that an attorney should be appointed for an indigent in a variety of situations. [See Form VI, question 8 and Form VIII, question 7, in volume 1, pages 228, 238.] For the sentencing of a defendant on his plea of guilty or on conviction after trial, the judges, by a preference of nearly two to one, thought that counsel should then be provided. Objections to this position included the fact of prior waiver, the capacity of the judge alone to protect the interests of the accused, and, in the case of the defendant guilty by plea, the right of the accused to withdraw and change his plea before sentencing. In each of the other situations, the judges divided almost three to two favoring the appointment of counsel. Those in favor of appointment generally were so because of the impending deprivation of liberty or property of the defendant or respondent; those objecting, particularly as to sexual psychopath hearings and civil commitments of the insane, narcotics addicts, and alcoholics, conceded that their position was substantially because of the civil, rather than criminal, aspect of the proceeding, and they repeatedly expressed the fear that intrusion in these areas might tend to "socialize" further the practice of law.

While the prevalent attitude of the judges was that they could pass adequately on a question of revocation of probation without impinging upon any of the defendant's rights, a slight majority professed the desirability of appointing counsel. Those objecting to appointment tended to regard the matter as essentially one of judicial discretion alone; the proponents conceded that the defendant's cause might be aided where he faced possible penalties. A middle ground was voiced to the effect that probation is a matter of grace, but if the revocation be based upon a criminal act then counsel should be appointed. As to postconviction remedies, although the division of opinion was nearly even under the supposedly ideal situation, nearly all thought that the indigent's rights were better protected at the trial. One judge favoring appointment indicated that he preferred to pass on a petition drawn by an attorney than on that of a fellow inmate of the defendant! As already indicated, the practice is fairly general, where the superior court has exclusive jurisdiction of both felonies and misdemeanors, to appoint counsel for indigent misdemeanants. The division of opinion of the judges as to the necessity of appointment reflected their own practices. The judges divided evenly on whether it would be unfair to refuse appointment, one attitude being that the offenses were not so severely punished as to justify such a conclusion, and the other, that the defendant still faces relatively severe sanctions. Concerning the attention to be given to these several situations, in terms of appointments to represent indigents, the consensus was that the question of representation in felonies must first be satisfactorily resolved, particularly as to compensation in noncapital cases. General reservations were also expressed as to the propriety of more uncompensated demands on members of the bar, and of furtherance of the notion that the state should do all things for all people.

On the general question of appointed counsel for indigents, the judges from the smaller rural counties, as well as the appellate judges with earlier experiences in such areas, tended to regard the acceptance of an appointment by an individual attorney as a necessary incident of the attorney's status as an officer of the court: a duty to society owed by this privileged professional. The concern for compensation was token at best. In the larger counties, and especially those in metropolitan areas, the duty of the attorney was conceded by the judges interviewed, but with them there was a pointed concern for the absence or inadequacy of compensation, except in Chatham County, as mentioned earlier. The consensus of these judges was that the responsibility for protecting the indigent defendant was one to be shared by the community in terms of financial support, and by the attorney in the rendering of his services. In this respect there was no suggestion that appointed attorneys be compensated on a scale commensurate with fees of retained counsel, but there was the opinion, often expressed, that the general aversion to criminal practice by the average city practitioner was due in part to the inordinate demand on his time with no pecuniary return therefor.

Not one judge interviewed expressed any difficulty in obtaining attorneys to serve, although one (in Fulton County) did register concern over the limited number of experienced attorneys who made themselves available for appointment. All but five judges reported that fewer than 10% of the attorneys appointed ever asked to be excused from the case and that usually the reason given was a good one. The judges all indicated that the attorney was excused upon request for good cause. Two causes cited were the desire of the accused to try the case himself rather than to be guided by the advice of counsel, and the fact that the accused had earlier sought to retain the attorney ultimately appointed but had failed because of disagreement as to a fair fee.

Each of the 35 judges was asked to compare the appointed attorney first with retained counsel in a similar case, and then with the solicitor-general. Six of the judges thought their appointees performed better than counsel retained by the accused. The reason to these judges was obvious: they could pick an attorney better than the defendant! Nine judges considered appointees less able, chiefly because of youth and lack of experience, although one judge attributed the disparity in performance to the caliber of attorney usually available for appointment—the unemployed attorney, often present in the courtroom and receiving the appointment by default. Significantly, eight of the nine judges who found the appointees substandard in performance by comparison with retained counsel all came from, or derived their experience on, the bench in populous counties. The other 20 judges considered appointees generally equal to retained attorneys. In rating the appointed defender against his prosecuting adversary, only one judge regarded the appointee as generally superior to the solicitor-general. Eleven judges regarded the prosecutor as better qualified and more experienced. The other judges found the appointees compared favorably with the prosecutor as to ability and experience, one judge noting that his appointees gave the solicitor-general "a fit." All of the judges acknowledged that the appointees generally performed with energy and diligence, and five remarked that appointed counsel were usually better prepared than the solicitor-general, although not necessarily better qualified.

All judges interviewed expressed general satisfaction with the Georgia system of appointed counsel, but a few suggested that a public defender system, particularly for the populous counties, might be desirable. In commenting on a public defender system in any county in Georgia, one judge (Fulton County) cautioned that defendants might easily regard such an officer as just another courthouse official helping to convict the accused, or even as a part of the office of the solicitor-general. One voice only was raised in favor of a private defender program, financially supported by the bar, perhaps as salve for its conscience in its general neglect of, or aversion to, criminal practice.

The first affirmative step towards the development of a defender system in the Atlanta metropolitan area was taken by the Metropolitan Legal Aid Society when it appropriated $500 for the purpose of developing a proposal for a defender program in Atlanta. While no definite commitment to a particular type of defender system has been made, it has been indicated that the program would be one initially sponsored by the Atlanta Legal Aid Society, employing the services of two full-time attorneys and two full-time investigators, augmented by volunteer attorneys and a part-time psychiatrist. The defender office would be located in the Fulton County courthouse.

Of the judges questioned, their legal experience ranged from 10 to 44 years since admission to practice and their tenure on the bench from less than one year to 38 years. Other than the attitude earlier noted as to the duty of the bar to serve, even without compensation, there seemed to be no significant correlation of age, experience, or tenure to the opinions expressed by the various judges.

D. OPINIONS OF THE PROSECUTING ATTORNEYS

Eleven prosecuting attorneys were interviewed. They were from 11 different judicial circuits embracing 39 counties and more than half of the state's population. Years of practice of this group ranged from 10 to 29. Their time in office as solicitors-general ranged from less than 1 to 21 years. All but one (Walton County) devote their full time to the office and all spend at least 30 hours or more per week on the job. In Georgia, the solicitor-general normally has but a few civil responsibilities, and in none of the counties surveyed did these entail as much as 10 hours per week.

Additionally, 29 solicitors were mailed questionnaires containing essentially the same questions as the personal interviews, and 15 responded. These officials had from 12 to 42 years of legal experience and from 1 to 40 years in office. Only six of these devoted full time to their offices.

In but one circuit of the 26 from which responses were received did the solicitor-general unqualifiedly consider allotted funds adequate for proper functioning of his office, although all maintained that the job required was being done, but not as well as it might be. Three needed more clerical assistance (a pointed need in view of the relative inaccessibility of data and information for this project!), one also desired additionally to employ an accountant (Fulton County), and two considered an investigator an essential addition to their staffs. One (Chatham County) expressed the feeling that his office should be allowed to control the funds allocated to him. He felt that his investigating machinery and staff could be more functional if he were allowed to determine his own financial needs. Others bemoaned inadequacy of funds for travel, office supplies, and secretarial assistance, and there was a general expression of a desire to retain a staff investigator. Perhaps the most cogent and lamentable comment was this one: "I depend entirely on officers and private citizens. I have no assistant, no secretary, no file clerk, no help in office or courtroom."

There was general satisfaction with the current system of appointment, although several voiced displeasure with an apparent attitude of the bar to avoid any more association than necessary with criminal proceedings. Only in Fulton County was a public defender system suggested as a real possibility, and there and in only one other county the performance of appointed counsel was deemed unfavorable in comparison with retained counsel. The solicitor-general in Walton County echoed the sentiment of several judges that the judge was better at selecting counsel than the defendant.

No prosecutor's approval was required to subpoena defense witnesses for an indigent accused.

With respect to discovery of the state's evidence, opinion was divided. One group felt that the state was "entitled to its secrets," and that the defendant should have no right to access to information in the prosecutor's hands, at least not until ordered by the court. One did state that he produced confessions if he thought it would lead to a plea of guilty. Most of the prosecutors, however, were willing to cooperate with defense attorneys on matters within their knowledge. One voiced the wish that defense attorneys would cooperate as much with him! In regard to the principle of discovery, one solicitor-general liberally allows the practice of discovery if he is satisfied that the defense counsel is really trying to find the truth, as opposed to "fishing." Another allows discovery if the defense counsel "is a gentleman." A third readily discloses any evidence directly coming from the defendant. All but five of the others professed that they normally disclosed such things as confessions, written statements of witnesses, physical exhibits, and reports of expert witnesses which were in their possession.

No prosecutor wanted to try a case against an unrepresented defendant. Those who had done so reported that it was awkward and required them to lean over backwards to avoid prejudicing the jury. They also indicated that the court usually kept a tighter rein on proceedings and carefully watched out for the defendant.

The prosecutors divided markedly as to the time, in an ideal system, when counsel should first be appointed for an indigent defendant (see Table 1). It is significant to note that only three of the solicitors considered the "ideal" time to be that now prevailing in Georgia, that is, after indictment but before arraignment. Most considered it unfair if the defendant were not afforded counsel at the time he indicated as ideal. None foresaw any additional financial problem. The prosecutors' opinions were also elicited as to the desirability of appointing counsel for indigents in a number of other situations. By nearly three to one they felt that a man should have counsel even though he pleads guilty, and that such counsel should assist him throughout the proceeding. Those differing usually treated the plea as a waiver of counsel. A slight majority opposed the initial appointment of counsel for sentencing when the accused had been convicted after trial, the prevailing sentiment being that the defendant has had his chance.

The great majority favored assignment of counsel in cases involving revocation of probation, considering the proceeding to be essentially a continuation of the trial, although several treated this as a matter exclusively within the discretion of the judge. A majority by a proportion of three to two favored appointment in misdemeanors; and in sexual psychopath hearings, all but four considered counsel desirable. The majority, again by a three to two division, opposed appointment of counsel in postconviction remedies other than appeal, and in civil commitments. The reasons paralleled those of the judges, both pro and con. As a practical matter, each prosecutor opposed appointment in these situations either because of the "socializing" effect upon the profession or the additional burden placed on members of the Bar. Several voiced the opinion that a public defender could appropriately represent the indigents in these situations, not all of which were purely criminal.

No correlation was noticeable between opinions and factors of age, experience, or location.

E. OPINIONS OF DEFENSE ATTORNEYS

Of 85 attorneys drawn from the sample counties, 41 responded to mail questionnaires, expressing their attitudes towards the system of indigent representation under which they had practiced for periods ranging from 2 to 50 years.

Fourteen who were appointed in 1962, the year under study, to represent indigents had participated in 50 cases or more before the appointment. All had had some prior experience, only three having tried less than five cases. Of the 35 who received appointments, 14 were assigned to more than 10 cases during 1962. These recent appointees were asked to indicate the stage of the proceedings at which they were appointed in the last case handled. Only 8 entered the case prior to indictment, but 1 of these entered before first appearance before a magistrate; 6 were not appointed until the time of trial; and 17 began their appointment at arraignment on the indictment, or later. Five attorneys indicated they did not have time to prepare an adequate defense. All of these were appointed after indictment, all but one at arraignment or later. Of the 35 appointees 24 received no compensation for their services, which collectively, according to the attorneys' own fee appraisal, would have amounted to $11,000. The 11 who did receive compensation (the statutory limit of $150) would have charged $13,550 for their services. Four attorneys were reimbursed in full for their out-of-pocket expenses, and two in part.

When asked about the present system for representing indigents and whether it was fair to the defendant, the attorneys divided almost evenly, a narrow majority regarding it as unfair. The comments ranged from "more than fair" to "deplorable." The principal grounds of unfairness were the tendency of the defendant to want to plead guilty to avoid lengthy pre-trial incarceration, and the normally brief period available to the appointed attorney to prepare an adequate defense.

There was no such division of opinion, however, about the fairness of the system to defense lawyers. By more than a two to one majority, the attorneys expressed their dissatisfaction. The objections were not entirely based on want of adequate compensation, although this was certainly present. There was a sense of imposition in that the appointed attorney could not always prepare his case adequately, or because of concentration in legal areas where they did not really feel competent, both views relating to professional integrity and the duty of the attorney to render first-class service to his client, even a non-paying one. There was also some sentiment to the effect that assurance to the professed indigent that he would have counsel led to a reluctance on the "indigent's" part to seek counsel at his own expense.

Thirteen of the attorneys favored earlier appointment, comments ranging from "as soon as possible" to at least 30 days before trial. Those who indicated a precise time procedurally favored a time before indictment.

There was little sentiment for appointment in misdemeanor cases or in other cases where an indigent might desire counsel (e.g., civil commitments, habeas corpus). Most attorneys expressed financial unhappiness with the system as it now exists, without adding new areas of attorney responsibility. Payment in noncapital felony cases, increased compensation in felony cases, and reimbursement for out-of-pocket expenses in all appointments were favored improvements in the present system. Two lawyers favored a practice similar to an undefined one by which medical practitioners are compensated for their services.

Several attorneys favored a more careful inquiry into the fact of indigency, there being considerable opinion that the usual modes of inquiry were too casual or too reliant on the word of the defendant alone.

The mode of selection of appointees received scant attention, although several deplored the practice of appointing young and inexperienced attorneys without also naming an experienced associate. Several also thought the judges should confine their appointments to those in active criminal practice.

Only six of the attorneys volunteered an opinion that a public defender system should be initiated. To these this approach answered most of the evils of present appointment practices, imposition on attorneys, and inadequate compensation.

F. COMPARISONS AMONG JUDGES, PROSECUTORS, AND DEFENSE ATTORNEYS

The survey disclosed differing attitudes among judges and prosecutors. These are summarized in Table 1.

TABLE 1

Views of Judges, Prosecutors, and Defense Attorneys

	Judges	Prosecutors	Defense attorneys	Total
Number responding	35	26	41	102
Ideal stage for first appointment of counsel:				
1. Between arrest and first appearance	11	6	0	17
2. At first appearance	7	5	0	12
3. Between first appearance and preliminary hearing	1	3	0	4
4. At preliminary hearing	1	6	0	7
5. After preliminary hearing, but before indictment	2	1	0	3
6. After indictment but before arraignment	11	3	0	14
7. At arraignment	2	1	0	3
8. No answer*	0	1	41	42
Is present compensation of lawyers adequate?				
Yes	13	12	0	25
No	16	14	25	55
No answer	6	0	13	19
Should out-of-pocket expenses be paid?				
Yes	26	22	20	68
No	0	3	0	3
No answer	9	1	21	31

*Answer does not conform to above tabulation.

G. DOCKET STUDY

Although a docket study was made in eight counties, as shown in the tabulation in Section A supra, the available information was so fragmentary in four of them that no meaningful tables could be constructed. (For the method of conducting the docket study see volume 1, pages 178-179.) In none of the counties was it possible to ascertain what percentage of defendants was released on bail or what the amounts of bail were. In none of the counties was it possible to get information about the proportion of defendants who had committal (preliminary) hearings. (The test for reporting was whether the information was available for 80% or more of the sample cases.)

Information about whether defendants charged with felonies had counsel was available for three counties, as shown in Table 2. The proportion of defendants without counsel was 8% in Catoosa, 22% in Cobb, and 85% in Walton. The most frequent assignment of counsel occurred in Catoosa, where 9 out of 12 defendants who had counsel had assigned counsel.

Table 3 shows dispositions of cases in four counties and a weighted percentage for the state as a whole, taking into account the limited information from the other four counties. For all the counties together 66% of the defendants pleaded guilty to the principal offense and 5% pleaded to lesser offenses. Also 21% of the cases went to trial, resulting in 14% convictions of the principal offense, 4% convictions of lesser offenses, and 3% acquittals. Most of the other cases had been dismissed or were still pending at the time of the survey. The highest percentage of guilty pleas was in Walton County (90%), while Cobb had 83%, Fulton had 65%, and Catoosa had only 38%.

Table 4 shows the sentences, if any, imposed in the four counties, with projected state-wide figures. For the state as a whole, an estimated 68% of the felony defendants were sentenced to prison, including county jail. Among the four counties the figure ranged from a low of 61% in Fulton to 73% in Cobb. Cobb also had the most frequent use of probation and fines. If a defendant had a combination sentence, such as fine and probation, he was counted under each heading. Walton and Fulton Counties had considerable numbers of defendants who drew suspended sentences without probation.

TABLE 2
Retained and Assigned Counsel in Felonies
Georgia, 1962

County	Total sample No.	Did defendant have counsel? Yes No.	%	No No.	%	Retained No.	%	Assigned No.	%	Combination or type unknown No.	%	No data No.	%*
Catoosa	16	12	92	1	8	3	23	9	69	0	0	3	19
Cobb	41	25	78	7	22	9	28	8	25	8	25	9	22
Walton	20	3	15	17	85	0	0	2	10	1	5	0	0

* % under no data refers to total sample; % in other columns refers to cases where data were available.

TABLE 3
Disposition in Felony Cases
Georgia, 1962

County	Total sample	Plea guilty	Plea lesser offense	Dismissed	Found guilty	Found guilty lesser degree	Acquitted	Mental commitment	Pending	Stet*	Other
Catoosa	16	5	1	3	5	1	1	0	0	0	0
Walton	20	16	2	0	1	1	0	0	0	0	0
Fulton	107	74	2	1	6	2	5	2	10	5	0
Cobb	41	34	0	0	5	1	0	0	0	0	1
Weighted total percentages		66	5	5	14	4	3	1	3	1	0

*Held on inactive docket.

TABLE 4*
Sentencing in Felony Cases
Georgia, 1962

County	Total sample	No sentence		Prison		Probation		Suspended sentence		Fine		No data		Miscellaneous combinations	
		No.	%	No.	%	No.	%	No.	%	No.	%	No.	%†	No.	%
Catoosa	16	4	25	11	69	3	19	0	0	0	0	0	0	0	0
Cobb	41	0	0	29	73	12	30	0	0	10	25	1	2	0	0
Walton	20	0	0	14	70	4	20	2	10	4	20	0	0	0	0
Fulton	107	21	20	65	61	19	18	11	10	9	8	0	0	3	3
Weighted total percentages			11		68		21		5		13		1		1

*If a defendant had a combination sentence, such as prison and fine, he is counted under both columns. Thus the total is more than 100%. The last column is cases of combination sentences that were not specified in the returns.
† % under no data refers to total sample; % in other columns refers to cases where data were available.

H. CONCLUSIONS AND RECOMMENDATIONS

1. The present impasse between the appellate courts and the legislature as to compensation for assigned counsel in appeals from conviction of capital felonies must be resolved. The statutory authorization for compensation and reimbursement for expenses should be implemented either by adequate appropriation of funds for these purposes to the appellate courts or by an authorization to counties to expend their own funds for this representation.

2. The authority for compensation and reimbursement for expenses, now available only in capital felony cases, should be extended to all criminal cases tried before the superior court, the judge thereof being granted discretion within the limitations now prescribed to determine the precise amount. The state or counties should be authorized to make the disbursement. Such an approach would permit individual circuits, and the judges therein, to continue or extend their present practices as desired, and at the same time distribute the social and constitutional obligation between the community and the legal profession.

3. Legislation should be enacted to authorize counties so desiring to establish an office of public defender, supported wholly by public funds, to be disbursed by the county affected.

4. In counties having county courts, such courts should by legislation, if necessary, be given sole authority for courts of inquiry or committal hearings for charges of felony. Further, it should be provided that the judges of such county courts shall have the power to appoint as counsel for an indigent accused of felony any attorney licensed to practice in that county.

5. In counties having no county courts, it should be provided, by legislation if necessary, that the magistrate before whom one accused of felony and determined upon inquiry by the magistrate to be indigent appears, shall, upon finding of indigency, suspend the proceedings, if so requested by the defendant, until the judge of the superior court of that county shall appoint counsel for the accused. The magistrate should not be precluded from allowing bail upon the charge alone, if it be bailable, and such should be authorized to prevent unnecessary restraint of an indigent. Provision should be made for speedy communication by the magistrate to the superior court judge.

6. The infinitely varied system of record keeping, such as it is, should be considerably overhauled to permit gathering of intelligible information for use by interested agencies of the legislature and the bar. Standardization of docket entries, or even case summaries, should be attempted, and some central source in each county should be designated.

7. There should be a system of screening the purported indigents to determine the verity of their claim of indigency. This need is particularly evident in the counties which do not permit any felony defendant to waive counsel. (In these counties it appears that the percentage of indigents greatly exceeds that in those counties which do not afford counsel so readily.) The success of this screening process would ease the burden on the appointed attorneys by diminishing the number of cases in which they are involved, thus enabling them to give more time to their indigent clients and to afford them better representation.

HAWAII

Daral G. Conklin, Honolulu

The small size of the state allowed the reporter to gather data personally and to conduct interviews, neither of which would have been possible without the cooperation that was found among all judges, lawyers, and clerks who were consulted, interviewed, or polled. No one person or staff can be singled out. The response was excellent.

A. INTRODUCTION

Hawaii, with a 1963 population estimated at 709,000, is composed essentially of six islands, the largest in size being Hawaii, and the largest in population being Oahu, where the state capital, Honolulu, is located. Each island is a county, except that one county, Maui, is composed of three islands, Maui, Molokai, and Lanai, these being in close geographic proximity.

Each county corresponds to a judicial circuit. Each judicial circuit has at least one judge presiding in the circuit court, the court of general trial jurisdiction. The circuits are divided into districts, each of which has at least one magistrate. Each county has an elected county attorney who is both prosecutor and civil counsel for the county, except on Oahu, where the offices are separate and appointive.

The counties selected for study were the city and county of Honolulu, embracing the whole of the Island of Oahu, and the county of Hawaii. The city and county of Honolulu, essentially urban, has about three-quarters of the entire state population; Hawaii County essentially rural, had a 1962 population of about 60,000, but is about six times larger in size than Oahu. A docket study was made for Honolulu.

B. CRIMINAL PROCEDURE AS IT AFFECTS INDIGENT PERSONS

Jurisdiction to return indictments and try felony cases is vested exclusively in the circuit court.

Most felony cases begin with the arrest of the suspect. Because Hawaii in 1960 adopted, with slight modification, the Federal Rules of Criminal Procedure, the suspect is required to be taken "without unnecessary delay" before a magistrate. The magistrate is always a lawyer; he almost always informs the suspect of the nature of the charge, the right to counsel, and the right to a preliminary hearing[1]; and the magistrate sets bail according to a schedule set by the circuit judge currently[2] handling the felony calendar. The schedule of amounts of bail is relatively stable from year to year.

Throughout Hawaii, the formal charge against the defendant is by grand jury indictment. In the city and county of Honolulu, however, it is occasionally by information filed with the defendant's prior consent. Although the Oahu grand jury is in continuous session, the time between arrest and indictment is longer than in the county of Hawaii: for Oahu the period is usually two to four weeks; for Hawaii, one to two weeks. In both counties, however, the period between indictment and arraignment is almost always one day and rarely more than three days.

By state law, only the circuit judge may appoint counsel for an indigent defendant and then only in felony cases pending in the circuit court. Since a felony case is not pending in the circuit court until an indictment has been filed, the effect of the law is that bail is rarely altered for an indigent before his indictment, and counsel can never be appointed for him until he is indicted.

Appointment of counsel varies somewhat between the two counties surveyed. In the city and county of Honolulu, the circuit judge generally asks the defendant if he wants an attorney and goes on to explain that counsel will be furnished gratis if the defendant lacks funds. In the county of Hawaii, the explanation is not made unless and until the defendant states that he does want counsel, but in capital cases, the Hawaii county judge will insist upon and immediately appoint counsel, at arraignment.

The determination of indigency also varies between the two counties: on Oahu, the judge's determination of indigency is usually based upon questions put to the defendant in open court together with the receipt of a signed affidavit of indigency, and often the judge may ask for an investigation and report on the defendant's financial resources by the Adult Probation Department.[3] In the county of Hawaii, only the series of questions by the judge is generally used.[4]

Compensation for appointed counsel is fixed by law: minimum $100 and maximum $250 in ordinary felonies; minimum $250 and maximum $750 in felonies punishable by more than 20 years' imprisonment.[5] There is no reimbursement for defense counsel's costs nor provision for defense investigation, and no further fee is provided if there is an appeal, although by law a full record on appeal is provided at state expense.

C. OPINIONS OF THE JUDGES

In Honolulu, since the felony calendar is rotated annually, it was considered appropriate to interview the three circuit judges who handled felonies for the years 1961 through 1963. Both judges in the county of Hawaii handle felony cases, so they were interviewed together.

All of these five judges[6] felt that under an ideal system counsel for an indigent should be appointed at the stage between arrest and first appearance, but all felt that an "ideal" system could hardly be practical. Four of the five felt that the lack of appointment at that stage would "not necessarily" be unfair to the defendant, and one said that it would. All felt that a public defender system, financed at the state level, would be beneficial.

All five judges stated that they tried to appoint the best defense counsel available. None has had any difficulty in getting lawyers to serve, and all felt that appointed lawyers generally compared quite favorably with the prosecutor. Four of the five judges believed that present rates of compensation for appointed lawyers are adequate,[7] but one stated they are "not adequate if trial is had," and three of the judges qualified their approval of the statutory fee schedule by remarking that there should be additional compensation on appeal and reimbursement for counsel's out-of-pocket expenses.

A questionnaire was mailed to the circuit judge of each of the two counties which were not surveyed. Both responded, and their views were similar to those of the judges personally interviewed, except that one of the judges responding by mail felt that present rates of compensation for appointed counsel are inadequate. Both judges thought the ideal stage for appointment of counsel was at arraignment on the indictment.

D. OPINIONS OF THE PROSECUTORS

The prosecutor for the city and county of Honolulu devotes full time to his job and has a staff of 13 attorneys. His office processes almost 500 felonies each year and about 200,000 misdemeanors, including traffic offenses. On the other hand, the Hawaii county attorney devotes most of his time to civil duties for the county and has a legal staff of three. He does not have what could be considered a serious crime problem, which is probably typical for many rural areas in the United States.

Despite this wide difference in size and scope, the similarity of their responses was quite dramatic.[8] Both thought that appointed counsel were generally equal to their staff attorneys, and both felt that the present method of selection of, and rates of compensation for, appointed counsel are adequate. Both agreed with the judges that under an "ideal" system, appointment of counsel should take place between arrest and first appearance, but both stated that such a system would not be practical. Both suggested that counsel should be appointed for indigents in certain unspecified types of misdemeanors and that the determination of indigency should be more carefully made. Both approved of the concept of a public defender system, financed at the state level by taxation.

Questionnaires were mailed to and answered by the prosecutors of the two counties that were not surveyed. Their responses were similar to the foregoing, except that neither felt that counsel for indigents was necessary in any misdemeanor cases, and both stated that the present methods for determination of indigency are "about right." One responded that present compensation for assigned counsel is inadequate, and the other agreed, where there was a "protracted trial." One thought that the appointment of counsel at the time of first appearance before a magistrate would be ideal and "within practical limits," although the other believed that the present system in Hawaii (appointment at time of arraignment) was sufficient.

E. RESPONSES OF DEFENSE ATTORNEYS

This part of the survey is based upon a questionnaire mailed to attorneys in Honolulu, each of whom had served as appointed counsel at least once in 1962.[9] Questionnaires were mailed to 30 attorneys, of whom 22 responded.[10] No attempt was made to canvass the entire bar of either of the selected counties.

Of the lawyers responding, 72% were satisfied that they had been appointed in time to represent the accused adequately, and only 40% said that lawyers should be appointed at an earlier stage of the case; 63% thought that the present system for appointment of counsel is fair to the indigent, but only 45% that the present system is fair to the lawyer; 72% felt that appointed counsel should be compensated for out-of-pocket expenses, and 54% said that lawyers should be paid more for their services.

F. DOCKET STUDY

A study was made of the court docket in Honolulu, consisting of a check for the year 1962 of cases involving 50 out of a total of 486 defendants. (For details on the method used see volume 1, pages 178-179.)

The docket study revealed that, among 48 defendants for whom the information was available, 15 had retained counsel, 17 had assigned counsel, and 14 had no counsel. The other two had different kinds of counsel at different times or had counsel but the records did not disclose whether retained or assigned. Twenty out of 49 defendants were officially found to be indigent, while 19 out of 50 were not released on bail, which is another indication of indigency. Eight of the defendants were white, 2 were Negro, and 36 were of other races (for four there was no information).

Preliminary hearings were held in only 8 of the 50 cases, having been waived in 40. In the other two cases the reason for omitting the hearing was unknown.

Of the 50 defendants, 41 pleaded guilty to the principal offense charged, none pleading to a lesser offense. Eight cases went to trial, resulting in four acquittals, three convictions of the principal offense and one of a lesser offense. Eighteen of the defendants were sentenced to prison, 26 were placed on probation (a relatively high proportion compared to other states), and one was required to pay a fine only. The other five were not sentenced.

G. CONCLUSIONS AND RECOMMENDATIONS

On the basis of the foregoing, the following conclusions and recommendations can be made:

1. Indigent defendants in Hawaii are represented by competent counsel, and no serious problem with regard to the defense of indigents exists in the state.

2. The present system for appointment of counsel to defend indigents is considered adequate.

3. Judges and prosecutors believe that a public defender system would be beneficial. However, if such a system is adopted, a full-time defender probably would not be needed in any county except the city and county of Honolulu, which probably would need more than one.

4. The methods of determining indigency vary from county to county and among individual judges and should be made more uniform.

5. If the assigned counsel system is retained in Hawaii, counsel should be reimbursed for out-of-pocket expenses and for certain costs of investigation, and they should be compensated for appeals.

6. If the assigned counsel system is retained in Hawaii, existing law should be amended so as to permit the circuit judges to appoint counsel at an earlier stage of the case than is presently allowed.

[Editor's note: since this report was written, the legislature in June, 1965, enacted a law authorizing each circuit to establish a public defender office on a local-option basis.]

NOTES—Hawaii

[1] As indicated by the docket study for Honolulu, almost all suspects without counsel waive preliminary hearing; the majority who do have counsel also waive.

[2] The first circuit (i.e., the city and county of Honolulu) has eight circuit judges, and the

felony calendar is rotated among seven of them annually. The eighth judge is in the juvenile court.

[3] But each of the Oahu judges apparently carries out or utilizes this procedure in an individual fashion.

[4] This is somewhat to be expected, since in the smaller and more rural community, the judge tends to be more familiar with the background of persons brought before him.

[5] Hawaii abolished capital punishment in 1957.

[6] All of them have been admitted to practice more than 17 years, and all of them had criminal law experience before taking the bench.

[7] Of the lawyers polled, 54% disagree.

[8] The two gentlemen interviewed were of different ages, ethnic groups, backgrounds, and experience. One is elected, the other appointed. Their respective offices and jurisdictional limits are on islands separated by 250 miles of open sea, inter-island travel being almost always by air. It is doubtful that they see each other more than a few times each year.

[9] Names were selected at random from vouchers showing payments to appointed counsel. Over 50% of the responding attorneys have been in practice more than 10 years; over 50% had handled 50 criminal cases or more prior to 1962; and only one has been in practice less than 6 years.

[10] Some of the responding attorneys are engaged in politics, but every one of the attorneys who did not respond holds political office, holds an appointive position, or actively participates in politics.

IDAHO

Eli Rapaich, Lewiston

The American Bar Association Committee for Idaho consisted of Sherman F. Furey, Jr., chairman, Salmon; Frank E. Chalfant, Sr., Boise; Cope R. Gale, Moscow; James B. Green, Pocatello; and James T. Knudson, Coeur d'Alene. The cooperation and assistance received from the persons interviewed, the bar, and the clerks of the various courts were most gratifying.

[Editor's note: since the following report was written, the Idaho legislature in 1965 adopted a statute (§ 19-803A) authorizing appointment of counsel for indigent defendants at the preliminary examination, on request of the defendant. The magistrate postpones the proceedings and notifies the clerk of the district court, who arranges for the district judge to appoint counsel. Such counsel are to be compensated.]

A. INTRODUCTION

Idaho had a population of 667,191 in 1960. The state is divided into 44 counties, which are organized into 13 judicial districts. All but four of Idaho's counties have populations of under 50,000, and these four have populations of less than 100,000. Each district has one or more district judges, and each county has its own prosecuting attorney. The counties selected for survey are shown in the following tabulation.

County	1960 population in thousands	Location in state	Remarks
Ada (D)	93	West central	State capital, agricultural-commercial center, state prison
Bear Lake	7	Southeast	Agricultural, phosphate mining and processing
Bingham (D)	28	East central	Agricultural, food processing, affected by Arco Atomic Energy installation, state mental hospital, Indian reservation
Cassia	16	Southwest	Agricultural, food processing
Nez Perce (D)	27	North central	Agricultural, pulp-paper-lumber manufacturing, commercial center, Indian reservation

(D) indicates that a docket study was made. Bingham County was substituted for Custer County because of the small number of criminal cases (8) in Custer County. Both are in the same region of the state.

The counties visited are an excellent cross section of Idaho geographically, economically, politically, and socially. Although the largest ethnic group is of north European extraction, there are substantial numbers of Indians, Basques, and Spanish-Americans, the latter being itinerant farm workers. Protestants,

Catholics, and Mormons were well represented in the counties surveyed. In considering the indigent defendant in Idaho, one should bear in mind that the state is not rich in terms of per capita income, that salaries of district court judges and prosecutors are modest, and that some counties have less than 1,000 people and few or no lawyers. In such counties the condition of the county roads is more important to the county commissioners than the economic condition of a defendant. Additional data about the counties surveyed follows.

County	Felony defendants, 1962	Lawyers in private practice	% of indigents estimates by judge	% of indigents estimates by prosecutor	% of indigents who waived* estimates by judge	% of indigents who waived* estimates by prosecutor
Ada	120	179	90	85-90	20	60
Bear Lake	12	2	80	50	60-75	90
Bingham	63	8	50	75	60	50
Cassia	42	14	46	75	45-50	40-50
Nez Perce	40	35	Refused Estimate	60		

*The survey reveals annual fluctuations in the number of requests for counsel by indigents. Some of this fluctuation can be attributed to the fact that in a particular period the county jail may be the lodging place of one of those gentlemen referred to as "jail house lawyers." On the other hand, this is really a very minor offset against the practice formerly prevalent in at least one of the counties surveyed, in which it was made known to the defendant that if he asked for counsel he was going to do much more "dead time" before going to trial, and it would likely be easier on him if he pleaded guilty rather than force the county to undergo the expense of a trial. This, and other practices of a similar nature, make an excellent practical argument that counsel should be appointed at the earliest possible stage in a criminal proceeding. These practices have a tendency to work to the detriment of a first-time offender who is inexperienced in the workings of the law. The experienced defendant is not swayed by jailhouse rumors. It is the reporter's experience as a defense attorney and a deputy prosecutor that the "con" never asks for a trial unless he is either innocent or thinks he has a very good chance of "beating the rap." The prosecutors personally interviewed indicated that this was also their experience.

B. CRIMINAL PROCEDURE AS IT AFFECTS INDIGENT PERSONS

The district court has general civil and criminal jurisdiction. Justice of the peace courts have jurisdiction over assault and battery, petit larceny, and minor criminal offenses where the maximum penalty is six months in jail or $300 fine or both. Justice courts also issue warrants and act as committing magistrates in felony cases. The probate court has concurrent jurisdiction with justice courts in criminal matters. The Supreme Court has appellate jurisdiction and original jurisdiction to issue the extraordinary writs, including habeas corpus.

Justices of the peace and probate judges need not be lawyers, and few of them are. They are compensated by salary rather than a fee system. Until four years ago justices were elected, but at that time the office was made appointive. The power to appoint rests in the county commissioners, but an appointee must be approved by the district court judge and the probate judge. District court judges have, wherever possible, used this power to cause the appointment of lawyers only. The work done by these legally trained justices has been excellent.

IDAHO

It is not always possible for the district court judge to use this power, however, because some of the counties have either no attorneys or only one attorney, and he is the prosecutor.

In practice most arrests for a felony are made under the authority of a warrant issued by a magistrate upon the complaint of a peace officer or other prosecuting witness. The arrested person is taken before the magistrate, who is required to inform him of the charge against him and of his right to the aid of counsel, and must allow reasonable time and assistance to the accused person in retaining counsel. (Idaho Code §§ 19-514, 19-801.) No provision is made for appointment of counsel for indigent persons in the magistrate's court.

The reporter's opinion, based on the interviews with judges, prosecutors, and members of the bar, and his own experience, is that most lay magistrates do not know what these rights are and do not appreciate the intricacies of the procedure laboriously arrived at through the centuries for the protection of a criminal defendant's rights. Most lay magistrates proceed on the assumption that the defendant would not be there if he were not guilty and that the sooner the defendant gets his just deserts the better. Like the general public, the magistrates are shockingly naive about the workings of the criminal law. They tend to see the process as the "good guys against the bad guys," and there is seldom any doubt about who falls in which category. A high percentage of these lay magistrates exhibit a very active and open hostility toward lawyers in general. They feel that defense counsel are "meddling" in something that is none of their business and appear for the sole purpose of "getting rich."

In those jurisdictions where the magistrate is a lawyer, the defendant is adequately advised of his rights with two possible exceptions: (1) the language used is often beyond the comprehension of the defendant and (2) the advantage of being represented by counsel is not fully explained. These two items become important in view of this recent language of the Supreme Court on what constitutes a waiver:

> Waiver is defined as the voluntary relinquishment of a known right. Thus, the accused not only must voluntarily manifest his intention to waive his right or rights but it must clearly appear that he is completely aware of the nature of the charge against him and is competent to know the consequences arising from his waiver of these rights. In this connection this court will indulge every reasonable presumption against a waiver of fundamental constitutional rights, and will not presume acquiescence in their loss. Davis v. State (Okla.) 368 P.2d 519. (State v. Thurlow, 85 Idaho 96, 375 P.2d 996 [1962]).

There would appear to be no undue delay in bringing most defendants before the magistrate for the defendant's initial appearance. The time element involved here is not really meaningful. The more cogent question is: how long was the defendant in police custody before he was actually arrested, formally charged with a crime, and fully advised of his rights?

The magistrate also sets bail except in capital cases. The amount of bail appears reasonable in the counties surveyed, except in Nez Perce, where the amount is uniformly very high. In most instances the district court does, upon proper motion, reduce the bail fixed by the committing magistrate. But this is a hollow right for the defendant who does not have counsel to prepare the necessary motions and orders, and the practice is to appoint counsel only at a later stage. Except in Ada County most bail is in the form of a property bond. A professional bondsman has an office in Ada County, and the docket study reveals that many defendants used his services.

As a practical matter the amount of bail fixed is of no consequence to most indigents. They cannot afford a bail bond, have no cash collateral of their own, and cannot find two property bondsmen. Under Idaho law the bondsman must have property, *over and above that which is exempt from execution by law*, in double the amount of the bail fixed. The statutory exemption is $10,000 on real property plus additional amounts on personal property.

Prosecutors did not appear to play much part directly in fixing the amount of bail except in cases where they wanted, for a variety of reasons, to keep the defendant confined. Indirectly, however, a prosecutor, perhaps not the incumbent, has likely had a hand in suggesting the amount of bail for various offenses. Lay magistrates are universally inclined to take the prosecutor's advice on all aspects of a criminal proceeding, including bail. In some instances the prosecutor is the only attorney in the county and may well be the only lawyer the magistrate knows. This again points to the need for representation by counsel at the earliest possible stage in the proceedings.

A preliminary hearing is held by the magistrate if requested by the defendant. The study indicates that the hearing is waived by most defendants who do not have counsel, but is invariably requested where the defendant has counsel.

Of the five district court judges who were personally interviewed, three make a regular practice, upon proper motion, of sending a case back for preliminary hearing where the defendant waived the preliminary or conducted his own defense at the preliminary. The fourth would do so for good cause shown. The fifth refuses to do so on the grounds that there is no statutory basis for such a practice. The other judges agree with this latter view but feel that they have the inherent power to remand since they are charged with the duty of protecting the defendant's rights.

Most of the prosecutors will not conduct a preliminary hearing where the defendant is not represented by counsel. The prosecutors feel not only that this is not fair to the defendant, but that it (1) may save the state money that would be expended on an unnecessary trial, (2) may dispose of cases the prosecutor did not really want to prosecute anyway, and (3) makes a better record on appeal.

Preliminary hearings held before lay magistrates leave much to be desired. Most of them are not able or willing to understand the fine distinctions that the criminal law draws and, if they do, their sympathies are with the prosecution. Unless one has had the experience of listening to an almost illiterate man read a criminal complaint to a defendant, the inherent viciousness of the lay magistrate system cannot really be appreciated. To this must be added the heartbreak of a "judge" turning to the prosecutor for rulings on questions of evidence and subsequently conferring with him privately on what the "judge's" decision ought to be. The prosecution actually has to reveal very little since the magistrate generally has a preconceived opinion that a crime was committed and that there is reasonable ground to believe that the defendant committed it.

As a consequence, the preliminary hearing in Idaho is often used as nothing more than a vehicle for causing the state to divulge at least part of its case.

It is to the credit of the majority of Idaho prosecutors that they will have no part in such practices and always seek to file their complaints before the best magistrates available to them.

In the district court the prosecution can be by indictment or information, but the general practice is by information. This reporter knows of no case prosecuted by indictment in the recent past.

After the filing of the information the defendant is arraigned before the district court. The code (§ 19-1512) provides:

> If the defendant appears for arraignment without counsel he must be informed by the court that it is his right to have counsel before being arraigned, and must be asked if he desires the aid of counsel. If he desires and is unable to employ counsel the court must assign counsel to defend him.

The trial court must make it clear that the defendant may have counsel appointed for him at the expense of the county if he is unable to pay for such services himself. *State v. Thurlow*, supra. The defendant may withdraw a plea of guilty at any time.

In this reporter's opinion four of the five judges personally interviewed thoroughly advise the defendant of his rights. The district judges have had a problem in that until the *Thurlow* case neither the statutes nor the court decisions provided any real guidance as to what the court should advise the defendant. Moreover the judges have had no satisfactory method, other than questions in open court, to determine the economic status of a defendant.

Many of the judges do a good job in selecting and rotating appointed counsel. In one of the counties surveyed, however, almost all the 1962 cases were assigned to the two newest members of the bar. One case was a capital case. Fortunately, both counsel were zealous and qualified members of their profession and performed excellent services for the defendants.

Compensation to appointed counsel is paid by the county, the district judge allowing such amount as he deems reasonable. In four of the five counties surveyed the court follows the minimum bar schedule, which allows $150 for an appearance and $150 a day for trial. In one of these counties the court allows only about one half the bar schedule for lengthy cases. In the fifth county the judge uses his own judgment. He has authorized fees from $50 to $1,000, the latter being for two counsel in a capital case. The adequacy of the amount of the fee awarded should not be judged against the bar minimum, but rather against the fact that in Idaho an experienced and competent lawyer in the bigger cities will not accept a felony case for less than a $500 retainer and, if the case goes to trial, the fee is $1,000 or more, with corresponding increases for more serious felonies and capital offenses.

Counsel is usually not provided for an indigent at sentencing, on either a plea of guilty or a conviction, even though when suggested by either party a hearing is held on circumstances in aggravation or mitigation of the punishment (code § 19-2515).

Since Idaho statutes do not provide for appointment of counsel for an indigent felon on appeal, competent appointed counsel in trial court will always perfect the appeal by filing the requisite notice, then advise the defendant to retain counsel or request appointment of counsel from either the district court or the supreme court. Some of the district courts have taken the position that they do not have the power to appoint counsel on appeal, since the statutes provide only for appointing counsel at the trial level. The supreme court has taken the position that the district courts can appoint counsel on appeal but has not promulgated a rule authorizing such appointments. The statutes provide for a full transcript and record at public expense upon the filing of the required affidavit of indigency by the defendant.

Writs of habeas corpus must be filed either in the supreme court or in the district court in the county where the defendant is incarcerated. This means that counsel for a convicted felon would often have to travel at his own expense to Boise, since the state prison is located there. No funds are available for payment of counsel for appeal or habeas corpus proceedings.

C. OPINIONS OF THE JUDGES

District judges in Idaho are elected for a four-year term on a nonpartisan judicial ballot. Their salary is $12,000 per year. All 13 senior district judges in Idaho were contacted, 5 personally. The tenure in office of these judges varies from a year to 15-19 years. They have been members of the Idaho bar from a minimum of 11 years to a maximum of 46, with an average of almost 25 years. Most of them have had an extensive private practice, and many of them have been prosecutors.

The judges with the shortest tenure uniformly favored appointment of counsel at an earlier stage than the present practice of appointing counsel at arraignment on information. Of the two judges with the longest service, one expressed satisfaction with the present system and the other merely stated that each case was dependent upon its own facts, declining further comment. The docket study in his county reveals the highest percentage of waivers of counsel by indigents of the five counties surveyed. Of the remaining 11 judges, 5 were of the opinion that counsel ought to be appointed between arrest and first appearance before a magistrate, 4 said that counsel should be appointed no later than the first appearance before a magistrate, and 2 between first appearance and preliminary. Ten judges thought that unless counsel were appointed at the stage designated, it was unfair to the indigent, two said not necessarily unfair, and one said not unfair.

Twelve of the judges thought that the system they recommended could be financed. One judge made no comment. The majority of the judges who commented felt that the financing should be on a county level by tax levy. Another suggestion was that part of the district court filing fees could be allocated to such a fund.

Two of the judges favoring appointment at an earlier stage commented as follows:

> 1. The possibilities of unfairness are frightening. Whether there is unfairness or not is a moot question. I dislike to see anyone accused of crime come into court without counsel. They often don't know what their rights are and what they are waiving. This is particularly true in a felony case.

186

2. The preliminary hearing is a very important process for the defendant. It is an important device for his protection under our system. This is particularly true in the absence of grand jury process.

In commenting on the question of unfairness another judge stated:

In our area, where the justices of the peace and other magistrates tend to accept the arresting officers' words verbatim, counsel should be provided so that the facts can be examined into and the case dismissed if need be.

This judge, a former prosecutor, pointed out the danger involved where an overzealous police officer tends to twist the facts when perhaps he does not have a case at all.

This judge reflected the view of the majority of the judges contacted when he pointed out that the assigned counsel system generally functions quite effectively in Idaho in the rural counties. The bar seems to accept responsibility without objection, and the services rendered are apparently uniformly good.

The majority of the judges personally interviewed, however, felt that in the urbanized areas some form of public defender system would be preferable. As one judge stated, the big problem in the assigned counsel system is often that of selecting competent counsel: the judge must not only request counsel to defend an indigent but also make certain that he does an adequate job. Sometimes the counsel may be offended by the court's criticism of his efforts, and this, the judge thinks, tends to create a split between the bench and the bar.

As to providing counsel in various cases and proceedings in an ideal system, the younger judges were again, by heavy preponderance, in favor of providing counsel in all of the categories listed under Question 8a, Form VI, and Question 7a, Form VIII. (For forms see volume 1, pages 228, 238.) However, four of the five judges personally interviewed were not in favor of counsel at sentencing, either where the defendant had pleaded guilty or where he had been convicted after trial, whereas seven of eight responding by mail thought that a defendant who had pleaded guilty should have counsel at sentencing, and six of eight thought he should have counsel if he were convicted after trial. On providing counsel for habeas corpus proceedings and other such postconviction remedies, the judges were in favor 10 to 2. Four of the judges personally interviewed favored appointment of counsel for hearings on revocation of probation, at least in some cases, and one was opposed. Of the 13 judges, 7 favored appointment of counsel for misdemeanors and 6 did not. All but one judge favored counsel for the commitment of the mentally ill. Throughout the state the probate courts, which have jurisdiction of competency hearings, appoint counsel almost invariably.

The majority of judges thought it would be unfair if the defendant did not have representation in the proceedings outlined above. It should be remarked, however, that the question whether something is fair bears several possible interpretations and is not a simple one to answer.

One judge responded that many defendants plead guilty out of mistaken belief and for that reason should have counsel when sentenced. He went on to comment, as to the other stages mentioned, that "our whole legal system needs interpretation at every stage of the proceedings—even the judges and attorneys become confused!"

187

One of the judges personally interviewed, whose thinking seemed to be in line with the majority of judges, stated that the defendant should not reach the point of sentencing either on a plea of guilty or after trial without having had counsel. In regard to hearings on revocation of probation he said, "I require my probation officer to file an affidavit setting out the alleged acts of violation. If the defendant denies them, then I would appoint counsel and have a hearing in any questionable case."

The views of the judges on financing appointment of counsel for the various stages under discussion reflected their views on financing the appointment of counsel at an earlier stage in the criminal proceedings. The philosophy of one judge toward the whole matter was succinctly and revealingly expressed when he said, "If we had nothing else to finance, it might be possible. Anything free is over-used." He went on to comment that some of the defendants who appeared before him were indigent, "but all would be if they got free legal advice."

The survey revealed that the judges are well aware of the fact that many of the criminal defendants who appear before them are indigent. Their average estimate is that 70% are indigent. They are further aware that a large percentage of defendants waive counsel: they estimate 45%. The docket study revealed too little information to say how many are indigent and how many waive counsel.

Idaho judges do not appoint a particular lawyer requested by an indigent, except possibly a lawyer who was retained at the preliminary hearing. If two defendants have conflicting interests most judges readily appoint two attorneys. The judges are not inclined to be sympathetic to a defendant's objections to appointed counsel. One judge recited an experience where the "indigent" fired appointed counsel and retained counsel of his own. The defendant was tried and convicted.

In arriving at a reasonable fee the judges have two distinct practices. Where counsel has done little more than make an appearance, there is a fixed fee and the judge will orally discuss the nature of the services rendered with counsel. In cases where considerable time and effort have been expended the court will ask for an itemized statement, generally in affidavit form. They always ask for an affidavit where counsel alleges that he has incurred out-of-pocket expenses.

All of the judges agree that counsel appointed for indigents should be compensated, but they disagree as to the amount. Almost all the judges consider the recommended state minimum bar schedule and some of them follow it explicitly. The opinion of the older judges on adequate fees is illustrated by the comment of one of them: "We don't make such practice attractive in fees."

The general opinion of the judges is that appointed counsel are adequately compensated. By this they do not mean that appointed counsel are paid enough for the services rendered, but rather that the bar should perform such service partially as a public service. Furthermore, their concept of adequacy is related to the size of the county budget.

All but one judge felt that counsel should be compensated for out-of-pocket expenses, and this judge thought that "it is part of their civic responsibility—if it becomes burdensome it should receive some consideration." However, he would provide counsel between arrest and first appearance before a magistrate, as well as under each of the categories under Question 7a, Form VIII. The judges feel that appointed counsel are as good as, or better than, retained counsel. One judge pointed out what the reporter feels to be a truism: that most of the bar considers an appointment as an obligation of the highest order and, as a consequence, renders a service commensurate therewith. The survey reveals that under 10% of counsel appointed ask to be excused and that those who do ask generally have good reason.

The judges feel that appointed counsel are as competent as the prosecutors— and perhaps more so. One judge took the position that most prosecutors are at the mercy of the defense attorney, but it should be noted that this judge is characterized by his bar as a "prosecuting judge."

Four of the judges personally interviewed will readily order compensation for counsel representing an indigent where an indigent can afford to pay only a small fee. The county pays the difference between what the client can pay and the usual counsel fee for cases of indigent defendants.

The question of what constitutes indigency has not really been considered in Idaho. There is no liaison between the district court and welfare agencies. The method generally used for determining indigency is to ask the defendant questions in open court. Some of the judges do get assistance from their prosecuting attorneys, but these judges are equally divided in their opinion as to the effectiveness of the assistance given. All of the judges expect appointed counsel to make a thorough investigation of the defendant's economic status and report to the court if they find that he is not indigent.

The judges, as a whole, do not consider the resources of parents or relatives, or even a spouse, in determining whether they will appoint counsel. As they point out, they really have no way of making these parties pay. On the other hand, the judges, as a general rule, seem to consider the various asset tests contained in Question 18b, Form VIII, and Question 9d, Form I. As one judge pointed out, it doesn't do much good to consider wages because the average defendant is in jail and can't work and, if he can afford bail, he can generally afford counsel. This same judge advanced what is probably as good a test of indigency as any presently in use in Idaho: "You can just about tell by looking at them."

Actually, a very basic question is, "Can the average Idahoan afford a properly conducted felony defense trial?" The cost would be considerably more than one half of the average per capita annual income in the state.

D. OPINIONS OF THE PROSECUTING ATTORNEYS

The state's attorney in Idaho is an elected official called the prosecuting attorney. His territorial jurisdiction is limited to one county which he represents in all civil and criminal affairs. Of the 44 prosecutors 5 were interviewed in person and 39 were contacted by mail. The response was 100%.

The average Idaho prosecutor has been a member of the bar for 14 years and has held his position as prosecutor for from 5 to 9 years. In only two of the counties is his position full time. The average prosecutor works between 20 and 30 hours per week in his official capacity.

The salary of prosecuting attorneys is fixed by the legislature, based on the population of the county served. Several of the prosecutors of the smaller counties pointed out how inadequate their salaries were. Some were less than $2500 per year. The prosecutors say that in small counties they do as much work as a prosecutor in some of the larger counties because in those he has one or more assistants.

Thirty of the prosecutors (68%) said they did not have adequate funds to run their offices. Almost all of the prosecutors must rely upon law enforcement agencies to do the investigative work connected with prosecutions. This work is often done so poorly that the prosecutor is very seriously handicapped. Frequently this results in complaints being filed which would never be filed if the prosecutor had a trained investigative staff of his own. Even in counties where an investigative fund is provided, the prosecutor can use it only with the approval of the district court.

Ten of the prosecutors thought that the ideal stage for appointing counsel would be between arrest and first appearance before a magistrate; 8, that the appointment should be at the first appearance before a magistrate; 11, between the first appearance and the preliminary hearing; 3, at preliminary hearing; 3, after the filing of the information; and 9, at the arraignment on the information. Thus all but 9 of Idaho's 44 prosecutors are in favor of appointing counsel at some stage prior to that presently provided by law, and the vast majority favor appointment of counsel at the preliminary hearing stage or well before.

It should be noted that many of the comments by these men stress the word "ideal" in Question 8a, Form IX, because of the practical problem of providing funds. Twenty-seven of the prosecutors were positive that a system providing for earlier appointment could be financed and only four were sure that it could not. In response to this question one mail respondent said,

> We have cases where commission of offense by defendant is so clear that no rights are lost if defendant is not represented prior to first appearance—in others where there is any question of commission of offense and of defendant's innocence then earlier representation is indicated.

One cannot but question this man's understanding of the essence of our criminal system.

Like the judges, the prosecutors were asked about providing counsel in miscellaneous proceedings under an ideal system. The responses were equally divided on the question whether counsel should be provided at the sentencing of a defendant who pleads guilty without counsel, but they favored, 22 to 16, providing counsel at the sentencing of a defendant who had been tried. Likewise, the prosecutors were closely divided, 22 answering "yes," and 19, "no," on the question of providing counsel during proceedings to revoke probation. More than 75% were in favor of providing counsel for proceedings concerning habeas corpus and the mentally ill, but only 39% favored providing counsel at the misdemeanor stage. Many of them pointed out the problem of financing appointments at this level, although for the other proceedings the great majority thought the problem of financing could be solved.

A heavy majority of the Idaho prosecutors thought that assigned counsel compared favorably in experience and ability with retained counsel. A number of them thought that assigned counsel were often the very best attorneys in their bar and were often more zealous than retained counsel. One prosecutor pointed out that his judge had a tendency to appoint only newly admitted attorneys. Only four prosecutors thought that assigned counsel did not compare well with retained counsel.

The prosecutors responding by mail estimated that 65% of the felony defendants were indigent and that of these indigents 52% waived counsel. The estimates of the prosecutors personally interviewed appear in the second tabulation in Section A above.

Although the prosecutors agreed that appointed counsel should be compensated, there was an interesting variety of opinions as to what the compensation should be:

Nominal fee	3
Bar schedule minimum fee	9
Reasonable fee	6
50% of regular fee	11
Time basis	1
$15-$25 per hour	1
$10 per hour	1
At same rate as prosecuting attorney is paid	2
No comment	5

One prosecutor stated,

> Definitely yes. I believe they should receive compensation at the regular bar schedule for their area. The lawyer is using this means of livelihood and should not be required to discount his charges any more than a grocer should be required to discount his charges for food to persons on relief.

Of the prosecutors personally interviewed, two thought the fees of appointed counsel were adequate and two thought not. One of the latter suggested that a statutory standard should be set. Two thought that the appointed counsel should be compensated in part only since he is rendering a public service. Two felt that the recommended fee schedule should be followed subject to the discretion of the court to fix fees after considering the amount of work done, the type of case, the quality of the work, and the county budget.

Of the prosecutors contacted by mail, 24 thought that appointed counsel received adequate fees, and 11 thought they did not. The feeling of the many members of the Idaho bar was well expressed by one of the prosecutors:

> Our present rates are not adequate, but I feel that the lawyers in the local bar are satisfied with them insomuch as they recognize the financial situation of the county government. They may not be entirely adequate, but a lawyer who represents an indigent defendant knows he will be paid.

Those answering the question were unanimously of the opinion that counsel for indigents should be compensated for out-of-pocket expenses. However, 17 of those responding by mail gave no answer on this question.

Idaho prosecutors state they are quite liberal in disclosing such things as confessions, statements of witnesses, reports of expert witnesses, and exhibits to defense counsel. The experience of the reporter and other lawyers is that many prosecutors will disclose at least a part of their file, particularly if they have a good case. An equal number of prosecutors will disclose only what the statutes and decisions require under a very limited criminal discovery procedure.

Most lawyers with any amount of criminal experience feel that Idaho needs a liberal criminal discovery procedure. There is nothing just, let alone fair, about appointing counsel to represent an indigent under a system that does not provide appointed counsel with funds to make an investigation and then denies him the information available to the prosecution. It is well to remember that all lawyers are officers of the court and that appointed counsel can be very well characterized as a semipublic official. Fortunately, many of the district court judges ameliorate some of the harshness of this situation by readily remanding cases for preliminary hearing once counsel is appointed.

Prosecutors are often maligned for a situation that is not of their own making. In the first instance, they have to avoid the pitfalls of those decisions holding that there must not be undue delay in criminal proceedings, and at the same time they must not violate the rule that a defendant must be given a reasonable time to protect his rights instead of being "shanghaied." If the prosecutor escapes the thrust of this legal horn, then he must avoid the other horn of the dilemma, which is that the prosecutor should never file a complaint unless he has made a thorough investigation and has good cause to believe that a complaint should be filed. All of this he must accomplish without falling afoul of the decisions that sharply caution him about talking to the accused because such conversations, often had in good faith and in an effort to help the defendant, may end up being labeled "coercion" and are often grounds for castigation, if not reversal. Many a prosecutor who is serious about his duty to protect the public and at the same time protect an innocent person really has a difficult problem here, particularly since he often cannot rely upon investigations conducted by police authorities of limited competence. It is for these reasons that the prosecutors overwhelmingly favored the appointment of counsel at an early stage in the proceedings.

E. OPINIONS OF DEFENSE ATTORNEYS

In the five sample counties questionnaires were mailed to 25 attorneys who were appointed to represent indigents in 1962, and 20 responded. They had been members of the bar for an average of 12½ years, and were appointed to represent an average of 3 indigents each in 1962. Two of the counsel were appointed on capital cases. These appointed counsel had tried an average of 22 criminal cases prior to being appointed to represent indigents in 1962, and all of them had had some experience in criminal practice prior to being appointed.

The responses showed that 8 of the 18 counsel who answered this question were appointed prior to the arraignment on information even though an indigent felon is not entitled by law to appointment of counsel before the arraignment. This indicates that the judges are actually appointing prior to the arraignment on information, in accordance with their views that this is desirable. Of the 18 appointed counsel, 12 thought they were appointed in time to represent the accused adequately, 5 thought they were not and 1 stated that it was questionable that he was appointed in time.

All but one of the appointed counsel were compensated for their services, but only seven were reimbursed for out-of-pocket expenses, and they were paid in full.

Appointed counsel stated that they would have charged their clients from $100 to as high as $20,000 for the services rendered. The latter fee was in an extremely complicated and lengthy first-degree murder case in which counsel had well over $1000 out-of-pocket expenses. His diligence in and toil on the case exemplified the highest standards of the bar. Except for this case, appointed counsel would have charged, had they been retained, an average of $475 plus expenses. This is a straight across-the-board average with no distinction between cases where counsel merely made an appearance and those where the defendant was tried. The average fee counsel would have charged for a trial was well in excess of $750 plus expenses, again excluding the one large fee.

Although appointed counsel thought by 12 to 8 that the present system was unfair to indigent felons, 12 out of 18 said they were appointed in time to represent the accused person adequately. It might well be that in the particular case involved appointment was made in due time, but that counsel thought the system was generally unfair. Eleven appointed counsel thought the system unfair to lawyers and eight thought it fair.

On the question of what changes they would recommend, 14 appointed counsel thought that the appointment should occur before the preliminary examination, 13 thought that lawyers should be paid for out-of-pocket expenses, 14 thought that lawyers should be paid more for their services, 6 thought that counsel should be appointed in additional kinds of cases such as serious misdemeanors, and 8 thought the system of selection of appointed counsel should be improved. Only one volunteered a recommendation for the public defender system.

One counsel stated that he felt the most important change was to "provide for indigent defendant's release from jail without expense of bond so he can help prepare case and make best impression at trial."

Another expressed a view widely held by appointed attorneys that since they are, in effect, acting as public officials they should be "entitled to full disclosure of prosecutor's case and have cooperation of officers in completing a full and fair investigation of both sides of the case. Additional investigative aid should be provided when necessary." It is a disquieting experience to willingly accept appointment, and then find that the judge is not the least bit liberal in allowing counsel to examine the state's file or, in the alternative, remand the case for preliminary hearing.

Several appointed counsel stressed the fact that in their jurisdictions competent and experienced attorneys were not always appointed. One said:

> Under the system now in use in this county lawyers are theoretically assigned by the judge's going down the list of the members of the bar. Many are not interested and most are not familiar with the criminal practice. Often this results in a poor representation for the indigent. However, this system is better than the former system where the judge usually assigned lawyers sitting in courtroom or hanging around the courthouse.

These tended to be practitioners who didn't have much practice and were at the courthouse hoping to be assigned defense of an indigent for the small fee involved. This probably resulted in poorer representation for indigents than is the case under our present system.

A factor not considered by the survey is the extent to which lawyers have represented indigent felons either gratuitously or for the most nominal fee. It is well known that many criminal defendants from the police court on up receive such assistance. At least two 1962 defendants were represented in very complex cases completely gratuitously on appeals to the supreme court and in the prosecution of all the extraordinary remedies allowed. This practice is not at all uncommon in the Idaho bar.

F. COMPARISONS AMONG JUDGES, PROSECUTORS AND DEFENSE ATTORNEYS

The survey reveals that judges, prosecutors, and appointed counsel are overwhelmingly of the opinion that the great majority of accused felons are indigent and that counsel should be appointed prior to the present stage of appointment in Idaho, which is at arraignment on the information. Most of them feel that this appointment should come no later than the preliminary hearing and many of them feel that it should come well before.

These men feel that it is unfair to the defendant to be denied the protection that counsel can give him throughout the early, and often vital, stages of criminal proceedings. They base their views on their experience that the criminal law is a technical thing both in procedure and in substance.

Likewise, a majority of these men feel that, except in the case of a misdemeanor, counsel should be provided for the indigent defendant in proceedings other than felonies. Their view on misdemeanors is that, although counsel is necessary and important, it is questionable that Idaho could finance a system of appointment.

Their majority opinion is that lawyers under Idaho's assigned counsel system are not adequately compensated, and with one exception all thought that a lawyer should be paid for out-of-pocket expenses.

The majority of judges, prosecutors, and appointed counsel felt that indigent felons are being adequately represented, that assigned counsel are doing a good job, and that the present assigned counsel system should be extended beyond its present scope, but that the system is unfair (1) to the appointed attorney in that he is not properly compensated and (2) to the attorney and to the indigent defendant in that neither funds nor facilities are provided to make the type of factual investigation necessary for a first-class criminal defense.

The question then is to what extent the bar should be called upon to subsidize the protection of civil rights in Idaho.

G. THE DOCKET STUDY

A study was made of the court dockets for sample felony cases in three of the five sample counties for the year 1962. (See volume 1, pages 178-179, for methods of research.) Results are summarized in Tables 1 to 5 below.

A considerable number of defendants had no counsel at all, as shown in Table

1. In Nez Perce County 69% of the defendants had no counsel, in Bingham 48%, and in Ada 33%. The projected figure for the state as a whole, based on a weighted average of these three counties, was 49%. Where defendants did have counsel, about half were retained and half were assigned.

Table 2, showing the frequency of release on bail, indicates that some defendants who were unable to make bail—usually a test of indigency—did not have counsel. This is because the percentage of defendants who were not released on bail is higher than the percentage who had counsel. In Nez Perce 84% of the defendants were not released, in Ada 64%, and in Bingham 52%, with a projected state-wide figure of 67%. This is rather high compared with other states.

Table 3 indicates that the great majority of defendants waived the preliminary hearing in all three of the counties, the state-wide average being 87%.

Dispositions of the sample cases are shown in Table 4. The projected state average shows that 84% of the defendants pleaded guilty, including 2% who pleaded to lesser offenses. In the few cases that went to trial all the defendants were convicted.

Table 5 shows the sentences, if any, that were meted out. The three counties vary quite widely in the relative frequency with which probation is granted in relation to sentences of imprisonment (including county jail). Probation is more common than imprisonment in Bingham, somewhat less common in Nez Perce, and much less common in Ada. (A few defendants in Bingham and Ada Counties who had a combination sentence are counted under more than one category, but the pattern is still clear.)

TABLE 1
Retained and Assigned Counsel in Felonies
Idaho, 1962

County	Total sample	Did defendant have counsel? Yes No.	%	No No.	%	Retained No.	%	Assigned No.	%	Combination or type unknown No.	%
Nez Perce	19	6	31	13	69	3	16	3	16	0	0
Ada	45	30	67	15	33	17	38	12	27	1	2
Bingham	21	11	53	10	48	5	24	6	29	0	0
Weighted total percentages			51		49		27		24		1

H. CONCLUSIONS AND RECOMMENDATIONS

1. The survey revealed that well over half the defendants charged with felonies were indigent and that of those charged a high proportion waived the appointment of counsel. These figures surely tend to substantiate the long held and often valid public opinion that there is no justice for the poor man. One is led to suspect that the reason the matter has gone on as long as it has with-

TABLE 2
Frequency of Release on Bail of Felony Defendants
Idaho, 1962

County	Total sample	Yes No.	%	No No.	%
Nez Perce	19	3	16	16	84
Ada	45	16	36	29	64
Bingham	21	10	48	11	52
Weighted total percentages			33		67

TABLE 3
Frequency of Preliminary Hearings in Felonies
Idaho, 1962

County	Total sample	Yes No.	%	No, waiver No.	%
Nez Perce	19	2	11	17	89
Ada	45	7	16	38	84
Bingham	21	2	10	19	90
Weighted Total percentages			12		87

TABLE 4
Disposition in Felony Cases
Idaho, 1962

County	Total sample	Plea guilty	Plea lesser offense	Dis- missed	Found guilty	Found guilty lesser degree	Ac- quitted	Pend- ing	Other
Nez Perce	19	15	0	1	1	0	0	1	1
Ada	45	37	1	3	2	0	0	1	1
Bingham	21	17	1	0	2	0	0	0	1*
Weighted total percentages		82	2	4	7	0	0	3	2

* No data.

out a drastic upheaval is that the average indigent criminal defendant is a second class citizen economically and socially, and that he is from a stratum of our society that generally has very little political power. This does not allow us to escape the truism that the system is only as good as what it does for the least one of us; nor the further truism that the failures of the judicial system are laid to "you lawyers" and that, as a result, the bar has lost prestige in the public eye.

2. The survey further revealed that there was no uniform practice in Idaho

TABLE 5*
Sentencing in Felony Cases
Idaho, 1962

County	Total sample	No sentence No.	%	Prison No.	%	Probation No.	%	Sentence pending No.	%	Fine No.	%
Nez Perce	19	4	21	9	47	6	32	0	0	0	0
Ada	45	6	13	31	69	9	20	1	2	0	0
Bingham	21	1	5	8	38	11	52	1	5	1	5
Weighted total percentages		13		52		34		2		2	

*If a defendant had a combination sentence such as imprisonment and probation, he is counted under both columns. Hence the totals are more than 100%.

for determining the eligibility for the appointment of counsel. Appointment is left exclusively to the discretion of the judge. A concerted study is needed to determine what standards should be applied in determining indigency. The standard should be prescribed in either a statute or a rule of the Supreme Court, preferably the latter.

3. The system for selection of counsel for indigents is not uniform, but appears to function moderately well. Some thought should be given, however, to the right of the indigent defendant to inquire into the experience and qualifications of his counsel. The general thinking of the Idaho district judges who were personally interviewed is that the defendant should not have this right. Fortunately, most of our judges do pick qualified counsel, but that fact does not restore the life or liberty of the defendant who did not have competent counsel.

It is recommended that each local bar association provide the judge with a list of its members qualified to conduct a criminal defense, and that counsel so appointed should have the right to request an appropriate committee of the bar association for the bar's assistance.

Furthermore, the Idaho bar should consider the establishment of a specialized criminal bar whereby those who want to hold themselves out as competent to practice criminal law should pass a state bar examination strictly confined to the criminal practice. It is from a list of lawyers who pass this examination that the district judge should appoint counsel. As an alternative the state bar would do well to undertake a program for the reform of the criminal code and the institution of some form of continuing legal education in criminal law with particular reference to the impact of federal decisions. Some judges revealed that they had taken little cognizance of the federal decisions in the area of a defendant's right to counsel.

4. There is little uniformity in the compensation received by appointed counsel throughout the state. A minimum fee should be established jointly by the Supreme Court and the state bar, with the maximum fee to be discretionary with the trial judge, but subject to review by the Supreme Court.

5. Funds must be made available for reimbursement of the costs of investigation and preparation of the trial. If funds are not made available for investigation, state-financed investigative facilities should be.

6. The system of keeping the dockets in Bingham and Ada Counties is excellent and should be examined by the district clerks of other counties.

ILLINOIS

Donald C. Dowling, Chicago, and John Yantis, Shelbyville

The A.B.A. Associate State Committee consisted of Thomas P. Sullivan, Chicago, chairman; Richard K. Bates, Danville; David E. Bradshaw, Chicago; James P. Chapman, Chicago; Marvin S. Lieberman, Decatur; Thomas F. Railsback, Moline; Jerold Solovy, Chicago; Robert B. Oxtoby, Springfield; and Morris J. Wexler, Chicago.

A. INTRODUCTION

Illinois had a population of 8,712,176 in 1960. The state is divided into 102 counties, 20 judicial circuits, and 5 Supreme Court judicial districts. Each judicial circuit has at least three circuit judges, depending upon the population of the circuit. With the exception of Cook County, the judicial circuits are roughly equal in population but unequal in area. In addition to the circuit judges in each circuit, associate circuit judges are assigned to assist the circuit judges. The number of associate circuit judges depends upon the population of the judicial circuit.

On January 1, 1964, the judicial amendment to the Illinois constitution came into effect. Under the amendment a far-reaching consolidation of the previously complex judicial system in the state has been accomplished. Prior to January 1, 1964, Illinois had a variety of trial courts, i.e., circuit and superior courts, county courts, probate courts, city and municipal courts, justice of the peace and police magistrate courts, and family and juvenile courts. All of the trial courts of Illinois in existence prior to the amendment have been consolidated into circuit courts sitting for each of the 20 judicial circuits in the state. All of the data in this report were gathered prior to the effective date of the new judicial article; however, the data gathered are fully consistent with the present criminal practice.

Each county has its own elected prosecuting attorney, known as state's attorney. The public defender system works in conjunction with the assigned counsel system in those counties which have elected to adopt the public defender law in their county under the statutory option granted to counties by the legislature. In counties which have not adopted the public defender law, only the assigned counsel system is in operation. A public defender is appointed by the resident circuit judge for the county.

The counties selected for survey in Illinois are presented in the table on page 200.

B. CRIMINAL PROCEDURE AS IT AFFECTS INDIGENT PERSONS

Jurisdiction to return indictments and to try felony cases is exclusively vested in the circuit courts. Typically, felony cases commence with the arrest of the suspect, promptly followed by a hearing before a judge or a magistrate. Occasionally a felony case starts with a grand jury investigation and direct indictment of an accused person who has not been arrested. If the felony case cannot be disposed of by either entry of a plea of guilty to a lesser charge, i.e., a misde-

199

County	1960 population in thousands	Location in state	Remarks
Cook	5130	Northeast	Chicago and environs
DuPage	313	Northeast	Adjacent to Cook County, farming, metropolitan
Will	192	Northeast	Farming, manufacturing, state penitentiary branch (Joliet)
Piatt	15	Central	Farming and light manufacturing
Madison	225	West central	Mississippi river county, manufacturing, industry
Sangamon	147	West central	State capital, commercial center
Peoria	189	North central	Manufacturing, industry

meanor, or by discharge, the defendant will either be bound over for action of the grand jury, or he will waive indictment and consent to the filing of an information.

At the time the defendant is bound over to the grand jury by the preliminary hearing judge or magistrate, or at the time the defendant consents to the filing of an information in lieu of indictment, bail will be fixed by the presiding judge according to the circumstances of the individual case. The indigent defendant who is unable to make bail is held in custody until he is arraigned upon the indictment or information in the circuit court. The practice of proceeding by information in lieu of indictment is almost never followed in Cook County, largely because the grand jury is in constant session in Cook County except for a short period during summer, and because the state's attorney of Cook County uses the grand jury as an investigative and preparatory device. Moreover, because counsel is not appointed until the arraignment, it is easier to obtain an indictment than it is to arrange for an effective waiver of indictment and filing of an information. Outside of Cook County, particularly in the smaller counties, the great majority of felony prosecutions are initiated by information upon waiver of grand jury indictment. This is largely because in smaller counties it is easier to arrange for appointment of counsel before indictment than it is to arrange for convening of the grand jury. In almost all counties other than Cook, the grand jury is called into session only three or four times a year for a few days at a time.

In the criminal division of the Circuit Court of Cook County (previously the Criminal Court of Cook County) counsel is provided to the indigent defendant when he is first brought into court for arraignment upon the indictment(s) filed against him. All indictments in Cook County are returned for arraignment thereon before the presiding judge of the criminal division. The typical indigent defendant will be brought to court for arraignment with perhaps 50 other inmates of the county jail. He will await his turn for arraignment in a jail area immediately adjacent to the courtroom. When his case is called he will appear before the presiding judge without counsel. The judge will ask him: "Do you have a lawyer?" If he answers "no," the judge will then ask: "Do you have money to hire a lawyer?" If the defendant says he does not, the court says: "Then I appoint the public defender to represent you." Whereupon the public defender assigned to the courtroom of the presiding judge will automatically acknowledge receipt of a copy of the indictment(s), waive formal reading of the indictment and enter a plea of not guilty on behalf of the defendant, bail having been fixed already on the prior return of the indictment. The presiding judge will then transfer the case to one of the judges assigned to the criminal division in the criminal court building. The defendant is immediately transported to the trial judge for setting a trial date and other proceedings in the case. An assistant public defender assigned to the courtroom of the trial judge will then meet the defendant he will represent.

Alternatively, the indigent defendant may inform the trial judge at the arraignment that he desires counsel other than the public defender, in accordance with his statutory right. Or the defendant may demand counsel other than the public defender after the case has been assigned to a trial judge. In either event, the judge before whom the request is made will continue the case in order to arrange for appointment of counsel.

In Cook County, as one might expect, the tremendous case load of the criminal division of the circuit court imposes a substantial responsibility on the bar to represent indigent defendants who demand counsel other than the public defender. A small group of the Chicago bar has accepted this responsibility willingly and effectively. The Chicago Bar Association has for many years maintained a Committee on Defense of Prisoners comprised of volunteer lawyers, until January 1, 1964, unpaid except in capital cases, who accept appointments to represent indigent defendants. This committee remains on a stand-by basis with the criminal division of the circuit court. Whenever a lawyer is needed to represent an indigent defendant who demands counsel other than the public defender, or in those cases where the public defender finds it impossible to represent the defendant (e.g., where a conflict of interest exists between co-defendants), the trial judge almost always contacts the secretary of the bar association committee (a full-time employee) who will in turn contact a committee member willing to accept the appointment. This system in Cook County has effectively supplemented the public defender system in providing counsel for indigent accused persons.

Prior to January 1, 1964, lawyers appointed to represent indigent defendants generally received no compensation for their services except in capital cases, where the statute allowed a fee not to exceed $250. However, in many counties outside of Cook, local practice had provided for payment of a fee to lawyers appointed in noncapital felony cases. These fees generally ranged from $50 to a maximum of $150, set by the trial judge either on his own motion or upon the filing by the appointed lawyer of a verified statement of services rendered. These fees were paid out of the county treasury.

On January 1, 1964, the Code of Criminal Procedure of 1963 became effective in Illinois. The new provision relating to counsel is hereafter set out. Section 49-4 of the Code provides:

(a) Every person charged with an offense shall be allowed counsel before pleading to the charge. If the defendant desires counsel and has been unable to obtain same before arraignment the court shall recess court or continue the cause for a reasonable time to permit defendant to obtain counsel and consult with him before pleading to the charge.

(b) In all noncapital cases if the court determines that the defendant is indigent and desires counsel the Public Defender shall be appointed as counsel. If there is no Public Defender in the county the court shall appoint counsel from among members of the bar. Upon filing with the court of a verified statement of services rendered the court shall order the county treasurer of the county of trial to pay counsel other than the Public Defender a reasonable fee stated in the order not to exceed one hundred fifty dollars ($150.00) for each defendant represented.

(c) In capital cases if the court determines that the defendant is indigent and desires counsel the court shall appoint one or more experienced and competent counsel from among members of the bar. Upon the filing with the court of a verified statement of services rendered the court shall order the county treasurer of the county of trial to pay counsel a reasonable fee stated in the order not to exceed two hundred fifty dollars ($250.00) for each defendant.

(d) In capital cases, in addition to counsel, if the court determines that the defendant is indigent the court may, upon the filing with the court of a verified statement of services rendered, order the county treasurer of the county of trial to pay necessary expert witnesses for each defendant reasonable compensation stated in the order not to exceed two hundred fifty dollars ($250.00) for each defendant.

The determination of indigency in Cook County generally consists of two questions in open court, asked by the judge: "Do you have a lawyer?" And if not, "Do you have funds with which to hire a lawyer?" The prevailing attitude of the Illinois judges toward the determination of indigency reflects the practice most often followed: if the defendant has not made bail by the time of arraignment, and if he says he is unable to hire a lawyer and wants one, then the court assumes that the defendant is indigent and freely appoints counsel for him. If the defendant were financially able, it is assumed, he would most probably have secured his release on bail and have retained his own attorney. The trial judges generally are not concerned with whether relatives of a defendant are able to employ counsel for the defendant because there is no legal obligation upon relatives to hire an attorney for him, regardless of the degree of kinship. However, rather common factors considered by many judges in determining indigency are employment of the accused and whether he owns an automobile or other valuable property.

The practice in the counties surveyed reveals a general hostility toward permitting a defendant to waive counsel. Although the defendant is usually asked whether he desires to have counsel appointed for him, in many counties counsel will be appointed for the indigent defendant whether he wants one or not. One judge, however, said that in 1962, 100% of the indigent defendants who came before him waived counsel. In Cook County it is the practice to appoint a lawyer in all cases. If a defendant in Cook insists upon trying his own case

202

he may do so, but even then the court probably will appoint counsel to remain in court with the defendant as an adviser if the defendant finds he needs one as the trial progresses. As one state's attorney commented, the state much prefers to try a case against a defendant with a lawyer than against a defendant pro se.

Almost all indigent defendants in Illinois are held in custody, having failed to make bail. The new Code of Criminal Procedure of 1963 directs trial courts to release an accused on his own recognizance when the circumstances indicate that the accused will appear in court as required. This provision is new. If it is applied by the trial judges as the legislature has directed, i.e., liberally, it can be expected that many defendants heretofore unable to make bail will be released pending the disposition of the charge against them. Other important new provisions of the Code of Criminal Procedure are those pertaining to bail. In lieu of the practice of posting 10% of the amount of bail with a professional bondsman as a premium for a surety bond, a defendant may now post 10% of the amount of bail with the clerk of the circuit court, 90% of which will be returned to the defendant if he performs the conditions of his bond. To illustrate, a defendant whose bond is set at $5000 may post $500 with the clerk. If he performs all of the conditions of his bond, $450 will be returned to the defendant at the conclusion of the case. Thus, the premium for bail bonds has been effectively reduced from 10% to 1%. It can be supposed that the new bail provision will encourage persons such as relatives to post bond for defendants. The amount refundable at the conclusion of the case might be applied toward payment of fees for retained counsel.

C. THE DOCKET STUDY

Tables 1 to 5 indicate the results of the docket study in 1962 on the kind of counsel in felony cases, the percentage of indigency, the frequency of release on bail of felony defendants, the dispositions of cases, and the sentences imposed. (Details of the method of conducting the docket study appear in volume 1, pages 178-179.) The figure at the bottom of each table is a projected state-wide total based on the weighted average of the figures for the sample counties.

Table 1 shows whether defendant had counsel and if so, what type of counsel. Only in Sangamon and Piatt Counties were any significant number of defendants without counsel. For the state as a whole, at least 40% of the defendants had privately retained counsel, while at least 48% were represented by either public defenders or assigned counsel.

Table 2 shows whether the defenders were officially determined indigent. For the state as a whole, 49% of the defendants were in this category. Results in one or two of the counties may reflect a local practice of finding indigency only when counsel is appointed, while this in turn depends on a local method of deciding when the defendant waives the right to have counsel appointed.

Frequency of release on bail is shown in Table 3. The proportion of defendants released varied quite widely among the sample counties, from 27% in Madison County to 75% in Cook and 80% in Sangamon, with a state-wide average of 68%. This is considerably above the median figure of 56% reported for 37 states (volume 1, page 8).

TABLE 1
Kind of Counsel in Felony Cases
Illinois, 1962

County	Total sample	Did defendant have counsel? % yes	% no	% retained	% assigned	% public defender	% combi- nation or type unknown	% no data°
Cook	249	100	0	38	6	47	4	2
DuPage	48	98	2	52	7	34	4	8
Madison	37	97	3	46	3	43	5	0
Peoria	20	100	0	47	0	53	0	5
Piatt	6	40	60	20	20	0	0	17
Sangamon	50	64	36	36	0	28	0	0
Will	20	100	0	50	5	45	0	0
Weighted total percentages		93	7	40	6	42	4	4

° % of no data refers to total number of cases sampled within county; % in other columns refers to cases for which data were available.

Table 4 indicates the dispositions in the sample cases, with numbers shown opposite each county and percentages at the foot of the table. For the state as a whole, 67% of the defendants pleaded guilty, including 7% who pleaded to lesser offenses. Of 18% of the cases that went to trial, 13% resulted in convictions, including 1% convictions of lesser offenses; and 5% of the defendants were acquitted. Will and Sangamon Counties had the highest proportion of guilty pleas.

Sentences are reported in Table 5. In 19% of the cases, no sentence was imposed, by reason of acquittals, dismissals, and pending cases. In 57% of the cases the defendant was sentenced to prison, including county jails and houses of correction, while 22% of the defendants were placed on probation and 3% were fined. Compared to other states, this is a relatively infrequent use of probation. However, among the sample counties there was considerable variation in the granting of probation: it was granted most frequently in DuPage and Madison Counties and least frequently in Cook and Peoria.

D. OPINIONS OF THE JUDGES

The study included personal interviews with seven circuit judges in the sample counties. In Cook County an additional interview was conducted with a circuit judge who previously served as Felony Court judge of the Municipal Court of Chicago. (Felony Court branch of the Municipal Court, prior to its abolition on January 1, 1964, the effective date of the new judicial article, was the major felony preliminary hearing court for Chicago.) Replies were received from 27 of the 42 circuit judges sent mail questionnaires (64%). The following data is a

TABLE 2*
Was Felony Defendant Determined Indigent?
Illinois, 1962

County	No. of cases	% yes	% no	% no data
Cook	249	55	45	4
DuPage	48	47	53	6
Madison	37	47	53	3
Peoria	20	53	47	5
Piatt	6	20	80	17
Sangamon	50	28	72	0
Will	20	50	50	0
Weighted total percentages		49	51	4

* % of no data refers to total number of cases sampled within county; % in other columns refers to total cases in which data were available.

TABLE 3*
Frequency of Release on Bail of Felony Defendants
Illinois, 1962

County	No. of cases	% yes	% no	% no data
Cook	249	25	75	7
DuPage	48	48	52	12
Madison	37	73	27	30
Peoria	20	53	47	5
Piatt	6	60	40	17
Sangamon	50	20	80	0
Will	20	39	61	10
Weighted total percentages		32	68	6

* % of no data refers to total number of cases sampled within the county; % in other columns refers to total cases in which data were available.

compilation of the information obtained from the personal interviews and mail questionnaires of the circuit judges.

All the judges interviewed were asked the following question: "Under an ideal system, at what stage do you think the indigent person should first be provided with a lawyer if he wants one?" The results are shown below.

	Personal interviews	Mail questionnaires
Total judges responding	7	27
Between arrest and first appearance	1	7
At first appearance before magistrate	0	3
Between first appearance and preliminary hearing	1	2

	Personal interviews	Mail questionnaires
At preliminary hearing	1	3
After preliminary hearing but before filing indictment or information	0	1
After filing of indictment or information but before arraignment thereon	1	7
At arraignment on indictment or information	2	4
After arraignment	0	0
No answer	1	

Of the judges who felt that appointment should be made at an earlier stage than the present system provides, i.e., at the arraignment prior to entry of plea, half thought that it is unfair to the indigent defendant if counsel is not made available at the earlier stage. Of the remaining judges who felt appointment should be made at an earlier stage, most thought it is not unfair to the defendant if he does not have counsel at the earlier stage and a few did not know whether it would be unfair. The majority of judges who felt that the ideal stage for appointment of counsel was just prior to entry of plea at arraignment also felt that it is unfair to the defendant if counsel is not made available to him at this time. A few thought that no unfairness would result if appointment of counsel were delayed beyond arraignment.

Of the judges responding by mail, 11 of those who favored appointment earlier than the present system provides thought such a system could be financed;

TABLE 4
Dispositions in Felony Cases
Illinois, 1962

County	Total sample	Plea guilty	Plea lesser offense	Dis- missed	Found guilty	Found guilty lesser degree	Ac- quitted	Mental commit- ment	Pend- ing	Stet*	Other
Will	20	17	0	0	1	0	2	0	0	0	0
DuPage	48	25	5	5	5	1	4	0	3	0	0
Cook	249	142	24	19	27	4	11	4	13	5	0
Piatt	6	4	0	0	1	0	0	0	1	0	0
Madison	37	15	3	7	5	0	1	0	5	0	1†
Peoria	20	9	0	0	4	0	0	0	4	3	0
Sangamon	50	37	5	0	4	0	3	1	0	0	0
Weighted total percentages		60	7	6	12	1	5	1	7	2	0

* Held on inactive docket.
† No data.

206

TABLE 5*
Sentencing in Felony Cases
Illinois, 1962

County	Total sample	No sentence No.	%	Prison No.	%	Probation No.	%	Fine No.	%
Cook	249	52	21	144	58	44	18	5	2
Will	20	2	10	14	70	7	35	1	5
DuPage	48	11	23	16	33	18	38	3	6
Piatt	6	1	17	4	67	2	33	0	0
Madison	37	12	32	11	30	14	38	1	3
Peoria	20	6	30	10	50	3	15	0	0
Sangamon	50	3	6	30	60	13	26	4	8
Weighted total percentages		19		57		22		3	

* If a defendant had a combination sentence, such as fine and probation, he was counted under each column, hence the totals may be more than 100%.

3 thought it could not be financed; and 2 did not know. The comments of the judges personally interviewed revealed that no financial barrier existed to appointment of counsel at the stages the judges, respectively, thought counsel should be provided to indigent defendants. One judge felt that the added cost of providing counsel at an earlier stage might not be worth the benefit it gives to defendants. Another suggested that the public defender system is best suited to bear the financial burden of providing counsel between arrest and first appearance before a magistrate.

The judges were asked the following question: "Under an ideal system do you think a lawyer should be made available to the indigent person in the following kinds of cases and proceedings?" The results are shown in the following chart:

Kind of case or proceeding	Yes	No	No answer
Sentencing of a defendant who pleaded guilty	26	4	1
Sentencing of a defendant convicted by trial	27	3	2
Habeas corpus, coram nobis, or other postconviction remedy	25	4	2
Hearing on revocation of probation	27	3	1
Sexual psychopath hearing	23	5	3
Misdemeanors	11	14	6
Civil commitment of the mentally ill, including alcoholics and narcotics addicts	17	8	6

Asked, "Do you think it is unfair to the indigent person if he does not have a lawyer for such cases and proceedings?", the judges replied as follows:

Kind of case or proceeding	Yes	No	No answer	Depends
Sentencing of a defendant who pleaded guilty	22	7	3	2
Sentencing of a defendant convicted by trial	22	8	3	1
Habeas corpus, coram nobis, or other postconviction remedy	21	7	3	3
Hearing on revocation of probation	24	6	3	1
Sexual psychopath hearing	27	3	4	0
Misdemeanors	14	13	5	2
Civil commitment of the mentally ill, including alcoholics and narcotics addicts	19	8	5	2

The judges were asked to comment on whether present rates of compensation for lawyers for services rendered to indigent defendants are adequate. The results are shown below.

	Personal interview	Questionnaire
Present compensation is adequate	3	9
Present compensation is not adequate	2	9
No response	2	9

In response to the question, "Do you think that lawyers should be reimbursed for their out-of-pocket expenses for investigation and preparation of cases for indigents?", the results were as follows:

	Personal interview	Questionnaire
Lawyers should be reimbursed	3	13
Lawyers should not be reimbursed	1	0
No response	3	14

The great majority of judges felt that appointed lawyers compare favorably in experience and ability both with lawyers retained by defendants and with the state's attorney.

The judges make their determination of indigency by asking the defendant a series of questions in open court. The most common factors considered by the judges on the eligibility of the defendant to have counsel appointed for him are: (1) salary of the accused, (2) ownership of automobile and other personal property, (3) ownership of real property, and (4) stocks, bonds and bank accounts owned by the accused. Less common factors considered by the judges were: (5) pensions, social security and unemployment compensation, (6) whether defendant is out on bail, (7) financial resources of parents or spouse, and (8) financial resources of other relatives.

In Cook County, however, whether the defendant is out on bail often determines whether the court will appoint counsel. Only in exceptional cases will a defendant who has posted a bond be given free legal services.

If a defendant is found ineligible for appointment of counsel, the great majority of the judges so inform the defendant and tell him that if he wishes to have a lawyer, he should retain his own.

The judges reported that they had no problem in getting lawyers to serve as appointed counsel. Lawyers have accepted the appointments responsibly. Less than 5% of the lawyers have asked to be excused and even in those cases the judges reported that the attorneys had good cause. Generally the tendency is to appoint younger lawyers. Some judges will appoint more experienced attorneys, or two attorneys, in capital cases.

The judges interviewed estimated, on the average, that about 75% of the total felony defendants are indigent. While the bulk of the judges estimated a percentage of indigency near 75%, the estimates ranged as low as 20% and as high as 98%.

E. OPINIONS OF THE STATE'S ATTORNEYS

Of the 102 Illinois state's attorneys (each county elects a state's attorney) 7 were interviewed personally, and 78 of the 96 who were sent mail questionnaires responded, making a total response of 83% of the state's attorneys in Illinois.

The response to the question, "Under an ideal system, at what stage do you think the indigent person should first be provided with a lawyer if he wants one?" is shown in the tabulation below.

Ideal stage for appointment	Number of state's attorneys
Total state's attorneys responding	85
Between arrest and first appearance	20
At first appearance before magistrate	5
Between first appearance and preliminary hearing	8
At preliminary hearing	6
After preliminary hearing but before filing of indictment or information	2
After filing of indictment or information but before arraignment thereon	30
At arraignment on indictment or information	9
After arraignment	0
At trial	0
No answer	5

The majority of state's attorneys stated that it is unfair to the indigent person if he does not get a lawyer at the stage when counsel should be provided under an ideal system. Several of the state's attorneys commented that the question of fairness, as it relates to the stage for appointment of counsel, depends upon the circumstances of the individual case. Of the 39 state's attorneys who felt appointment should be made at an earlier stage than the present system provides, 15 thought fairness required earlier appointment, 15 thought that it would not be unfair if appointment were not made at the ideal stage, and 9 did not answer the question. Twenty-three thought fairness required appointment by the time of arraignment.

Of the 36 state's attorneys favoring appointment at an earlier stage than the present system provides, 15 thought that earlier appointment could be financed, 12 thought that it could not be financed, and 12 either did not respond or found the question difficult to answer.

The following table shows the answers received to the question, "Under an ideal system do you think a lawyer should be made available to the indigent person in the following kinds of cases and proceedings?"

Kind of cases or proceeding	Yes	No	Don't know	No answer
Sentencing of a defendant who pleaded guilty	53	29	0	3
Sentencing of a defendant convicted by trial	63	17	0	5
Habeas corpus, coram nobis, or other postconviction remedy	60	19	1	5
Hearing on revocation of probation	62	18	0	5
Sexual psychopath hearing	71	10	0	4
Misdemeanors	21	55	0	9
Civil commitment of the mentally ill, including alcoholics and narcotics addicts	29	46	0	8

To the question, "Do you think it is unfair to the indigent person if he does not have a lawyer in such cases?" the replies were as follows:

Kind of cases or proceeding	Yes	No	Don't know	No answer
Sentencing of a defendant who pleaded guilty	22	34	5	24
Sentencing of a defendant convicted by trial	30	22	5	28
Habeas corpus, coram nobis, or other postconviction remedy	35	19	3	28
Hearing on revocation of probation	37	18	2	28
Sexual psychopath hearing	43	10	2	30
Misdemeanors	11	40	3	31
Civil commitment of the mentally ill, including alcoholics and narcotics addicts	19	31	5	30

The great majority of state's attorneys felt that assigned counsel compared favorably in experience and ability with lawyers retained by defendants. Eight of the state's attorneys answered that assigned counsel are less experienced and able than the public defender, however.

On the question whether assigned counsel should be compensated for their services to indigent defendants, the results are as follows:

Lawyers should be compensated	66
Lawyers should not be compensated	1
No answer, undecided, or qualified answer	18

Of the state's attorneys 34 thought that present rates of compensation for assigned counsel were inadequate, 39 thought that present rates were adequate, and the remainder either did not answer or did not express an opinion.

Fifty-one state's attorneys thought that assigned counsel should be reimbursed for out-of-pocket expenses for investigation and preparation of cases for indigent defendants; 5 thought assigned counsel should not be reimbursed; and 29 did not answer the question.

The state's attorneys interviewed estimated, on the average, that 60% of all defendants were indigent. Based upon actual count, two state's attorneys said that they had not prosecuted any indigent defendants in 1962. The bulk of the responses indicated that between 50% and 90% of the defendants were indigent.

F. OPINIONS OF DEFENSE ATTORNEYS

Formal and informal interviews were conducted in the sample counties and in other counties with lawyers who had been appointed to represent indigent defendants either as public defender or as assigned counsel. All of the attorneys interviewed had been appointed after the filing of the indictment or information but before arraignment thereon, or, in the case of an information, prior to consent to proceed by information in lieu of indictment. The experience in years of practice of these attorneys ranged from 1 to 45 years.

The defense attorneys feel that appointment at arraignment provides adequate opportunity to represent a defendant properly. However, if a defendant has made a statement without knowing that he could refuse to do so, certainly the defense attorney is less able to defend fully than if he could have advised the defendant not to make a statement.

One of the public defenders interviewed made this observation on appointing counsel prior to arraignment: "If the system provides for appointment of counsel at the earliest opportunity, then the bar may rightly complain that the defender service is impinging upon the province of the organized private bar."

None of the assigned counsel were reimbursed for out-of-pocket expenses incurred. It was felt that these expenses should be paid in order to be fair to the appointed lawyer and to enable him to investigate properly and prepare the assigned case.

Although the Illinois legislature has now provided for compensation for assigned counsel, as already noted, a need remains to provide adequate compensation in lengthy cases. It is not unusual for an assignment to require an expenditure of one to three months in preparation and trial. One young attorney interviewed was required to spend three months over a four-month period in one case in which he was appointed. He received no compensation for either his services or expenses incurred and, as a result, a year after the conclusion of the case, still suffers from the financial hardship thrust upon him and his family as a result of the appointment. In the last analysis, providing free legal services to indigent defendants costs money. There is no reason why the lawyers, individually, should have to bear this expense which rightly belongs to society as a whole.

G. CONCLUSIONS AND RECOMMENDATIONS

On the basis of the foregoing report and the data gathered during the Illinois survey, the following conclusions and recommendations are submitted:

1. The present discovery procedure in Illinois in criminal cases provides both indigent and non-indigent defendants with equal opportunity to prepare a defense. From the point of view of fairness, it may be concluded that no basic unfairness inures to an indigent defendant merely because counsel is appointed at the arraignment, prior to entry of the plea.

2. Provision should be made to reimburse assigned counsel for out-of-pocket expenses in investigating and preparing the defense of an indigent defendant. There seems to be no adequate reason why assigned counsel should, individually, be called upon to bear the cost of assuring justice to indigent accused persons.

3. Indigent defendants who are proper risks should be released upon their own recognizance. Once so released, they should be required to account for income received during their liberty. To the extent that the court finds that an indigent defendant is able to afford to pay his assigned counsel, he should be required to do so.

4. The methods employed in Illinois for determining indigency and eligibility for appointed counsel, while informal, adequately provide for free representation when it is needed. Perhaps the present system overprovides counsel in some cases.

5. The majority of persons interviewed agreed that the ideal stage for appointment of counsel is at the arraignment prior to the entry of the plea. However, a substantial number of persons interviewed felt that appointment should be made at some earlier time. The reporters feel that the added expense involved in making counsel available to defendants after arrest and before preliminary hearing would be prohibitive in Cook County and perhaps in many other counties. The benefits to be derived from appointment at the earliest possible stage in the criminal proceeding do not seem to warrant this expense.

6. The bar has readily assumed the responsibility of defending indigent persons accused of crime. The Illinois legislature has taken a step in the right direction in providing for payment of a fee to assigned counsel in all noncapital cases. However, the limitation of $150 for each defendant is unrealistic in many cases. Provision should be made to compensate assigned lawyers at least fairly, i.e., with some relation to the bar schedule of minimum fees. The duty to provide adequate representation to indigent defendants belongs to society as a whole, not only to the legal profession.

7. Consideration should be given to the possibility of requiring parents and spouses to pay for legal services and costs in connection with the defense of indigents, perhaps similar to the statutory reimbursement provisions which require certain relatives to pay for the care of patients in state hospitals.

INDIANA

Richard H. Huston, Indianapolis

The members of the A.B.A. Associate State Committee were of great assistance in gathering data for this report and also made valuable suggestions as to the content of this report. The committee consisted of Jerry P. Belknap, Indianapolis, chairman; Frederick T. Bauer and N. George Nasser, Terre Haute; Charles E. MacGregor, New Albany; James D. Nafe, South Bend; Edmond A. Schroer, Hammond; Richard P. Tinkham, Jr., Indianapolis; and Robert H. Hahn and K. Wayne Kent, Evansville. In addition, the judges, prosecutors, office of the state public defender, and county public defenders who were personally interviewed were of great help in preparation of the material for this report. The probation division of the department of correction and the Indiana state police were of invaluable assistance in compiling some of the statistics included in this report.

A. INTRODUCTION

Indiana had a population of 4,662,498 in 1960. It is estimated by the State Board of Health that the population in July, 1962, reached a total of 4,751,100. The state is divided into 92 counties and 86 judicial districts. A few of the districts include two counties. Each judicial district has one circuit court and some have superior courts, probate courts, juvenile courts, and criminal courts. Each judicial district has its own prosecuting attorney. Public defenders have been established in nine counties having a population of 100,000 or more (see Section E infra). The counties selected for the survey are shown in tabular form below, and the subsequent tabulation gives additional information about them.

County (city)	1960 population	Location in state	Remarks
Elkhart (D) (Elkhart)	106,790	North	Medium manufacture, farming
Henry (New Castle)	48,899	West Central	Manufacture, farming
Lake* (Gary)	513,269	Northwest	Heavy industry
Marion (D) (Indianapolis)	697,567	Central	State capital, commercial and industrial center
Porter (D) (Valparaiso)	60,279	Northwest	Farming, small business
Tipton (D)	15,900	North central	Farming
Vanderburgh (Evansville)	165,800	Southwest	Manufacture

(D) indicates that a docket study was made.

*Lake County was not included in the original sample, but was added because of its large population, heavy industrial economy, and some unique problems which do not occur elsewhere in the state. The state reporter felt it should not be left out and it was therefore included as an addition to the survey.

213

County	Felony defendants, 1962	% indigent	% of indigents who waived counsel	Lawyers in private practice	No. of appointments of counsel in felonies, 1962	No. of lawyers who served	Typical payment for felony guilty plea
Elkhart	151	10-75[1]	90[1]	66	no data	1	Public defender
Henry	144	10-20[2]	0	30	18	1[3]	$50
Lake	707[4]	50	0	279	385[5]	1	Public defender
Marion	1187	40-75[6]	less than 1	1183	no data	7[7]	Public defender
Porter	72	50	5-50[8]	54	4	3	—[9]
Tipton	30	25-33	0	7	20[10]	4	$100
Vanderburgh	224	50-75	0	163	121[11]	1	Public defender

[1]Prosecuting attorney and superior court judge estimated that 33%-50% of defendants were indigent. Per cent waiving counsel in superior court is very small.
Circuit court judge estimated 10% of the defendants were indigent; deputy prosecutor estimated 75%. Judge estimated 90% waive counsel; deputy prosecutor estimated 75%.
[2]Judge estimated 10%-20% of the defendants were indigent. Prosecutor said per cent was very small. No waiver of counsel is permitted.
[3]Present judge uses several attorneys as pauper counsel, but prior judge used only one.
[4]Estimated.
[5]These are the defender's statistics. Prosecutor's statistics indicated 309.
[6]One judge estimated as many as 75%; defenders in each court estimated 30%-40%.
[7]Three defenders in one court and four defenders in the other court.
[8]Judge estimated 50% waived. Prosecutor estimated 5% waived.
[9]Judge who handles most of the felony cases said each case was different and he could not estimate a typical fee.
[10]Includes some misdemeanors.
[11]Defender was appointed on some 10 to 15 misdemeanors also.

214

B.   CRIMINAL PROCEDURE AS IT AFFECTS INDIGENT PERSONS

Jurisdiction to return indictments and try felony cases is generally vested in the circuit court, except for Lake and Marion Counties which have criminal courts with exclusive criminal felony jurisdiction. In some counties, the superior court has concurrent jurisdiction to try felony cases.

A great majority of felony cases begin with the arrest of the suspect. The accused is required to be taken promptly before a magistrate. In most counties the committing magistrate is the circuit court judge, criminal court judge, or superior court judge if that court has criminal jurisdiction. In some of the counties surveyed, the defendant's first appearance before a judge is at the time of arraignment. At that time he is informed of the nature of the charges against him and of his right to counsel; and if he so desires, counsel is appointed to represent him. In some of the counties surveyed the defendant is brought before the judge prior to arraignment, at which time an inquiry is made into his financial circumstances and whether he would desire to have counsel appointed. At that time bail may be modified or increased, and counsel is assigned to the indigent defendant.

Only in Marion County are preliminary hearings used extensively. There a defendant is brought before a municipal court judge or magistrate court judge generally within 24 hours of his arrest, at which time a preliminary hearing is conducted unless waived by the defendant. Although the right to counsel is generally explained to the accused before the municipal or magistrate court judges, the courts have no provision or facilities for appointing counsel at that time. In all of the counties surveyed, bail is set according to a schedule by the committing judge whether in circuit court, criminal court, superior court, municipal court, or magistrate court. Bail schedules vary from county to county and from judge to judge within the same county and also may vary from year to year as different judges are elected or appointed. In only one of the sample counties surveyed does the first appearance before a magistrate usually occur as early as within 13 to 24 hours after arrest. In the other counties the period is usually much longer, and in one court it is estimated that the first appearance after arrest would be within 8 to 14 days after arrest. In most other courts the first appearance is within seven days after arrest.

In most counties other than Marion the formal charge against a defendant is generally made by affidavit (information). Grand juries are rarely used in these counties except where required by law in capital cases. In Marion County indictments by grand jury are used much more extensively than elsewhere in the state, generally for the more serious felonies, sex crimes, etc.

In all the counties surveyed except two, counsel is first appointed for the indigent defendant at the time of arraignment on the indictment or affidavit. In Lake and Vanderburgh Counties the judges call the defendants in for an informal proceeding prior to arraignment and inquire into their ability to employ counsel. If it is determined at that time that they are indigent, the court assigns the pauper counsel, or public defender. In most of the counties surveyed, except Marion, counsel is appointed within one or two weeks after arrest either at the time of arraignment or during an informal proceeding prior to arraignment.

In Marion County it is possible that the arraignment on an indictment will not occur for two to three months after the defendant is first arrested and bound over to the grand jury after a preliminary hearing. The exact time depends upon the case load before the grand jury and how fast it acts upon each case. Arraignments in Marion County are scheduled by the two criminal court judges within a very short time after the indictments are returned, but this is the first time that counsel is appointed for the indicted defendant.

The procedure for appointment of counsel is basically the same in all the counties surveyed. The judge determines the indigency of the defendant by asking a series of questions concerning his financial circumstances. If satisfied that the defendant is indigent, he then appoints a public defender in counties in which there is one, or assigns counsel in the other counties. Generally speaking, there is no independent investigation of the financial status of the defendants either by the prosecutor or the defense counsel. The normal policy of most of the judges in the counties surveyed was to accept the defendant's word that he is indigent and to resolve any doubt in his favor. In Tipton County, the judge requires the defendant who says he is unable to employ private counsel to sign an affidavit-type questionnaire setting out his financial status and declaring that he is indigent. In none of the counties surveyed were there any specific standards or rules for determining indigency. The public defender enabling statutes provide "that the county attorney shall bring suit on behalf of the county at the request of the judge of said court or any division thereof for recovery of a reasonable sum for the service of the public defender rendered on behalf of any such poor person wherever it appears to the court that said person has sufficient means to employ an attorney" (Ind. Stat. Ann. §§ 4-2316, 9-3501).

Practice varies in the surveyed counties as to what constitutes waiver of counsel. In Henry, Marion, Tipton, and Vanderburgh the judges said that they would not allow an indigent defendant to waive counsel, but would insist that he be represented by counsel. In Elkhart County, where two courts have criminal jurisdiction, the circuit court judge informs the indigent defendant that he is entitled to be provided with counsel only if he says he is not guilty or if he asks for counsel. The superior court judge makes a much greater effort to insure that the defendant who wants counsel is provided with one by the court. He explains the significance of the arraignment and tells the defendant that counsel will be provided at no cost to him. In Porter County, the court explains the significance of the arraignment to the defendant, mentions the maximum sentence for the crime, and asks the defendant if he wants to have counsel appointed. An automatic plea of not guilty is entered which may be withdrawn at a later date so that technical objections to the affidavit or indictment may be raised. In Lake County the court asks the defendant if he wants to have counsel appointed for him, explaining that counsel will be provided at no cost to him, and further urges the defendant to accept appointment of counsel.

There is a widespread discrepancy among the counties in practices respecting offer of counsel. In one group are the four counties in which the judges will not accept a waiver of counsel by the indigent defendant, and Marion County, in which a waiver is accepted only after a thorough interrogation of the defendant to make sure that he understands what he is doing. In the other counties surveyed, a large percentage of the indigent defendants do waive counsel. In these counties, generally speaking, the judges neither insist nor urge the defendant to accept pauper counsel.

Compensation for attorneys differs widely among the counties surveyed. In those using the assigned counsel system the amount paid to counsel per case varies greatly. In Marion and Vanderburgh Counties the statute provides the maximum that may be used by each court for a public defender. In Marion County each of the two criminal courts has a budget of $12,500 for public defender service. Each criminal court judge apportions this among the attorneys he appoints as public defenders; one court has four defenders and the other has three. In Vanderburgh County the statutory maximum is $10,000. However, the county council will appropriate only $7500 for the defender and $500 for a secretary. In Lake County an item of $8100 for the public defender is included in the court budget. In Elkhart County the defender is paid $1000 by the circuit court and $1500 by the superior court. Among the counties using the assigned counsel system, the smallest county surveyed provides a budgetary amount of $750 per year for use of the court, and in some of the other counties as much as $1200 is provided. (In the county which has a yearly budget of $1200 for assigned counsel, it was noted that in 1961 in the trial of a first degree murder case a fee of $1500 was awarded to the pauper counsel. In the following year the standard fee in felony cases was only $50 per felony.) No provision is made in any of the counties for reimbursement of defense counsel's cost of investigation, preparation, and expert witnesses.

None of the public defenders has the funds to employ investigators. In none of the sample counties is counsel provided for misdemeanors that are brought either in the justice of the peace, city, magistrate, or municipal court. This is generally the practice throughout the state according to members of the associate committee.

In Tipton, Henry, and Vanderburgh Counties counsel is provided on misdemeanors in the circuit court. However, in Vanderburgh County only misdemeanor appeal cases are brought in circuit court. This is true also of Elkhart County. In Marion County, one criminal court judge said he would not appoint counsel on misdemeanor appeals but the other indicated that he would. In Porter County, the prosecuting attorney and the superior court judge said that counsel was not provided on misdemeanor cases and the circuit court judge said that counsel was provided. In Lake County, the prosecutor and pauper counsel said counsel was provided for misdemeanor defendants who came before the criminal court, but the criminal court judge indicated that counsel was not provided. In five of the seven counties surveyed, counsel is usually appointed for the defendant who pleads guilty. These are the counties in which the judge is insistent that the indigent defendant accept the appointment of counsel. In the other two counties, differing answers were given as to whether the defendant who pleaded guilty was provided with counsel. In some instances the judge said yes, if the defendant requested it, and in the same instances the prosecutor said that counsel was not provided. Where a trial was held and the defendant was convicted, in five of the sample counties the practice was to require the appointed counsel, or public defender, to be present at the time of sentencing. In Elkhart County, however, in the circuit court, counsel is provided at sentencing only if the defendant asks for counsel, but none has ever done so. In the superior court, counsel is provided at sentencing after the trial. In Porter County, the prosecuting attorney said counsel was provided at sentencing after trial, but the circuit judge said only if the defendant asks for one.

The tabulation below shows the replies of the judges to the question: "Is counsel provided in trial court in the following kinds of proceedings?"

It may be seen from this table that there was a wide variation of answers concerning the appointment of counsel to handle appeals. Some of the judges were not sure they had the authority to appoint counsel for appeal and to compensate counsel on appeal. In some of the smaller counties a request for an appeal to the Indiana Supreme Court may occur only once every two or three years. After discussing this with several of the more experienced judges, public defenders, and other learned defense counsel, this reporter was able to determine that the law in Indiana is that an indigent person has the right for an appeal and to be assigned counsel for this.

After completion of the case, the attorney assigned the appeal petitions the court for an order for attorney fees; the court determines the amount of compensation to be paid, and then orders the proper county officials to issue a check drawn upon the county. The amount of compensation in these cases varies widely depending upon the amount of time and effort spent by appellate counsel in preparing the case. Fees in these cases may vary from $500 to $2000. If an appeal is authorized by the court, a free transcript of the trial proceedings is also authorized by the court. The practice in Marion County is for the trial judges to appoint counsel other than the public defenders to handle the appeals. The practice in pauper appeals in Vanderburgh County is to appoint the public defender, who is compensated additionally for this service.

In Indiana until the case of *Lane v. Brown* (372 U.S. 477 [1963]), and the new Supreme Court Rules (2-40 and 2-40a) promulgated in September of 1963, the basic postconviction remedy was the writ of error coram nobis. The writ was usually sought by petition in the court which originally tried the convict. Such proceedings for indigent convicts were generally filed by the state public defender. By statute he is the only person who can obtain a free transcript for appeal purposes in a coram nobis proceeding. Prior to *Lane v. Brown,* the state public defender had always had the discretion as to whether to accept a case; and also, it was discretionary with him as to whether an appeal should be taken from a coram nobis hearing in the trial court. In *Lane v. Brown* the United States Supreme Court held that a petitioner in a coram nobis proceeding in Indiana was entitled to a transcript regardless of whether the public defender thought that he had grounds for a meritorious appeal. This was based upon the

Type of proceeding	Elkhart County	Henry County	Lake County	Marion County	Porter County	Tipton County	Vanderburgh County
1. Appeals	Yes[1]	Yes[1]	No[8]	Yes	Yes	Yes	Yes
2. Habeas corpus, coram nobis, and other post-conviction remedies	Yes[2]	Yes[2]	Yes[2]	Yes[2]	Yes[2]	Yes[2]	Yes[2]
3. Hearings on revocation of probation	See[3] below	Yes	See[9] below	See[11] below	Yes[13]	Yes	Yes
4. Sexual psychopath hearings	Yes[4]	Yes	Yes	Yes	Yes[13]	Yes	Yes
5. Misdemeanors	Yes[5]	Yes[6]	Yes[10]	See[12] below	See[14] below	Yes[16]	Yes[17]
6. Civil commitments of mentally ill, alcoholics, and narcotics addicts	No	Yes[7]	No	No	Yes[15]	No	Yes

[1]One judge was unsure on this. The other has appointed counsel to handle appeals. The law is clear that the courts have the authority and duty to appoint counsel for pauper appeals and to compensate counsel for this work. [2]These proceedings are handled by the state public defender. In some counties the judges and prosecutors were not certain of the function of the state public defender. Rules 2-40 and 2-40a of the Indiana Supreme Court substantially change the procedure and substance of postconviction remedies. [3]Circuit judge said counsel was provided if the defendant asked for it. Counsel is provided in superior court. [4]There were a variety of answers on this, also. The majority interviewed thought counsel was provided. [5]Counsel was provided only on the misdemeanors which reach circuit court or superior court. [6]Only on misdemeanors filed originally in circuit court. [7]Judge requires the prosecutor to appear for the defendant in some insanity proceedings. [8]It was indicated that the state public defender handled appeals. This is not correct, as explained later in the report. [9]Judge said counsel was not provided; pauper counsel said he handled these; prosecutor did not know. [10]Counsel was not provided in city court, judge said counsel was provided in criminal (felony) court; prosecutor and pauper counsel stated that counsel was provided in criminal court. [11]One judge said counsel was provided; the other judge said counsel was not provided in his court because of an Indiana Supreme Court case holding that the defendant has no rights in a probation proceeding. [12]Counsel is not provided in the municipal or magistrate courts. The criminal courts hear misdemeanor appeals. One judge provides counsel in these appeals; the other does not. [13]Under some circumstances the defendant is represented. One judge stated that counsel was not provided. [14]Prosecutor and superior court judge said no; circuit judge said counsel was provided. [15]Both judges said counsel was provided if requested; prosecutor said no. [16]Counsel provided on misdemeanors in circuit court if requested. [17]Only for misdemeanor appeals in circuit court.

reasoning that if the defendant had financial assets he would be able to appeal and obtain a transcript for appeal purposes regardless of merit. As a result of this holding and some other holdings in this case, the Indiana Supreme Court has promulgated two new rules in postconviction remedies. Under Rule 2-40, the court has abolished the writ of error coram nobis and substituted a belated motion for new trial. Under Rule 2-40a, the court has set out certain guidelines for the state public defender and provided how his rejection of a case may be appealed for a judicial review by the Supreme Court. Some of the problems arising under the new rules will be discussed later in this report.

C. OPINIONS OF THE JUDGES

This study began with an interview with Chief Justice Walter Myers of the Indiana Supreme Court and included interviews with the judges having criminal felony jurisdiction in the seven counties surveyed. In each of three counties, two judges were interviewed, and in each of the other four counties, one judge was interviewed. Mail questionnaires were sent to the remaining 79 circuit judges. Replies were received from 51 of them, a response rate of 64.5%.

Question 7 of the judges' interview was: "Under an ideal system at what stage in a criminal case do you think the indigent person should first be provided with a lawyer if he wants one?" Seven of the 10 judges interviewed thought that the appointment should be at the stage in proceedings that the current system provides. One judge thought counsel should be provided between arrest and arraignment. (Current practice in his county is appointment at arraignment.) Two judges indicated that appointment should be prior to the arraignment. In their counties, however, arraignments are held once each week and when counsel is appointed, the arraignment is continued until a later date so that counsel can have adequate time to prepare. On the question of unfairness to the indigent person if he does not get a lawyer at the stage designated by the judge, eight of the judges interviewed indicated that it would be unfair. One indicated it would "not necessarily" be unfair. The other judge said it would not be unfair in his court not to provide counsel even at arraignment "since I read a ritual to him explaining his constitutional rights and offering him counsel even before he makes his plea."

On the same question propounded in the mail questionnaire, 24 judges indicated that counsel should be provided at an earlier stage in proceedings and 27 stated that the present system was satisfactory. On the question of unfairness to the indigent person if he does not get a lawyer at the stage designated, 39 of the judges agreed it would be unfair; 7 judges said it was not unfair, and the others stated no opinion. Answers to these two questions are shown in tabular form below. Concerning the question of financing such a system, 52 judges thought it could be financed, 2 definitely said it could not be financed, and the others declined to comment. Several judges using the assigned counsel system indicated a preference for a public defender system as a more economical means of providing competent counsel for the indigent.

As set out in the tabulation below, there was a widespread variation in opinion among the judges as to whether, under an ideal system, counsel should be provided in certain proceedings. The second phase of this question called for comments as to whether it was unfair if counsel were not provided in these cases. Most of the comments could be reduced to a "yes" or "no" answer and have been included in the tabulation. A great majority of judges (42) thought that the indigent accused should be represented at a sexual psychopath hearing. One may conclude from the answers tabulated that the judges in Indiana are not of one mind on providing counsel for the indigent and that opinion is pretty evenly divided in many instances.

One judge said he would provide counsel at certain stages only if the defendant asked for it. Another, who provides counsel in most of the proceedings set out, commented that he did not understand how some of the smaller counties could get away with using assigned counsel or with allowing a defendant to waive counsel. He felt strongly that the assigned counsel system would not provide competent counsel as does the public defender system. He further pointed out that the failure to provide counsel on misdemeanor cases in the city courts and municipal courts is contrary to Indiana law; and lack of representation in the courts having juvenile jurisdiction was a sad commentary upon the state of justice in Indiana.

Another judge, in a county where a public defender system is utilized, commented that he could not get busy counsel to take the job with the money provided. He further stated that in his opinion the fairest way would be the appointment of counsel in individual cases. When asked why he continued to use the old system when he did not regard it as the fairest method of providing counsel, he replied that "the old system saves money so I use it—indigents get adequate defenses."

Case or proceeding	Under an ideal system do you think an attorney should be provided in the following cases?		Do you think it is unfair to the indigent person if he does not have a lawyer for such cases?	
	Yes	No	Yes	No
Sentencing of defendants who plead guilty	30	25	28	24
Sentencing of defendants convicted by trial	38	20	28	24
Habeas corpus, coram nobis or other post-conviction remedy	37	16	29	21
Hearing on revocation of probation	30	28	19	25
Sexual psychopath	42	5	38	10
Misdemeanors	31	25	26	29
Civil commitment of mentally ill, alcoholics, narcotic addicts	23	34	23	34

Of the 10 judges interviewed, only 2 came from counties of less than 50,000 population, which for purposes of this report are classified as rural counties. The judges from these counties seemed concerned with protecting the rights of the indigent accused. Both said they would like to have a public defender system set up in their counties. The judges interviewed from the larger counties had varied views on this subject. Some were interested in protecting the rights of the indigents, and others apparently were giving mere lip service to this principle. In counties of 150,000 population, the courts had a public defender system, and the rights of the accused were pretty well protected by the defenders after their assignment. In Vanderburgh and Lake Counties, this assignment was prior to arraignment, and in Marion County assignment was made at arraignment.

An attempt was made to make a rough evaluation of all the mail questionnaires as to the interest of the judge in protecting the rights of the accused. This was arrived at by their answers to question 6 on the ideal stage for appointment of counsel. In counties of over 50,000 population, nine of the judges seemed to regard the rights of the indigent important; the other four were less than idealistic in their answers and comments concerning the rights of the accused. In counties of less than 50,000 population, 27 of the judges seemed genuinely concerned with the rights of the indigent person and 11 judges were not so concerned.

A more objective indication might well be the per cent of waiver of counsel by the indigent accused. Of those personally interviewed, the two judges of counties of 50,000 or less population did not allow waivers. In counties of over 50,000 population, six judges estimated a waiver of counsel by indigents to be very small, 10% or less; however, one judge indicated that 90% of the indigents waived counsel; and one other judge estimated that 50% waived counsel. In answer to the waiver question in the mail questionnaires, nine of the judges in counties of over 50,000 population reported that they either did not allow waiver or that waiver occurred in less than 25% of the cases involving indigent defendants; one judge indicated that 50% waived counsel and one that 75% of the defendants waived counsel; two declined to estimate. In counties of 50,000 population or less, 20 of the judges estimated that less than 50% of the defendants waived counsel. Many judges stated that they did not allow waivers; 28 indicated that 50% or more of the indigent defendants waived counsel; and 3 judges did not estimate.

Of the judges interviewed, four who had served four years or less were satisfied with the present system of providing counsel, and one thought the present system could be improved. Of the judges with five years of service or more, two made suggestions of improving the present system of representation. One judge with over 15 years' service was quite concerned with the quality of representation and its extent all over the state. He felt that it could be greatly improved by representation at the city, municipal, and juvenile court levels. Three judges with over five years' service indicated satisfaction with the present system.

In commenting on the present public defender system in his county, one judge stated that he usually got younger boys just out of school as pauper counsel. He added that he always tried to get them with at least one year's experience but that sometimes he had to take them without experience.

On the evaluation of the mail questionnaires, the judges were again divided into two groups, those who had served for four years or less and those who had served five years or more. Many of the judges serving their first term had more than 20 years of experience in the practice of law. Of the first group of judges, 11 indicated that the present system could be improved by providing counsel at an earlier stage of proceedings and 6 expressed satisfaction with the present system (of these 6, 5 had been admitted to practice prior to 1938, and the other had been admitted in 1959). The second group (judges who had served five or more years) was fairly evenly divided: 18 judges thought the present system could be improved and 16 were satisfied with the present system.

D. OPINIONS OF THE PROSECUTING ATTORNEYS

In the six sample counties and in Lake County, the seven prosecuting attorneys were interviewed. In one county the deputy prosecuting attorney was also interviewed, since the two courts having criminal jurisdiction were in separate cities and the prosecutor handled cases only in superior court, his deputy handling cases in circuit court. Questionnaires were mailed to the prosecuting attorneys in the remaining 79 circuits. Replies were received from 43 of them (54%).

On question 101 of the prosecutor's interview, "Under an ideal system, at what stage in a criminal case do you think the indigent person should first be provided with a lawyer if he wants one?" four of the eight interviewed thought that appointment should be at an earlier stage than the present system provides. One thought the appointment should be between arrest and first appearance before a magistrate; one thought it should be at first appearance before a magistrate; and two thought it should be at the preliminary hearing. The other four were satisfied with the present system of providing counsel at the time of arraignment. Seven of those interviewed felt it would be unfair not to have counsel provided at the stage indicated, and the remaining prosecutor indicated it would be all right if counsel were not provided.

Of the 43 prosecutors who returned questionnaires, 25 thought that counsel should be provided at an earlier stage of the proceeding than is encompassed by the present system and 18 felt the present system was adequate. As shown in the tabulation below, 10 felt counsel should be furnished between arrest and first appearance before a magistrate; 8 thought counsel should be furnished at the first appearance before the magistrate; 4, that counsel should be furnished between first appearance and preliminary hearing; 1, that counsel should be furnished at the preliminary hearing; and 2, that counsel should be furnished after preliminary hearing but before filing of indictment or affidavit. Thirty-two of the prosecutors indicated that it was unfair to the accused if counsel were not furnished at the stage indicated in the first part of the question; nine said it was not unfair; and two declined to comment. On the problem of financing such a system, three of the prosecutors who advocated earlier representation and were personally interviewed felt that financing would be difficult. One prosecutor suggested that such a program be privately financed since the taxpayers were overburdened with taxes. Another thought financing the present system in his county was difficult. Three thought it could and should be done. One said, "We have money for less important things. When personal liberties are involved, it's important." Another stated, "This is no problem. The counties build bridges and half a bridge would pay for a good pauper attorney for a year."

Also set out in the tabulation below are the prosecutors' answers to the question "Do you think it is unfair to the indigent person if he does not have a lawyer for the following cases and proceedings?" The last two columns of the tabulation also include their comments as to whether they feel it is unfair if counsel is not provided. Since most of their comments were in a "yes" or "no" form, it was thought proper to include their comments in this fashion. Some did not answer all parts of the question, which explains the discrepancy in the numbers.

A great majority favored furnishing counsel in postconviction remedy cases and in sexual psychopath hearings. A majority indicated that counsel should not be furnished in misdemeanor cases. Several expressed the view that providing counsel in misdemeanor cases would be much too expensive. A majority felt that the defendant should be represented at hearings on revocation of probation. On the question whether it was unfair if counsel were not provided in such cases, the pattern of answers was much the same as in the first part except that many prosecutors did not answer all parts of the question.

Case or proceeding	Under an ideal system do you think an attorney should be provided in the following cases?		Do you think it is unfair to the indigent person if he does not have a lawyer for such cases?	
	Yes	No	Yes	No
Sentencing of a defendant who pleaded guilty	25	23	20	23
Sentencing of a defendant convicted by trial	27	16	26	15
Habeas corpus, coram nobis or other post-conviction remedy	38	9	34	8
Hearing on revocation of probation	28	20	23	19
Sexual psychopath hearing	41	6	32	8
Misdemeanors	19	29	13	29
Civil commitment of mentally ill, including alcoholics and narcotics addicts	31	17	22	19

The prosecutor's questionnaires were divided up according to population and their answers were tabulated as to certain questions. In counties of over

50,000 population, nine of the prosecutors stated that their offices did not have adequate funds and eight thought they had sufficient funds. Five thought defense counsel for the indigent were adequately compensated and 10 thought they were not. Seven prosecutors indicated counsel should be provided at an earlier stage in proceedings than in the present system, and 11 said it was unfair if counsel were not provided at the stage indicated, while 5 did not feel it was unfair.

In counties with population under 50,000, the prosecutors were evenly divided on the question of adequate funds for their offices. A majority of 21 to 12 thought defense counsel were adequately compensated. The same ratio appeared on providing counsel at an earlier stage in proceedings and also on the question of unfairness to the accused.

The prosecutors from the smaller counties are much more interested in providing counsel at an earlier stage of proceedings than are those from the larger counties. Perhaps this may be attributed in part to the cost of providing counsel at an earlier stage in the larger counties, which would make it prohibitive.

Prosecutors with five or more years' experience indicated the following: 10 said they had adequate funds for their offices and 13 said they did not; 12 replied that defense counsel was adequately compensated and 9 said no; 14 thought counsel should be appointed at an earlier stage in proceeding and 10 did not feel an earlier appointment was necessary; 16 said it was unfair if counsel were not appointed at the stage indicated and 6 said it was not.

Prosecutors with four years or less of experience in office indicated the following: 16 said they had adequate funds for their offices and 12 said they did not; they were evenly divided on the question of adequacy of funds for defense counsel (13-13); 17 indicated a desire for counsel to be provided at an earlier stage in proceeding and 11 indicated no; 19 said it was unfair to the indigent if counsel were not provided at the stage chosen and 5 said it was not unfair.

As may be seen from the above answers there was no great variation between prosecutors based upon experience in office. A few more of the prosecutors with four years or less of experience indicated a desire that counsel be appointed for the indigent defendant at an earlier stage in proceedings than did prosecutors with more experience. Many of the prosecutors who indicated that they did not have adequate funds were desirous of additional investigating facilities. Also, many of the prosecutors in counties employing a public defender suggested that the defender needed an investigator.

Among the eight prosecutors interviewed, four said they made a full disclosure of confessions, exhibits, etc., three said they did not, and one said sometimes. Two prosecutors said they cooperated more fully with the defender than retained counsel, and three indicated they did not give any preferential treatment to the defender.

E. THE PUBLIC DEFENDER SYSTEM IN INDIANA

Indiana has two classes of public defenders: (1) those who are appointed by the judge in the trial court to represent indigent accused persons at the trial level; and (2) the public defender of Indiana, who is appointed by the

Supreme Court to represent pauper inmates of prisons after their time for appeal has expired.

The Indiana courts have held on many occasions that a poor person is entitled to counsel and that an attorney appointed to represent a poor person in a criminal case could not be compelled to serve without just compensation. (See *Blythe v. State*, 4 Ind. 525 [1853]; *Webb v. Baird*, 6 Ind. 11 [1854]; *Board of County Commissioners v. Pollard*, 153 Ind. 371, 55 N.E. 87 [1899].) The courts have the inherent power to appoint attorneys to defend poor persons charged with crime (*Stout v. State*, 90 Ind. 1 [1883]). More recently the courts have held that the court must have the power to appoint counsel and to order that they be compensated, and the right to compensation cannot be made to depend upon the will of the legislature or the county council. (See *Knox County Council v. State*, 217 Ind. 493, 29 N.E. 2d 405[1940].) The courts have further held that the right to paid counsel also extends to appeals.

Indiana has two statutes authorizing public defenders at the trial level. Ind. Stat. Ann. §§ 4-2316 et seq. authorizes $12,500 per year in each criminal court or division thereof in counties of over 400,000 population. Sections 9-3501 et seq. authorize courts in counties of 100,000 to 175,000 population to expend up to $10,000 per year on such services. One or two counties have established public defenders without the aid of a statute. As of March 1, 1965, nine counties had public defenders.

The criminal courts in Marion County have budgeted $5000 per court per year for payment of pauper appeals. In most instances the defense counsel for the indigent, whether he is employed on a per-case or a salary basis, is permitted to engage in the private practice of law, and his job as a defender is only a part-time position.

The office of the state public defender was created by the Indiana legislature in 1945 as an outgrowth of numerous cases filed pro se by inmates of the Indiana prison. In 1944, the federal court of appeals had held that habeas corpus was not an adequate remedy in Indiana and would not have to be used before filing an action in federal court. It was further held that a pauper prisoner without the ability to obtain counsel or a transcript did not need to exhaust the state remedy of coram nobis before going into federal court (*Potter v. Dowd*, 146 F. 2d 244 [7th Cir. 1944]). As a result of this decision, the bill creating the state defender was enacted in 1945 (Ind. Stat. Ann. §§ 13-1401 et seq.). The defender is appointed by the Supreme Court for a four-year term. He may appoint deputies with the consent of the court. He has one deputy. Section 13-1402 provides:

> It shall be the duty of the public defender to represent any person in any penal institution of this state who is without sufficient property or funds to employ his own counsel, in any matter in which such person may assert he is unlawfully or illegally imprisoned, after his time for appeal shall have expired.

The defender may order transcripts at the expense of the state (Id., § 1405).

The defender's office has supplied the prisons with questionnaires which are called "Request for Interview with the Public Defender." These are filled out by the inmates and mailed to the defender's office at the state capitol. Actually, the defender will look into any request by a prisoner even if it is on a post card.

After receiving a request for help, the defender investigates the case by looking at the record of the trial court and checking with trial counsel and others. If the defender finds merit in the prisoner's contention that he was denied his constitutional rights, an action is brought to set aside the conviction and to obtain a new trial. A writ of error coram nobis was usually used in these cases. The defender can also bring an action to correct an erroneous sentence. If the defender finds no merit in the inmate's contention, he gives the prisoner a statement of his findings and the applicable law.

As a result of the decision in *Lane v. Brown*, (372 U.S. 477 [1963]), the Indiana Supreme Court on September 11, 1963, enacted new rules concerning postconviction remedies. Rule 2-40 abolishes the writ of error coram nobis and provides that the remedy included in the writ shall be obtained through a motion for new trial. (Proper time for filing a motion is 30 days after verdict or judgment.) If a timely motion is not filed, the rule provides this may be considered as evidence that no meritorious grounds exist for a new trial or appeal, or, if meritorious grounds did exist, that there is an acquiescence. A belated motion for new trial may be filed by petition where the grounds for said motion first came to the knowledge of the party after the time for filing a motion has expired. If a belated motion for new trial is filed in forma pauperis, the state public defender shall represent the petitioner if he finds, after diligent inquiry, merit to the petition and motion.

Rule 2-40a provides that rulings on petitions to file belated motions for new trial and rulings on belated motions for new trial may be reviewed by the Supreme Court on petition for a writ of certiorari. It shall be the duty of the state public defender to represent inmates after their time for regular appeal has expired, if requested to do so, in filing petitions for delayed appeals, petitions for belated motion for new trial, and petitions for writs of certiorari, if after diligent inquiry he finds any grounds to file such proceedings. If he fails or refuses to represent, a petition may be filed in the clerk's office of the Supreme Court setting up such facts, and a citation to show cause shall be issued to the public defender. He then files his response and report and the court determines whether he should be ordered to represent the petitioner. The petitioner may file a reply within 10 days after the filing of the response.

There are several problems that the new rule presents:

(1) The time for filing a regular motion for new trial is 30 days; the time for filing a timely appeal is 90 days after judgment or the overruling of a motion for new trial. The new rules do not provide for representation of a pauper prisoner in these proceedings between the expiration time for filing a timely motion for new trial and the expiration time for a regular appeal. The new rule merely provides that the state defender shall represent after time for a timely appeal has expired.

(2) If the state defender refuses to take a case, the inmate may petition the Supreme Court to require him to act, and the defender then files a response. Query: does this in effect become an adversary proceeding with the scales heavily weighted in favor of the defender's side?

If the defender is ordered to represent the inmate after he has refused to do so, can he with enthusiasm and due diligence advocate the inmate's cause when he has already determined it to be non-meritorious? What effect will this have on the judges when they know that the defender has already decided that the inmate did not have a meritorious cause for appeal and when they have read and examined his response and report to the petition? It may be that as a result of *Lane v. Brown* the United States Supreme Court has obtained substantial justice for Lane but has reduced what was perhaps the best system in the United States of postconviction remedies for pauper inmates to a mere summary proceeding.

F. OPINIONS OF DEFENSE ATTORNEYS

In the six sample counties and Lake County, four of the counties had public defenders and three had assigned counsel. One defender was interviewed in Elkhart, Lake, and Vanderburgh Counties, and one in each of the two Marion County criminal courts. Questionnaires were mailed to 14 attorneys in the other three counties where the judges had indicated they appointed attorneys in pauper cases, and 9 responded. Two of the questionnaires from Tipton County and two from Henry will be used in this report only for the answers given to Question 7, since the attorneys were not assigned any cases in 1962, the sample year. Other questionnaires to be used are: Tipton, one; Henry, two; and Porter, two.

Of the five public defenders interviewed, four thought counsel should be appointed at an earlier stage than the present system provides. Four thought counsel should be provided ideally between arrest and first appearance before a magistrate. Indeed, one felt that counsel should be appointed as soon as an indigent was taken into custody for questioning. One defender indicated that counsel should be provided after the filing of indictment or affidavit but before arraignment. (Practice in his court is to appoint counsel at arraignment and then continue the arraignment.) Four defenders indicated it was unfair if counsel were not provided at this stage. One said it was not unfair. On the question of the cost of financing such a system, three defenders indicated this might be prohibitive; the other defender said it would not, as it would only need the services of one other attorney.

The five defenders were asked, "Under an ideal system do you think a lawyer should be provided in the following cases and proceedings?" They indicated that counsel were already provided in sentencing of a defendant who pleaded guilty; sentencing of a defendant convicted by trial; habeas corpus, coram nobis, and other postconviction remedies; hearing on revocation of probation; and sexual psychopath hearings. One said "yes and no" to representation on revocation of probation, indicating counsel was not always provided. In Vanderburgh, Lake, and one court in Marion, the defender represents on misdemeanors in the felony court but not at the municipal or city court levels. In the other Marion court the defender does not handle misdemeanors. None of the defenders represented indigent persons in civil commitment cases. All thought it was unfair if the indigent accused were not represented in these proceedings except for hearings on revocation of probation. One defender from Marion County thought

228

this was not necessary, nor did he think it was necessary to provide counsel in misdemeanor cases. The defender from Lake County indicated that counsel should be provided for a misdemeanor if the penalty called for incarceration. The two defenders from Marion felt that the legal aid society should represent the indigent in civil commitment cases. On the problem of financing such a system, two of the defenders, from Marion and Vanderburgh, indicated that the cost of providing counsel on misdemeanor cases in the municipal and city courts would be quite high. One said it would be so costly as to be almost prohibitive.

All the defenders but one had 2 to 4 years of experience as a defender and had been admitted to practice for more than 10 years. The four defenders with more experience were more defense minded than the defender with little experience. Three of them had served previously as deputy prosecutors, and the other had practiced criminal law for some 10 to 14 years. The defender with less experience did not think it unfair if counsel did not appear at sentencing. His idea was that with an ideal probation system and a good report, counsel would not be necessary. He also indicated that counsel need not be provided at sexual psychopath hearings since this was a voluntary proceeding. (This is erroneous.)

Two of the defenders indicated that they had adequate funds; three said they did not. Of the three who indicated need for additional funds, two stated they needed funds to employ investigators. The other defender indicated salaries should be higher, but said that if more time were required on defender cases, he would have to resign. All the defenders interviewed were employed on a part-time basis.

Of the attorneys answering by mail, two indicated they were appointed between arrest and first appearance before a magistrate, two were appointed at first appearance, and one was appointed at time of arraignment on the information. The attorney who was appointed at the arraignment said he was not appointed in time and recommended a 24-hour committing magistrate hearing, with defense counsel appointed at that hearing. The other four attorneys said they were appointed in time to represent the defendant adequately. One of these four attorneys indicated that an earlier appointment would have been helpful. Six attorneys stated the present system was fair to the indigent accused; two attorneys said it was not fair to the accused; and one attorney said it was "partially" fair to the accused.

Five of the nine attorneys answering by mail indicated that the present system was not fair to the lawyer appointed as assigned counsel; one attorney said it was "partially" fair; and the other three attorneys said it was fair. The six attorneys who were dissatisfied all cited inadequate fees as the main problem. The other three attorneys did not recommend any changes in the present system.

G. COMPARISONS AMONG JUDGES, PROSECUTING ATTORNEYS, AND PUBLIC DEFENDERS

For the purpose of comparison, the judges were divided into two groups according to years of service in their present courts. The half who had served for less than nine years are called junior judges and the remainder are called senior judges. The prosecutors were divided into two groups according to years of service, also. Prosecutors with less than four years of service are designated as junior prosecutors and the remainder are called senior prosecutors. Results are shown in Table 1.

TABLE 1
Comparison Among Judges, Prosecutors and Defenders
Indiana, 1962

	Senior judges	Junior judges	Senior prosecutors	Junior prosecutors	Public defenders	Total
Total responding	26	33	23	28	5	115
Ideal stage for first appointment of counsel						
Between arrest and first appearance	5	4	6	5	4	24
At first appearance	3	8	2	8		21
Between first appearance and preliminary hearing	1	3	2	2		8
At preliminary hearing	2	1	2	1		6
After preliminary hearing but before indictment			1	1		2
After indictment but before arraignment	5	6	5	3	1	20
At arraignment on indictment	9	10	5	7		31
After arraignment on indictment	1	1		1		3
Is present compensation of lawyers adequate?						
Yes	20	20	11	15	2	68
No	5	11	10	12	3	41
No answer	1	2	2	1		6
Should out-of-pocket expenses be paid?					Not	
Yes	9	9	10	14	applicable	42
No	1				Question	1
No answer	16	24	13	14	was not asked	67

H. THE DOCKET STUDY

A study was made of representative felony cases in the court dockets of four of the sample counties for 1962. Porter and Elkhart Counties had separate samples for the circuit and superior courts. (For details of method of research see volume 1, pages 178-179.) Results are shown in Tables 2 to 6.

Unfortunately the records were so incomplete in certain counties that it was impossible to tell whether some of the defendants had counsel. Table 2 shows this information insofar as it was available. (If data were missing for over 20% of the defendants in the sample, the court was omitted.) For Marion County, where 97% of the defendants had counsel, slightly over half were represented by the public defender or assigned counsel. In the Elkhart superior court, where again virtually all defendants had counsel, only one-third were represented by the public defender and none by assigned counsel. That these figures are an accurate indication of the extent of indigency is confirmed by two other findings. Table 3 shows that the proportion of defendants found indigent was 54% in Marion County and 33% in the Elkhart superior court. Another indication is the percentage of defendants who are not released on bail, as shown in Table 4. In Marion the figure was 67%, in Elkhart 41%. This may include a few defendants who were held without bail because they were charged with very serious crimes.

Table 5 shows the disposition of the sample cases in all the courts where a docket study was made, with a projected figure for the state as a whole based on the weighted average of the county samples. Taking the state as a whole, 31% of the defendants pleaded guilty, including 7% who pleaded to lesser offenses. The highest rate of guilty pleas, 59%, was in the Elkhart superior court. The statewide rate of dismissals, 22%, was relatively high compared to other states: the rate in Marion County was 29%. In counties other than Marion an unusually large number of cases commenced in 1962 were still pending at the time of the docket study in the late summer and fall of 1963. Of the 11% of the defendants whose cases went to trial, 9% were convicted, including 1% convicted of lesser offenses, and 2% were acquitted. In Marion County the great majority of the trials were without a jury.

Sentences imposed, if any, are shown in Table 6. For the state as a whole, 23% of the defendants drew prison sentences, 16% were placed on probation, 4% were given suspended sentences without probation, and 14% had fines imposed. The most frequent use of probation was in Elkhart County. A few defendants who had a combination sentence, such as fine and probation, were counted under more than one heading, but the basic pattern is the same.

I. CONCLUSIONS AND RECOMMENDATIONS

On the basis of the foregoing report the following conclusions and recommendations are submitted:

1. Practice respecting determination of eligibility for appointment of counsel varies widely, so that it is possible for a defendant to be eligible in one place and ineligible in another. A uniform system or set of financial eligibility stand-

TABLE 2

Retained and Assigned Counsel in Felonies
Indiana, 1962

County	Total sample	Did defendant have counsel?				Retained		Defender		Assigned		Combination or type unknown		No data*	
		Yes		No											
		No.	%	No.	%	No.	%	No.	%	No.	%	No.	%	No.	%
Marion	105	99	97	3	3	38	37	51	50	2	2	8	8	3	3
Elkhart (S)	22	21	96	1†	5	13	59	7	32	0	0	1	5	0	0

(S) means superior court.

* % of no data refers to total sample; % in other columns refers to cases for which data are available.

† waived counsel.

232

TABLE 3
Was Felony Defendant Determined Indigent?
Indiana, 1962

County	Total sample	Yes No.	%	No No.	%	No data° No.	%
Marion	105	56	54	46	46	3	3
Elkhart (S)	22	7	33	14	67	1	5

(S) means superior court.
° % of no data refers to total sample; % in other columns refers to cases for which data are available.

TABLE 4
Frequency of Release on Bail of Felony Defendants
Indiana, 1962

County	Total sample	Yes No.	%	No No.	%	No data° No.	%
Marion	105	35	33	68	67	2	2
Porter (C)	13	5	45	6	55	2	15
Elkhart (S)	22	13	59	9	41	0	0

(C) means circuit court.
(S) means superior court.
° % of no data refers to total sample; % in other columns refers to cases for which data are available.

ards would be of great benefit to the trial courts. Some flexibility should be allowed in the system so that the trial judges would have discretionary power to see that borderline persons would be represented by counsel. This could be accomplished by the Supreme Court under its rule-making powers.

2. The practicing of allowing an indigent defendant to waive counsel varies widely between the circuits. In some the judges will not allow waiver, and in others as many as 75% to 90% waive the appointment of counsel. It is recommended that the Supreme Court adopt rules prescribing the trial judges' responsibility and duties in this area. A requirement should be made that the defendant who desires to waive counsel should be required to sign a written waiver similar to the ones used by the federal district courts in this area.

3. The use of preliminary hearings is not widespread in this state. It is suggested that legislation be enacted requiring every person arrested on felony charges to be brought before a magistrate or judge within 24 hours of his arrest and at that time be informed of the charge against him; the state should be required to show by competent evidence that probable cause exists; and the committing magistrate should set bail. It would be desirable that counsel be appointed to represent pauper defendants at this stage in proceedings.

4. It is recommended that counsel be appointed for indigent persons charged with serious misdemeanors at the municipal, magistrate, and city court levels.

TABLE 5
Disposition in Felony Cases
Indiana, 1962

County	Total sample	Plea guilty	Plea lesser offense	Dismissed	Found guilty	Found guilty lesser degree	Acquitted	Mental commitment	Pending	Other
Marion	105	28	9	30	23	5	3	1	2	4
Porter (C)	13	3	0	3	0	0	1	0	5	0
Porter (S)	7	0	0	0	0	0	0	0	7	0
Elkhart (C)	27	7	0	11	4	0	0	0	4	1
Elkhart (S)	22	9	4	2	1	0	0	2	2	2
Tipton	19	4	3	3	0	0	0	0	7	2
Weighted total percentages		24	7	22	8	1	2	1	30	0

(C) means circuit court.

(S) means superior court.

TABLE 6

Sentencing in Felony Cases
Indiana, 1962

County	Total sample	No sentence No.	No sentence %	Prison No.	Prison %	Probation No.	Probation %	Suspended sentence No.	Suspended sentence %	Fine No.	Fine %	Driver's license suspended No.	Driver's license suspended %	No data* No.	No data* %
Marion†	105	40	38	40	38	14	13	7	7	23	22	3	3	0	0
Porter (C)	13	10	77	1	8	1	8	1	8	1	8	0	0	0	0
Porter (S)	7	7	100	0	0	0	0	0	0	0	0	0	0	0	0
Elkhart (C)	27	15	56	4	15	8	30	0	0	5	18	0	0	0	0
Elkhart (S)	22	6	27	9	41	7	32	0	0	4	18	0	0	0	0
Tipton	19	11	61	4	22	3	17	1	5	2	11	0	0	1	5
Weighted total percentages			56		23		16		4		14		1		1

(C) means circuit court.

(S) means superior court.

* % of no data refers to total sample; % in other columns refers to cases for which data are available.

† Two additional defendants had combination sentences.

This could be accomplished by the inherent powers of the court to protect the rights of the accused. Also, the state bar and the Supreme Court should see that enabling legislation is passed to accomplish this purpose.

5. It is recommended that the establishment of a public defender system (part-time or full-time as the situation warrants) be considered for each county. Each of the several circuit courts has the inherent authority to do this. The trial judges association might be the appropriate vehicle to inform the judges of this possibility and explain their authority.

6. Minimum compensation of counsel should be increased, and all compensation be made uniform throughout the state. Funds should be made available for reimbursement of costs of investigation and preparation. Where public defenders are used they should be provided with offices and secretarial staff commensurate with case load. The Supreme Court, working with the state bar, should prescribe minimum fees.

7. Because of the apparent inexperience and lack of knowledge by some trial judges of their authority and responsibilities in this area, it is recommended that the state bar and the judges association undertake a program of continuing legal education in criminal procedure and criminal substantive law.

8. Due to the relative inexperience of trial counsel in a few of the counties surveyed, it is recommended that the state bar undertake a program of continuing legal education in criminal law in cooperation with the Indiana University Law Schools.

9. The system of keeping docket records should be more uniform throughout the state. More complete data about each case should be kept in a central file and statistical reports should be sent to a central agency operating under the direction of the Supreme Court. The state bar should investigate the systems used in some of the sister states.

10. There is no central repository of the number of investigations, arrests, or charges brought by the various law enforcement agencies throughout the state. It is recommended that appropriate legislation be enacted requiring that such reports be made to the state police or department of correction, and that the information be published in a consolidated report.

11. The state bar should appoint a study committee to consider the problem of bail and to recommend corrective legislation or corrective court procedures in setting bail.

IOWA

Ronald L. Carlson, Davenport

The chairman of the A.B.A. Associate State Committee, Earl R. Jones, was most helpful in publicizing this project to the lawyers and judges throughout the state. Invaluable was the assistance of Clarence A. Kading, judicial department statistician, whose compilations form an integral part of this study. The support of Chief Justice Theodore G. Garfield, at whose kind invitation this reporter was able to attend the Judicial Conference of the district judges of Iowa, was much appreciated. Attorney General Evan Hultman and his staff provided much needed information. Finally, the splendid cooperation of the judges, prosecutors, and defense attorneys throughout the state was a primary factor in the successful completion of this report.

A. INTRODUCTION

Iowa had a population of 2,757,537 in 1960. Its 21 judicial districts cover the 99 counties of the state. Each district has two or more district judges, and the largest district has nine. Each county has its own county attorney.

The counties selected for survey are shown in the following table:

County	Chief city	1960 population in thousands	Location in state
Benton*		23	East central
Clarke (D)		8	South central
Des Moines (D)	Burlington	45	Southeast
Dickinson		13	Northwest
Polk (D)	Des Moines	266	Central
Scott (D)†	Davenport	119	East central
Story	Ames	49	Central

(D) indicates that a docket study was made.

* Substituted for Marshall County, which was in the original sample. Both are farm counties in the same judicial district, but Marshall is contiguous to Story, which is also in the sample.

† Substituted for Dubuque County, which was in the original sample. Both are Mississippi River counties in adjoining judicial districts. Dubuque had a population of 80,048 in 1960.

The following table gives additional information about the counties surveyed.

B. CRIMINAL PROCEDURE AS IT AFFECTS INDIGENT PERSONS

Jurisdiction over felony matters is vested exclusively in the district court.[1] Indictable misdemeanors are also within the jurisdiction of the district court, but in the 13 counties that have cities with a municipal court, such cases are usually heard there, since the jurisdiction is county-wide.[2]

Most felony cases begin with the arrest of the suspect, who must be taken without unnecessary delay to the committing magistrate. In most counties this is a justice of the peace, but in counties where a municipal court is in operation the preliminary stages of felony procedure are handled primarily there. The municipal judge must be a lawyer, but the justice of the peace need not be.[3]

County	District court criminal cases commenced 1962*	Cases disposed of without trial	Cases disposed of by trial to jury	Cases disposed of by trial to court	Average months from filing of information to trial by jury†	No. of cases in which preliminary hearing was held‡
Polk	910	840	56	133	4.9	567
Scott	395	390	7	0	3.1	158
Story	67	65	0	0	0	4
Benton	63	52	4	3	1.6	3
Des Moines	62	50	3	0	0.5	7
Dickinson	39	37	0	0	0	5
Clarke	15	10	1	4	2.5	0

* If a man is arrested but is discharged upon preliminary hearing, he will not show up as a separate case. A defendant appears as a district court case when the preliminary information and transcript from the lower court are filed in the district court. Since this is prior to indictment or the filing of a county attorney information, the district court clerk would report this as a commenced case even though the information might be dismissed later. Where two or more defendants are on a single information, each is counted separately.

† Filing means the date of the return of the indictment or filing of the county attorney's information in the district court clerk's office.

‡ This figure includes all preliminary hearings held, including cases which resulted in dismissal or other disposition without being filed in district court. For example, in Polk County the 567 preliminary hearings cover 1205 pre-grand jury cases docketed in the inferior courts during 1962.

Polk County (Des Moines) has had the longest experience with a municipal court, and its four judges sit on a rotating basis in the criminal branch. Preliminary hearings are conducted promptly here, and counsel are appointed in cases involving indigent defendants. Although no provision is made under Iowa law for compensation of attorneys for work done prior to arraignment in district court, the court in Polk County has arranged to appoint an attorney previously appointed in the case by the municipal court, and to allow compensation for representation there.

In the smaller counties there is a serious problem respecting appointment of counsel at the magistrate level. Attorneys are not appointed and preliminary hearing is frequently waived. Salutary efforts by some county attorneys to conform justice of the peace practices to the requirements of current law have met with limited success. In one sample county the county attorney circulates instruction sheets to the justices with a checklist of procedural steps to follow in criminal cases. State law requires that when an arrested person is brought before the magistrate, he must immediately be informed of the offense charged and of his right to counsel in every stage of the proceedings.[4] The magistrate is required by statute to afford the defendant time to obtain counsel, and must adjourn for that purpose if necessary.[5] Bail is set at this stage, generally in accord with a customary rule of thumb for the particular offense in each county. The county attorney usually participates by recommending the amount of bail.

One formula used occasionally for bail is $1000 for each year of the maximum sentence for the crime involved.

The county attorney's information is the usual vehicle for making a formal charge against a defendant in lieu of indictment. Polk County uses indictment more than other counties studied. In Polk the grand jury is in session all year. Elsewhere indictment is used less often. One county attorney interviewed proceeds by indictment only where public opinion or a vexed citizen pushes prosecution of a case that he feels is of doubtful merit. The grand jury can then refuse to indict so that the onus of dismissal does not rest on the county attorney. In other counties the grand jury is seldom used except where a capital offense or other serious crime is involved. Here the county attorney may want the strength of an indictment to fortify his case.[6]

In the sample counties the period between the filing of an indictment or information and jury trial in a district court case averaged 4.3 months. Generally, trial to the court in these same counties proceeded within 5 months. New legislation affords protection for the indigent here. As amended in 1963, the law provides that, except where a trial has been postponed upon application of the defendant, the defendant must be brought to trial at the next term of court or within 60 days after indictment, whichever occurs first, unless good cause to the contrary be shown.[7] This statute restricts the local incarceration of the defendant pending disposition of his cause on penalty of dismissal of the action. The statute further provides that "an accused not admitted to bail and unrepresented by legal counsel shall not be deemed to have waived his privilege of dismissal. . . ." A recent Iowa attorney general's opinion points out that, where the defendant is represented by counsel, his attorney must demand early trial of the case in order to avail the accused of the provisions of this section as under prior law.[8]

Appointment of counsel is required at district court arraignment.[9] The defendant is asked whether he can employ counsel of his own. His answers generally control, and in most cases an attorney will be appointed without independent investigation of indigency. In some smaller counties the county attorney advises the court that counsel should be appointed. The general practice, however, is to make the appointment pursuant to questions raised in open court. Individual assignment is made since Iowa has no public or private defender system.

In each of the surveyed counties the judges refuse to permit waiver of counsel in felonies. If a defendant wants to plead guilty without counsel he is given an attorney before being allowed to plead.[10] A defendant who insists on trying his own case is provided counsel to sit with him for consultation and advice through the trial. In one recent trial where a defendant insisted on representing himself, he got only as far as the opening statement when the court continued the case and directed counsel to be present and undertake further conduct of the defense. One judge estimated that 50% of the indigent felony defendants in his district attempt to waive counsel. For such defendants injustice might result from taxing them with appointed attorneys' fees. Although none of the sample counties followed the practice of taxing attorneys' fees as costs, this idea met with a favorable response from several of the judges and county attorneys interviewed. It was pointed out that this practice would have special merit as a condition of a bench parole, wherein the defendant is placed on parole at the time of sentencing. Although this procedure would accomplish the worthwhile objective of reimbursing the county for funds expended on behalf of an indigent defendant who may go to work and earn the funds needed to make such reimbursement, it nevertheless forces the defendant who asks that no counsel be appointed to represent him to pay for something he does not want.

Compensation for attorneys is provided by statute at the rate of $50 a day for time actually occupied in court in homicide cases or offenses punishable by life imprisonment.[11] Representation in other felonies is compensated at the rate of $25 for all services, with no per diem allowance. By amendment in 1959, the statute permits the court to allow such additional sums as it may determine to be necessary. All fees are paid by the county upon affidavit from the appointed lawyer that he has not received compensation from any other source.[12]

The provision allowing remuneration in the court's discretion over and above the stipulated $25 fee alleviates some of the hardship caused by this limit. The $25 limit is applied by most judges where the representation consists of appearance by the attorney and entry of a plea of guilty. Where an extensive investigation and preparation precede the plea, however, or if the case is tried, an upward adjustment is generally made. How far upward depends on the locale. Some counties attempt to approximate one-half of the fee specified in the local bar association minimum fee schedule for similar services. In one county the court attempts to fix fees at the lower level of the fee schedule. Complaints were received from attorneys in several counties that they had been compensated in unrealistically low rates for appointed work.

Provision is made for appointment of counsel in indictable misdemeanor cases with compensation at the rate of $15 in full for services.[13] Waiver of counsel in such cases is allowed in some counties. In ordinary misdemeanors no provision is made for appointment of counsel, and the sample indicated that only where a municipal court was in operation would counsel be readily available if the defendant should request one.

Current law leaves it to the discretion of appointed counsel whether to pursue an appeal. Several jurists interviewed cited as a problem the divergence between the requirements of the *Douglas* and *Lane* decisions[14] and existing law respecting appeals. The statute recites that an appointed attorney need not follow a case into the Supreme Court but, if he does so, he shall receive enlarged compensation commensurate with the Code section setting fees for appointed attorneys.[15] It is to be noted that district court judges estimated the number of indigent defendants appearing before them as 50% to 60% of all defendants. This estimate is confirmed by the docket study conducted in four sample counties. The Supreme Court clerk's office reported that 15 criminal cases in the court in 1962 involved indigents. The attorney general's office estimated that about 20% of the criminal cases on appeal involve indigents. Thus it appears that indigent matters, although they make up a large portion of the district court criminal work, have not been appealed with the frequency of causes involving retained counsel.

A statute specifically authorizes payment of transcript expense.[16] It provides that if a defendant in a criminal case satisfies the district court from which the appeal is taken that he is unable to pay for a transcript of the evidence, the court may order the same made at the expense of the county.

In Iowa habeas corpus is the vehicle for postconviction relief. The petition for the writ must be filed with the court nearest the applicant in point of distance.[17] For this reason the district court in Lee County is a primary depository for writ applications, since it is the home of Fort Madison Penitentiary. The same is true to a lesser extent in Jones County, where the men's reformatory is located. Resistance to the writ must be supplied by the county attorney of the county where the defendant was convicted. As a practical matter the county of conviction often hires resident counsel in the county where the correctional institution is located. No provision is made under Iowa law for appointment of counsel to represent the petitioner in habeas corpus proceedings.

C. OPINIONS OF THE JUDGES

The study included interviews with Chief Justice Garfield and Justice Moore of the Supreme Court, as well as district and municipal court judges in the seven sample counties. In Polk County four district court judges and two municipal court judges were interviewed. In each of the other counties one district court judge was interviewed, and in Scott and Des Moines Counties a municipal court judge was also interviewed. Where the resident judge in a particular county was not present at the time of the survey, the judge of that district who was sitting in the county was interviewed with special emphasis on his work in that county. Questionnaires were mailed to 38 district court judges in the counties not covered by personal interview, and replies were received from 28 of them (74%).

In the judge interview the question was posed: "Under an ideal system, at what stage in a criminal case do you think the indigent person should first be provided with a lawyer if he wants one?" The response in almost every instance was that counsel should be afforded sooner than under the present system. This reaction was also received on the mail questionnaire. The problem was discussed in some detail during the judicial conference of the district judges of Iowa in June, 1963, with the recommendation that efforts be made to insure counsel for preliminary hearings in felony cases. As shown in Table 1, there is no great dissimilarity in views on this matter among judges of varying years of service on the bench.

Counsel is readily provided by the court at arraignment pursuant to the requirements of the Code and, generally, the statements of the defendant relative to indigency control the situation. One jurist noted that he asks a defendant if he can afford counsel, and when the defendant indicates that he is unable *or unwilling* to do so the court will appoint counsel. Most of the judges do not go this far, and where a defendant clearly has the means he is directed to retain counsel. Exploratory questions range from a perfunctory one as to whether the defendant can afford counsel to a searching inquiry by the court relative to the financial circumstances of the defendant and his relatives. Doubtful cases gen-

TABLE 1
When Counsel Should First Be Provided

	Senior prosecutors	Junior prosecutors	Senior judges	Junior judges	Total
Ideal stage for first appointment of counsel:					
Between arrest and first appearance before a magistrate	7	13	7	9	36
At first appearance before a magistrate	7	8	3	8	26
Between first appearance and preliminary hearing	4	5	1	0	10
At preliminary hearing	2	1	0	2	5
After preliminary hearing but before the filing of an indictment or information	2	1	0	0	3
After the filing of an indictment or information but before arraignment thereon	4	7	2	0	13
At arraignment on indictment or information	1	3	0	1	5
After arraignment on indictment	0	0	1	0	1
At trial	0	0	0	0	0
No answer	1	0	0	0	1
Total	28	38	14	20	100

erally are resolved in favor of indigency. In the rural counties the problem of determining indigency is often obviated by general community knowledge of the defendant's means. Although most judges felt it would be impracticable, they responded favorably to the suggestion that the probation department or other independent agency conduct a summary investigation of indigency.

With infrequent exceptions, the judges report no particular problem in obtaining counsel for defense appointments. Most attorneys are willing to serve. Eleven judges (34%) replied that none ask to be excused, and another 13 (41%) replied that the number is 1% to 9%. The judges consider that the attorneys feel it their duty as members of the bar to perform this function. Perhaps this is the reason why the reporter noted no great tide of sentiment favoring a public defender system among judges. The obvious advantage to the court of a system that provides readily available defense counsel at state expense is somewhat less attractive in a jurisdiction where no significant problem is reported in obtaining such services from the organized bar. Only in the municipal court of the largest county in the state, where the case load is considerably increased, was support for a public defender unequivocal.

The method of selecting attorneys for appointment varies greatly throughout the state. Of 33 judges who answered this question, 11 said they used a roster of all attorneys admitted to practice; 9 said they used their own list; 6 said they used a list supplied by the local bar association; and 7 said they used other methods of selection. In the more populous counties the court will often appoint defense counsel from the judge's list of names, which includes attorneys he knows are willing to accept appointments. In the smaller counties a broader spread of representation in criminal appointments is generally noted. Here the judges tend to make appointments from the whole roster of the county bar association.

Replies of judges as to providing counsel for miscellaneous cases and proceedings under an ideal system were as follows:

Type of case or proceeding	Provide counsel* No.	%	Unfair if not provided† No.	%
Sentencing of defendant who pleaded guilty	32†	97	27	90
Sentencing of defendant convicted by trial	29	91	26	93
Habeas corpus or other postconviction remedy	19	61	17	68
Hearing on revocation of probation	16	52	16	59
Sexual psychopath hearing	28†	95	22	85
Misdemeanor	11†	37	8	38
Civil commitment of mentally ill	31	100	24	100

* An answer of "already provided" is counted as "yes."
† A few persons who said "sometimes," "depends on circumstances," "if requested," etc., are counted here.

Although 75% of the judges indicated that compensation rates for indigent representation were adequate, and 70% of the senior prosecutors agreed, only 46% of the junior prosecutors felt that current rates were satisfactory. (Junior prosecutors are those with less than five years' experience in office.) The more recent association of these persons with representation of indigent defendants may account for their closer kinship in views with the defense attorneys (see Table 2).

D. OPINIONS OF THE PROSECUTING ATTORNEYS

Response was strong from the county attorneys. In addition to those covered by personal interview, 63 of a possible 92 (68%) responded by mail. Like the judges, the county attorneys were asked: "Under an ideal system, at what stage in a criminal case do you think a lawyer should first be made available to the indigent person?" The results are shown in Table 1.

The support for early representation is consistent with the general response received to the question: "What do you think about trying a case when the defendant does not have counsel?" Every county attorney interviewed indicated a preference for an attorney in this situation. One county attorney noted that law enforcement officers are cautious with the rights of a defendant in direct proportion to the amount of contact they have with defense counsel. Therefore, carelessness prevails at the misdemeanor level, as well as at any stage of a felony proceeding where counsel is not present.

Of the reporting county attorneys, 33% stated that the available funds were not adequate to run their office. A chief complaint was inadequate staff, especially with the civil case load which must be carried by these offices as a result of increasing welfare cases. In addition, funds for investigation are unavailable in many counties. One county attorney pointed out that the sheriff's office is not qualified to investigate a complex fraud or embezzlement case. In such instances he states that funds should be available to the county attorney to finance investigations. However, the majority of responding county attorneys took the position that available funds were adequate to carry out their duties and to pay any investigation expenses, in many cases.

The estimates of the percentage of felony defendants who were indigent ranged from 5% to 95%, with the mean running slightly below that indicated by the judges, which was 60.5%. Fourteen prosecutors (22%) were critical of the present tests of indigency as too lenient, although 48 (76%) felt the test was about right. One county attorney suggested that a system of parent and child responsibility for attorney's fees be applied in indigent cases similar to the liability of close relatives imposed under the social welfare laws.

Several county attorneys, in comparing the appointed lawyer to one retained by a defendant, made the point that because of the smaller size of their jurisdictions, appointed counsel had more impetus to do a good job because their reputation would suffer otherwise. Especially in a county where little negligence and other trial work goes on, as one county attorney observed, an appointed attorney's work in defending a criminal case is well publicized.

Disclosure of certain information by the county attorneys to defense counsel is compelled by statute. At the time of filing an information, the county attorney is required to attach thereto the names of the witnesses he expects to call at trial, as well as a summary of their expected testimony. A copy of these minutes of evidence is delivered to the accused along with the information at or prior to the arraignment. If the state is proceeding by way of indictment, the names of all witnesses on whose evidence the indictment is found and the minutes of their evidence are made available to defense counsel. A bill of particulars is available to the defendant should the above information be insufficient. Four days before trial, the state must present to the defense attorney a summary of testimony of each witness whom the state has determined to call, including his name, residence, and occupation. With regard to confessions, witness statements, and technical reports and exhibits, many county attorneys indicated they disclose these to defense counsel where a plea of guilty may be possible. Where a trial of the case is certain, however, such disclosure is often withheld. The Supreme Court has recently held that civil discovery rules are not available to a defendant in criminal proceedings.[18]

On the question of providing counsel in miscellaneous cases and proceedings under an ideal system, the responses of prosecutors agreed generally with those of the judges, as indicated below. The least popular cases for providing counsel were misdemeanors, followed by hearings on revocation of probation and petitions for habeas corpus.

Type of case or proceeding	Provide counsel* No.	%	Unfair if not provided† No.	%
Sentencing of defendant who pleaded guilty	59	91	48	81
Sentencing of defendant convicted by trial	59	91	48	81
Habeas corpus or other postconviction remedy	47	72	35	67
Hearing on revocation of probation	40	62	32	58
Sexual psychopath hearing	56	86	45	85
Misdemeanors	15	24	15	28
Civil commitment of mentally ill	54	90	42	79

* An answer of "already provided" is counted as "yes."
† A few persons who said "sometimes," "depends on circumstances," etc., are counted here.

E. OPINIONS OF THE DEFENSE ATTORNEYS

Questionnaires were sent to 90 defense attorneys in the sample counties, and 54 of them responded (60%). These included attorneys who had over 20 district court appointments in 1962 and ranged to those who were appointed in only one case during the same period. One of the most consistent responses from the defense attorneys was the recommendation that additional funds be provided for both investigation expenses and increased attorneys' fees. One defense counsel pointed out that an attorney should feel free to spend the same amount of money in an indigent case as he would on another important case, including expenditures for photographs, long distance telephone calls, drawings, exhibits, etc. He pointed to a general feeling that a lawyer in an indigent case is expected to get along without the necessity of expenses of this nature. Several defense attorneys referred to appointment work as a burden which should be spread more evenly among the members of the bar. Several noted they were hampered in making an adequate investigation because of lack of funds. Table 2 illustrates the attitude of defense attorneys, prosecutors, and judges on the question of whether present rates of compensation for lawyers' services to indigent persons are adequate.

A strong body of opinion existed among defense attorneys that lawyers should be assigned at an earlier stage in the case than is the present practice. However, a majority of the assigned counsel felt that they were appointed in

TABLE 2
Compensation of Assigned Counsel

Is present compensation of lawyers adequate?*	Defense attorneys	Senior prosecutors	Junior prosecutors	Senior judges	Junior judges
Yes	10	17	17	12	15
No	41	7	20	2	2
No answer	3	1	1	0	4

* The question was posed directly to the prosecutors and judges as to whether present rates of compensation were adequate. In the defense attorney questionnaire counsel was asked what changes the attorney would recommend in the area of indigent defense. It is from the attorneys recommending that lawyers be paid more for their services that the defense attorney figures in the above table are derived. The attorneys who did not indicate that appointive fees should be increased are reflected as affirmatively supporting current rates of compensation. Senior prosecutors here are those with five or more years as county attorneys, and senior judges are those with 10 or more years of service on the bench.

time to make an adequate defense. Of those responding to this question, exactly 60% replied that their appointment came soon enough to do so. Several added the caveat that protection of the indigent's rights and preparation of his case would have been enhanced by a more prompt appointment.

TABLE 3
Retained and Assigned Counsel in Felonies
Iowa, 1962

| | | Did defendant have counsel? | | | | | | | |
County	Total sample	Yes No.	%	No No.	%	Retained No.	%	Assigned No.	%
Des Moines	20	20	100	0	0	8	40	12	60
Clarke	15	9	60	6	40	8	53	1	7
Scott	52	45	87	7	13	26	50	19	37

TABLE 4
Frequency of Release on Bail of Felony Defendants
Iowa, 1962

County	Total sample	Yes No.	%	No No.	%	No data* No.	%
Des Moines	20	7	35	13	65	0	0
Clarke	15	8	53	7	47	0	0
Scott	52	31	60	21	40	0	0
Polk	79	48	67	24	33	7	9
Weighted total percentages			53		47		2

* % of no data refers to total sample; % in other columns refers to total cases for which data were available.

TABLE 5
Disposition in Felony Cases
Iowa, 1962

County	Total sample	Plea guilty	Plea lesser offense	Dis- missed	Found guilty	Ac- quitted	Pend- ing
Des Moines	20	16	0	1	3	0	0
Clarke	15	9	0	2	3	1	0
Scott	52	44	4	1	1	1	1
Polk	79	43	6	4	19	4	3
Weighted total percentages		70	4	6	15	3	1

F. DOCKET STUDIES

Court dockets were examined for representative felony cases commenced in 1962 in four of the seven sample counties, and results are shown in Tables 3 to 6. (For details of methods of research see volume 1, pages 178-179.)

Information about whether defendants had counsel was available in three of the counties (see Table 3). In Des Moines County all defendants had counsel; in Clark, 60%; and in Scott, 87%. Table 4 shows the percentage of defendants who were released on bail in each county. The percentage varied from 35% in Des Moines County to 67% in Polk. As a rough test of indigency, the proportion not released would therefore range from 65% down to 33%, with a projected state-wide average of 47%. When Table 3 is compared with Table 4, the inference is possible that in Des Moines and Scott Counties virtually all indigent defendants had counsel assigned to represent them, but this did not occur in Clarke County.

Table 5 indicates the disposition of the cases. For the state as a whole, 74% of the defendants pleaded guilty, including 4% who pleaded to lesser offenses. Of the 18% of the cases that went to trial, 15% resulted in convictions. The highest rate of guilty pleas was in Scott County and the lowest rate in Polk County.

Sentences, if any, are shown in Table 6. For the state as a whole 54% of the defendants were sentenced to prison including county jails, and 27% were placed on probation. Iowa had a high proportion of fines and suspension of driver's licenses compared with other states.

G. CONCLUSIONS AND RECOMMENDATIONS

On the basis of the foregoing report the following conclusions and recommendations are submitted:

1. A uniform system of making attorneys available at the preliminary stages of criminal procedure should be provided. In many areas a defendant who expresses a desire for appointment of counsel and a preliminary hearing conducted by counsel on his behalf is denied this opportunity. There is no statutory provision for appointment of counsel prior to district court arraignment or for payment of attorney fees for work done in justice or municipal court. As noted previously, the district court in one county appoints the lawyer who participated

TABLE 6
Sentencing in Felony Cases*
Iowa, 1962

County	Total sample	No sentence		Prison		Probation		Suspended sentence		Fine		Suspended driver's license		Sentence pending		Miscellaneous	
		No.	%	No.	%	No.	%	No.	%	No.	%	No.	%	No.	%	No.	%
Des Moines	20	1	5	12	17	9	45	0	0	6	30	4	20	0	0	0	0
Clarke	15	3	20	11	73	2	13	0	0	10	67	7	47	0	0	0	0
Scott	52	3	6	12	23	17	33	1	2	21	40	0	0	0	0	0	0
Polk	79	24	30	48	61	13	16	1	1	23	29	10	13	1	1	1	1
Weighted total percentages			15		54		27		1		42		20		0		0

* If a defendant had a combination sentence, such as fine and probation, he is counted under both columns. Thus the total adds to more than 100%.

248

in the case at the preliminary stages. This is a worthy example of progressive judicial attack on this problem. A standard procedure for appointment of counsel at the magistrate level, with adequate financing, should be developed.

2. The prescribed fees for felony representation should be increased and funds should be made available for reimbursement of the cost of investigation and preparation. In certain larger counties consideration should be given to suggestions that a defense investigator be retained to assist defense counsel, on either a full-time or part-time basis as local conditions require.

3. In conformity with the opinions of judges, county attorneys, and defense counsel throughout the state, the appointed lawyer system should be retained. The establishment of a public defender system, even on the basis of one office for each judicial district, is not a practical solution to the problems of indigent defense. Improvement of the existing system appears to be preferable.

4. Evidence indicates that indigent cases have not been appealed with the frequency of cases involving retained counsel. Perhaps this is a justifiable situation based upon the merits of the individual cases involved. This matter should be studied, however, and efforts made to standardize appeal practice to insure the right of counsel-conducted appeal to indigent defendants.

5. The current practice in several counties is to place the onus of criminal assignments on the junior members of the bar. Because of the inexperience of appointed counsel in these instances, it is suggested that the state bar association undertake a program of clinical study and practical training in criminal law in cooperation with the law schools of the state. Establishment of a legal internship program, with actual case participation by the involved students, will better equip those younger members of the bar for the duties of appointed counsel which fall so frequently upon them.

NOTES—Iowa

[1] *Iowa Code Ann.* § 753.2 (1962).

[2] *Iowa Code Ann.* §§ 602.15, .16 (1962). If the county is divided into two districts, the jurisdiction of the municipal court is the same as the district in which it is located.

[3] *Iowa Code Ann.* § 605.14 (1962).

[4] *Iowa Code Ann.* § 761.1 (1962).

[5] Ibid.

[6] County attorney informations are dealt with in *Iowa Code Ann.*, ch. 769 (1962); indictments in ch. 772.

[7] *Iowa Code Ann.* § 795.2 (1962), as amended by H.F. 52, Laws of the 60th General Assembly, 1963.

[8] *Ops. Att'y Gen.*, Oct. 28, 1963.

[9] *Iowa Code Ann.* § 775.4 (1962).

[10] *Iowa Code Ann.* § 775.12 (1962).

[11] *Iowa Code Ann.* § 775.5 (1962).

[12] *Iowa Code Ann.* § 775.6 (1962).

[13] *Iowa Code Ann.* § 775.5 (1962).

[14] Douglas v. California, 372 U.S. 353 (1963); Lane v. Brown, 372 U.S. 477 (1963).

[15] *Iowa Code Ann.* § 775.5 (1962).

[16] *Iowa Code Ann.* § 793.8 (1962).

[17] *Iowa Code Ann.* §§ 663.4, .5 (1962).

[18] State v. District Court, 253 Iowa 903, 114 N.W.2d 317 (1962). See also State v. McClain, 125 N.W.2d 764 (Iowa 1964).

KANSAS

Prof. Paul E. Wilson, Lawrence

The following Kansas lawyers served as members of the A.B.A. Associate State Committee: Everett E. Steerman, Emporia, chairman; John W. Brand, Jr., Lawrence; Carl L. Buck and Stanford J. Smith, Wichita; Gerald L. Goodell and Ernest J. Rice, Topeka; Miles D. Mustain, Kansas City; and Maurice P. O'Keefe, Jr., Atchison. The committee demonstrated a real interest in the project and its contribution was substantial.

A. INTRODUCTION

Kansas had a population of 2,178,611 in 1960, which has increased slightly each year since. There are 105 counties, which are organized into 41 judicial districts; 34 of the districts have one judge each, while 7 districts have multiple divisions with two to seven judges. The county attorney in each county is the chief prosecutor for the state. Eight counties were personally visited by the reporter and an inquiry was carried on by mail in the remaining counties. Information concerning the eight sample counties is shown in Table 1.

B. CRIMINAL PROCEDURE AS IT AFFECTS INDIGENT PERSONS

The jurisdiction to try felony cases is vested exclusively in the district courts of the state. Substantially all felony prosecutions are tried upon information. Although the statutes authorize the use of grand juries under exceptional circumstances, experience indicates that the grand jury is seldom employed.

Most felony cases commence with the arrest of the suspect. An arrested person must be taken before a magistrate of the county, who is required to conduct a preliminary examination "as soon as may be." (Kan. Gen. Stat. Ann. § 62-614 [1949].) While judges on all levels are authorized to sit as examining magistrates, preliminary hearings are usually conducted by an officer of justice of the peace level. The name given the officer and the designation of his court varies from one county to another. In Sedgwick County, the largest county of the state, the preliminary examination is ordinarily held before a judge of the court of common pleas. Three judges sit on this court, all of whom are required to be lawyers. In Brown, Edwards, and Butler Counties, preliminary examinations are conducted before the judge of the county court. The probate judge of the county is ex-officio judge of the county court. In Butler County the probate judge is a lawyer; in Brown and Edwards he is not. In Shawnee, Leavenworth, and Wyandotte Counties, the judge of the city court acts as examining magistrate. In Kansas City, Leavenworth, and Topeka, as well as in several other cities, city courts have been established which are in fact state courts exercising justice of the peace jurisdiction. The courts of Topeka and Leavenworth each have one judge, while the city court of Kansas City has two judges. All the judges of these courts are lawyers. Labette County has neither a county court nor a city court; hence, preliminary examinations are conducted before lay justices of the peace.

At his first appearance before a magistrate, an arrested person is informed of

251

TABLE 1
Sample Counties

County	Chief city	Location in state	1960 population in thousands	Lawyers in practice	Felony defendants, 1962	% of felony defendants indigent*	Economic base
Brown† (D)	Hiawatha	Northeast	13	9	13	92	Agriculture
Butler† (D)	El Dorado	South central	38	33	153	70	Agriculture, oil production and refining
Edwards	Kinsley	Southwest	5	5	9	33	Agriculture
Labette	Parsons	Southeast	26	16	23	30	Agriculture, light industry
Leavenworth‡ (D)	Leavenworth	Northeast	49	22	56	75	Military post, state and federal prisons, agriculture
Sedgwick† (D)	Wichita	South central	343	485	402	25	Industry and commerce, oil production, agriculture
Shawnee† (D)	Topeka	East central	141	300	246	30	State capital, industry and commerce, agriculture
Wyandotte	Kansas City	East	185	223	198	30	Industry and commerce

(D) indicates that a docket study was made.
* Estimate based on docket studies and opinions of judges and prosecutors.
† Mail survey of appointed counsel was made.
‡ The original sample included seven counties only. Leavenworth was added because of special local conditions there.

the crime with which he is charged and his bail is fixed if the offense is bailable. At this time the defendant is informed of his right to a preliminary hearing, and the date for the hearing is set unless it is waived by the defendant. The hearing may not be adjourned for more than 10 days without the consent of the accused. The laws of Kansas make no provision for the appointment of counsel prior to or at the preliminary hearing. The right to appointed counsel does not arise until the defendant is about to be arraigned in the trial court. Nevertheless, in three of the counties visited, counsel are commonly appointed at or prior to the preliminary hearing. In Sedgwick every felony defendant who appears for preliminary hearing without counsel has an attorney appointed to represent him. In Shawnee and Wyandotte counsel are assigned in cases where the penalty may be death or a long imprisonment, or where special circumstances are present.

Bail is set by the examining magistrate. Although the magistrates ordinarily do not have formal schedules, practice is uniform within each jurisdiction. In Sedgwick County, for example, bail in felony cases is set at $1000 unless unusual circumstances indicate a higher bond. In all of the counties the first appearance before the magistrate regularly occurs within 24 hours following the arrest, except when the defendant has been arrested on a weekend or on the evening preceding a holiday. Then he may not be able to appear before the magistrate until the next business day.

Although preliminary hearings are available to all defendants charged with felony, it appears that they are actually held in only about 20% of the cases. In Butler County the district judge indicated that when a preliminary hearing has been waived without assistance of counsel before the magistrate the defendant has an opportunity to withdraw his waiver after appointment of counsel in the district court. In the event of withdrawal the case is remanded to the magistrate for a preliminary hearing, which is usually held within 10 days after the arrest unless a longer time is requested by the defendant. Waivers are usually accepted forthwith. After the hearing is held or waived, the magistrate makes an order binding the defendant over to the district court for trial. Thereupon, the information is filed and the defendant is arraigned. Ordinarily, the defendant is tried during the first term that commences after he is bound over for trial. Each district court has three terms per year. Thus the defendant may be tried within a few days, or he may have to wait for nearly four months. It is apparently the usual practice to file the information immediately after the defendant is bound over, but to delay arraignment until opening day of the term in which he is to be tried. If the defendant indicates a desire to plead guilty, he is not required to wait until the following term to appear and enter his plea.

Procedure for the appointment of counsel varies from one county to another. In Sedgwick, Shawnee, and Wyandotte, when an attorney is appointed in the preliminary hearing by the examining magistrate, the attorney is usually reappointed in the district court. In the other counties, counsel may be appointed either prior to or at the time of arraignment on the information, depending on the circumstances. In no county is a thorough investigation made of the question of indigency. Ordinarily, when the defendant appears before the court for arraignment, the judge inquires whether he has counsel or the means with which to employ one. No other investigation is made. If this interrogation satisfies the judge that the defendant is indigent, counsel is appointed.

There is no provision in the law for the compensation of appointed counsel for services performed at the preliminary hearing. Payment from the county treasury is made for services in the trial court. Until July 1, 1963, the allowance was limited to $10 per day (Kan. Gen. Stat. Ann. § 62-1304 [Supp. 1961]). Since that date the trial judge has been authorized to fix a reasonable fee in each case (*Laws 1963* ch. 305). At the time of the survey, the new law had been operative for only a few weeks. Experience was so limited that it was not feasible to generalize as to fees allowed in any county. In several counties schedules of compensation were under consideration by the judges and local bar associations. Suggested minimums for trial work have ranged from $25 to $150 per day. It seems likely that most courts will establish a standard fee which will not exceed $50 per day. In the past some of the judges seem to have taken a liberal view of the statutory allowance of $10 per day. Although the statute contemplated payment only for days spent in court, it has been a common practice to honor claims for time spent in the investigation and preliminary hearing. Padding of claims seems often to have been overlooked. Also, it appears that rural judges have been more conservative in fixing fees than judges in the urban areas. (See Appendices I and II.)

The procedure for appointment of counsel is prescribed by law. Section 62-1304 of the General Statutes Supplement, as amended, makes it the duty of the court to inform a defendant who appears for arraignment without counsel that he is entitled to counsel, and to give him an opportunity to employ counsel of his own choosing if he is able to do so. If he is not able to employ an attorney and does not ask to consult a particular one, the court must appoint counsel to represent him unless he waives in writing and the court finds that the appointment of counsel over his objection would not be to his advantage. A transcript of these proceedings must be prepared and placed in the case file. The statute is apparently followed closely in the Kansas courts. Counsel is seldom waived. Only one of the judges interviewed indicated that he had ever accepted a waiver. All the other judges said that they will not honor waivers even though the defendant desires that he be not represented. Apparently, Kansas judges are usually unwilling to make the finding that the appointment of counsel over the defendant's objection would not be to his advantage. Hence, procedure for waiver is of academic interest only.

In none of the counties visited is counsel provided for defendants charged with misdemeanors in courts inferior to the district court. Although the district court has jurisdiction over misdemeanors as well as felonies, in practice few misdemeanor cases are filed there. When filed in that court they are prosecuted on information. Since the statute requiring appointment of counsel applies to all defendants about to be arraigned on an information or indictment, three of the district judges interviewed took the view that appointment is required in misdemeanors as well as felonies. Hence, a few appointments are made in misdemeanors. Other judges apparently believed that the statute applied to felony cases only. Since the vast majority of misdemeanors are processed in courts of the magistrate level, where no provision exists for appointment of attorneys, most indigent defendants have no statutory right to the assistance of counsel.

The statutes of Kansas provide for appointment of counsel on appeal only for a defendant convicted of murder in the first degree and sentenced to death. (Kan. Gen. Stat. Ann. § 62-1304 [Supp., 1961] as amended.) Thus it was necessary that additional provision for appointed counsel be made following *Douglas v. California*, 372 U.S. 353 (1963). On April 16, 1963, the Supreme Court of Kansas adopted Rule 56, as follows:

> When any defendant has been convicted of a felony and he is without means to employ counsel to perfect an appeal to the Supreme Court, he may make affidavit to that effect, stating that he intends to appeal and requesting the appointment of counsel. The judge of the court in which the defendant was convicted shall, when satisfied that the affidavit is true, appoint counsel to conduct such appeal.

No provision is made for the compensation of counsel appointed under Rule 56 in noncapital cases. However, in a memorandum dated May 1, 1963, the attorney general advised all district judges and county attorneys that his office had conferred informally with legislative leaders and that they had informally agreed that pending the enactment of legislation providing compensation for appointed appellate attorneys, claims of appointed appellate counsel for services and expenses should be presented to the Claims and Accounts committee of the Legislature at the 1964 budget session. Such claims have been honored, although a limit of $300 has been observed. Later, the 1965 session of the Legislature will be asked to amend the law to provide for compensation to such appointed attorneys.

There is no provision for appointment or compensation of attorneys who represent petitioners in habeas corpus or other postconviction proceedings.

C. OPINIONS OF THE JUDGES

The study included interviews with district judges and with magistrates in the eight sample counties. In six of the counties, one judge was interviewed; in Butler County, two judges; and in Sedgwick County, three judges. Questionnaires were mailed to at least one judge in each of the other districts of the state. Of 38 questionnaires sent out, 28 were returned (74%). Judges of 36 of the state's 41 judicial districts took part in the survey either in person or by mail.

One of the objectives of the interview was to determine the attitudes of judges as to procedure that might be employed in an ideal situation. Each judge interviewed was asked the following question: "Under an ideal system, at what stage in a criminal case do you think the indigent person should first be provided with a lawyer if he wants one?" A similar question was included in the mail questionnaire. Each judge was requested to indicate at which of several indicated stages he thought counsel should ideally be provided to the indigent felony defendant. The results are summarized in Table 2. Of the 38 judges reached by the survey, 18 expressed the view that the defendant should be provided with counsel at or prior to the time of his first appearance before a magistrate. An additional 10 indicated that counsel ought to be provided subsequent to the first appearance before the magistrate but at or before the preliminary hearing. One would provide counsel subsequent to the preliminary hearing but before the filing of the information. Seven indicated satisfaction with the present practice of providing appointed counsel between the filing of the information and the time of the arraignment. Two judges did not answer specifically, but each of them indicated that counsel should be provided at an early stage in the proceedings, the exact point to depend on the discretion of the court in each case. In summary, the vast majority of trial judges reporting believe that ideally counsel should be provided at some point earlier in the felony proceedings than now provided by Kansas statute.

Whatever the stage designated for the appointment of counsel, the great majority of both groups of judges, those interviewed and those questioned by mail, agreed that the defendant who does not have counsel at that stage is then treated unfairly. A few said "not necessarily" or left the question blank. Also, most judges felt that the system could be financed. In a few cases, some concern was expressed as to the problem of unduly burdening the public treasury. Apparently, all the judges assume that this burden will continue to fall on county government. The only expression of sentiment in favor of state appropriations for this purpose was heard in Leavenworth County, where a substantial percentage of the cases involve inmates of state institutions located in the county. Most of the answers in this phase of the survey were quite summary. Since up to this time the cost of this item of government has been relatively little, it may be inferred that no great amount of thought has been given to the problem.

There is virtual unanimity of opinion concerning the appointment of counsel in several other kinds of cases. The laws of Kansas seem to require that counsel be provided for those defendants who appear for sentencing after conviction on plea of guilty. The courts universally comply with this requirement. On the other hand, the law makes no provision for appointment of counsel to handle habeas corpus, coram nobis, or other postconviction remedies. Only a small minority of the judges feel that counsel is necessary in these proceedings. Moreover, some of those judges who favored appointment did so upon the ground that the appearance of counsel would insure a more orderly and responsible presentation of the matter rather than on the basis of the requirements of justice to the petitioner. In at least two instances, judges stated with candor that they favored the appointment of counsel in such cases as a convenience to the court. With respect to revocation of probation, the usual practice seems to require that notice be given by the court to the attorney who represented the defendant at the time of his conviction. In most cases, the attorney appears at the hearing upon receipt of notice. On the other hand, the statute makes no provision for his compensation, and in routine cases the judges do not hesitate to proceed without counsel.

The sexual psychopath hearing in Kansas is in the nature of a postconviction proceeding. The statute applies only to a defendant who has been convicted or has pleaded guilty, and the only issue is what disposition will be made of him. In such proceedings he is represented by counsel.

Most judges feel that it is unnecessary to appoint counsel in misdemeanor cases. A few believe that counsel should be appointed for serious misdemeanors, such as driving while intoxicated, negligent homicide, and others where a substantial penalty applies. As a matter of practice, most district courts have little concern with misdemeanor cases, since almost all such cases are prosecuted in the courts of inferior jurisdiction.

Civil commitments of the mentally ill are generally within the jurisdiction of the probate courts of Kansas. The judges surveyed universally approve the Kansas law that provides counsel for the patient in such cases.

No significant differences in attitudes appear between judges in rural counties and those in urban counties. Practice does differ, however, particularly with respect to appointment of counsel in preliminary hearings, as described above. The rural judge or magistrate is inclined to take a more literal view of the statute providing for appointment of counsel. Also, the rural judge is more conservative in fixing fees. As an illustration, under the former statute that authorized payment of $10 per day as counsel fees, rural judges would adhere strictly to the statutory schedule, whereas urban judges deviated considerably from the letter of the law, allowing more realistic payments to appointed counsel. These differences in practice may be attributable not to the attitudes of the judges, but rather to the fact that in urban areas a more aggressive and vigorous segment of the bar is interested in the criminal practice. In the rural counties, where substantially all practice is civil, lawyers often regard criminal appointments as charitable contributions of service. Hence, few seem to expect adequate compensation.

The judges' opinions varied somewhat according to age and years on the bench. Sixteen of the judges contacted had served 10 years or more, whereas 22 had served for less than 10 years. Although the responses of each group vary only a little, there is some indication that the junior judges desire appointment of counsel at an earlier stage in the proceedings, and that they are more concerned about inadequacy of fees paid to counsel.

With respect to the quality of appointed counsel, 27 of 38 judges felt that the assigned attorney was equal in performance and experience to the employed attorney in the same court. Ten felt that the appointed counsel did not perform as effectively as employed counsel, while one judge suggested that appointed counsel was generally better than employed counsel. On the other hand, 25 judges thought that appointed counsel was usually equal in ability and experience to the county attorney. Nine felt that appointed counsel was usually better, and only three felt appointed counsel was at a disadvantage when compared with the prosecuting attorney.

D. OPINIONS OF THE PROSECUTORS

Eight county attorneys were interviewed. In addition, 68 of the remaining 97 replied to mail questionnaires (70%). The views of the county attorneys were not unlike those expressed by the judges. Thirty-three thought that counsel should be provided between the arrest and the first appearance before the magistrate; 20 said after the first appearance but not later than the preliminary hearing; 2, between the preliminary hearing and the filing of the information; 20, between the filing of the information and the arraignment thereon; and one did not answer this item. Fifty-six of those replying (74%) thought that present compensation of assigned lawyers is inadequate; nine, that present fees are adequate; and one failed to answer the question. Fifty-six of the county attorneys viewed appointed counsel as about equal to those employed by the defendant, 17 considered appointed counsel in some respects inferior, while only 2 felt that appointed counsel are better. Substantially all the county attorneys felt that counsel should be provided in felony cases for the several postconviction procedures. Most would require appointed counsel for sentencing, revocation of probation, sexual psychopath hearings, and in mental commitment proceedings in the probate court. Few, however, would require appointment of counsel for trial of misdemeanor cases.

Almost all county attorneys complained of the inadequate funds for the financing of their own offices, resulting chiefly in lack of sufficient professional staff, lack of investigative staff, and inadequate salaries. It was frequently suggested that in most counties the county attorney should be paid a salary sufficient to enable him to refrain from private practice. At present, most county attorneys spend far more time in private than in official pursuits. A good many deplore the necessity for this division of their loyalty.

All county attorneys reporting indicated their willingness to cooperate as fully with appointed counsel as with employed counsel. Many of them indicated a willingness to make full disclosure of confessions, statements of witnesses, exhibits, and other matters of evidence. Some made a distinction between the routine case and the one likely to receive publicity: in the routine case, full disclosure usually is made; in the other, disclosure is made with greater reluctance. The county attorneys interviewed often indicated that they felt that disclosure was significant in that it frequently assisted defense counsel to advise his client to plead guilty or to waive preliminary hearing. In no case did the county attorneys admit to cooperating more with employed counsel than with counsel appointed by the court.

E. OPINIONS OF DEFENSE COUNSEL

Questionnaires were sent to 37 attorneys who had served as defense counsel during the year 1962, and 22 replied (59%). These attorneys represented five of the eight sample counties (see Table 1, note †). Although the number is small, the views expressed may have some significance. Most attorneys reported that they had been appointed to represent 5 or fewer cases in 1962, but a few reported a larger number, and one attorney reported 19. Generally, those who responded to the questionnaire were experienced defense counsel. None had been practicing for less than three years, and 12 had been in practice for five years or more. The attorneys were asked to comment specifically on their last appointment. Although the Kansas statute contemplates appointment of counsel at the time of arraignment on the information, only 2 of the 22 attorneys reported an appointment at that time. One was appointed after the arraignment, and the others were appointed at various times prior to the arraignment. This reflects the local practice in Sedgwick and Shawnee Counties reported above in Section B.

Each attorney was asked to indicate whether in his last case the appointment had been made in time to prepare adequately for the trial. Thirteen attorneys indicated that they had had adequate time; seven indicated that time had been insufficient; two did not answer the question. Only one of the 10 attorneys who replied from Sedgwick and Shawnee Counties, where counsel is provided at the preliminary hearing, complained of insufficient time. On the other hand, 6 of the 12 who answered from the other counties had felt unable to prepare adequately. Nine of the attorneys thought the system now employed in Kansas is fair to the accused while 13 thought it unfair. On the other hand, only 3 felt that the system is fair to appointed counsel, whereas 19 stated that the system is unfair to such counsel. Services rendered in the cases commented on were valued by the attorneys at from $150 to $1500. Only four valued their services at less than $300. This service was rendered during the period when the nominal fee of $10 a day was authorized. Actual compensation ranged from zero to $50.

Twenty of the 22 attorneys who replied recommended that the system might be improved by more adequate compensation of defense counsel. Fifteen said that out-of-pocket expenses should be reimbursed, and nine said attorneys should be appointed at an earlier stage. Nine also felt that counsel should be provided in other kinds of cases, such as serious misdemeanors and habeas corpus. And seven expressed the view that it would be helpful to the system for the judges to prepare and employ a new system in the selection of appointed counsel.

The last item merits additional comment. In some counties both defense counsel and prosecuting attorneys indicated dissatisfaction with the procedure for selection of counsel. Young lawyers are appointed to represent routine felony defendants. They are often inexperienced. For capital offenses an effort is usually made to obtain the best counsel available. There is a feeling in some counties, not necessarily verified by references to cases, that certain attorneys are given unduly large numbers of appointments. The problem has two aspects. In most instances, attorneys regard the representation of indigent defendants as a disagreeable chore that is not financially rewarding. Therefore, they object when the burden seems unequally distributed. On the other hand, there are instances, particularly in the larger cities, where attorneys actively seek appointments of this kind. They may become a matter of political patronage for a judge who has friends who need and are interested in this kind of business. There is no evidence that counsel so selected render an inferior kind of service, but there is the possibility of abuse. It becomes a matter of concern in view of the recent legislation which permits more adequate compensation to appointed counsel. With counsel assured of a reasonable fee for his service, appointments ought to be rotated regularly among all members of the bar who are competent and willing to undertake service of this kind.

F. COMPARISONS AMONG JUDGES AND PROSECUTORS

An analysis of comparable attitudes among judges and prosecutors may be of interest. For the purpose of comparison, the judges were divided into two groups.

Those who have served 10 years or more in their judicial position are designated as senior judges, and the others as junior judges. Similarly, prosecutors with five or more years of experience were designated as senior prosecutors and the others as junior prosecutors. The attitudes and views of the judges and prosecutors with respect to several aspects of the survey are shown in Table 2 below.

TABLE 2
Views of Judges and Prosecutors

	Senior judges	Junior judges	Senior county attorneys	Junior county attorneys	Totals
Total responding	16	22	38	38	114
Ideal stage for first appointment of counsel:					
Between arrest and first appearance	6	12	14	18	50
Prior to or at preliminary hearing	6	4	10	10	30
Between preliminary hearing and filing of information		1	1	1	3
Between information filing and arraignment	3	4	12	9	28
No answer	1	1	1	0	3
Is present compensation of lawyers adequate?					
Yes	11	8	10	9	38
No	3	11	27	29	70
No answer	2	3	1	0	6
Should out-of-pocket expenses be paid?					
Yes	9	15	28	23	75
No	0	0	1	0	1
No answer	7	7	9	15	38
Comparison with employed counsel					
Poorer	3	7	11	6	27
Equal	12	15	27	29	83
Better	1	0	0	2	3
No answer	0	0	0	1	1

G. DOCKET STUDY

A study was made for 1962 of representative felony cases in five of the eight counties selected for survey. (Methods of research are explained in volume 1, page 178.) The results are shown in Tables 3 to 8.

Table 3 confirms that virtually every defendant had counsel. This table also shows a striking variation in the percentage of defendants who retained their own counsel. The figures were as low as 14% in Brown County and 18% in Leavenworth, with a range upward to 67% in Shawnee County (Topeka) and 69% in Sedgwick (Wichita). The weighted average of the five counties, which is a projected figure for the state as a whole, was 41% retained counsel.

As shown in Table 4, an average of 58% of the defendants in the state were officially determined to be indigent. This figure corresponds closely to the proportion of defendants who had assigned counsel (at least 56%), and, as shown in Table 5, the proportion who were not released on bail (63%). (In 3% of the cases no bail was set, usually where the defendant was charged with a very serious crime.) The figures for the individual sample counties also correspond closely.

Table 6 shows that preliminary hearings were relatively uncommon in the state as a whole, although the frequency varied in different counties. The highest proportion occurred in Sedgwick County. Further analysis indicates that although the majority of defendants represented by either assigned counsel or retained counsel waived the hearing, the proportion of defendants with retained counsel who had a hearing was somewhat higher. In Sedgwick County, 22 out of 53 (42%) of clients of retained counsel had a preliminary hearing, while only 1 out of 19 (5%) of clients of assigned counsel had one.

Table 7 shows the way in which the sample cases were disposed of by the court. For the state as a whole an estimated 75% of the defendants pleaded guilty, including 17% who pleaded to lesser offenses. The highest rate of guilty pleas occurred in Brown County, followed by Sedgwick (82%) and Leavenworth (74%). Butler County had an unusually high percentage of dismissals: only about 5% of the cases went to trial.

The proportion of pleas to lesser offenses, which is relatively high as compared with other states, may be a function of the high proportion of defendants who have counsel, since a defendant without counsel is less able to bargain with the prosecutor for a lesser plea.

Table 8 shows the final sentences, if any, imposed on the defendants. For the state as a whole, 40% of the original sample of defendants were sentenced to prison (including county jail); 37% were placed on probation; 1% were given a suspended sentence without probation; and 2% were fined. The most frequent use of probation vis-à-vis imprisonment was in Leavenworth and Shawnee Counties, and the least frequent use was in Brown County.

H. RECOMMENDATIONS

On the basis of the foregoing report, the following recommendations are made.

1. A uniform schedule of fees for appointed counsel should be established in each judicial district. This schedule should be consistent with the schedule adopted by the State Bar Association, after taking into account local variations in economic conditions and fee schedules for other legal services. Expenses incident to investigation and preparation of defense should be reimbursed.

2. Because of the relative inexperience of assigned counsel in many counties,

TABLE 3
Retained and Assigned Counsel in Felonies
Kansas, 1962

County	Total sample	Did defendant have counsel? Yes No.	%	No No.	%	Retained No.	%	Assigned No.	%	Combination or type unknown No.	%	No data° No.	%
Brown	14	14	100	0	0	2	14	12	86	0	0	0	0
Leavenworth	23	22	100	0	0	4	18	18	82	0	0	1	4
Butler	50	41	98	1	2	14	33	25	60	2	5	8	16
Shawnee	80	79	100	0	0	53	67	23	29	3	4	1	1
Sedgwick	79	77	100	0	0	53	69	20	26	4	5	2	3
Weighted total percentages		100		0		41		56		3		5	

° % of no data refers to total sample; % in other columns refers to total cases for which data were available.

TABLE 4
Was Felony Defendant Determined Indigent?
Kansas, 1962

County	Total sample	Yes No.	%	No No.	%	No data° No.	%
Brown	14	12	86	2	14	0	0
Leavenworth	23	18	82	4	18	1	4
Butler	50	26	62	16	38	8	16
Shawnee	80	26	34	50	66	4	5
Sedgwick	79	21	28	55	72	3	4
Weighted total percentages		58		42		6	

° % of no data refers to total sample; % in other columns refers to total cases for which data were available.

TABLE 5
Frequency of Release on Bail of Felony Defendants
Kansas, 1962

County	Total sample	Yes No.	%	No No.	%	No data° No.	%
Brown	14	1	7	13	93	0	0
Leavenworth	23	9	39	14	61	0	0
Butler	50	18	37	31	63	1	2
Shawnee	80	39	52	36	48	5	6
Sedgwick	79	40	51	38	49	1	1
Weighted total percentages		37		63		2	

° % of no data refers to total sample; % in other columns refers to total cases for which data were available.

262

TABLE 6
Frequency of Preliminary Hearings in Felonies
Kansas, 1962

County	Total sample	Yes No.	%	No, waiver No.	%	No data* No.	%
Brown	14	1	7	13	93	0	0
Leavenworth	23	2	9	21	91	0	0
Butler	50	10	21	38	79	2	4
Shawnee	80	15	20	61	80	4	5
Sedgwick	79	24	31	54	69	1	1
Weighted total percentages			18		82		2

* % of no data refers to total sample; % in other columns refers to total cases for which data were available.

TABLE 7
Disposition in Felony Cases
Kansas, 1962

County	Total sample	Plea guilty	Plea lesser offense	Dis- missed	Found guilty	Found guilty lesser degree	Ac- quitted	Mental com- mit- ment	Pend- ing	Other
Brown	14	10	4	0	0	0	0	0	0	0
Leavenworth	23	12	5	5	0	1	0	0	0	0
Butler	50	20	6	21	0	0	0	0	2	1
Shawnee	80	44	9	9	6	2	3	3	3	1
Sedgwick	79	55	10	4	2	1	1	2	1	3
Weighted total percentages		58	17	16	2	2	1	1	2	1

TABLE 8*
Sentencing in Felony Cases
Kansas, 1962

County	Total sample	No sentence No.	%	Prison No.	%	Probation No.	%	Suspended sentence No.	%	Fine No.	%
Brown	14	0	0	10	71	4	29	0	0	0	0
Leavenworth	23	5	22	7	30	11	48	0	0	1	4
Butler	50	24	48	13	26	9	18	1	2	4	8
Shawnee	80	18	23	22	28	36	49	1	1	0	0
Sedgwick	79	8	10	37	47	34	43	0	0	0	0
Weighted total percentages		20		40		37		1		2	

* In a few instances, the defendant had a combination sentence, such as fine and probation. If this occurred he is counted under both headings; hence, the totals are slightly over 100% for some of the counties.

it is recommended that the State Bar Association undertake a program of continuing legal education in criminal procedure in cooperation with the law schools of the state.

3. It is suggested that an appropriate agency consider possible amendments to the statutes to provide for the appointment and compensation of counsel at stages prior to arraignment on the information. The survey shows that the judges, prosecutors, and the defense attorneys of the state believe that counsel should be provided to the indigent accused not later than the preliminary hearing. This would seem to be an appropriate matter for a study by the Judicial Council.

4. Some consideration should be given to the problem of providing counsel for a defendant in a misdemeanor case where the penalty is substantial. Also, the problem of supplying counsel in habeas corpus and other postconviction proceedings ought to be explored.

5. Standards of indigency should be defined, and effective procedures for applying such standards should be developed and employed.

6. The system of keeping docket records should be more uniform throughout the state. More complete data about each case should be kept in one central file in the county. Also, records as to arrests and other data should be made available to the public in a report published by the officers who make arrests.

7. Under existing conditions in Kansas, there is no apparent need for a public defender in any community. Hence, it is recommended that the assigned counsel system be retained but that it be implemented and improved as suggested herein.

APPENDIX I

PREAMBLE TO DECENT REQUEST

WHEREAS, the Criminal Practice and Procedure Committee of the Wichita Bar Association has met several times to attempt to work out a practical solution to the problems of defending indigent criminals and under the new edicts of the Supreme Court of the United States, and

WHEREAS, the committee has investigated and found that the average lawyer, besides being plagued with office rent ranging from $2.50 to $4.50 for a square foot of office space, a secretary that costs between three to four hundred dollars a month, the continuing cost of various legal periodicals, let alone the claims made on his time for charity work and contributions, plus contributions of time and money to all sorts of political campaigns and

WHEREAS, and because of the above, plus the demands of taxes and living expenses, the average lawyer has expenses that exceed $1000.00 a month, which must be paid regardless of the demands made upon him,

NOW, THEREFORE, this Committee thinks it is unconscionable for courts or members of the public to require lawyers to represent indigent clients in felony cases unless the following provisions are enacted by the Bar and adhered to by the courts:

FIRST: A decent, realistic fee schedule should be enacted, and it should at least provide the following:

1. For representation of the indigent criminal on a felony matter in the Court of Common Pleas, regardless of the number of the appearances but where the preliminary hearing is waived, that fee should be ....$ 50.00

2. To representation of the indigent criminal on a felony matter in the Court of Common Pleas, regardless of the number of appearances but where a preliminary hearing is had, the fee should be ....$ 100.00

3. To representation of the indigent criminal on a felony matter in the District Court, regardless of the number of appearances, but where a plea is entered

KANSAS

without the necessity of a trial or hearing .... $ 100.00
4. To representation of the indigent criminal on a felony matter where the case is
tried to a court or jury, the per day fee on trial should be no less than $150.00
a day .... $ 150.00
5. Where an appeal of the case of an indigent criminal is taken to the Supreme
Court of Kansas, the total sum allowed, including expenses of briefing, abstracting, printing and traveling to Topeka to argue the matter should not be less
than $1200 .... $1200.00
SECOND: In determining who is an indigent person for whom counsel should be appointed
by the court, besides the other rules now used, the following should be mandatory:
1. No prisoner who can make bond that requires a surety is to be considered an indigent
person.
2. Every prisoner claiming to be an indigent person and requesting that counsel be appointed to represent him should sign a confession of judgment whereby the court can
enter a judgment against him for the amount of the attorneys' fees and expenses that are
incurred in his behalf to bring the case to a conclusion. Said confession of judgment
would be entered on the records of the Clerk of the Court so that execution could be
issued thereon. The counsel in whose favor the judgment is entered shall be charged with
the duty of attempting to collect the judgment, and thus to reimburse the county for the
sums paid on behalf of said indigent criminal. (It should be noted that a system of this
sort is in successful operation in Butler County, Kansas.)
THIRD: On or before January 1, of each year, members of the Wichita Bar Association
desiring or willing to accept appointment in criminal felony cases, and who are qualified
by trial experience to do so, shall submit their names to the assignment judge of the 18th
judicial district. The names will be placed upon a list in the exact order received and
appointment will be made from that list by strict rotation.
(a) To be qualified to be placed on the list, the applicant must be a member of the
Wichita Bar Association and must, in the opinion of the majority of the judges, be
competent to adequately try a criminal felony jury case. In the event any lawyer, who
is a member of the Wichita Bar Association, feels that he has been wrongfully refused
a place on the appointment list by the members of the judiciary, he has the privilege of
appealing such decision to the Criminal Practice and Procedure Committee of the Wichita
Bar Association, whose decision in the matter shall be final.
In the event there are insufficient applicants from the Wichita Bar Association, willing to
undertake the defense of indigents, then and in that event, the Criminal Practice and Procedure Committee of the Wichita Bar Association along with the judges of the 18th Judicial
District shall compile a list of lawyers that are members of the Wichita Bar Association, and
who in the opinion of both bodies are well qualified to defend felony cases. These names will
be added to the list of those already willing to accept such appointments and indigent clients
with felony cases will be likewise assigned to those counsel on a strict rotation basis. No lawyer
so selected shall refuse the appointment except on the following grounds:
1. Poor health;
2. Personal acquaintance with the party or witness involved;
3. If the lawyer be over the age of 50 years, he has the right to refuse the appointment.

CONCLUSION

This committee realizes that the above recommendations will not achieve any panacea.
We do believe that their adoption will result in a favorable and more adequate defense of
the indigent criminals, whose only resources are those which his court-appointed attorney
is willing to donate to his client, while the prosecution has almost unlimited resources to draw
from. Secondly, we feel the end result will be a more economical solution to the problem than
to have an office of public defenders which could only result in another government agency
with its usual great appetite for public funds and administrative personnel.

Respectfully submitted,
THE CRIMINAL PRACTICE AND
PROCEDURE COMMITTEE

DEFENSE OF THE POOR

APPENDIX II

REPORT OF CRIMINAL LAW COMMITTEE,
KANSAS BAR ASSOCIATION, OCTOBER 11, 1963

"WHEREAS, it has now become more apparent due to recent court decisions that indigent individuals accused of felony crimes must be represented by competent legal counsel at all stages of the proceedings, and

"WHEREAS, it is felt that individual practitioners appointed by the various courts of this state can and will handle such matters as conscientiously and more efficiently and economically than public defenders, and

"WHEREAS, compensation to a degree should be allowed those attorneys appointed by the courts to represent indigent persons accused of felony crimes which will partially compensate said practitioners for the time spent and responsibilities of defense work;

"NOW, THEREFORE, BE IT RESOLVED, that the following suggested minimum fee schedule be considered as a minimum, reasonable fee for court-appointed counsel in representing indigent individuals accused of felony crimes:

1. Representation in magistrate courts including waiver of preliminary hearing regardless of number of appearances: $ 50.00
2. Representation in magistrate courts where a preliminary hearing is had, regardless of number of appearances or days in trial: 100.00
3. Representation in district court regardless of number of appearances where a plea is entered without the necessity of trial or hearing other than hearing on application for parole: 100.00
4. Representation in District Court where trial to the court or jury is held, a total of $100.00 for appearances and preparation for trial, plus $150.00 per day or part thereof of trial.
5. Appeals to the Supreme Court of the State of Kansas including briefing, abstracting, docketing, and pleading: 600.00
6. Travel to Topeka and argument of the case (except Topeka lawyers): 600.00
7. In the case of Topeka lawyers: —

The foregoing suggested minimum shall apply to all cases where felony charges are filed even though the final disposition reflects the case is a misdemeanor or the case is dismissed.

"BE IT FURTHER RESOLVED, that courts appointing counsel to represent indigent persons accused of felony crimes make careful examination as to whether or not such individuals are in truth and in fact indigent and that no person admitted to bond or bail shall be considered indigent unless a special finding by the court is made as to why it is possible for such an individual to be upon bond and still be indigent.

"BE IT FURTHER RESOLVED that courts in appointing counsel for indigent persons accused of felony crimes carefully consider the capabilities and desires of the various practitioners at the bar where such appointments are made.

"BE IT FURTHER RESOLVED that indigent persons accused of crimes are entitled to the same highest caliber of representation whether they be accused in metropolitan areas or rural areas and that responsibilities of defense counsel and their capabilities are the same regardless of size of the county where felony cases are prosecuted.

"BE IT FURTHER RESOLVED that in the event of exceptional cases the courts in their discretion shall grant fees in addition to the suggested minimum above outlined."

KENTUCKY

Prof. Wallace A. MacBain, Louisville

The A.B.A. Associate State Committee consisted of Thomas E. Gates, Louisville, chairman, and Maubert R. Mills, Madisonville.

A. INTRODUCTION

Kentucky is a state neither North nor South but partaking of both. Only 44% of the state's population of 3,038,156 is "urbanized"[1] and, as in many other states, this is reflected in the composition of the state legislature. Louisville, the state's largest city, has a larger population than the next 20 largest cities combined.

Reflecting a political division of somewhat advanced age, the state has 120 counties, divided into 48 judicial circuits. The circuit court has general civil and criminal jurisdiction. One circuit, the 12th, takes in six counties, while in Jefferson County, the 30th circuit, in which Louisville is located, 11 circuit judges preside. In each circuit there is a commonwealth's attorney who serves as prosecutor for the state. As well as a proliferation of counties, there are a great number of courts, as illustrated in the following chart.

Jurisdiction

Court	Trial	Examining court
County	Exclusive: fines up to $20 Concurrent: fines up to $500 (With circuit court) imprisonment up to 12 months	Any public offense within county and exclusive in all cases of homicide
Quarterly (Presided over by county judge)	Same	Same, except homicide
Justice	Same	Same
Police	Same except exclusive jurisdiction of violation of city ordinances	City of first class: exclusive jurisdiction of all offenses in city limits; other cities: same, except homicide
Circuit	General criminal jurisdiction	

By means of random sampling, seven counties were selected to be surveyed personally by the state reporter. In those counties the circuit judge and the commonwealth's attorney were to be interviewed. Three attorneys in each of these counties and the circuit judges and commonwealth's attorneys in the. remaining circuits were surveyed through use of a mail questionnaire. The results are embodied in this report.

The counties personally surveyed and some pertinent facts about each are shown in Tables 1 and 2.

TABLE 1
Sample Counties

County	Largest city	1960 population in thousands	Location in state	Land area in square miles	Remarks	Per capita income
Boyd	Ashland	52	Northeast	159	Primarily manufacturing and transportation, federal correctional institute	$1948
Daviess	Owensboro	71	Northwest	152	Manufacturing, retail and wholesale trade, agriculture	1846
Jefferson (D)	Louisville	611	North central	375	Manufacturing, transportation, retail and wholesale trade, U.S. Naval Ordnance Plant, General Electric (employs 11,150)	2348
Letcher	Whitesburg	30	Southeast	339	Primarily coal mining	1215
Madison (D)	Richmond	33	Central	446	Agriculture, retail and wholesale trade, Blue Grass Ordnance Depot	1392
Monroe (D)	Tompkinsville	12	South central	334	Primarily agricultural	763
Pulaski (D)*	Somerset	34	South central	630	Agriculture, retail and wholesale trade, manufacturing, tourist (Cumberland Lake)	930

(D) indicates that a docket study was made.
* Pulaski County was substituted for Rockcastle, which was drawn in the original sample. The two counties are contiguous and are in the same judicial circuit.

TABLE 2
Additional Information

County	Felony defendants, 1962	% indigent estimated by: commonwealth's attorney	judge	No. of lawyers in private practice	No. of lawyers who served as assigned counsel, 1962
Boyd	87	55	55	96	9
Daviess	200*	50	75	85	15
Jefferson	1480	75	50	1491	ND
Letcher	94	60	75	12	ND
Madison	20*	60	55	34	6
Monroe	20*	40	25	6	ND
Pulaski	75*	10	25	20	15 to 20

ND means no data.
* Estimate.

B. CRIMINAL PROCEDURE IN PROSECUTION OF FELONIES

When the suspect is arrested, he is taken before a magistrate, usually a police judge or the county judge,[2] who may be but usually is not an attorney. This first appearance generally takes place within 24 hours, but in one county, Madison, up to seven days may elapse. No explanation was offered for this and none could be elicited. The preliminary hearing may be held immediately, set at a later date, or waived at the defendant's election. In most jurisdictions the hearings are held regularly in all felony cases, though there is a tendency to waive if counsel has been retained. Counsel is rarely, if ever, appointed at the preliminary hearing, though when Rule 8.04 of the present Rules of Criminal Procedure was under discussion, the committee agreed that appointment of counsel should be required at the preliminary hearing. However, it was concluded that until provision for compensation of counsel is made, such a requirement would place an intolerable burden on the practicing attorney.

At the hearing, when held, the state attempts to show probable cause to believe that an offense has been committed and that the defendant committed it; the defendant may cross-examine, put on witnesses of his own, and make a statement in his own behalf. If the hearing is waived, or if the magistrate finds that probable cause exists, the defendant is held to answer before the circuit court and is committed to jail or admitted to bail. The amount of bail is determined at least nominally by the magistrate but he usually leans heavily on the advice of the prosecutor. The nature of the crime and the past record of the accused are also taken into account. Two counties use schedules of a sort, one pegging the minimum bail in a felony case at $2500 and the other at $5000. In most rural counties professional bondsmen are nonexistent.

In Kentucky all felonies are prosecuted by means of indictment as required by the state constitution (§ 12). Upon the return of a true bill by the grand jury, the defendant is arraigned in circuit court. This may transpire up to 90 days after arrest, though only 14 days after filing of the indictment. This is because many rural circuit courts have only four terms a year at three-month intervals.

At his appearance in open court the defendant is read the indictment or is given a copy and is asked to plead. The Rules of Criminal Procedure (Rule 8.04) provide for assignment of counsel to the indigent at the "arraignment or thereafter." The survey indicates that generally counsel is assigned before the defendant is asked to plead. The judge makes the determination of indigency. Four of the seven judges interviewed accept the defendant's statement that he cannot afford to retain counsel, including two who do so because the defendant or his family are known to the judge or an officer of the court. The other three develop the situation through a series of questions in open court. In two circuits no appointment will be made if the defendant is out on bail.

Unless the defendant pleads guilty, a jury is impanelled within two weeks, except in Jefferson County, and the trial ensues. It appears that in Jefferson County up to 60 days may elapse between arraignment and trial, usually due to the tactics of defense counsel. All felony trials in Kentucky must be by jury. The following table illustrates the type of proceeding in which counsel is and is not assigned in the counties surveyed.

	Counsel appointed	
Type of proceeding	Yes	No
Sentencing of a defendant who has pleaded guilty	7	0
Sentencing of a defendant who has been convicted after a trial	7	0
Appeal*	6	1
Habeas corpus, coram nobis, and other postconviction remedies†	1	6
Hearing on revocation of probation	2	5
Misdemeanors‡	2	5
Civil commitment of the mentally ill	7	0

* Though in six counties the judges indicated they had or would appoint on appeal, this is evidently unusual. Where it does happen, the assigned attorney continues to serve.

† Coram nobis has been abolished in Kentucky. Before one may petition for writ of habeas corpus, the court of appeals has held under Rule 11.42 of the Rules of Criminal Procedure that a motion to vacate, set aside, or correct sentence must be made in the court which imposed sentence. In this rule, provision is made for appointment of counsel. This has stemmed the flood of writs which previously engulfed the circuit courts in Lyons and Oldham Counties, where the two state penitentiaries are maintained.

‡ Again, even in the two counties in the "yes" column, appointment is the exception rather than the rule.

On appeal a full transcript and record is generally provided at public expense, though in Monroe County a bystander's bill of exceptions is used quite often. It should be emphasized that in Kentucky no provision is made for compensation of counsel or reimbursement of his expenses. One attorney interviewed described a recent successful appeal taken on behalf of an indigent. He said he was out of pocket more than $400. He observed: "One more such victory and I am undone."

C. OPINIONS OF THE JUDGES

Judges in 7 of the 48 judicial circuits were personally interviewed.[3] In addition, questionnaires were mailed to 48 circuit judges and returns were obtained from 28 (58%). The returns indicate that counsel is usually appointed at arraignment on the indictment. No provision is made for compensation of counsel or reimbursement for expenses incurred, which would certainly tend to inhibit adequate representation. This is particularly true in a highly urbanized area such as Louisville, where extreme dissatisfaction was voiced by the two circuit judges who have criminal jurisdiction, the commonwealth's attorney, and prominent members of the criminal bar who were interviewed.

It is not surprising that generally the judges, who are responsible for administering the present system, evidence only slight dissatisfaction with its operation, again excepting Louisville. Only three of seven judges interviewed thought that counsel should be appointed at an earlier stage than arraignment on indictment, the present practice. However, 25 of 28 judges responding by mail believed appointment should come at an earlier stage, 17 urging such appointment between arrest and first appearance before a magistrate or at first appearance at the latest.

Four of seven judges interviewed felt that it would be feasible to finance such a system. They indicated such financing should be by the state legislature, and administered by the circuit judges in accordance perhaps with fee schedules promulgated by the state or local bar associations. Of the 28 judges replying by mail, 18 agreed with this in substance, and 4 did not answer. Of all the judges, 74% thought reasonable compensation desirable, aside from feasibility, and 88% indicated that reasonable expenses actually incurred by counsel should be recoverable. The judges dissenting thought that such representation is an inherent part of the attorney's professional responsibility to the public. This view was held, for instance, in Madison County, where the caseload is extremely small, and in other smaller counties, such as Pulaski. It may be suggested that when the litigation becomes unduly burdensome, this wholly admirable position might tend to break down. One judge, though opposed to compensation, indicated that he rewards cooperation by appointments as guardian ad litem, which he refers to as his "plums." Another judge opposed compensation for appointed counsel on the ground that "it would tend to encourage crime."

For selection of counsel four methods are used. Of the 35 judges, 14 (40%) appoint from a roster of all attorneys admitted to practice subject to exceptions for age, infirmity, etc. An effort is made to rotate the assignments so as to distribute the burden equitably. Commonly, in more serious cases, co-counsel is appointed. Ten of the judges (28%) appoint from their own list. This list is developed through either their own intimate knowledge of the local, usually small, bar associations, or a list of attorneys recently admitted to the bar. Such representation, it is said, serves as an apprenticeship program, a rather dubious boon to the indigent. In Daviess County, for instance, the judge has a list of the 15 attorneys most recently admitted, this number being determined by designating one attorney for each 5000 residents, as determined by the most recent census and updated by chamber of commerce estimates. Eight of the judges (23%) appoint counsel from the attorneys present in court at the time, and the remaining 3 (9%) from a bar association list.

Twenty-three (60%) of the judges sampled either do not allow felony defendants to waive appointment of counsel or have never had a defendant who attempted to do so. Of the other 10 judges who answered the question, only one had waivers exceeding 10% (Pike County, 75%).

The following table reflects the opinions of all the judges contacted concerning the types of proceeding in which they consider appointment of counsel desirable in an ideal system.

Type of case or proceeding	Number of judges	Counsel should be appointed		Unfair if not appointed		
		No.	%	Yes	No	No answer
Sentencing of a defendant who has pleaded guilty	35	27	77	17	12	6
Sentencing of a defendant who has been found guilty by a jury*	35	25	71	14	14	7
Habeas corpus, coram nobis, or other postconviction remedy	35	17	49	13	17	5
Hearing on revocation of probation	35	21	60	12	20	3
Sexual psychopath hearing†	35	18	51	11	15	9
Misdemeanor‡	35	12	34	6	24	5
Civil commitment of the mentally ill, including alcoholics and narcotics addicts	35	30	85	22	7	6

* Sentence is determined by jury in Kentucky.
† No statutory provision for such a proceeding, but results are included for possible interest.
‡ Judges personally interviewed indicated that for serious misdemeanors appointment should be required and it might be unfair not to appoint.

The judges in both personal interviews and mail questionnaires were asked to compare appointed counsel with retained counsel as to ability and experience. Twenty of the judges felt that appointed counsel compared well on this basis; 10 judges reacted with designations of "fair" or "poor" (7 and 3, respectively); and 5 judges failed to answer. The question is somewhat ambiguous in that it may have been interpreted as pertaining to counsel's ability and experience generally and not to their conduct of cases in which they were appointed. This is borne out by the observation made by several judges, that appointed counsel were not as highly motivated or conscientious as retained counsel. The widespread tendency to appoint younger members of the bar would also seem to belie the favorable comparison regarding experience. The largely favorable reaction of the judges to representation of the indigent as currently afforded may perhaps be explained by the fact that the judges appoint and supervise counsel, and a poor performance would reflect on their administration of the program. The following table shows the number of years on their present court of the circuit judges

No. of years	No. of judges
1	0
2-4	5
5-9	13
10-14	8
15-19	3
20 or more	6

D. OPINIONS OF THE COMMONWEALTH ATTORNEYS

The prosecution for the state is conducted by the commonwealth attorney, who is elected for a six-year term (Ky. Const. § 97). The maximum salary is $6000, plus $250 a month expenses (Ky. Rev. Stat. Ann. §§ 64.510, .515). For the purpose of this report he will be referred to as the prosecutor. He deals with no civil business for the county but is required to represent the state in any action in his circuit to which the state is a party.

Seven prosecutors were personally interviewed and the remaining 41 were polled by means of a mail questionnaire, returns being received from 22 (54%). Including those personally interviewed the results here summarized represent the opinions of 60% of the prosecutors in Kentucky.

Only 10 of the 29 prosecutors felt that they were granted adequate funds to run their respective offices. Twenty indicated that they had no funds available for investigation. Where funds are available they usually take the form of salaries for investigators or the expense allowance mentioned above. State and local police resources are available but are not subject to the control of the prosecutor. The degree of assistance rendered depends on the cordiality of the relationship between the officers involved.

In Kentucky counsel is usually appointed at arraignment on indictment. Under an ideal system, 24 of the prosecutors thought appointment should be made at an earlier stage of the proceedings and 22 thought such appointment should be made at or before the preliminary hearing. Of the 29 prosecutors, 21 believed that it would be feasible to finance the system they designated. Twenty-two also believed that compensation of counsel is highly desirable, and 27 indicated that, at the very least, the attorney should be reimbursed for out-of-pocket expenses incurred in investigating and preparing the case. The prosecutors opposed to compensation seemed to agree with those judges who indicated that representation of the indigent was an exercise in professional responsibility. One prosecutor felt that any further burden on an already "oppressed" taxpayer was "indefensible." Of the seven prosecutors interviewed personally, four said that financing was possible and one declined to answer. Of the four, three indicated that state money should be used, but one was unalterably opposed to this, stating that such a system should be financed locally. One prosecutor responding by mail suggested that appointed counsel should be granted a lien against the indigent defendant—a right of doubtful value. Nineteen of 25 of the prosecutors who answered as to the possibility of financing a system to provide representation in such case felt that it would be feasible.

The following chart indicates the types of cases and proceedings in which, in an ideal system, the prosecutors believed appointment of counsel necessary:

Type of case or proceeding	Appoint counsel			Unfair to indigent if not appointed		
	Yes	No	No answer	Yes	No	No answer
Sentencing of a defendant who pleaded guilty	21	7	1	17	7	4
Sentencing of a defendant convicted by trial*	24	4	1	19	5	4
Habeas corpus, coram nobis, or other postconviction remedy	19	8	2	15	7	6
Hearing of revocation of probation	19	8	2	18	4	6
Sexual psychopath hearing†	19	4	6	16	3	9
Misdemeanors‡	6	21	2	5	17	6
Civil commitment of the mentally ill, including alcoholics and narcotics addicts	19	5	5	17	4	7

* Sentence is determined by jury in Kentucky.
† No statutory provision for such a proceeding, but results are included for possible interest.
‡ Result may have been different if question had read "serious misdemeanors."

The seven prosecutors personally interviewed were asked to state their opinion of the present system of providing counsel to the indigent. Three indicated satisfaction, one because of excellent cooperation of the local bar and another because of sound exercise of judgment by the circuit judges. Four of the prosecutors voiced extreme dissatisfaction with the present system, citing inadequate preparation and investigation, failure of the local bar association to participate or cooperate, and the predominance of appointment of fledgling attorneys, fresh out of law school.

All of the prosecutors were asked to compare the performance of assigned counsel with that of counsel retained by defendants. Twenty felt the comparison was favorable, eight thought appointed counsel compared poorly and one failed to respond. Once again, this question may have been misunderstood, as the same attorneys serve as both retained and appointed counsel and it may have been felt that the question required an assessment of the attorneys as such and not of their performance when assigned to represent the indigent. It might also be suggested that prosecutors might be reluctant to downgrade the performance of their adversaries as this would indirectly reflect on their own performance. Those questioned personally pointed out that assigned counsel possessed little incentive to properly represent the interest of their clients and had seldom fully prepared or investigated cases to which assigned. Often such preparation consisted, at best, of only a 10-minute interview in the back of the courtroom. Fourteen of the prosecutors felt that the present system for determining indigency, usually a series of questions addressed to the defendant in open court by the judge, was too lenient, and the other 14 indicated that it was satisfactory. None criticized the method or practice of the judge as too strict. In a number of smaller counties it was pointed out that the judge is usually personally familiar with the defendant or his family and is well acquainted with their financial position.

Estimates of the percentage of indigents among felony defendants varied widely, ranging from 5% to 75%; 16 of 29 prosecutors estimated indigency at 50% or over. The following table indicates the range of responses received.

Estimated % indigent felony defendants	No. of estimates
0-20	4
21-40	8
41-60	9
61-80	8
81-100	0

In 15 of the 29 circuits sampled, waiver of counsel by felony defendants is not permitted or does not occur. Only in five circuits was it estimated that waiver occurs in over 10% of felony cases involving indigent defendants.

Twenty-two prosecutors said that counsel should be compensated, while six were opposed, usually again on the ground that this was a matter of professional responsibility. There also seemed to be overtones of "economy in government," i.e., any proposal which will serve to increase taxes is undesirable. Those who responded as to quantum of compensation referred to formulation of schedules by the local bar association[4] or a determination by the trial judge made in light of time spent in preparation and trial of the case. One prosecutor suggested that fees should be pegged at one-half of the minimum schedule fixed by the local bar, assuming such schedule had been adopted. Of the 29 prosecutors, 28 favored reimbursement for out-of-pocket expenses.

A rather surprising degree of cooperation with defense counsel was indicated. Twenty-five prosecutors said that they make full disclosure to the defense of such matters as confessions, statements of witnesses, reports of expert witnesses, and exhibits. Another four make partial disclosure, usually limited to confessions. One prosecutor commented that he limited such disclosure due to "the low calibre of the local criminal bar." Another opens his file only to assigned counsel, perhaps empathizing with the plight of his brethren.

The seven prosecutors personally interviewed were queried as to their views on trying a case when the defendant is unrepresented by counsel. Their reaction varied only in intensity. Four answered that they preferred the defendant to be represented; two were completely opposed to such procedure; and one stated that he would not be a party to a proceeding of that nature.

Finally, the prosecutors in both categories were asked for their comment on how the present system for providing counsel might be improved. As already noted, a consensus urged compensation of appointed counsel and reimbursement for expenses incurred. Also suggested were appointment of counsel at an earlier stage in the proceedings and a more active participation by the local bar, perhaps through the creation of a greater awareness of, and sensitivity to, the existence of the problem. The creation of this awareness would seem to be primarily a responsibility of the local and state bar associations.

E. OPINIONS OF THE DEFENSE ATTORNEYS

Questionnaires were sent to 21 attorneys, 3 in each of the counties personally surveyed. Twelve attorneys responded[5] from six of the seven counties. The names of the attorneys were obtained from judges and prosecutors who indicated that they had participated extensively as assigned counsel in felony cases. Due to this direct interest it cannot be said that they accurately reflect the views of the bar as a whole, but they are certainly familiar with the problems involved.

The attorneys responding had been practicing for from less than one year to 39 years, the average being approximately 10 years. The years of practice and previous experience in criminal cases are indicated below.

Years of practice	No. of attorneys	No. of criminal cases before 1962	No. of attorneys
1 or less	1	0	2
2	1	1-4	1
5	2	5-9	0
6-9	2	10-19	0
10-14	5	20-49	1
15-29	0	50 or more	6
30-39	1	no answer	1

Eleven of the 12 had served as assigned counsel in 1962 in a state court of general criminal jurisdiction. They appeared in from 2 cases (one attorney) to 30 or more cases (two attorneys). Seven of the 11 represented defendants charged with crimes punishable by death or life imprisonment; one attorney had more than 10 such cases.

Questions were directed to the last case in which each of the 11 had represented an indigent accused. The 11 cases involved ranged from assault, embezzlement, forgery, grand larceny, and armed robbery to two charges of murder. As to the stage of the proceedings at which appointment took place, the following results were obtained.

Stage of proceedings	No. of appointments
Prior to preliminary hearing	1
After filing of indictment but before arraignment thereon	3
At arraignment on indictment	4
After arraignment but before trial	2
At trial	1

Only 2 of the 11 felt that they had been appointed in time to represent the accused adequately, and one of these was appointed prior to the preliminary hearing. Even he was concerned because interrogation had been completed before he entered the case and his client's chances were accordingly jeopardized.

Ten of the 11 received no compensation for their efforts in the accused's behalf, and none were reimbursed for out-of-pocket expenses. The one attorney who was compensated received a small sum from the defendant. The average fee estimated in these cases, had counsel been retained rather than appointed, was more than $800 (see table following). Thus the estimated value of legal services donated in these few cases alone was nearly $9000.

Crime charged	Estimated fee
Death by auto	$ 300
Murder	2500
Manslaughter	500
Assault, grand larceny	200
Armed robbery	1000
Embezzlement and forgery	1500
Embezzlement	250
Armed robbery	1000
Murder	750
Burglary	250
Grand larceny	500
	$ 8950

Only one of the lawyers felt that the present system was fair to the indigent, and he indicated that he had not been appointed in time to represent his indigent client adequately, which would seem to involve a contradiction. That the system was unfair to the lawyers involved was a unanimous conclusion.

Finally, the attorneys polled were requested to suggest means of improving the present system. All approved reasonable compensation of assigned counsel; 7 favored reimbursement for out-of-pocket expenses; 11 felt that appointment must be made at an earlier stage of the proceedings; 5 disapproved of the system used by the judge in selecting assigned counsel; and 4 indicated that counsel should be provided in additional kinds of cases. Further, it was suggested that investigative facilities and personnel be provided to the defense. It may be of interest to note that nowhere is the term "public defender" mentioned.

F. THE DOCKET STUDY

A docket study was attempted in four of the sample counties (see Table 1). Unfortunately, the records were so incomplete in most counties that it was not possible to obtain such information as whether the defendant was released on bail, and whether a preliminary hearing was held. (For methods of research on the docket study see volume 1, page 178.) Results of the docket study appear in Tables 3 to 6.

Table 3 indicates that in the three counties for which information was available, virtually all felony defendants had counsel. In Jefferson County just over 50% of the defendants had assigned counsel. Table 4 shows that about the same number of defendants were found indigent as were represented by assigned counsel in each of the three counties. For instance, the figures for Jefferson County were 53% and 55%. The docket study also showed that in Jefferson, 30% of the defendants were not released on bail; thus some of those who managed to effect their release were nonetheless given assigned counsel.

Table 5 shows the disposition of the sample cases. For the state as a whole, based on a projection from the weighted averages of the county samples, 52% of the defendants pleaded guilty. Jefferson County was the only one where any defendants pleaded to lesser offenses. A relatively high proportion of cases went to trial compared with other states: 30%, which resulted in 24% convictions and 6% acquittals. Most of the remaining cases were dismissed.

Sentences, if any, are shown in Table 6. For the state as a whole, 58% of the defendants were sentenced to imprisonment, including terms in the county jail, while 10% were placed on probation and 4% had suspended sentences without probation. Probation and suspended sentence are relatively infrequent compared with other states.

TABLE 3
Retained and Assigned Counsel in Felonies
Kentucky, 1962

County	Total sample	Did defendant have counsel? Yes No.	%	No No.	%	Retained No.	%	Assigned No.	%	Combination or type unknown No.	%	No data* No.	%
Monroe	13	13	100	0	0	4	31	9	69	0	0	0	0
Madison	10	8	89	1	11	5	56	3	33	0	0	1	10
Jefferson	103	86	97	3	3	37	42	45	51	4	4	14	14
Weighted total percentages		96		4		33		46		17		12	

* % of no data refers to total sample; % in other columns refers to total cases for which data were available.

TABLE 4
Was Felony Defendant Determined Indigent?
Kentucky, 1962

County	Total sample	Yes No.	%	No No.	%	No data* No.	%
Monroe	13	9	69	4	31	0	0
Madison	10	3	38	5	63	2	20
Jefferson	103	47	55	38	45	18	17

* % of no data refers to total sample; % in other columns refers to total cases for which data were available.

TABLE 5
Disposition in Felony Cases
Kentucky, 1962

County	Total sample	Plea guilty	Plea lesser offense	Dis-missed	Found guilty	Found guilty lesser degree	Ac-quitted	Mental commit-ment	Pend-ing	Stet°	Other
Monroe	13	7	0	1	5	0	0	0	0	0	0
Pulaski	20	12	0	2	3	1	2	0	0	0	0
Madison	10	4	0	3	2	0	1	0	0	0	0
Jefferson	103	46	15	6	4	0	4	4	7	15	2
Weighted total percentages		51	1	15	22	2	6	0	1	2	0

° Held on inactive docket.

TABLE 6
Sentencing in Felony Cases
Kentucky, 1962

County	Total sample	No sentence No.	%	Prison No.	%	Probation No.	%	Suspended sentence No.	%	Fine No.	%	No data° No.	%
Monroe	13	1	8	10	77	1	8	0	0	1	8	0	0
Pulaski	20	4	20	13	65	0	0	2	10	1	6	0	0
Madison	10	3	33	4	44	2	22	0	0	1	11	0	0
Jefferson	103	37	37	35	35	17	17	9	9	3	3	2	2
Weighted total percentages			21		58		10		4		6		0

° % of no data refers to total sample; % in other columns refers to total cases for which data were available.

G. CONCLUSIONS AND RECOMMENDATIONS

It is undeniable that in implementing the following suggestions a number of practical problems would arise, but they are not insurmountable. Perhaps the most difficult problem is public apathy. As with reform of a penal system, the man on the street does not empathize with or perhaps realize the plight in which the person accused or convicted of a crime finds himself.

1. *Reimbursement of expenses.* There is virtual unanimity among those interviewed, on both sides of the bench, that reimbursement of expenses is not only desirable but necessary. That an attorney who is not to be compensated will be under-motivated seems obvious. Idealism has its limits. When, in addition to time expended, the attorney is forced to undergo further financial sacrifice, the result is unconscionable both to the attorney and to his client. When it is remembered that the major part of such representation falls on a small

segment of the bar, usually the younger attorney who can ill afford the outlay of time and money involved, the situation is further aggravated. Few could often afford the $400 plus appeal already referred to.

2. *Compensation.* Closely allied to the problem of expenses is that of compensating assigned counsel. Most of what has been said above applies here as well. The problems involved are how much compensation, source of funds, and administration. Suggested fee schedules for criminal cases should be formulated by the local bar associations, with maximum and minimum limits. Within those limits the judge would then determine the fee to be paid counsel, on the basis of time spent in preparing and trying a case, and, if necessary, taking an appeal. That an attorney might be less ardent than otherwise in provoking one who is later to fix his compensation is certainly possible. Placing over-all supervision of the system under the court of appeals might alleviate this difficulty.

It is apparent that the funds to finance such a system must come from the state. Those areas in which the problem is most critical will tend to be the areas that cannot finance the system properly due to lack of tax resources.

3. *Investigatory facilities.* The need for proper investigation, voiced by a number of attorneys interviewed, could be met in at least two ways: by providing the necessary funds to the defense (or reimbursement for funds already expended for this purpose), or by requiring that the prosecutor fully divulge to the defense the results of his investigation. As already indicated, most prosecutors claim to make full disclosure now. Some attorneys, however, do not feel that the cooperation accorded is satisfactory. A requirement of full divulgence would certainly engender vigorous protest from many prosecutors.

4. *Appointment at an earlier stage.* Aside from remuneration, a grievance most often voiced was that appointment came too late to benefit the client. It will be recalled that assignment of counsel at the arraignment on the indictment is prescribed by the Rules of Criminal Procedure. The rules may be made or changed unilaterally by the Court of Appeals. It would appear to be desirable to make such a change regarding time of appointment. At the latest, counsel should be appointed at the inception of the defendant's first appearance before a magistrate.

5. *Appointment by type of proceeding.* Though Kentucky's record is generally good as to the range of appointment, there are weak spots, principally in misdemeanors, appeals, and hearings on revocation of probation. Apparently, appointments seldom are made in these areas, and no change is contemplated as a result of *Douglas v. California.* Unless compensation is provided, the bar probably would object to a broadening of its already onerous responsibility. But as one prosecutor observed: "representation by competent counsel should be provided an indigent in any proceeding in which his freedom is at stake."

6. *Record keeping.* Perhaps a more ancillary matter is the inadequate keeping of records. It was virtually impossible in most counties to determine the number of felony indictments in a given period, or their disposition. In one instance four members of a county clerk's staff spent two hours determining the fate of one batch of indictments. It was finally learned that they had all been dismissed on one court day. A notable exception to the general rule was the

Boyd County circuit clerk's office, where all pertinent information was readily available.

7. *Bar associations.* If any or all of the foregoing suggestions are acceptable, they may be accomplished only through the organized bar, both state and local. The lay public is either unaware of or insensitive to the problems involved. The attorney is directly affected, both in his practice and in his professional responsibility. Committees have been formed recently to study the situation in Kentucky and to report back to their respective organizations. It is too soon to appraise their effectiveness.

Where a local bar association assumes its responsibility in this respect the problems are at least met if not conquered. Once again, to cite Boyd County, a list of all active attorneys under the age of 55 is supplied to the circuit judge, and appointments are rotated accordingly. By this means, an undue burden is not placed on any one group, particularly the younger attorneys, and representation should be of a higher quality. The ensuing benefits should enlist the support of all who are interested in the improvement of their profession.

NOTES — Kentucky

[1]A rather loose classification adopted by the U.S. Bureau of the Census, and including urban, suburban, and surrounding unincorporated areas.

[2]An elective official in whom administrative and judicial functions are combined. In Jefferson County his duties are administrative only.

[3]In Kentucky the circuit judge is an elected official by virtue of the state constitution (§129). He serves a six-year term and has a salary of $14,900. Recently, efforts have been made to remove this office, to some extent at least, from the political arena, but to little avail. A table showing length of service of the judges responding appears at the end of this section.

[4]Insofar as could be determined there have been no such schedules formulated.

[5]While many other attorneys were informally consulted in the course of the survey, only the responses of these 12 are analyzed here.

LOUISIANA

Harry F. Connick, New Orleans

The A.B.A. Associate State Committee consisted of Robert E. LeCorgne, Jr., New Orleans, chairman; J. Bennett Johnston, Jr., Shreveport; Robert L. Kleinpeter, Baton Rouge; Richard F. Knight, Bogalusa; and Jack L. Simms, Leesville.

A. INTRODUCTION

In 1960, Louisiana had a population of 3,257,022, according to the official census. The state is divided into 64 parishes (counties) and 31 judicial districts, plus the Parish of Orleans (composed of the city of New Orleans) which constitutes, in effect, another judicial district. Each district has at least one judge and a district attorney. Except in four districts, the district attorney has one or more assistants. The 31 district courts have general criminal and civil jurisdiction. The Parish of Orleans, however, has a separate civil district court and criminal district court. A court of general criminal jurisdiction, the latter is composed of eight sections, with a judge for each section.

Six sample parishes for the survey were selected on the basis of geography and volume of serious crimes, as follows:

Parish	1960 population of parish in thousands	Location in state
Ouachita (D)	101	North
Jefferson (D)	207	Southeast
Jefferson Davis	30	Southwest
Tangipahoa (D)	59	Southeast
Terrebonne	60	South
Orleans (D)	628	Southeast

(D) indicates that a docket study was made.

The table on page 284 gives additional information about the six parishes surveyed.

B. CRIMINAL PROCEDURE AS IT AFFECTS INDIGENT PERSONS

1. *Felony cases.* The Louisiana Code of Criminal Procedure[1] provides that all prosecutions may be by indictment and that all prosecutions for noncapital offenses shall be by indictment or information.[2] All indictments are to be returned in the district court;[3] an information may be filed either in open court or in the office of the clerk of the court having jurisdiction.[4] The district courts, therefore, have exclusive jurisdiction of all felony cases. The district attorney has entire control of every criminal prosecution instituted or pending in any parish wherein he is district attorney.[5]

The law provides that after arrest, with or without warrant, the arrested person shall be conducted immediately to the nearest jail or police station and there booked.[6] When a peace officer makes an arrest with a warrant the prisoner, after being booked, must be brought without unnecessary delay before the judge designated in the warrant.[7] If the arrest is made without a warrant the prisoner, after being booked, is to be brought without unnecessary delay, "if

283

the charge be such as to entitle the accused to a preliminary examination," before the judge having authority to sit as a committing magistrate in the case, or before the judge having trial jurisdiction thereof.[8] The Code does not say what is meant by "unnecessary delay." The Code specifically provides for committing magistrates and preliminary examinations.[9] The magistrates have authority to commit an accused for trial, discharge him, or release him on bail.[10] The preliminary examination does not, however, necessarily follow every arrest. It must be demanded by either the defendant or the district attorney. In the surveyed parishes, it is rarely demanded by either, the usual procedure being arrest, formal charge by the district attorney, and arraignment. An accused is entitled as a matter of right to a preliminary examination prior to indictment or filing of information, but after indictment or information is filed, it becomes wholly discretionary with the court whether to order a preliminary examination.[11] In Orleans Parish, in the few cases where a preliminary examination has been requested by the accused, the district attorney has immediately formally charged the accused, which made the granting of a preliminary examination discretionary with the judge. Past experience has indicated that the judges rarely order preliminary examinations after formal charges have been filed.

The procedure in cases involving felonies, from the arrest to the termination of the case, is the same, with slight variations, in the sample parishes: the suspect is arrested and brought to the police station or to the parish jail, where he is booked.[12] In some instances the arrestee is brought directly to the scene of the crime, where he may be questioned by the arresting officer or viewed by the victim for possible identification. The arresting authority—the city police, the

Parish	Felony defendants, 1961	% indigent	% indigent who waived counsel	No. of lawyers in private practice	No. of lawyers who served
Ouachita	150	50*	0	107	40
		75†			
Jefferson	1290	no data	no data	160	25
Jefferson Davis	78	75*	less than 5	15	10
		60†			
Tangipahoa	459	85†	0	38	8
		70*			
Terrebonne	96	50*	1/3 of 1	40	27
Orleans‡	2294	60*	0	1900	40
		30-40*	1/2 of 1		
		80*	0		
		50†	0		

* Average of judges' estimates.
† District attorney's estimate.
‡ The Parish of Orleans is the only parish with a defender system. The Legal Aid Bureau, a private defender system supported by the United Fund, represented 473 individuals in 694 cases in 1961, or approximately 35% of defendants who were determined indigent. In 1962, the bureau represented 526 individuals in 894 cases.

parish sheriff's office, or the state police—makes a report of the matter and sends the report to the district attorney's office. The report is a detailed factual statement upon which the charge is based. In Orleans Parish it is not uncommon for an accused to be arrested for vagrancy, having no visible means of support, or some other minor charge as a pretense for holding him for 72 hours or longer while the police conduct an investigation.[13] Under the state law the accused is allowed to use the telephone after his arrest. He may contact his family or an attorney, who can make arrangements for a bond to be set. This bond can be set by district judges or committing magistrates upon the request of an attorney.[14]

If the accused has neither attorney nor someone to assist him with bail, he remains in jail, and bond usually is not set until charges are accepted by the district attorney. In Jefferson Davis Parish, where warrants for arrest are used in most cases, the amount of bond is determined by the district judge at the time he signs the warrant for arrest.

In Orleans Parish, after arrest and booking, and acceptance by the district attorney of the charge against the accused, the district attorney formally charges the accused and sets the amount of the bond. The district attorney may use the same amount set by the judge, or he may set an amount depending on the nature of the charge, the past record of the accused, etc. The amount of the bond set by the district attorney is subject to reduction by a district judge upon request by the attorney for the accused.

Most charges in Louisiana are by bill of information, except in capital cases, where the charge is made by an indictment returned by the grand jury.

Usually, the first time an accused sees a judicial officer in a criminal proceeding in Louisiana is when he is arraigned before the judge. This practice is common throughout the sample parishes due to the lack of use of the preliminary examination and of the committing magistrate as such.

With rare exception, therefore, the first judicial figure the accused sees after his arrest is the district judge, and this is at arraignment, where the accused is called upon to plead to the charge after the accusation against him has been read.[15] The accused is entitled by law to a formal arraignment in all criminal cases arising under state laws and parish ordinances.[16] The time between arrest and arraignment varies in the different parishes from 2 to 3 days in Ouachita Parish to 20 to 30 days in Orleans Parish.

Under Louisiana law the accused in every instance has the right to defend himself and to have the assistance of counsel.[17] Whenever an accused person charged with a felony makes an affidavit that he is unable to retain counsel, the law states that the court shall immediately assign counsel.[18] Assigned counsel in capital cases must have at least five years' actual experience at the bar.[19]

The practice currently employed in all of the sample parishes is to appoint counsel for indigent defendants in all felony cases shortly before or at the time of formal arraignment. (This practice was well established in a few parishes, but in the remaining parishes it seems to have been the direct result of the *Gideon* decision.) An accused is usually not formally arraigned in felony cases unless and until he is represented by counsel, although this is done in some parishes. Some of the judges in the parishes surveyed usually will order an arraignment continued or postponed until the defendant has obtained counsel for himself or the court has appointed counsel to represent him.

It is at the arraignment that inquiry into the indigency of the accused is made. In all parishes surveyed the question of indigency is determined solely by the judge. There seems to be little formality attached to this determination. In spite of the requirement of the affidavit of poverty, Orleans Parish is the only place where an oath of poverty is required before counsel is appointed, and not all judges in Orleans Parish require such oath.

The usual procedure for determining whether the accused is indigent is as follows.

The accused is brought into court for arraignment. If he is not represented by counsel, the judge inquires of him whether he has counsel. If he says he does not, the judge asks whether he intends to employ an attorney. If the accused answers "no," the court inquires whether he can pay for counsel, and usually appoints counsel if the answer is in the negative. (Orleans Parish, as stated above, often requires execution of an oath of poverty before appointment is made.) None of the surveyed parishes appears to employ a definite criterion for determining indigency, nor do any of the judges make inquiry into whether the accused can pay a moderate fee. In the so-called country parishes surveyed (Ouachita, Tangipahoa, Jefferson Davis, and Terrebonne), the judges and district attorneys stated that they grew up and practiced law in the parish and many of the accused or their families were known to them. Because of this, there was no need to inquire extensively into the financial status of the accused.

The only parish in the state with a defender system is Orleans Parish, where the Legal Aid Bureau, a private defender system supported by the United Fund, operates. In all other sample parishes the method of assigning counsel on a case-by-case basis is used.

Generally, persons who are in jail and are not represented by counsel are unquestionably considered indigent. Where the accused is out on bail the courts usually withhold the appointment of counsel until it appears that the matter will not proceed further unless such appointment is made. Waiver of appointment of counsel in felony cases is not permitted, according to the judges who were interviewed personally, and generally the case does not proceed until counsel is appointed. Assigned counsel are not compensated, except in West Feliciana Parish.[20]

In respect to appeals, when the court appoints an attorney to represent the accused, the same attorney remains in the case until a final determination is made. However, other counsel has been appointed, according to the judges interviewed, where the original attorney was unable to proceed with the case. The law allows the convicted indigent to prosecute his appeal at no cost.[21] In capital cases resulting in convictions the entire transcript of the trial is furnished the indigent at no cost to him and must be presented to the Supreme Court.[22] In other felony cases only those portions of the evidence that are needed to prepare his appeal properly are furnished the indigent at no cost.[23] In Louisiana appeals in criminal cases in which the penalty of death or imprisonment with hard labor may be imposed, or in which a fine exceeding $300 or imprisonment exceeding six months has actually been imposed, are direct to the Supreme Court.[24] The rules of the Supreme Court require that briefs be printed or multi-lithed, except where the litigant is not financially able to furnish a printed brief. In such cases, typewritten briefs may be filed.[25]

2. *Misdemeanor cases.* There are no provisions in Louisiana law for assignment of counsel to indigents in misdemeanor cases. The general practice in the parishes surveyed is that counsel is seldom appointed for indigent defendants in misdemeanors, and then only in serious cases.

The district courts have appellate jurisdiction in all appeals from sentences imposing fines or imprisonment by a mayor's court or by a city or a municipal court. These appeals are tried de novo and without juries.

C. OPINIONS OF THE JUDGES

Personal interviews were conducted with nine judges in the six sample parishes, located in six separate judicial districts. Questionnaires were mailed to 41 judges in the remaining 26 judicial districts, and were completed and returned by 20 judges from 17 districts. A total of 23 of the 32 districts, therefore, are represented, with 29 judges participating.

Each judge contacted personally was asked this question: "Under an ideal system, at what stage in a criminal case do you think the indigent person should first be provided with a lawyer if he wants one?" (Unless otherwise indicated, all answers refer to felony cases only.) In response, five judges said between arrest and first appearance before a magistrate; two said at first appearance before a magistrate; one, after the filing of an indictment or information but before arraignment thereon; and one, at arraignment on indictment or information.

Each judge contacted by mail was asked virtually the same question. In response, one judge answered between arrest and first appearance before a magistrate; three said at first appearance before a magistrate; two, between first appearance and preliminary hearing; one, at preliminary hearing; eight, after the filing of an indictment or information but before arraignment thereon; three, at arraignment on indictment or information; and two, after arraignment on indictment.

Thus all judges favored appointment of counsel to represent the indigent defendant at some point prior to trial, but there was little agreement on the particular stage of the proceedings.

Five judges who were interviewed personally thought that it was unfair to the indigent person if he did not get a lawyer at the designated stage, and four thought it not unfair. Of the judges answering by mail, 13 thought that it was unfair; 5 thought that it was not unfair; and 2 did not answer.

Eight of the judges in the personal interviews thought that a system could be financed that would provide lawyers for indigents at the designated stages, while one judge felt this would be impossible. Among the 20 judges replying by mail, 12 answered affirmatively; 2 replied "no"; one was doubtful; and 5 did not answer. More than 50% of all of those who thought the system could be financed felt that such financing should come from state and parish sources.

The data tabulated below, relative to providing a lawyer in certain kinds of proceedings under an ideal system, were obtained from personal interviews with nine judges.

Kinds of cases and proceedings	Provide counsel*			Unfair if not provided*	
	Yes	No	Already provided	Yes	No
Sentencing of a defendant who pleaded guilty	1	1	7	7	1
Sentencing of a defendant convicted by trial	3	0	6	7	0
Habeas corpus, coram nobis, or other postconviction remedy	7	0	2	7	1
Hearing on revocation of probation	5	4	0	4	5
Sexual psychopath hearing	5	1	2	6	1
Misdemeanor	3	4	1	2	7
Civil commitment of the mentally ill, including alcoholics and narcotics addicts	5	3	0	3	3

*Some did not answer all categories and some answers were not relevant.

The same judges were asked: "What do you think about the problem of financing a system that would provide counsel in these kinds of cases and proceedings?" Two answered that the state should bear the cost; five felt the state and parish should pay; one said it would be impossible to finance; and one said it would be very expensive, without indicating how such a system could be financed.

Mailed responses to similar questions were as follows:

Kinds of cases and proceedings	Provide counsel*		Unfair if not provided*	
	Yes	No	Yes	No
Sentencing of a defendant who pleaded guilty	8	12	4	13
Sentencing of a defendant convicted by trial	8	12	4	11
Habeas corpus, coram nobis, or other postconviction remedy	12	8	9	8
Hearing on revocation of probation	7	13	5	13
Sexual psychopath hearing	7	12	6	11
Misdemeanor	0	19	0	17
Civil commitment of the mentally ill, including alcoholics and narcotics addicts	7	13	4	14

* No answers given in some categories.

To the question on financing, "Do you think it would be possible to finance a system to provide counsel in these kinds of cases and proceedings?" 10 of the 20 judges responding by mail answered "yes"; 5 answered "no"; 3 did not answer; and one was doubtful.

As to the percentage of defendants who are indigent and the percentage of indigents who waive appointment of counsel, the nine judges participating in the personal interviews answered as follows:

% indigent*	% indigent who waive appointment*	Section of state in which judicial district located	Population of judicial district in thousands
50	1/3 of 1	South	228
30-40	1/2 of 1	Southeast	628
80	0	Southeast	628
60	0	Southeast	628
70	0	Southeast	95
75	less than 5	Southwest	110
50	0	North	228
no answer	no answer	Southeast	207
no answer	no answer	Southeast	207

* All figures are estimates.

The table on the following page shows data supplied by the 20 judges who answered by mail.

When asked about their system for finding lawyers to appoint in ordinary criminal cases, seven of the nine judges interviewed said they use their own list of names; two use a bar association list. Of the 20 judges who answered by mail, 5 used only their own lists of names; one used his list in combination with the local bar association list; 10 used a roster of all attorneys admitted to practice in the district, subject to exemptions for age, infirmity, etc.; and 3 used the local bar association list of names. Only one judge stated that he used any attorney present in court at the time.

In Orleans and in several other parishes the judge's own list of names is composed of attorneys who practice criminal law, who are familiar with criminal law and procedure, and who have volunteered to have their names put on the list. In many parishes it is the practice for young attorneys to request to be put on the judge's list for appointments. Several judges stated that they appoint only lawyers who practice criminal law. Several judges in districts where the court has criminal and civil jurisdiction make it a practice to make civil (paying) appointments for curatorships only to those attorneys who accept criminal (nonpaying) appointments. In several of the districts with a small bar membership all attorneys are on the judge's list.

Eight of the 9 judges who were interviewed personally, and 16 of the 20 answering by mail, stated that they have a special system for appointing attorneys in very serious cases, such as crimes punishable by death or a long prison sentence. The other five judges said they do not have a special system. A state statute governs the practice in capital cases[26]: the appointed lawyers must have at least five years' practice. Most of the judges appoint more than one lawyer in capital cases.

In the personal interviews, when asked: "If the indigent person asks for a lawyer by name do you appoint him?" three of the nine judges said "yes," three said "no,'" and three said that this had never happened. All nine judges stated that if there are two defendants who have interests that may conflict, they appoint separate lawyers for each. If the defendant objects to the lawyer who is appointed, three of the judges said they insist that he keep that lawyer, unless he has a good reason for not wanting him. Three appoint someone else. Three stated that this had never happened, but if it did happen they probably would appoint someone else.

Two of the nine judges who were interviewed personally said that they had a problem in getting lawyers to serve as appointed counsel, and a third judge said he had trouble only in capital cases, where approximately 70% of the requested attorneys declined to accept appointments. The six remaining judges said getting lawyers to serve as appointed counsel was no problem, but one of them felt that appointment was an imposition.

To the same question on the mail questionnaire, 16 judges answered that they had no problem in getting lawyers to serve; 2 experienced a problem; one

No. of felony defendants per year*	% indigent*	% indigent who waive appointment†	Section of state in which judicial district located	Population of judicial district in thousands
350	90	90	unknown‡	unknown‡
55	50	90	Northwest	228
6	85	90	North central	52
50	50	25	North central	52
75	50	50	North central	46
75	70	75	Northeast	64
40	60	0	Central	30
more than 100	75	0	Central	46
50-100	75	1-2	Central	37
200	20	0	Southwest	150
87	10	95	Southwest	150
15	75	0	South central	130
35-50	99	0 in pleas of not guilty	Central	285
300	25	75	Central	32
25	66	cannot waive appointment	Southeast	82
97	50	0	Southeast	82
60-70	25	0	Northwest	96
150-250	75	95	Northwest	96
200	25	70	Southeast	39
50	90	10	West	37

* All figures are estimates.
† Note the extremes in the percentages of indigents who waive appointment of counsel to represent them.
‡ Mail questionnaire returned without identifying postmark.

judge said that he sometimes had a problem; and one judge did not answer. In the personal interviews, four judges said that no lawyers asked to be excused. (One of these said, however, that in capital cases approximately 70% of the lawyers asked to be excused.) Four of the nine judges said 1% to 9% asked to be excused. One judge in Orleans Parish stated that 25 to 35 regular criminal lawyers never refused but others, who do not regularly practice criminal law, frequently asked to be excused. Six judges said they would excuse an attorney who had a good reason. Three judges did not reply.

Of the 20 judges responding by mail, 11 replied that no lawyer had asked to be excused; 7 said 1% to 9%; and 2 said 10% to 29%. Of these 20, 12 excuse attorneys for reasons varying from "good" to "valid" or "serious"; two judges did not have this problem; two said they excuse them without requiring a reason; one said he did not excuse them; and three did not answer this question.

Five judges in the personal interviews said that assigned counsel should be compensated for their services to indigent persons, two of these five specifying amounts as shown below. Four did not answer.

1. $ 25 . . . misdemeanor cases
       50 . . . cases where punishment is with or without hard labor
     100 . . . cases where punishment is with hard labor
  500-1000 . . . capital cases
2. $ 25-50 . . . misdemeanor cases
     200 . . . felony cases, plus more for appeal
     300 . . . capital cases, plus more for appeal

Sixteen of the 20 judges contacted by mail stated that lawyers should be compensated for their services; 4 were opposed. Nine of the 16 did not fix an amount. Of the remaining seven who said lawyers should be compensated, two believed they should be compensated for costs; one, for costs, plus an unspecified amount; one indicated a nominal fee; one felt they should be granted appointments as curators in civil cases; one thought they should be compensated, but a part of the financial burden should be assumed by the appointed attorney; one considered they should be reasonably compensated in serious cases but not in minor cases. Two judges answered specifically on the amount as follows:

1. $ 25 . . . lesser felonies
      50 . . . felonies
     100 . . . capital cases
2. $ 100 . . . for each day of trial work

All 9 judges in the personal interviews and 16 of the 20 answering by mail favored reimbursement of lawyers for out-of-pocket expenses for investigation and preparation of cases for indigents. Two replying by mail were opposed, and two did not answer.

In the personal interviews seven of nine judges said that appointed lawyers compare favorably with lawyers retained by defendants. One said the paid lawyer does a more respectable job and one said it varies.

When these nine judges were asked how appointed lawyers compared with the district attorney, one said very well; three said favorably; one said that on serious cases appointed lawyers are about the same but on less serious cases appointed lawyers do not compare as well; one said the appointed lawyers are at a greater disadvantage than the district attorney; one said it varies; one said they compare favorably except for those appointed lawyers who do not practice criminal law; and one said not as well.

To the same question on the mail questionnaire, 13 judges said appointed lawyers compare favorably with retained lawyers; one said they are the same lawyers; one said retained lawyers are more able; three that appointed lawyers are not as experienced but work hard; and two did not answer. Comparing appointed lawyers with the district attorney in experience and ability, these 20 judges replied as follows: 12 said they compare favorably; one said they compare more favorably; 5 said they are less experienced but work hard and are of equal ability; and 2 said it varies.

Orleans Parish is the only one that has a private defender system. Three of eight judges were questioned relative to this system. Asked "What do you think of the private defender's office?" the three judges stated the Legal Aid Bureau attorneys are efficient, but the bureau is understaffed and limited in its resources. The judges also pointed out that it has filled a terrible void in the defense of indigent prisoners. Two judges did not know whether the Legal Aid Bureau had adequate financial support; one felt it did not. All three judges said the private defender's office compared favorably with the retained lawyers in criminal cases. One judge added that while the present defenders are very good, he feels he has to be tolerant and helpful due to a frequent change in personnel, which brings in new, inexperienced attorneys.

Comparing the private defender with the district attorney, the judges felt the present defenders are "capable of combating the district attorney in the trial of anything."

The nine judges who were interviewed personally were asked: "Do you care to comment on the problem of providing a lawyer for the person who can pay a moderate fee?" Five judges said, without elaborating, that a moderate fee should be paid if the person can pay it; one said such a person should hire his own attorney; one said he requires payment on an installment basis according to means; one that he appoints an attorney, tells the attorney the defendant can pay, and lets the attorney and the client work out an arrangement themselves; and one did not answer.

The following data from the responses to the mail questionnaires deal with the question of determining whether the defendant is eligible for free legal counsel. The determination is made by the judges, and most of them (16 of 20) ask the defendant a series of questions in open court. The factors taken into consideration are:

Factor	No. out of 13 judges who consider this factor
Salary or wages of accused	13
Ownership of automobile and other personal property	10
Ownership of real property	12

LOUISIANA

Factor	No. out of 13 judges who consider this factor
Stocks, bonds, and bank accounts	11
Pensions, social security, and unemployment compensation	6
Whether defendant is out on bail	7
Financial resources of parents or spouse	9
Financial resources of other relatives	4

Relative to the question "Does any one of the following factors, standing alone, preclude a finding of indigency?" the answers by mail were as follows:

Factor	No. out of 20 judges who consider this factor
Defendant is out on bail	1
Defendant owns an automobile	3
Financial resources of parents are adequate	5
Financial resources of spouse are adequate	7
Financial resources of other relatives are adequate	0

To the question "If you find the defendant is ineligible to have counsel provided for him as an indigent, what happens then?" 12 judges of 20 said they advise the defendant to retain his own lawyer if he wishes to be represented by counsel.

Of the 29 judges, 15 commented generally about the problem of providing lawyers for indigent persons. Most felt that attorneys should be provided for indigent defendants in all felony cases, but, as a practical matter, need not be provided in misdemeanor cases. One judge stated that more and more defendants claim they are unable to afford a lawyer.

The judicial administrator of the Supreme Court of Louisiana recently compiled a report on court reporters and furnished the following information regarding court reporters and transcripts. Fifty-one judges participated in the report, Orleans Parish judges not included. Under the law each district judge is entitled to appoint a court reporter[27] and according to the report, 33 judges have done so. In felony cases, 28 judges specified that testimony is recorded and 18 stated that in their courts it is not. In misdemeanor cases, 38 judges stated that in their courts testimony is not recorded, and 13 stated that in theirs it is not recorded unless requested. Twenty-six judges reported that in their courts transcripts are furnished to indigent defendants in felony cases; in the courts of 25 they are not.

Generally, the judges do not make appointments in misdemeanor cases. In Louisiana there is no jury trial in misdemeanor cases. The feeling among some of the judges is that they are reluctant to impose on already overworked attorneys. Some judges feel that since misdemeanor cases are heard by a judge without a jury, the judge can serve in the dual capacity of judge and defense attorney.

D. OPINIONS OF THE DISTRICT ATTORNEYS

There is one district attorney for each of the 31 judicial districts and one for the parish of Orleans. Five district attorneys and one first assistant were interviewed personally. Questionnaires were mailed to the other 26 district attorneys, and 14 replied. All but 2 of the 20 district attorneys stated that their territorial jurisdiction extends to two or more parishes. Six district attorneys serve in a territory with a population of under 50,000; 7 where the population is 50,000 to 90,000; 6 where it is 100,000 to 399,000; and one where it is 630,000.

Relative to the number of years served as district attorney or as assistant district attorney, one district attorney said he had served for one year or less; five said from 2 to 4 years; seven, from 5 to 9 years; six, from 10 to 14 years; and one, for 15 years or longer. Of the district attorneys interviewed personally three had practiced criminal law for from 10 to 14 years and three for 15 years or longer.

Five of the six district attorneys interviewed personally stated that they devote full time to their duties as district attorney; one devotes part time. Five stated that they are also required to take care of civil business for the parish. One of the five spends over 30 hours per week on civil duties; three, from 10 to 19 hours; and one, under 10 hours. The district attorney in Orleans Parish does not perform civil duties.

Five of the 14 district attorneys answering by mail devote full time to their duties as district attorney; 8 devote part time; and one did not answer. Five of the 14 spend, on the average, over 30 hours a week in their capacity as district attorney. One spends from 10 to 19 hours; two, under 10 hours; and six did not answer this question.

Concerning adequacy of funds, two of the district attorneys interviewed personally said funds were adequate, and four said they were not. Of those answering the same question by mail, four said "yes," eight said "no," and two did not answer. Six said they have no funds for investigation; one said such funds are limited; one stated that while there are sufficient funds available for investigation, more are needed to hire additional assistants; one said he did have funds available for investigation; and five did not answer.

In the personal interview, in answer to the question "Under an ideal system, at what stage in a criminal case do you think the indigent person should first be provided with a lawyer if he wants one?" one district attorney said between arrest and first appearance before a magistrate; one said at first appearance before a magistrate; three said after the filing of the indictment or information but before arraignment thereon; and one said between arrest and arraignment on indictment or information, without designating the stage at which it should be done. Four of the six district attorneys said they thought it unfair to the indigent if he did not get a lawyer at the stage indicated and two said it was not unfair. Five of these district attorneys said a system of appointing lawyers for indigents at the stage of the proceedings suggested by them could be financed, and one did not respond to this question.

In answer to the same questions, 5 of the 14 district attorneys replying by mail said a lawyer should first be made available to the indigent person at first appearance before a magistrate; one said at first appearance and preliminary hearing; one said at the preliminary hearing; 5 said after filing of indictment or information but before arraignment thereon; and 2 said at arraignment on indictment or information. Nine of the 14 thought it unfair to the indigent person if he does not get a lawyer at the designated stage; one said it is sometimes unfair; and 4 said it is not unfair. Seven of the district attorneys thought it possible to finance such a system; five thought it not possible, and two did not answer.

Relative to providing a lawyer to the indigent defendant in certain kinds of cases, the combined results of personal and mail replies showed the following. (Two did not answer this question, and some did not answer all categories.)

Kinds of cases and proceedings	Provide counsel?		Unfair if not provided	
	Yes	No	Yes	No
Sentencing of a defendant who pleaded guilty	10*	8	5	12
Sentencing of a defendant convicted by trial	12*	5	9	9
Habeas corpus, coram nobis, or other postconviction remedy	11	5	9	6
Hearing on revocation of probation	8	10	7	10
Sexual psychopath hearing	11	6	7	8
Misdemeanor	0	18	1	14
Civil commitment of the mentally ill, including alcoholics and narcotics addicts	9	9	9	8

* Four district attorneys stated in the personal interviews that this is already provided.

In answer to the question "How do you think assigned counsel compare in experience and ability with lawyers retained by the defendant?" one district attorney personally interviewed said he thought they compare favorably; two said assigned lawyers are the same attorneys who appear as retained lawyers; one said they are not as thorough and not as experienced; one said they compare unfavorably except in capital cases; and one said it varies with the attorneys. Of those replying by mail, nine district attorneys thought assigned counsel compare favorably with retained lawyers; two said they are better and more experienced; one said they are not as experienced; one said they are the same attorneys; and one did not answer.

In evaluating the Legal Aid Bureau of Orleans Parish, the prosecutor said the bureau compared very favorably with lawyers retained by the defendants. It was said that "without exception, every man who has been in the Legal Aid Bureau has represented defendants with sometimes more vigor than if he were being paid a fee." It was said also that appointed lawyers in Orleans compared, in general, unfavorably with the private defender. The first assistant district attorney stated that his office cooperated no more with the defender than with retained or assigned counsel.

Of the six district attorneys personally interviewed relative to the present system for determining eligibility for free counsel, five felt it is too lenient, and one that it is about right. Three district attorneys who answered by mail said it is too lenient, eight said it is about right, and three did not answer. No district attorney thought that the present system is too strict.

In answer to the questions concerning the percentage of felony defendants who are indigent and what percentage waive appointment of a lawyer to represent them, the personal and mail responses were as follows:

Population of district	% indigent*	% indigent who waive appointment*
1. under 50,000	75	30
2. 50,000- 99,999	66 2/3	50
3. under 50,000	20	80
4. 100,000-399,999	no answer	0
5. under 50,000	5	0
6. 50,000- 99,999	no answer	0
7. 100,000-399,999	no answer	fairly large majority
8. 100,000-399,999	25	75
9. 100,000-399,999	85	0
10. 50,000- 99,999	75	0
11. 50,000- 99,999	50	0
12. under 50,000	90	50
13. 50,000- 99,999	80	25
14. under 50,000	15	5
15. 50,000- 99,999	50	60
16. 100,000-399,999	75	0
17. under 50,000	60	−1
18. 50,000- 99,999	85	0†
19. 100,000-399,999	no answer	0
20. 400,000-999,999	50	0†

* All figures are estimates.
† Defendant not allowed to waive in felony cases.

Assigned counsel in Louisiana are not compensated for representing indigent defendants.[28] The six district attorneys personally interviewed feel that lawyers should be compensated. Relative to the suggested amount of compensation, one said in misdemeanor cases not less than $50 per case and in felony cases not less than $200 per case; one said the lawyer should be compensated for his expenses and time in an amount to be determined by the court; and the other four did not suggest an amount. All six thought that lawyers should be reimbursed for their out-of-pocket expenses for investigation and preparation.

The same questions were answered by mail as follows: 10 district attorneys felt that assigned lawyers should be compensated; 3 felt they should not be; and one did not answer. Few commented on the amount which should be paid in these cases. One who did comment said the minimum fee should be $50 and the maximum $300, depending on the grade of the offense. Two said compensation should be commensurate with the work performed. One said not less than $100 a day. Eleven thought counsel should be reimbursed for out-of-pocket expenses; two thought they should not be; and one did not answer.

Replies to the question dealing with disclosure by the district attorney to defense counsel of confessions, statements of witnesses, reports of expert witnesses, exhibits, etc., showed that all 20 district attorneys disclose written confessions.[29] That is all that two of the district attorneys personally interviewed disclose; one said that more than the written confession is disclosed if a guilty plea is indicated but not otherwise; one said expert witness reports are disclosed but not the statements of other witnesses; one said statements of witnesses with firsthand knowledge are disclosed; and one district attorney said nothing is withheld and that his entire file is made available to defense counsel.

On the mail returns, three district attorneys said that the written confession is all they disclose; one district attorney stated that this is all he discloses unless he has an "airtight" case against the accused; seven stated that in addition to the written confession they furnish the defendant with exhibits, statements of accused and of witnesses, reports, etc.; one discloses everything except the statements of witnesses; one said his disclosures depend on no set rule but on each particular case, without specifying what is disclosed and what is not; one stated that appointed counsel for indigents are furnished information other than the written confession of the accused, whereas retained counsel are furnished only this.

Four of the six district attorneys who were interviewed personally said that the person who can pay a moderate fee should pay the appointed lawyer according to his ability to pay; one said he should get his own lawyer, and one did not comment.

The district attorneys personally interviewed were asked what they thought about trying a case when the defendant does not have counsel. Without specifying felony or misdemeanor cases, three district attorneys said they do not like to do this; one said he refuses to do it in felony cases but said the defendant is much better off in misdemeanor cases where the judge "defends" the accused; one said this is not done in felony cases and he prefers that it not be done in misdemeanor cases; and one said the defendant can get a fair trial in his parish whether represented by counsel or not.

Four of the six district attorneys in the personal interviews, when asked: "What do you think of the present system of providing counsel for the indigent accused?" stated that it is inadequate and that they do not like it, giving the following reasons:

It is an unwarranted imposition on the bar (not because the representation isn't adequate).

It is antiquated—unfair to attorneys who are appointed. The attorneys are asked to make personal sacrifices of time and money to defend these accused. There should be a fee and expense system to compensate attorneys who are appointed to represent indigent defendants . . . In rural areas, there is not enough work to justify a full-time public defender.

It is completely inadequate. The Legal Aid Bureau is completely understaffed for the amount of work assigned to it by the court. Practicing attorneys are generally reluctant to accept appointments and in many instances do not or cannot allot the necessary time to the handling of a case. There is no system for determining whether or not a defendant is in fact indigent and therefore many defendants who can afford counsel are abusing the present system.

It isn't good but it is the best we can do under the law and the circumstances—assigned attorneys share the burden.

The fifth district attorney said that the system in his parish is very good and that the court appoints the attorney on a case-by-case basis to represent indigent defendants. These appointments are made, in all felony cases, prior to arraignment. The sixth district attorney said the system is "adequate."

When asked how the present system for providing counsel for indigent defendants might be improved, one district attorney personally interviewed said the present system in his parish is adequate; one said it cannot be improved except by paying appointed attorneys at least out-of-pocket expenses; one said the system can be improved (1) by establishing a public defender system or by increasing the salaries and facilities of the private defender office, (2) by establishing some method of reimbursing appointed counsel at least for expenses, and (3) by providing facilities for investigation of alleged indigency; two said they were in favor of establishing a public defender system; one said the present system could be improved by paying a fee to appointed attorneys.

Only 3 of the 14 district attorneys replying by mail gave opinions as to how the present system might be improved. Excerpts are given below.

Due to the apparent increase in criminal matters in every jurisdiction, I believe that a case is made out for the justification of a public defender who specializes in criminal matters and who is paid to do so.

I believe that the best system to provide an indigent accused with counsel is the assigned counsel system . . . The lawyers in a given community, town or city should be grouped by the court or local bar association into defense teams with two, three or more lawyers on a team. Thus a law firm may constitute a team. These teams should be placed on a permanent revolving roster to be appointed to represent indigent accused in appropriate cases, due consideration being given to the nature of the charge and the experience and ability of the lawyers to be appointed . . . Thus, by appointment of the court, an indigent accused can be assured of adequate representation so that he would get a fair and impartial trial. I do not believe that the accused is entitled to any specific attorneys or to be granted the most skilled criminal lawyers in the community . . .

By having a public defender in all felony cases.

E. OPINIONS OF DEFENSE ATTORNEYS

1. *Assigned counsel.* Questionnaires were mailed to 25 lawyers in the six sample parishes, and 17 replied. A personal interview was held at the Legal Aid Bureau, the private defender system in Orleans Parish.

One of the 17 lawyers had been practicing for 30 to 39 years; 4, for 15 to 29 years; 3, for 10 to 14 years; 2, for 6 to 9 years; one, for 5 years; one, for 4 years; 4, for 2 years; and one, for one year. All 17 were appointed during 1962 to serve as counsel for an indigent person accused of crime. The number of indigent persons represented was as follows:

No. of attorneys	No. of indigent defendants
1	1
3	2
1	3
1	4
1	5
4	6-9
3	10-14
1	20-29
2	30 or more

Of the 17 attorneys, 10 had at least one case where the penalty was death or life imprisonment. One of the 10 had two such cases and one had three.

Two of the 17 lawyers stated that they had no experience in criminal practice before the first case in which they were appointed in 1962. One lawyer had experience in 1 to 4 cases; two, in 5 to 9 cases; one, in 10 to 19 cases; three, in 20 to 49 cases; and eight, or about 50%, had handled 50 cases or more. These eight who had experience in over 50 cases represented 10 of the 13 defendants where the crime was punishable by death or life imprisonment.

As stated previously, the system of committing magistrates is not used in Louisiana. Appointments generally are made, therefore, by the district judge. The stages at which the 17 lawyers were appointed in their last appointed case in 1962 were as follows:

Stage of proceeding	No. of attorneys appointed
After the filing of an indictment, information, etc., but before arraignment thereon	5
At arraignment on indictment, information, etc.	6
After arraignment on indictment or information, but before trial	6

Most of the lawyers (13) answered that they were appointed in time to represent the accused person adequately. Two answered that they were not, one of the two stating that the person he represented confessed before he was appointed. Two did not answer this question.

When asked about the crime or crimes with which the defendant was charged in their last appointed case in 1962, the 17 lawyers answered thus:

Crime	No. of attorneys
Assault	1
Auto theft	1
Burglary	4*
Forgery, bad check, counterfeiting	1
Grand larceny, grand theft (except auto theft)	1
Murder	4
Narcotics, possession	1
Armed robbery	1*
Aggravated battery	1
Theft	1

*One defendant was charged with both a robbery and a burglary.

On two of the returns, the answer to this question could not be determined. All 17 lawyers stated that they were not compensated for their services in this case. Three stated that they were paid in part for out-of-pocket expenses.

To the question "How much would you have charged a client who retained you for your services in this case?" the replies were as follows:

Crime	Fee lawyer would have charged
Murder	$2500
Murder	5000
Murder	1500
Murder	2500
Forgery, bad check, counterfeiting	250-500
Burglary	500
Grand larceny, grand theft (except auto theft)	300
Grand larceny, grand theft (except auto theft)	150 without trial; $750 with trial
Assault	150-200
Aggravated battery	350
Burglary / Armed robbery / Theft	3500*
Auto or motor vehicle theft	350
Narcotics, possession	300
Burglary	1000

*One defendant was charged with three crimes.

Five of the 17 represented indigent defendants on appeal in a state court in 1962. One of the five represented two different defendants on appeal. Four of the five received no compensation.

Four of the 17 attorneys represented indigent defendants in postconviction matters in 1962. Two of the four represented defendants in three such cases each. None of the four were compensated.

On the question of whether the present system for assignment of lawyers to represent indigent persons accused of crime was fair to the indigent person, 9 of the attorneys expressed the opinion that it was fair, and 8 said it was not. All 17 said the system was not fair to lawyers. Recommended changes are reported in the following pa.agraphs.

Five of the attorneys said that the lawyer should be appointed at an earlier stage in the case, one of the five stating that this should be done immediately after arrest. Ten said that out-of-pocket expenses of lawyers incurred in investigation and preparation should be reimbursed. Twelve recommended that lawyers be paid fees for their services. Two favored providing lawyers in additional kinds of cases, such as serious misdemeanors. Three advocated improving the system which the judge uses in selecting lawyers to be appointed.

Three of the lawyers suggested that the defender system be employed to handle cases involving indigent defendants. One of the attorneys stated that in Louisiana appointed lawyers in civil cases are paid fees, whereas in criminal cases they are not, which indicates to him that the law is more interested in economic rights than in individual freedom. One of the lawyers sent a letter with his completed questionnaire and made several observations about representation of indigents. He said he felt that the system of no compensation was not fair, particularly in capital cases. He cited a case of aggravated rape where he was appointed to represent the accused, who confessed shortly after his arrest and before counsel was appointed to represent him. The trial lasted for three days and the defendant was convicted. The case was appealed to the Louisiana Supreme Court, after which a writ of certiorari was refused by the United States Supreme Court. A habeas corpus proceeding was instituted in the federal district court and is currently on appeal to the Court of Appeals for the Fifth Circuit. Both the state Supreme Court and the federal court are a considerable distance from the attorney's home parish, necessitating considerable expense in attending court. This attorney said: "I believe it to be only fair, particularly in capital cases, that the attorney be appointed immediately upon arrest and that the confession obtained prior to consultation with an attorney should not be allowed. . . ."

2. *Legal Aid Bureau—Orleans Parish.* The attorney in charge at the Legal Aid Bureau in Orleans Parish has served in this capacity for two years and has practiced criminal law for that length of time. He devotes full time to his duties and spends, on the average, 30 hours a week or more in his capacity as defender. He feels that the present system of providing counsel for indigent defendants is "adequate based on existing laws and the procedures used by the Orleans Parish Criminal Court in court appointments for indigents." His annual salary is $7000. The budget for the defender office is approximately $28,000. In 1962, 526 defendants in 894 cases were represented by the Legal Aid Bureau, with the following staff: two full-time lawyers and one part-time lawyer, two full-time secretaries, and one investigator. The first stage at which the Legal Aid Bureau enters a case is after the filing of an indictment or information but before or shortly after arraignment thereon. This private defender office, in addition to felony cases, also handles misdemeanors, habeas corpus proceedings, and hearings on revocation of probation. The number of the latter type cases is included in the total number of cases handled.

There are not adequate funds to run the office, but, according to the attorney in charge, additional staff is not needed. Funds are available for investigation. The budget of the Legal Aid Bureau is determined by a board of directors composed of local attorneys who supervise the activities of the bureau.

To become a member of the Legal Aid Bureau one must be a member of the state bar with prior experience in criminal law. There are no career opportunities available to defenders and this is due primarily to the lack of good salaries. Those who work for the bureau do so for an indefinite time, which averages approximately two or three years.

According to the attorney in charge, the indigent person under an ideal system should first be provided with a lawyer, if he wants one, at the first appearance before a magistrate. He said he does not think that it is unfair to the indigent person if he does not get a lawyer at this stage, saying that the rights of the accused should be protected by the court at this stage of the proceeding. Regarding financing, he stated that the main problem in this area would be to avoid political patronage if revenues were available from the government.

When questioned about the present system for deciding whether a person is eligible for the defender service, the defender answered that the system is about right. He estimated that 35% of felony defendants are indigent and that none waive appointment of a lawyer to represent them. He also estimated that 25% of all felony defendants are not able to make bail, and added that those who do make bail are not eligible for the services of the Legal Aid Bureau because once a man can afford bond, he has a duty to obtain private counsel.

Regarding the relationship with the district attorney's office, the attorney in charge of the Legal Aid Bureau stated that his office is given the same consideration as outside counsel and that the district attorney's office is generally cooperative in disclosing pertinent facts about cases. Legal Aid is not, however, allowed to use the district attorney's investigating facilities.

F. COMPARISONS AMONG JUDGES, DISTRICT ATTORNEYS, AND DEFENSE ATTORNEYS

For purposes of comparison, certain parts of the survey are presented below.

	Judges	District attorneys	Defense attorneys
Total responding	29	20	17
Ideal stage for first appointment of counsel:			Received last appointment at this stage:
Between arrest and first appearance before a magistrate	6	1	
At first appearance before a magistrate	5	6	
Between first appearance and preliminary hearing	2	1	
At preliminary hearing	1	1	
After filing of indictment or information but before arraignment thereon	9	8	5
At arraignment on indictment or information	4	2	6
After arraignment on indictment	2	0	6
Between arrest and arraignment—no stage designated	0	1	

	Judges	District attorneys	Defense attorneys
Is it unfair to the indigent if he is not represented at the designated stage?			
Yes	18	13	
No	9	6	
No answer	2	0	
Sometimes	0	1	
Should lawyers be compensated for their services?			
Yes	21	16	
No	4	3	
No answer	4	1	
Should out-of-pocket expenses be paid?			
Yes	25	17	
No	2	2	
No answer	2	1	

G. DOCKET STUDIES

Docket surveys were conducted in four parishes for the year 1962. The following tables show some of the results of the survey. (For method used, see volume 1, pages 178-179.)

The third table shows that the proportion of defendants not released on bail varied from 40% in Tangipahoa and 43% in Orleans to 78% in Ouachita Parish.

The fourth table shows disposition of the sample cases. The weighted average for the four parishes together, which is also a projection for the state as a whole, shows that 50% of the defendants pleaded guilty, including 4% who pleaded to lesser offenses. Another 25% of the cases were dismissed and 17% were pending, both rather high percentages of these categories compared with other states. Orleans had an unusually high number of dismissals and Jefferson had a high number of cases pending. Only 5% of the cases went to trial.

The fifth table shows that in 46% of the cases no sentences were imposed, usually by reason of dismissals, acquittals, or pending cases. Twenty-eight per cent of the cases resulted in prison sentences, including terms in parish prisons, while 19% of the defendants were placed on probation, 4% were given suspended sentences without probation, and 3% were fined. The frequency of imprisonment versus probation or suspended sentence varied greatly among the four parishes. Jefferson had the lowest proportion of prison sentences and Orleans the highest.

Change of Bail

Parish	Total sample	Yes No.	%	No No.	%	No data* No.	%
Orleans	218	39	20	155	80	24	11

* % of no data refers to total sample; % in other columns refers to total cases for which data were available.

Sex and Race of Defendants

Parish	Total sample	Male		Female		No data*		White		Negro		No data*	
		No.	%	No.	%	No.	%	No.	%	No.	%	No.	%
Tangipahoa	48	45	94	3	6	0	0	24	50	24	50	0	0
Ouachita	46	38	86	6	14	2	7	28	64	16	36	2	4
Orleans	218	184	87	23	11	11	5	96	45	115	55	7	3
Jefferson	106	74	91	7	9	25	24	—	—	—	—	—	—

*% of no data refers to total sample; % in other columns refers to total cases for which data were available.

Frequency of Release on Bail

Parish	Total sample	Yes		No		No data*	
		No.	%	No.	%	No.	%
Tangipahoa	48	26	60	17	40	5	10
Ouachita	46	8	22	29	78	9	20
Orleans	224	112	57	83	43	29	13

*% of no data refers to total sample; % in other columns refers to total cases for which data were available.

Dispositions

Parish	Total sample	Plea guilty	Plea lesser offense	Dismissed	Found guilty	Found guilty lesser charge	Acquittal	Mental commitment	Pending	Stet†	Other
Tangipahoa	48	19	1	10	0	1	0	1	11	3	2
Ouachita	46	37	2	4	0	0	0	1	1	1	0
Orleans	224	74	8	87	8	0	8	1	32	0	6
Jefferson	106	27	6	33	4	0	4	0	29	0	3
Weighted total percentages		46	4	25	2	1	2	1	17	2	1

†Refers to cases that are held on the calendar by the district attorney to await further action, e.g., where a witness is unavailable or another case is pending against the defendant.

Sentencing

Parish	Total sample	No sentence No.	No sentence %	Prison No.	Prison %	Probation No.	Probation %	Suspended sentence No.	Suspended sentence %	Fine No.	Fine %	No data* No.	No data* %
Tangipahoa	48	23	50	15	33	5	11	2	4	1	2	2	4
Ouachita	46	7	16	17	38	20	44	1	2	0	0	1	2
Orleans	224	116	57	70	33	12	7	3	2	10	7	0	0
Jefferson	106	67	64	11	10	16	15	8	8	3	2	0	0
Weighted total percentages			46		28		19		4		3		2

* % of no data refers to total sample; % in other columns refers to total cases for which data were available.

The following statistics, furnished by the department of institutions, deal with probation cases in three of the parishes where the personal survey was conducted.

Probation Cases, 1961-62

	Orleans Parish			Jefferson Parish			Terrebonne Parish			Remaining on probation at end of year
	New cases	Terminated	Revoked	New cases	Terminated	Revoked	New cases	Terminated	Revoked	
1961	171	115	20	83	28	7	9	2	0	91
1962	155	100	19	133	38	9	4	0	1	125

H. CONCLUSIONS AND RECOMMENDATIONS

The following conclusions and recommendations are based on the information contained in the survey:

1. The system of committing magistrates is not used in Louisiana even though provided for in the procedural law of the state. As a result of this failure the arrested subject, if indigent, usually remains in a police station for 3 to 10 days before being formally charged by the district attorney's office. This practice is common in Orleans, Jefferson, and Tangipahoa Parishes.

It is recommended that the system of committing magistrates be utilized so as to prevent the police from holding a suspect while they make their case against him, to prevent unfounded or inappropriate charges from being accepted against the accused by the district attorney, and to speed up the process of judicial proceedings.

2. Even though the judges responding to the mail questionnaire stated that they determine indigency by asking a series of questions in open court and also consider other factors, it is apparent from the personal interviews and responses by mail that no verification is made of alleged indigency.

It is suggested that a uniform system should be established to determine indigency. It is felt that if this were done, it would either reduce the number of indigents or provide information which would allow for the "indigent" to pay at least a moderate fee to appointed counsel or to pay his out-of-pocket expenses. The appointed attorney should be able to make a determination based on his own investigation.

3. Generally, only a small percentage of the bar participates in the representation of indigents (e.g., Orleans Parish). Appointed counsel are not paid a fee for their services, nor are they reimbursed for out-of-pocket expenses incurred in defending clients.

Either appointed counsel should be paid a fee for their services in indigent cases and/or out-of-pocket expenses or all attorneys should be required by law to participate in the program of representing indigents. In Orleans Parish, for example, approximately 40 attorneys receive most of the assignments in appointed cases. The other members of the bar practicing in Orleans Parish rarely, if ever, appear in criminal court and few ever volunteer their services to represent indigents.

If assigned counsel are to be paid, most of the judges and district attorneys participating in the survey feel that the funds for such payment should come from parish and state funds.

4. All lawyers participating in the survey stated that the present system for assignment of counsel is not fair to the lawyer.

It is suggested that assigned counsel should be appointed earlier in the proceeding, as shortly after arrest as possible. (By employing the system of committing magistrates recommended above, it would be possible to assign counsel at this stage of the proceeding.)

Other recommendations are set forth above.

NOTES—Louisiana

[1] La. Rev. Stat. Ann. tit. 15 (1950). The Louisiana Code of Criminal Procedure is presently under revision by the Louisiana Law Institute.

[2] La. Rev. Stat. Ann. tit. 15, § 2 (1950).

[3] La. Rev. Stat. Ann. tit. 15, § 4 (1950).

[4] La. Rev. Stat. Ann. tit. 15, § 5 (1950).

[5] La. Rev. Stat. Ann. tit. 15, § 17 (1950).

[6] La. Rev. Stat. Ann. tit. 15, § 77 (1950).

[7] La. Rev. Stat. Ann. tit. 15, § 79 (1950).

[8] La. Rev. Stat. Ann. tit. 15, § 80 (1950).

[9] La. Rev. Stat. Ann. tit. 15, §§ 153-156 (1950).

[10] La. Rev. Stat. Ann. tit. 15, § 153 (1950).

[11] La. Rev. Stat. Ann. tit. 15, § 154 (1950).

[12] La. Rev. Stat. Ann. tit. 15, § 70 (1950).

[13] The only "holding" statute in Louisiana is found in La. Rev. Stat. Ann. tit. 15, § 84.5, which allows a peace officer, a merchant, or a merchant's employee, to detain, for not longer than 60 minutes, any person who he has reasonable grounds to believe has committed a theft of goods displayed for sale by the merchant. This "holding" is not considered an arrest.

[14] La. Rev. Stat. Ann. tit. 15, § 78 (1950).

[15] La. Rev. Stat. Ann. tit. 15, § 254 (1950).

[16] La. Rev. Stat. Ann. tit. 15, § 254.1 (1950).

[17] La. Rev. Stat. Ann. tit. 15, § 142 (1950).

[18] La. Rev. Stat. Ann. tit. 15, § 143 (1950).

[19] Ibid.

[20] La. Rev. Stat. Ann. tit. 15, § 868 (1950). The state penitentiary is located at Angola, West Feliciana Parish. In 1956, a special law was passed to compensate attorneys appointed to represent inmates in the state penitentiary. In Jefferson and Terrebonne Parishes, the judges follow the practice of appointing those attorneys who serve without fee in criminal cases to serve in civil cases where a fee is paid. In Terrebonne Parish, only those attorneys who serve on criminal cases receive appointments in civil cases.

[21] La. Rev. Stat. Ann. tit. 13, §4529 (1950).

[22] U.S. ex rel. Weston v. Sigler, 308 F. 2d 946 (5th Cir. 1962). See La. Rev. Stat. Ann. tit. 15, § 332.2 (1950).

[23] State v. Freeman, 160 So. 2d 571 (1964); State v. Daley, 146 So. 2d 798 (1960).

[24] La. Const. article 7, § 10 (5).

[25] La. Sup. Ct. R. IX, Sec. 5 (adopted February 13, 1962).

[26] La. Rev. Stat. Ann. tit. 15, § 143 (1950).

[27] La. Rev. Stat. Ann. tit. 13 § 961 (1950). See also La. Rev. Stat. Ann. tit 15, § 332.2 (1950), which states that in felony cases the entire proceedings of the trial and testimony shall be taken down and reported by a court reporter. See, too, La. Rev. Stat. Ann. tit. 15, § 555

(1950), dealing with right of accused to have testimony taken down and provisions for paying therefor. Read also U.S. ex rel. Weston v. Sigler, 308 F. 2d 946 (1962).

[28] See note 20, supra.

[29] Louisiana law allows pre-trial inspection of written confessions. See State v. Darsey, 207 La. 928, 22 So. 2d 273 (1945). See also State v. Bickham, 239 La. 1094, 121 So. 2d 207 (1960).

MAINE

Edward T. Richardson, Jr., Portland

The reporter wishes to note the interest and help received from Hon. Robert B. Williamson, chief justice; Hon. Richard S. Chapman, chief judge of the district courts; and especially the genial assistance and complete cooperation of the clerks of court and their staffs in the various counties.

A. INTRODUCTION

Maine had a population of 969,265 by count in the 1960 census. Since growth is very slow, the population is estimated not to have reached one million as yet. The state is divided into 16 counties, and the nine superior court judges may sit in any of these counties. In Cumberland, the largest, the court sits 10 months, 3 of them devoted exclusively to criminal trials; in Lincoln and Piscataquis, the 2 smallest counties, there are only 2 terms a year.

The superior court system, although organized in reference to the counties, is a state system, and the practice is uniform throughout, particularly because the judges travel from county to county. These judges are under the administrative direction of the chief justice of the Supreme Judicial Court. Each county has its own prosecuting attorney, known as the county attorney, and in the larger counties he has one or more assistants.

In addition to the superior court, where jury trials are held, the lower court system until 1961 was made up of urban municipal courts and rural trial justices. In 1961 a district court system was created to replace the older system, and it is functioning in several areas of the state at the present time, being set up in a given area as the terms of the incumbent justices run out. The old system will be entirely eliminated during 1965. For the purposes of this system, the state is divided into 13 districts and 33 divisions. These are set up on a statewide basis, rather than by counties. In this survey, however, the emphasis is on the superior court.

The following two tables describe the counties selected for study in Maine and summarize some of the information contained in the forms for the counties surveyed (all data for 1962).

County	Felony respondents	Number of appointments of counsel	No. of lawyers who served	Maximum number by one lawyer	Estimated number of lawyers in county
Cumberland	187	111	40	9	300
Kennebec	100	36	19	6	150
Androscoggin	83	41	23	4	150
Penobscot	132	77	22	14	200

County	Chief city	1960 population in thousands	Location	Remarks
Cumberland (D)	Portland	183	Southwest	Largest in population, commercial and recreational center
Kennebec (D)	Augusta	89	Southwest central	Location of capital; agricultural and commercial, recreational
Androscoggin	Lewiston	86	between above counties	Industrial and agricultural
Penobscot	Bangor	126	Central	Big area; lumbering, manufacturing, wilderness recreation, reaches into north central part of state

(D) indicates that a docket study was made.

Since it is a rarity to have an indigent respondent refuse the appointment of counsel the number of appointments of counsel would represent the number of respondents found indigent.

Pay to counsel in the superior court is at the discretion of the sitting justice. The average for an appearance, no trial, is $50 to $75. For trial in the usual felony it is $150 to $200, assuming one to two days. In one instance $1400 was allowed for a murder trial lasting six days in Cumberland County. This would be a maximum. There is no specific allowance for expenses, and counsel must do his own investigating.

B. CRIMINAL PROCEDURE AS IT AFFECTS INDIGENT PERSONS

The procedure is uniform throughout the state. The majority of felony cases begin with the arrest of the suspect. He is then taken before a municipal court, a trial justice, or the district judge. The trial justices need not be lawyers; the judges are lawyers.

There is a preliminary hearing, and in general the justices are mindful to inform the respondent of his rights. The purpose of this hearing in felony cases is to find "probable cause," and, if such is found, the man is bound over to the grand jury. Bail is set, but in default of bail he is committed to the county jail until the next criminal term. There is no regular practice in these lower courts for the providing of counsel; however, a new law effective Sept. 21, 1963, (R.S. 1954, ch. 148, § 11) provides for counsel, without pay, in the district court. (A copy of the law is appended to this report.)

Between the time of binding over and arraignment the respondent may indicate a desire to plead by information, in which case he sends word through the jailer to the county attorney, who undertakes to see that an attorney talks to the man. If it appears that he is likely to be found indigent, the attorney comes before the court with the indigent respondent, the court formally appoints him to be counsel, the respondent is required to waive his rights to indictment and trial by jury, in open court in writing, and he is then allowed to plead to the charge. The courts have been scrupulous to instruct such respondents of their rights and to make certain that they understand what they are giving up.

The new law requires that in felony cases counsel be appointed before arraignment. In the past that had been the prevalent practice. Although the formal appointment was made on the date of arraignment, in practice the attorney had been procured and had seen his client informally several days before arraignment, and if necessary could procure an extension of time for investigation, etc. This reporter has represented many men on informations, and he has always had ample time to investigate the case, and has found both the judges and county attorney to be cooperative and reasonable.

The grand jury, upon presentation of the state's case, returns an indictment. The case is then brought to trial promptly, ordinarily at the next regular term at which criminal causes are heard. Of course, in some of the smaller counties this may mean considerable time between the preliminary hearing and trial, and the information procedure is extensively used by respondents who want to get on with serving their sentence.

Most respondents who come up on information are indigent, and all have counsel assigned. Only in the most exceptional circumstances, when some eccentric respondent absolutely insists on not having counsel, is there an exception to this.

Indigency is determined by the judge through inquiry in open court, sometimes assisted by information from the county attorney, sheriff, or probation department. In some cases where the respondent has had some, but insufficient funds, he has paid what he could to counsel, and the court has supplemented this by an order on the county. This was done on a theory of inherent powers of the trial court. There have been cases of a man put on probation on condition that he repay the county. Payment is made to the probation office and it goes into general county funds.

It is entirely up to the indigent's counsel to provide investigation, witnesses, etc. This can be a hardship. In most cases, however, the county attorneys are cooperative in disclosing appropriate matter to the respondent's counsel. In extraordinary situations, it appears that the courts have allowed a sum large enough to embrace extra expenses.

In each county is a cadre of attorneys who handle most of the criminal cases, whether on fee or on appointment. Therefore, the assigned attorneys are generally those experienced in this type of case. They appear to the court willing and ready, and, Maine being a rather small state, the judges are likely to be familiar with the competence of the attorneys available for appointment. Many young attorneys, of course, get their chance at informations and the lesser felonies, but, for a graver crime, it is likely to be the experienced criminal counsel who is appointed. There is not so much criminal business in Maine that these attorneys would not welcome appointments. As a result, although a minority of the bar actually participate, indigents get experienced defense.

The expenses of counsel and cost of a record in a murder appeal are paid for by the county. In felonies other than murder the cost for indigent persons is met through a legislative appropriation for the operation of the courts. For the past several years the Supreme Judicial Court has extended this to postconviction appeal cases such as habeas corpus and coram nobis. No payment for counsel is provided, however, at hearings on postconviction remedies. A new law specifically provides for counsel (but not for payment to him) for indigents bringing habeas corpus in good faith. Most indigent appeal cases go up to the Supreme Judicial Court on one copy of the transcript and the original papers, thus keeping down the costs. This whole field is within the control of the Supreme Judicial Court, and it has for many years been zealous in the protection of appellants in these cases.

In the past no provision has been made for appointment of counsel in misdemeanor cases, but the new law provides for this at the discretion of the court, but without payment to counsel. It is widely assumed that appointment of counsel below would be followed by appointment of the same counsel above, but nothing seems to require this, and practice is not yet established.

C. JUDGES

The reporter had an interview with the Chief Justice, Robert B. Williamson, who expressed great interest in the survey. This is summarized as follows:

Under our new law providing protection of rights of indigent criminal respondents, the provisions for their defense, both where required in the lower courts, and in the higher courts, would seem to provide substantially that protection contemplated by the Constitution of the United States. The new law provides for paid counsel in the superior court in felony cases, and a very important provision is for representation before arraignment. The law had already adequately provided for murder cases.

The cooperation of the bar would seem to be assured; the chief justice strongly favors a very general participation by the bar in the defense of indigent respondents, and feels sure that the past excellent cooperation of the bar in this regard will continue. Given this situation, there would seem at present to be no need for a public defender system.

While it would be good, indeed, if counsel in the municipal and district courts could be paid for their services, as they are in the superior court, the financial problem is one for the legislature, and the members of the bar ought to, and generally do feel it their duty to defend indigents where counsel is needed.

The bench and bar are in some counties already working with the new district court system, which will soon be in operation throughout the state. It is anticipated that this will further improve the administration of justice in Maine.

The reporter also had an interview with Hon. Richard S. Chapman, chief judge of the district court system. He indicated that while it was too soon to know how the new law would work out in the district court, he felt sure that it would better protect the rights of indigents. He indicated that, since this is a state system, and was intended by the legislature to pay its own way, that payment of counsel is impossible at present, although it certainly is desirable that some arrangement be made to take care of such payment as soon as possible.

Three of the nine superior court trial judges responded, and they were in general agreement that counsel should be provided either at or before the first hearing before a magistrate; they disagreed, however, on whether lack of such counsel would prejudice the respondent. (Two thought it would.) They agreed that counsel ought to be present at sentencing either upon plea or at conviction. One judge set forth his reasons at some length, indicating that the technical nature of the proceedings, excepting revocation of probation and misdemeanor hearings, required that an average layman respondent needed the advice and explanation of counsel. All three judges approved of a broad base for choice of attorneys, in which position they were in agreement with the chief justice, and it could be inferred from the responses that they felt that respondents were receiving reasonably good representation, making it clear that they expended some care on the choice of counsel. One judge, especially, emphasized what is indicated elsewhere in this report, that the number of available counsel is relatively few, and as the judges travel circuit they soon become personally familiar with these counsel and able to form an opinion of their abilities. One of the judges felt that the remuneration generally allowed was insufficient, obviously considering his discretion in the matter somewhat circumscribed by custom among the members of the bench. One responding judge had served 10-14 years, one 5-9 years, and the other 2-4 years.

D. COUNTY ATTORNEYS

The response here was excellent, being 11 out of 16. Four found their funds inadequate, but all but one found the present system of determining eligibility for appointment as counsel to be about right, the exception finding it too lenient. All indicated a liberal policy of disclosure to appointed counsel, with differences in detail, and one made the remark that he disclosed more freely to local counsel than to those from other counties, an echo of a fortunately dying Maine tradition that the fellow from another county is a "furriner."

All agreed that counsel should ideally be provided either before or at the first hearing before a magistrate, but all but two felt no counsel was necessary at a misdemeanor hearing. Only one thought a public defender would be cheaper than the present system, the financing of which all agreed could be practical. There was some sentiment that because of the statewide organization of the trial court system, and of the supervening district court system, a state system of financing ought to be instituted.

In reviewing the reports from the county attorneys there appeared no startling differences of opinion, rather of detail only. There certainly was no appreciable sentiment for a public defender system among them.

E. DEFENSE ATTORNEYS

Of 25 questionnaires sent to defense attorneys in the sample counties, 13 were returned. Although not all were wholly responsive, certain conclusions can be inferred. Only four were appointed before indictment, but all of the others were appointed before arraignment, reflecting the general custom. Seven thought that appointment ought to be at an earlier stage, but most thought that they had been able to provide an adequate defense. In spite of this, three had doubts about the system being fair to the respondent and three thought it definitely unfair to the lawyer assigned. All indicated that if privately hired they would have charged more than they received. One who defended a murder case would have charged $5000; most on regular felonies would have charged from $150 to $250, two running higher.

There was general sentiment for payment of out-of-pocket expenses, which are not now paid except in murder cases. There was also some feeling that the system of choosing attorneys ought to be changed. Some complaint arose of the custom of appointing young attorneys so that they might get experience. It was felt by some that too often this resulted in an attorney being chosen who was insufficiently experienced for the case he had to handle.

One attorney stated flatly that a public defender system ought to be set up.

While generally the attorneys seemed to feel that the respondent was adequately taken care of, one did note that in those cases where a confession was received at the preliminary hearing before a magistrate, this could be introduced, after indictment, at the trial. With representation from the outset, this could be avoided.

F. COMPARATIVE STUDIES

It is difficult to make any convincing generalizations from the returns; however, one difference of opinion that does come to attention is the feeling among several of the defense attorneys that the method of choosing among them is inadequate, whereas the judges, who do the choosing, seem to feel it all right. One may well allow for a slight bias in each group.

Generally speaking the county attorneys seem more satisfied with the system than do the defense attorneys, yet only one among each group reporting favored a public defender system. Most of both groups felt the present system was workable and practical, but that it needed some adjustments. The most nagging complaint came from defense attorneys relative to remuneration, which obviously has not kept up with the scale of pay an attorney has a right to expect for his services by present valuation.

G. THE DOCKET STUDY

A study was made of court records for 1962 in representative cases in Cumberland and Kennebec Counties. (For details about methods of research see volume 1, pages 178-179.) Results are shown in Tables 1 to 4, listed by counties and as a weighted average, which is also a projection for the state as a whole.

As shown in Tables 1 and 2, every defendant had counsel in the sample cases, with the proportion of indigents averaging 69%. (Informed sources, however, indicate that for the state as a whole the proportion of indigent defendants is about 50%.)

Table 3 shows the disposition of cases. For the combined figure 81% of the defendants pleaded guilty, including 6% who pleaded to lesser offenses. Table 4 shows the sentences, if any, that were meted out. The figures for the two counties are rather similar, averaging out to 45% of the original group of defendants being sent to prison, including county jail or reformatory, and 34% placed on probation.

TABLE 1
Retained and Assigned Counsel in Felonies
Maine, 1962

County	Total sample	Did defendant have counsel? Yes No.	%	No No.	%	Retained No.	%	Assigned No.	%	Combination or type unknown No.	%
Cumberland	50	50	100	0	0	14	28	35	70	1	2
Kennebec	19	19	100	0	0	6	32	13	68	0	0
Weighted total percentages			100		0		30		69		1

TABLE 2
Was Felony Defendant Determined Indigent?
Maine, 1962

County	Total sample	Yes No.	%	No No.	%
Cumberland	50	35	70	15	30
Kennebec	19	13	68	6	32
Weighted total percentages			69		31

TABLE 3
Disposition in Felony Cases
Maine, 1962

County	Total sample	Plea guilty	Plea lesser offense	Dis-missed	Found guilty	Found guilty lesser degree	Ac-quitted	Stet°
Cumberland	50	41	1	0	1	0	1	6
Kennebec	19	13	2	2	1	0	0	1
Weighted total percentages		75	6	5	4	0	1	9

° Held on inactive docket.

TABLE 4
Sentencing in Felony Cases
Maine, 1962

County	Total sample	No sentence No.	%	Prison No.	%	Probation No.	%	Fine No.	%	Alterna-tive sentences° No.	%
Cumberland	50	7	14	24	48	18	36	0	0	2	4
Kennebec	19	4	21	8	42	6	32	1	5	0	0
Weighted total percentages		18		45		34		3		2	

° e.g., fine or imprisonment. May also be recorded under other columns.

H. CONCLUSIONS AND RECOMMENDATIONS

The clearest conclusion reached is that there is a very general sentiment throughout both bench and bar that a public defender system is not a present necessity in Maine.

Two problems of the present system are pointed up: if the base for choice of assigned counsel is too large, that is, substantially all practicing lawyers, then some of them are going to be incompetent or unwilling properly to represent the respondent in a criminal trial; if the base of choice is too narrow, then only a small cadre will get all the assignments, which raises the question of a practically professional defender group, without any systematized control. The only present answer is the individual integrity of any attorney concerned in either situation.

There is a very generally accepted opinion throughout the profession that the new changes in the law will improve the protection of the indigent's rights, while aggravating the individual attorneys' problems relative to unpaid representation.

As to this financial problem, a few years will bring out its extent and hopefully provide material for presentation to the legislature from which source funds would have to come.

As this study is preliminary the following recommendations must be tentative.

1. A further study is needed of the base for choosing assigned counsel.

2. A further study is needed to determine if there is some person or officer who, through an examination of alleged indigents prior to arraignment, could assist the court in determining indigency, there being a very high rate of indigency and some suspicion in some quarters that concealment may exist in some cases.

3. A further study is needed relative to rates of compensation of counsel directed to the provision, especially of funds for expenses, and, assisting the judges in the exercise of their discretion, perhaps a schedule of rates such as most bar associations now have.

4. It was found that generally the docket records in the various counties, while roughly uniform, usually left a great deal to be desired from the point a view of statistical study. It is submitted that the ideal docket on any respondent ought to outline the essential history of the case from its inception by arrest. Kennebec County was found most complete in this regard.

APPENDIX

A. THE CRIMINAL COURT SYSTEM

Supreme Judicial Court: Chief justice and five associate justices. Court of highest appeal to which in criminal matters a· e addressed post conviction matters.

Superior Court: Nine justices under the administrative direction of the chief justice of the Supreme Judicial Court. Only court for jury trials, jurisdiction of felonies. Organized by county, judges travel circuit, sitting in different counties in terms set up by months.

District Court: In course of organization. Two judges at large and ultimately 14 judges. A state court; 13 districts with 33 divisions. Jurisdiction of misdemeanors; juvenile court; power to find probable cause for holding for grand jury indictment in case of felonies.

Municipal Courts and Trial Justices: In process of replacement, to be complete in 1965, by district court; similar jurisdiction.

B. NEW LAWS RELATING TO INDIGENT RESPONDENTS

Amendment to R.S. 1954, c. 148, s.11, effective Sept. 21, 1963:

Before arraignment, competent defense counsel shall be assigned by the Superior or District Court unless waived by the accused after being fully advised of his rights by the court, in all criminal cases charging a felony, when it appears to the court that the accused has not sufficient means to employ counsel. The Superior Court shall order reasonable compensation to be paid to counsel out of the county treasury for such services in the Superior Court. No compensation shall be allowed for such services in the District Court. The Superior or District Court may in cases charging a misdemeanor appoint counsel when it appears to the court that the accused has not sufficient means to employ counsel, but no compensation shall be allowed counsel in such cases.

Amendment to R.S. 1954, c. 126, ss. 1-A, 1-G, additional; effective Sept. 21, 1963: (Relating to habeas corpus and post conviction procedure in criminal cases.)

317

DEFENSE OF THE POOR

Sec. 1-E. Appointment of counsel for indigent petitioners. Such justice may appoint an attorney for an indigent petitioner when a petitioner so requests upon a determination that the petition is filed in good faith, has merit, or is not frivolous . . .

(Petition may be heard by a justice of either the Superior or Supreme Judicial Courts.)

C. SUMMARY STATISTICS DRAWN FROM REPORT OF ATTORNEY GENERAL OF MAINE FOR YEAR ENDING NOV. 1, 1962

1. Trends:
Percentage of *decrease* over last preceding biennium:

Murder	25
Manslaughter	22
Felonious Assault	19

Percentage of *increase* over last preceding biennium:

Rape	17
Breaking, entry and larceny	27
Embezzlement	13
Robbery	1
Forgery	14
Arson	33 1/3
Sex offenses	6

2. Totals: (Entire State)

Total indictments and appeals		3149
Acquitted:	91	
Nol prossed, etc.	990	
Pending	268	
Plea of guilty	1759	
Plea of not guilty	132	
Fine	727	
Fine and prison	53	
Prison	598	
Probation	420	

3. Statistical Projection by Reporter:
Since the attorney general's statistics combine felonies and appeals, they do not serve our purpose exactly. Projecting the findings in the four counties studied indicates the following:

Approximately *one* indicted felon per *thousand* population.

Inferred total for state:	970*
Inferred total found indigent:	475

It should be noted that in Maine a felony is defined as an offense punishable by imprisonment in the state prison. Such punishment is always for one year or more. Misdemeanors are punished by probation, fine, or imprisonment in county jails or reformatories. Of course felons may be given probation or placed in reformatories in some cases.

4. Budgets: (1962) (source: Annual Statements of Counties)

Cumberland County, court-appointed attorneys:	$ 9,675.00
Penobscot County, court-appointed attorneys:	5,015.00
Cumberland County Attorney - salary	6,000.00
1st assistant	4,500.00
2nd assistant	4,000.00
clerk hire and expenses	6,117.80
Penobscot County Attorney - salary	5,000.00
assistant	4,000.00
clerk hire and expense	4,945.16

* Note: The figures for total indicted felons used in this study refer to individuals indicted; the attorney general's figures refer to total number of indictments, not the same thing. In our study, according to directions, we counted but one where there might be several indictments for the same offense, against the same man, arising out of the same incident. If the man was indicted for unrelated felonies, of course he might appear statistically more than once.

318

MARYLAND

Profs. John M. Brumbaugh and John W. Ester, Baltimore

We wish to acknowledge the helpful support and assistance of the A.B.A. Associate State Committee, which consisted of Fred E. Weisgal, Baltimore, chairman; Hon. J. Harold Grady, Hon. Charles D. Harris, Alan H. Murrell, Baltimore; and Austin W. Brizendine of Towson. We are also grateful to the director of the Maryland Administrative Office of the Courts, Frederick W. Invernizzi, and his staff for much valuable information. We also wish to thank Chief Judge Brune of the Maryland Court of Appeals and all of the other judges, attorneys, and clerks who gave generously and cheerfully of their time in submitting to interviews or answering questionnaires.

A. INTRODUCTION

Maryland had a population of 3,100,689 in 1960. It is estimated by the state department of health that the population in 1963 was 3,315,673. The state is divided into 23 counties and the independent city of Baltimore, and the judiciary is divided into eight judicial circuits. Except in one circuit, where there are four judges for five counties, there is at least one circuit judge for each county. Each county has its own state's attorney. The counties selected for study are shown in the following tabulation.

County	1960 population in thousands	Location in state	Remarks
Allegany (D)	84	Western	Farming, mining, railroad junction in Cumberland
Baltimore City (D)	939	Central	Port, commercial center, industry, state penitentiary
Baltimore County (D)	492	North central	Suburban, industry, farming
Prince George's	357	South central	Suburban, farming
Worcester	24	Southeastern	Truck farming, tourist industry

(D) indicates that a docket study was made.

B. CRIMINAL PROCEDURE AS IT AFFECTS INDIGENT PERSONS

Criminal jurisdiction is shared by the circuit courts on the one hand and by the trial magistrates in the counties and the judges of the municipal court of Baltimore City on the other.[1] The jurisdiction of the circuit courts is general, except for the criminal court of Baltimore City, where the municipal court has exclusive original criminal jurisdiction under some circumstances. (2 Md. Code Ann., Art. 26, § 109 [Supp. 1962].) Most cases which are to be tried before the circuit courts begin with the arrest of the suspect, who is required to be taken promptly before a magistrate. The latter, except in Baltimore City, need not be a lawyer and seldom is. At the first appearance of the accused, the

The following table gives additional information about the counties surveyed:

County	Felony defendants 1961-62[*]	% indigent[†]	% of indigents who waived counsel[‡]	Lawyers in private practice[§]	No. of appointments of counsel in 1961-62[¶]	No. of lawyers who served[**]	Typical payment[††]
Allegany	73	55	5	45	21	17	$75
Baltimore City	4959	60	2	2600	1219	no data	$72.35
Baltimore County	1115	65	3	300	176	84	$50
Prince George's	345	70	2	255	no data	30	$50
Worcester	108	70	1	12	19	12	$50

[*] The felony-misdemeanor distinction is not meaningful in Maryland for the purposes of this survey. The figures given represent criminal prosecutions before the circuit courts, not including appeals from magistrate's decisions and bastardy and desertion cases.

[†] These figures are an average of estimates supplied by judges and state's attorneys.

[‡] These figures are an average of estimates supplied by judges and state's attorneys.

[§] These figures are based on an actual count of trial attorneys in Worcester County, an estimate by the state's attorney in Allegany County and Baltimore City, and on an estimate from Martindale-Hubbell for Baltimore County and Prince George's County.

[¶] These figures are based on an actual count. The figures for Baltimore City and Baltimore County are for the calendar year 1962.

[**] These figures are based on an actual count in Allegany, Baltimore, and Worcester Counties, and on the estimate of the state's attorney in Prince George's County. 2 of the 12 lawyers who were appointed in Worcester County came from Wicomico County.

[††] The figure for Baltimore City is the average amount paid to assigned counsel in the calendar year 1962.

magistrate or municipal court judge sets bail, either with the advice of the state's attorney or according to a schedule. The usual elapsed time between arrest and first appearance before a magistrate varies from less than 12 hours in Baltimore City to more than three days in Baltimore County. In Worcester County it is 25 to 48 hours; in the other two counties it is 13 to 24 hours. Except where the accused is not arrested until after indictment, preliminary hearings are held regularly for felonies and serious misdemeanors, unless waived. In Baltimore City the state's attorney doubts the power of a defendant to waive preliminary hearing under the new Municipal Court Act. Since, in most cases, the indigent accused is not represented by counsel at the preliminary hearing, he is not permitted to enter a guilty plea in a case which is to come before the circuit court.

In Baltimore City and Baltimore County, formal charges in cases to come before the circuit court are made exclusively by indictment; in Prince George's County indictments are used most of the time. In the other counties informations are more common since the grand juries meet less frequently. In all of the counties the normal time between arrest and arraignment on the indictment or information is less than 30 days.

Maryland Rule 719 (as amended, August 7, 1963) does not require appointment of counsel for indigents prior to arraignment. However, in Allegany County the state's attorney usually learns of a claim of indigency and so informs the court prior to arraignment, and counsel is frequently appointed as soon as the judge can pass on the claim. In Worcester County, the judge at least once a week canvasses the jail population awaiting trial and promptly appoints counsel in indigent cases, often prior to preliminary hearing. Elsewhere, as required by Maryland Rule 719, the accused, if he appears at arraignment without counsel, must be advised of his right to counsel, and, unless he is financially able to obtain counsel or elects to proceed without counsel, the court must assign counsel unless the maximum penalty is less than six months' imprisonment and less than a $500 fine, or unless the charge is desertion or non-support. The court may assign counsel in other cases at its discretion. Counsel is allowed a reasonable time to plead, and the arraignment may be adjourned for this purpose. Rule 719 requires that affirmative compliance with its provisions appear on the transcript or docket entries.[2]

Just prior to the appointment of counsel, the judge makes a determination of indigency, usually by asking a series of questions about financial status, either in open court or in chambers. Allegany County uses a sworn questionnaire, and the local bar association is working on such a questionnaire in Worcester County. Generally, no further investigation is made of claims of indigency; occasionally an investigation will be made by telephone in Baltimore City. In less populous counties the judge or state's attorney may have personal knowledge of the accused's financial status. Standards for determining indigency seem universally to be flexible: no judge reported any simple test rigidly applied, but the fact that the accused is out on bail makes a finding of indigency unlikely in most counties.

In Allegany County assigned counsel are selected from a state's attorney's list and in Baltimore City from a list maintained by the judge; elsewhere all attorneys are assigned unless excused for cause. Compensation for assigned counsel is fixed by the judge. Minimum fees for simple cases vary from $25 to $75; in a complicated case, fees may exceed $500. The Prince George's County judges have set up normal fees for all indigency cases; these may be augmented by petition to a panel of three or more judges. In general, ordinary expenses of counsel are not compensated over and above the flat fee, but in all of the counties some additional compensation may be available for extraordinary expenses. Prince George's County, for example, allows an additional $25 where a prisoner must be visited in an institution outside the county.

Whether or not there is a trial, assigned counsel represents the accused on sentencing if he is found guilty. Under Maryland Rule BK 42, indigent prisoners are entitled to counsel on request in a postconviction proceeding at the trial court level in the county where the defendant was originally convicted (Maryland Post Conviction Procedure Act, 3 Md. Code Ann., Art. 27, § 645 A-S [Supp. 1962], and Rules BK. 40-48). Sometimes counsel is appointed in habeas corpus proceedings. Counsel is ordinarily not appointed in civil commitment proceedings or hearings on revocation of probation, although one judge in Allegany County frequently requests that the counsel originally appointed at the trial appear at a revocation proceeding without additional fee.

Since counsel for indigents on appeal is provided by the court of appeals itself, the practice is uniform. Counsel in the trial court is authorized to note an appeal, and his appointment is sometimes continued for the appeal.[3] The court of appeals sets a fee for counsel's services on appeal: from $100 to $300 in most cases, with $200 being the usual fee. In postconviction proceedings on appeal the usual fee is $50 to $75. The state either pays or waives the cost of as much of the transcript of the record as counsel requests, and the costs of printing the records, briefs, and exhibits. Travel costs are borne by counsel.

C. OPINIONS OF THE JUDGES

One resident circuit court judge was interviewed in each of the following counties: Allegany, Baltimore, Prince George's, Worcester, and Baltimore City. In the remaining counties mail questionnaires were sent to 18 judges. Replies were received from 12 of them (67%).

When asked to indicate the stage in a criminal case when, under an ideal system, an indigent person should first be provided with a lawyer, three of the five judges interviewed were satisfied with the present system: appointment between first appearance before a magistrate and preliminary hearing in one county, at preliminary hearings in the second county, and at arraignment in the third county. The other two judges thought that their present system of appointing counsel at arraignment is too late in the proceedings to guarantee fairness. One of these judges suggested that counsel should be appointed between arrest and the accused's first appearance before a magistrate, although he had doubts as to the practicability of such a system in Baltimore City and the larger counties. The other judge felt that counsel should be appointed at preliminary hearing, and could foresee little if any additional expense to the county or inconvenience to the bench and bar.

None of the 12 judges responding by mail questionnaire thought that appointment should be delayed until after arraignment. Under an ideal system, five of these judges would appoint counsel at first appearance before a magistrate, two would appoint between first appearance and preliminary hearing, two would appoint after the filing of an indictment or information but before arraignment, one would appoint between arrest and first appearance before a magistrate, one would appoint at preliminary hearing, and one would appoint after preliminary hearing but before the filing of an indictment or information. On the question of unfairness to the indigent person, only 3 of the 17 judges contacted by interview and mail questionnaire thought that there is no unfairness even if appointment occurs at a stage later than that designated as "ideal." The other 14 judges agreed that there might be unfairness because of the problem of gathering and preserving evidence, statements which the accused might make without the advice of counsel, and the like. In regard to financing appointment at an "ideal" stage, three judges felt that it might be impossible to finance such a system, particularly in Baltimore City and the large counties, while the other 14 judges could foresee no serious problem. One judge suggested that earlier appointment might be financed by allowing a nominal additional fee or no additional fee at all.

In regard to the competency of assigned counsel, 15 of the 17 judges agreed that the average assigned and retained lawyer are about equal in ability and experience, although 2 judges thought that the average appointed lawyer is below par. Only one judge thought that appointed lawyers are not equal in ability to the state's attorney's office; the other judges noted that the state's attorney's office may have more experience, but appointed lawyers seem to be about equal in ability. In fact, several judges commented that many assigned lawyers are more zealous than retained counsel or the state's attorney's office, partially because of the unfortunately large number of postconviction petitions challenging the competency of assigned counsel. These judges also pointed out that such petitions rarely have any basis in fact.

D. OPINIONS OF THE STATE'S ATTORNEYS

Personal interviews were conducted with the state's attorney in the five sample counties. Mail questionnaires were sent to the other 19 state's attorneys, and replies were received from 14 (74%).

All 24 of the state's attorneys contacted agreed that appointment should be made at least as early as arraignment. Under an ideal system, six of them thought that counsel should be appointed after the filing of an indictment or information but before arraignment, and four thought appointment should be at the accused's first appearance before a magistrate. Of the remaining 14 state's attorneys, 3 suggested appointment between arrest and first appearance before a magistrate, 3 suggested appointment at preliminary hearing, 2 would appoint counsel after preliminary hearing but before the filing of an indictment or information, and one thought that appointment at arraignment would be best. On the question of unfairness to indigent persons, 13 state's attorneys thought there might be unfairness if counsel is not appointed at the "ideal" stage designated, 6 were not convinced that unfairness would result, and 5 failed to comment. Eleven thought that their "ideal" system could be financed, 3 thought there would not be enough money, and 5 failed to comment. Two state's attorneys voluntarily suggested a public defender as the means for financing earlier appointment.

E. OPINIONS OF DEFENSE ATTORNEYS

Mail questionnaires were sent to a random sampling of 93 assigned lawyers located in the five political subdivisions selected for study. Responses were received from 64 of them (68%). Based on these responses, it appears that a lawyer is most commonly appointed in Maryland when the accused appears for arraignment.[4] Most of these lawyers thought that there was no essential unfairness to indigent persons under the existing system; 86% agreed that they were appointed in time to represent their clients adequately, and 82% thought that the existing system was "fair to indigent persons." Nevertheless, 27 of the 64 lawyers responding (42%) thought that it might be advisable to appoint counsel at an earlier stage.

Although most lawyers questioned were convinced that there was no essential unfairness to an indigent person under the existing system, 54% thought that there was some unfairness to the lawyer. Of those who specifically indicated how the system was unfair to the lawyer, 31 complained of the lack of reimbursement for out-of-pocket expenses, and 37 suggested that appointed counsel should be paid more for their services. Excluding the more serious cases involving crimes punishable by death or long imprisonment, $305 was the average fee which an appointed lawyer would have charged if he had been retained. When this figure is compared with the $50 to $75 which is usually paid in less serious cases, the reason for this complaint becomes apparent.

F. COMPARISONS AMONG JUDGES, PROSECUTORS, AND DEFENSE ATTORNEYS

The survey revealed several differences in attitudes among judges and prosecutors. For the purpose of comparison, judges with 10 or more years of service on their present courts are called senior judges and the remainder are called junior judges, and those state's attorneys who have served as state's attorney or assistant state's attorney for 5 years or longer are called senior prosecutors and the remainder are called junior prosecutors. Results are shown in Table 1.

TABLE 1
Views of Judges and Prosecutors

	Senior judges	Junior judges	Senior prose-cutors	Junior prose-cutors	Total
Total responding	6	11	11	8	36
Ideal stage for first appointment of counsel:					
Between arrest and first appearance	2	3	1	2	8
At first appearance	1	1	3	1	6
Between first appearance and preliminary hearing	2	1	0	0	3
At preliminary hearing	0	2	3	0	5
After preliminary hearing but before indictment or information	1	0	2	0	3
After indictment or information but before arraignment	0	2	2	4	8
At arraignment	0	2	0	1	3
Are present rates of compensation adequate?					
Yes	2	6	6	3	17
No	3	4	5	5	17
No answer	1	1	0	0	2
Should out-of-pocket expenses be paid?					
Yes	2	6	6	4	18
No	0	0	0	0	0
No answer	4	5	5	4	18

In regard to the ideal stage at which counsel should first be appointed, it is interesting to note that none of the 6 senior judges and only 2 of the 11 senior prosecutors would delay appointment until after the filing of an indictment or information, but 4 of the 11 junior judges and 5 of the 8 junior prosecutors would wait until this stage. This suggests that judges and prosecutors with the longest service tend to favor earlier appointment.

In respect to adequacy of compensation, approximately 50% of all judges and prosecutors who responded to this question thought that present rates are inadequate. Of the attorneys contacted by mail questionnaire, 59% thought that rates of compensation are too low. This tends to indicate a roughly equal division of opinion among judges, prosecutors, and attorneys as to whether the present rates of compensation should be increased. However, nearly all agreed that lawyers should be reimbursed for out-of-pocket expenses.

G. DOCKET STUDIES

A docket study was conducted in Baltimore City, Baltimore County, and Allegany County for representative cases in 1962. Results are summarized in Tables 2 to 6. A weighted total, which is also a projected average for the state as a whole, appears at the foot of each table. (For methods of research see volume 1, pages 178-179.)

As shown in Table 2, all defendants in Allegany County and 91% in Baltimore City had counsel, but in Baltimore County, only 63%. In Baltimore City 32% of the total defendants had assigned counsel, while in Baltimore County, 16%, and in Allegany, 60%. In part, these figures reflect different economic conditions in the three jurisdictions. In Baltimore City, 35% of the defendants were officially determined to be indigent (see Table 3) and 56% were not released on bail (see Table 4). In Allegany County 60% were determined to be indigent and 85% were not released on bail. In Baltimore County 48% were not released on bail, but information was insufficient to make a report about official findings of indigency. (In some instances defendants were kept in jail not because they were unable to afford bail but because bail was denied on account of the seriousness of the crimes charged, e.g., Baltimore City had six murder cases in the sample.)

The docket study also showed that preliminary hearings were held in 90% of the cases in Baltimore City. Data were insufficient to make a report for the two counties, except it is known that such hearings were held in at least 63% of the cases in Baltimore County and probably more.

Information about race, available only for Baltimore city, shows that 38% of the defendants were white and 62% were Negro. These figures are based on data from 84% of the total sample cases.

Dispositions of cases are shown in Table 5. For the state as a whole, 37% of the defendants pleaded guilty, plus another 6% who were placed on probation before verdict[5]; 46% of the defendants had trials, resulting in 33% convictions and 13% acquittals. This is a relatively high proportion of trials in comparison with other states.

Table 6 shows the sentences, if any, imposed in the sample cases. For the state as a whole, 39% of the defendants were sentenced to prison, including a term in county jail, 31% were placed on probation, and 3% were given a suspended sentence without probation. Baltimore County had a relatively frequent use of probation, while Baltimore City imposed a considerable number of fines.

TABLE 2
Retained and Assigned Counsel in Felonies
Maryland, 1962

County	Total sample	Did defendant have counsel? Yes No.	%	No No.	%	Retained No.	%	Assigned No.	%	No data° No.	%
Baltimore City	250	222	91	22	9	145	59	77	32	6	2
Baltimore County	110	69	63	41	37	51	46	18	16	0	0
Allegany	20	20	100	0	0	8	40	12	60	0	0
Weighted total percentages			87		13		53		34		1

° % of no data refers to total sample; % in other columns refers to cases for which data were available.

TABLE 3
Was Felony Defendant Determined Indigent?
Maryland, 1962

County	Total sample	Yes No.	%	No No.	%	No data° No.	%
Baltimore City	250	79	35	147	65	24	10
Allegany	20	12	60	8	40	0	0
Weighted total percentages†			39		60		13

° % of no data refers to total sample; % in other columns refers to cases for which data were available.
† Includes Baltimore County.

TABLE 4
Frequency of Release on Bail of Felony Defendants
Maryland, 1962

County	Total sample	Yes No.	%	No No.	%	No data° No.	%
Baltimore City	250	108	44	140	56	2	1
Baltimore County	110	50	52	46	48	14	13
Allegany	20	3	15	17	85	0	0
Weighted total percentages			39		61		3

° % of no data refers to total sample; % in other columns refers to cases for which data were available.

TABLE 5
Disposition in Felony Cases
Maryland, 1962

County	Total sample	Plea guilty	Plea lesser of-fense	Dis-missed	Found guilty	Found guilty lesser degree	Ac-quit-ted	Mental com-mit-ment	Pend-ing	Stet*	Proba-tion before verdict†
Baltimore City	250	79	0	8	100	2	26	13	8	1	13
Baltimore County	110	32	0	5	21	0	24	0	2	17	9
Allegany	20	13	0	0	5	0	1	0	0	0	1
Weighted total percentages		37	0	3	33	0	13	3	1	5	6

* Held on inactive docket.
† See footnote 5.

TABLE 6
Sentencing in Felony Cases*
Maryland, 1962

County	Total sample	No sentence No.	No sentence %	Prison No.	Prison %	Pro-bation No.	Pro-bation %	Sus-pended sen-tence No.	Sus-pended sen-tence %	Fine No.	Fine %	Sentence pending No.	Sentence pending %
Baltimore City	250	58	23	113	45	62	25	9	4	30	12	0	0
Baltimore County	110	49	45	10	9	42	38	5	5	7	6	1	1
Allegany	20	2	10	10	50	8	40	0	0	0	0	0	0
Weighted total per-centages			25		39		31		3		8		0

* Some defendants in Baltimore City and Baltimore County had a combination sentence, such as fine and probation. They are counted under both columns, hence the total is more than 100%.

H. CONCLUSIONS AND RECOMMENDATIONS

On the basis of our investigation and the foregoing report, the following conclusions and recommendations are submitted:

1. It is too soon to be sure whether Maryland's assigned counsel system, even with the adjustments which have been made and will be made in the future, will prove adequate to meet the demands which will be made upon it. Recent Supreme Court decisions have prompted changes extending the system to many

of the less serious cases, and some experimentation with providing counsel at the magistrates' courts level is taking place. We cannot yet be sure just how much the additional burden on the bar will amount to, or whether fundamental changes will be required to get the job done. The most serious strain is likely to occur in the more populous areas, where the criminal case load is the greatest.

2. We found little enthusiasm for a public defender system at the present time. In most of the counties, the assigned counsel system can be made to work for the foreseeable future. A step suggested to us which we think might give the present system the best chance of workable operation in Baltimore City, is the appointment of an experienced lawyer as an administrative officer. He would maintain the list of attorneys to be assigned, assist the judges in making assignments, make any necessary investigations of indigency, assist in settling fees and expenses of assigned counsel, and perhaps make himself available to advise those assigned counsel who are inexperienced in trying criminal cases.

3. We recommend the statewide adoption of a rule of evidence to the following effect:

> No plea or statement by an accused person in a criminal proceeding had before a magistrate or judge of the Municipal Court of Baltimore City shall be admissible in evidence (as an admission) in any criminal proceeding before a Circuit Court, unless, at the time of making such plea or statement, such accused person had been informed of his right to be represented by counsel, and was either (1) actually so represented, (2) able to afford counsel, or (3) unwilling to accept the assistance of counsel, such assistance, free of charge, having been offered him.

Such a rule would appear to solve the problem presented by *White v. Maryland,* 373 U.S. 59 (1963). It would probably be an adequate solution to the problem of providing counsel at the magistrates' courts level. In view of the right of the accused to obtain a trial de novo before a circuit court, it is difficult to see what constitutional considerations would require counsel if the evidentiary situation can be handled.

4. Unless the view is taken that the accused should be represented by counsel before any police statement is taken from him, we see no consideration of fairness which would require appointment of counsel prior to arraignment, provided our recommendation in paragraph three is accepted. Reasons of efficiency, however, suggest that it would be desirable if, at the time of arraignment, counsel could have been appointed for indigent persons a sufficient time in advance to be prepared to enter a plea, and thus avoid adjournment of the arraignment proceeding or hasty consultation in the courtroom. We see no reason why judges should not, as some already do, hold hearings on indigency and arrange for appointment of counsel one or more days before arraignment. An administrative officer like the one suggested in paragraph two might handle much of the routine.

5. For each county a master list of attorneys eligible to represent indigent defendants should be maintained, showing each appointment made. Judges should consult this list prior to making appointments to assure fairness in distribution of cases. Determination of eligibility is a difficult problem. Unless the list is to be restricted to attorneys of proved competence and experience in the trial of criminal cases, discretion in appointment will have to be exercised to

match the experience and ability of the attorney with the difficulty and seriousness of the case.

6. There is some disagreement as to the adequacy of compensation to attorneys representing indigent persons. The feeling that lawyers should, to some extent, absorb costs of representing indigents and the variations from one case to another in the time, effort, and skill needed and actually expended make some disagreement inevitable. It is our feeling that since the large burden of representing indigents in relatively serious or difficult criminal cases will fall, in the larger counties, by necessity on the relatively small group of experienced criminal lawyers of proven ability, the burden cannot be shared approximately equally among all practicing lawyers. We think that fees, particularly in the more serious and more difficult cases, should be higher. We think that the Maryland Bar Association might appropriately study the question with a view of probation, while Baltimore city imposed a considerable number of fines.
to recommending fee schedules and considering whether any increased costs of representation ought not to be borne wholly or in part by the whole practicing bar, as a part of its proper contribution to the public good. Whatever is done about fees, it appears clear to us that attorneys for indigents should be fully reimbursed for proper out-of-pocket expenses, over and above office overhead. When the appointed attorney feels it necessary to incur such extraordinary expenses as the hiring of investigative or expert assistance, he should be required to petition the court for approval in advance. He should submit an itemized statement of his expenses at the time of application for his fee, and such expenses should be paid.

NOTES—Maryland

[1] Procedure before the trial magistrates or municipal court judges is relatively informal and no more than three years' imprisonment for a single offense may be given. Demand for a jury trial results in a transfer of the case to the circuit court: any convicted defendant has a right to an appeal to the circuit court and a trial de novo there. Jurisdiction is limited to certain offenses: generally the trial magistrates (as justices of the peace) can try only non-penitentiary offenses not involving felonious intent. (The distinction between felonies and misdemeanors in Maryland is based on the common law, except as specific statutes have worked changes.) The jurisdiction of the municipal court of Baltimore City is set out in detail in the statute, and is similar. There is no tradition of free counsel in cases tried before trial magistrates or municipal court judges, but in view of recent Supreme Court cases, there is a tendency to reconsider this situation. With the cooperation of the local bar association, unpaid volunteer counsel have been appointed in some cases before the municipal court of Baltimore City. At least one judge has stated his intention to appoint counsel in more serious magistrate's cases, those involving possible imprisonment of 6 months or more, or a fine of $500 or more, if the accused so requests when notified of his rights and of the fact that appointment will probably delay disposition of the case. For statutory material relating to the jurisdiction, etc., of these courts, see 1 Md. Code Ann., art. 5, 9, § 43 (Supp. 1962); 2 Md. Code Ann., art 26, §§ 109-11 (Supp. 1962); 3 Md. Code Ann., art. 27, § 708 (1957); 5 Md. Code Ann., art. 52 §§ 13 (Supp. 1962), 15 (1957).

[2] Prior to the August, 1963, revision of Maryland Rule 719, the judge was not required to appoint counsel for indigents when the maximum term of imprisonment was under 5 years, although he had discretion to do so. This discretion appears to have been exercised liberally, and, since Gideon v. Wainright, the judges have begun to appoint counsel in all but trivial cases, a practice now confirmed in the new Rule 719.

[3] In postconviction proceedings, counsel is not at present appointed on appeal until after an application for leave to appeal is granted. This may require change.

[4] If the accused is not represented by counsel when he appears for arraignment, the court resolves the issue of indigency and appoints counsel, if necessary, before any plea is taken. Arraignment is postponed if counsel is appointed.

[5] 3 Md. Code Ann., art. 27, § 641 (1957) authorizes the court, "before conviction of any person accused of crime with the written consent of the person so accused . . . and after conviction or after a plea of guilty or nolo contendere, without such consent . . . to: (1) suspend the imposition of sentence; or (2) place such person on probation without finding a verdict; and (3) make such conditions of sentence and probation as the court may deem proper."

MASSACHUSETTS

Prof. Sanford J. Fox, Boston

The A.B.A. Associate State Committee consisted of Edward J. Duggan, Boston, chairman; LaRue Brown, Thomas E. Dwyer, Frank L. Kozol, Frederick H. Norton, Jr., and Samuel A. Wilkinson, all of Boston; and Frederick S. Pillsbury, Springfield.

A. INTRODUCTION

Massachusetts had a population of 5,148,578 in 1960. The state is divided into 14 counties. There are 72 district courts around the state, some of which are known as municipal courts. Each district court has at least one full-time judge. Judges of the Superior Court are rotated in their assignments from county to county. District court judges are sometimes assigned to the trial of misdemeanor cases in the Superior Court. There are nine district attorneys in the state, three of whom have jurisdiction in more than one county.

As shown below, four counties were selected for detailed survey:

County (city)	1960 population in thousands	Location in state	Remarks
Suffolk (D) (Boston)	791	East	State capital, commercial center for northern New England
Worcester (D)	583	Central	Largest county in area; largest city, Worcester, is almost 5 times as large as next largest. Manufacturing and farming
Norfolk (D) (Quincy)	510	East	Suburban, state prisons
Middlesex (Cambridge)	1239	Northeast	Suburban, truck farming

(D) indicates that a docket study was made.

B. CRIMINAL PROCEDURE AS IT AFFECTS INDIGENTS

In Massachusetts a felony is defined as an offense for which a term of imprisonment for more than two and one-half years is authorized. This term is the minimum state's prison sentence. Imprisonment for two and one-half years or less (for misdemeanors) must be in a county jail or house of correction. Thus, the definition of "felony" used in this study, i.e., "a crime defined as a felony by state law and any other crime punishable by imprisonment for longer than one year," includes many offenses classed as misdemeanors under the Massachusetts statutes. A frequently occurring example of such inclusion is the offense of operating a motor vehicle under the influence of intoxicating liquor,

331

for which imprisonment for two years is authorized (Mass. Gen. Laws c. 90, § 24 [1] [a]).

All felonies for which the punishment is not more than five years in the state prison, some offenses involving theft from a dwelling or from a railroad car where the penalty is not more than 10 years, and forgeries where the loss is not more than $50 are triable in the district courts. These courts cannot, however, sentence to the state prison even for an offense for which a state prison term is authorized, and they cannot sentence an offender to a house of correction for more than two and one-half years, even though the statutory penalty may be five years. Thus, for a single offense, the district courts may commit an offender to a jail or house of correction for the period authorized by statute, not exceeding two and one-half years. For multiple offenses, there may be consecutive two and one-half year sentences to these institutions: the maximum number of sentences is not controlled by statute.

The district courts may also commit male offenders to the Concord reformatory for an indefinite five-year term for any offense in which a jail or house of correction sentence is authorized, provided the offender has not received more than three prior sentences for felonies. Women may be sentenced by the district courts to an indefinite five-year term at the Framingham reformatory. A person convicted in the district court may appeal to the Superior Court, where he is entitled to a trial de novo before a jury.

In addition to trying cases, the district courts also hold probable-cause hearings, binding over to the grand jury those cases in which the sentence may be to the state prison. In 1857 the Supreme Judicial Court decided that the Massachusetts Bill of Rights required the commonwealth to proceed by indictment in such cases. The accused may, however, waive his right to an indictment and be arraigned in the Superior Court on a complaint. Since the trial jurisdiction of the district courts includes cases in which a state prison term is authorized by statute and an indictment thereby required, these courts can theoretically proceed to trial in such cases only when there has been a waiver. The fact that there appear to be few, if any, of these district court trials is probably a function of the scarcity of offenses carrying a penalty of more than two and one-half years but less than five years and one day.

The Superior Court has original jurisdiction over all crimes and the appellate de novo jurisdiction described above. Any sentence authorized by law may be imposed by the Superior Court.

Most felony cases begin with the arrest of the accused. Prosecutors indicate that he is usually taken before the district court on the next morning, or, in some cases, on the same day on which a formal charge has been made. In Middlesex and Worcester Counties an accused may be released from jail on bail by the bail clerk of the court. In Norfolk and Suffolk Counties the bail is usually set by the district court judge. Nowhere does there appear to be a schedule of bail amounts in use. The size of the bail required is a function of the seriousness of the offense, the character of the accused, and the nature of his past record.

Except in Suffolk and Middlesex, the superior court does not continuously sit for criminal business in any county. In most counties there are two sittings a year, thus making it possible that a person bound over just at the end of one sitting would have to wait several months in jail if he could not raise bail.

Procedure for appointment of counsel is fairly uniform throughout the commonwealth. When a person accused of a capital crime appears in the district court for the probable-cause hearing, he usually petitions for appointment of counsel. This petition is generally granted at this time, although the Supreme Judicial Court has said "There is nothing in the statutes of Massachusetts giving a person accused of a capital crime or any other crime a right to counsel before being brought into court" (*Commonw. v. McNeil*, 328 Mass. 436, 104 N.E. 2d 153 [1952]). Frequently this petition is to have a named counsel appointed, and such a request is always granted if the lawyer is available. A statutory fee of up to $1000 is allowed assigned counsel in capital cases, and the Superior Court, on motion, may allow additional amounts as expense for the defense. The statutes and rules of the Superior Court relating the details of assignment of counsel to indigents accused of first degree murder (the only capital crime in Massachusetts) are set forth in Appendix 1.

Appointment of counsel for indigents in noncapital cases is more complex. The Massachusetts Defenders Committee must first be considered.

In 1960 the legislature authorized the Judicial Council to appoint 11 unpaid committee members. (The appointing power is now with the Supreme Judicial Court.) This committee, in turn, has chosen the staff of defenders which is compensated from appropriated state funds. The state-wide staff consists of 11 full-time and 8 part-time lawyers. In spite of extremely low salaries, there are four or five applicants for each position on the staff. The chief counsel makes the initial hiring decisions with ultimate responsibility residing in the committee. The chief counsel and 9 of the other 10 full-time lawyers work from the Boston office of the committee and cover the courts in Suffolk, Middlesex, and Norfolk Counties. The other counties are covered as follows: one part-time lawyer each to Essex, Berkshire, and Worcester; one covering Bristol, Dukes, and Nantucket; two for Plymouth and Barnstable; and one full-time and one part-time for Franklin, Hampden, and Hampshire.

The enabling statute requires the committee counsel to appear "at any stage of a criminal proceeding, other than capital, in any court of the commonwealth provided the laws of the commonwealth or rules of the Supreme Judicial Court require that the defendant in such proceedings be represented by counsel, and provided, further, that such defendant is unable to obtain counsel by reason of his inability to pay" (G. L. C. 221, §34D). In other words, defenders are required whenever law (from any source, constitution, statute, decision, or rule) requires representation of indigent accused.

There is no Massachusetts legislation identifying when such requirements exist. There is, however, Rule 10 of the General Rules of the Supreme Judicial Court, which formerly required an offer of counsel for all indigent, noncapital felony defendants in the Superior Court and for indigent persons accused on any noncapital crime in any court if the judge of that court "in his discretion determines that the gravity of the charge or other circumstances require" counsel. The rule was amended in June, 1964, to apply to any court and to any crime "for which a sentence of imprisonment may be imposed." The full text of this rule, including its provisions and forms for waiver of counsel, is included in Appendix 2. Before the 1964 amendment the noncapital felony indigent had a right to counsel only when he first appeared in the Superior Court. Before that appearance, assignment of counsel was up to the judge. The indigent accused of a misdemeanor had no right to counsel in any court.

In a decision antedating the 1964 amendment to Rule 10, the Supreme Judicial Court denied a constitutional right to counsel in a district court probable-cause hearing on both felony (10 years) and misdemeanor ($25 fine) charges in the absence of any showing of prejudice. The chief justice, speaking for the court, added that

> . . . the prudent course for a District Court Judge is to appoint counsel for an indigent defendant in every case where there is to be a probable cause hearing unless the defendant declines the assistance of counsel, in which event preservation of proof of that fact should be made. See Rule 10 of the General Rules, as amended on December 21, 1962 (345 Mass. 792). Even where a district court holds a trial of a case within its jurisdiction, it would be wise to offer to appoint counsel except for the most trifling offenses for which no sentence of imprisonment may be imposed (*Commonw v. O'Leary*, 198 N.E. 2d 403, 405 [Mass. 1964]).

In order to help provide counsel for indigent persons in misdemeanors, 30 law students from Boston University are serving under the supervision of an experienced criminal lawyer in the Roxbury district court. The program is financed by a grant of funds from the National Legal Aid and Defender Association.

During the fiscal year July 1, 1962, to June 30, 1963, the defenders represented 1561 persons in the Superior Court and 75 in the district courts. Details of these operations appear in Table 1.

The stage at which the defender reaches the accused varies. In the Boston area (Suffolk County and most of Middlesex and Norfolk Counties), persons being held in jail for a district court appearance are asked if they want the services of an attorney. This is done through cards distributed by the jailers and filled out by those desiring representation. The return of these cards is initially followed up by Harvard law school students who interview jailed persons, referring cases of indigents likely to be bound over to the Superior Court to the Massachusetts Defenders. These students also represent indigents in district court trials under the authority of Rule 11 of the Supreme Judicial Court, described in the 1962-1963 annual report of the Harvard Voluntary Defenders. A copy of this report is provided in Appendix 3. In the Boston municipal court students from the Boston University Voluntary Defenders represent indigents. These are mostly misdemeanor cases with a few probable-cause hearings concerning felonies. They annually represent approximately 75 defendants. A copy of the indigency questionnaire they use is in Appendix 4.

Who determines indigency varies somewhat from judge to judge in the Superior Court. It appears to be the common practice to refer persons appearing without counsel to the defender, who inquires as to the accused's financial status. Most judges accept the defender's conclusions, although some interrogate the accused themselves. Among those who do so, the criteria for indigency vary.

TABLE 1
Persons Represented by Massachusetts Defenders
July 1, 1962 - June 30, 1963

Superior Court

Pending July 1, 1962:	60
Received during the year:	1621
Disposed of during the year:	1561
Pending June 30, 1963:	120

Dispositions

County	Persons	Trials	guilty	Verdicts not guilty	guilty lesser offense
Suffolk	910	85	50	52	5
Middlesex					
Norfolk					
Bristol	151	12	18	9	1
Dukes					
Nantucket					
Essex	91	3	4	2	0
Plymouth	145	13	11	10	0
Barnstable					
Worcester	135	18	44	16	0
Franklin	106	9	13	5	0
Hampden					
Hampshire					

District court

County	Persons
Suffolk	63
Norfolk	
Middlesex	
Worcester	8
Franklin	4
Hampden	
Hampshire	

Indigency is not worked out according to any fixed schedule. If an accused is free on bail, however, he is usually determined to be ineligible for the defender. The source of the bail is taken into account and if it has been supplied by friends, relatives, or any source not also available for the payment of a counsel fee, then the fact of bail does not preclude indigency. The affidavit that defenders have their clients sign is in Appendix 5.

The problem of the accused person who can pay a small fee, but one not considered to be the going rate for a competent attorney, is handled in a laissez-faire manner. The rules and regulations of the Massachusetts Defenders Committee forbid referral by a defender counsel in any case. As a matter of practice, judges and prosecutors also leave this accused to his own ingenuity in finding a lawyer. The Boston bar association does maintain a referral service, primarily for civil matters, but also for criminal cases. The number of referrals made in criminal cases in 1962 was 115, while in 1961 there were "over 200." There is, however, no institutional means or need perceived by prosecutors to connect an accused of moderate means to the referral service. On this point, two of the district attorneys interviewed commented that any good civil lawyer can do a good job defending a criminal case. Chief counsel for the Massachusetts Defenders, on the other hand, advised that a bar association referral panel would be very desirable.

Indigents were being provided counsel in misdemeanor cases by virtue of the operation of the former version of Rule 10, which, however, merely restated the discretion any judge has to appoint counsel in appropriate cases. The chief counsel of the Massachusetts Defenders indicated that they did, in fact, receive appointments in misdemeanor cases although no estimate of the number of such cases was available. Defenders are also from time to time appointed for indigents in habeas corpus, writs of error, hearings on revocation of probation, and sexually dangerous persons cases. In respect to appeals, counsel who has been appointed by the trial court continues to serve through to the disposition of the appeal.

C. OPINIONS OF THE JUDGES

The judges interviewed included Chief Justice Wilkins of the Supreme Judicial Court, Associate Justice Reardon of the same court, formerly chief justice of the Superior Court, Chief Justice Tauro of the Superior Court, and two associate justices of the Superior Court.

Mail questionnaires were sent to 51 of the district court judges. Replies were received from 15 (29%).

The Superior Court judges felt that counsel should be supplied earlier in the criminal process than is now usually the case. The consensus was that if the accused appears first in the district court (as he does in all cases except those involving secret indictments), he should there be provided with a lawyer. One judge suggested that indigents be assigned counsel after they have been arrested but before they have appeared in any court. He acknowledged that a problem then arises concerning determination of indigency in the police station, but proposed that an affidavit form be used with perjury penalties to be explained by the police in each case.

The mail replies of the district court judges were of the same tenor on this question. Seven thought counsel should be granted at the first court appearance; five opted for counsel between arrest and first appearance; one indicated arraignment on the indictment as the proper time; one suggested "after arraignment"; and another replied "at trial."

Not all judges thought it was always unfair to the indigent person if he did not get a lawyer at the early stages indicated above. The qualifications appended to their replies concerning when it would be unfair included, "if he asked for a lawyer," "in felonies and serious misdemeanors," and "in some cases." An opinion of no unfairness was expressed by two district court judges, one of whom had suggested counsel before first appearance while the other had indicated an ideal of assignment at the first appearance.

All of the judges, save three, thought that a system of supplying counsel at or before first appearance could be financed. One of these said he didn't know. Wherever the judges made further comments, they stated that financing was properly a function of government. Some made explicit the corollary that the burden should not fall on the bar.

As to the kinds of cases and proceedings in which counsel ought to be furnished to the indigent accused, the judges' opinion was divided. The proportion of "yes" and "no" replies for each type is tabulated below:

	% yes	% no
Sentencing of a defendant who pleaded guilty	52	48
Sentencing of a defendant convicted by trial	71	29
Habeas corpus, writ of error, or other postconviction remedy	89	11
Hearing on revocation of probation	55	45
Sexually dangerous person hearing	76	24
Misdemeanors	56	44
Civil commitment of the mentally ill, including alcoholics and narcotics addicts	45	55

The above compilation reveals substantial disagreement among the judges, there being an almost even division of opinion on four of the seven entries. A strong view in favor of the presence of counsel is discernible only for sentencing after trial, in postconviction cases, and in sexually dangerous persons proceedings. Seven of the judges provided a "yes" answer to all types of cases. These seven were quite heterogeneous, ranging, for example, in date of bar admission from 1905 to 1949 and in years on the bench from 2 to 4 to over 20 years.

As to unfairness if counsel is not furnished, the replies of the judges tended to follow their replies as shown in the preceding tabulation. Two judges, however, reported that it would not be unfair to refuse counsel even where they had indicated there ought to be representation, e.g., in postconviction cases and in sexually dangerous persons hearings.

All but four of the judges replying to the problem of financing representation in these kinds of cases said that it could be done.

There was a variety of replies to the question relating to the source of attorneys appointed to represent indigents. In the Superior Court, of course, the Massachusetts Defenders carry the responsibility for noncapital felonies. In capital cases the accused usually requests a named attorney who is appointed. In the district court the judges indicated that they appoint from their own list of lawyers, the Massachusetts Defender, "any qualified lawyer," from a bar association list, or any attorney present in court. Relatively little difficulty is experienced by district court judges in getting counsel to serve. All but two of the judges replying to the question relating to this said they had no problem in getting lawyers to serve. All of the judges who revealed their policy concerning lawyers who ask to be excused said that they did excuse.

Counsel assigned by the district court (other than the Massachusetts Defenders) serve without compensation. Judges commenting on this generally indicated that the lawyers ought to be paid a reasonable fee or one set by the bar association. As to the financial support of the Massachusetts Defenders, most judges made no comment. Of those who did reply, eight deemed the support inadequate, while two thought it was adequate.

The replies of district court judges concerning the percentage of felony defendants who were indigent varied from zero to 60, reflecting apparently the economic conditions of the area in which the courts sit. The responses concerning the proportion of indigents who declined an offer of counsel made by these judges also varied: here, from zero to 50%.

The judges interviewed indicated that if an accused requested a named lawyer, such an appointment would be made and, further, that if the accused objected to the lawyer appointed for him, another would be offered. One judge said he had sometimes responded favorably three times to this kind of objection, although another judge required a good reason before making another appointment.

The comments by the judges concerning the quality of the Massachusetts Defenders were strongly favorable, in both an absolute and a relative sense. A question seeking general comments elicited such replies as "excellent" and "very good." There were no negative comments, the ones scored as not clearly positive or favorable including "it depends," or "more money needed." When the judges compared the defenders with retained attorneys and with the district attorneys the responses were seven to one for a favorable comparison with the former and three to one for a favorable comparison with the latter. The Superior Court judges were unanimous in praising the performance of the defenders. Several commented, however, that a lack of experience was a handicap to the quality of representation provided by the defenders. None of the judges thought that the *public* status of the defenders in any way diminished their zeal or independence.

There was some indication by Superior Court judges that the system of representation of indigents in capital cases is not functioning properly. The quality of representation could stand improving and a better means is needed for insuring that an attorney requested by the indigent capital defendant has not solicited the case.

The means employed to determine indigency varied among the judges from simply asking the accused if he is able to pay for a lawyer to inquiring as to his salary or wages, ownership of an automobile or other personal property, stocks, bonds or bank accounts, his receipt of pensions, social security or unemployment compensation, and the financial resources of his parents, spouse, or other relatives. The most frequent variation on this detailed inquiry was by way of excluding consideration of the resources of parents, spouse, and other relatives.

As to which of the above factors, standing alone, preclude a finding of indigency, the responses ranged from "none" to "all." Some of the responses were qualified, indicating, for example, that the resources of the parents would be determinative depending on the age of the accused, or those of the spouse only if they are living together.

Upon finding an accused ineligible, most of the judges tell him to retain his own lawyer if he wishes to be represented. Some judges indicated that they would refer him to the local bar association or lawyer referral service for assistance, while others replied that if the accused did not know a lawyer the judge would appoint one who would then make his own arrangements for a fee.

Final comments by the judges were few. There was frequent indication in the replies of a need for more defenders. Several of the district court judges thought defenders were needed particularly in the district court. One said he doubted their value at the district court level.

D. OPINIONS OF THE DISTRICT ATTORNEYS

Of the nine district attorneys in Massachusetts, four were interviewed personally. Questionnaires, of which two were returned, were sent to the other five. Of these six all but one devoted part time to their duties as district attorney. Among these five the average weekly time spent in these duties varied as follows: 10 to 19 hours (1), 20 to 29 hours (1), over 30 hours (3). The office of district attorney does no civil business for the county.

Four of the six indicated that they lacked adequate funds to run their offices. Two of these four felt quite strongly about the need for funds for more investigators. Moreover, one of the positive responses—indicating adequate funds—conceived of the office as a prosecuting one, not one devoted to investigating. The other positive reply was qualified by the need for a part-time secretary.

When the district attorneys compared the defenders with retained lawyers, four indicated a favorable comparison while two replied that the retained lawyer is generally better. In comparing the defender with appointed lawyers, the six responses were evenly divided between a favorable or "as good" answer and an answer which rated appointed counsel higher. In regard to appointed counsel in capital cases, some concern was voiced concerning the quality of representation and the fear that cases may in fact be solicited in violation of law. The defender's relative lack of experience was frequently mentioned as a negative characteristic, while great zeal and a willingness to fight hard were cited as positive ones.

The prosecutors were also evenly divided in their opinions on the present system for determining indigency. Three felt that it was about right and three felt that it was too lenient.

The prosecutors' estimates concerning the percentage of felony defendants who are indigent varied greatly. Their responses were 25%-33⅓%, 30%, 50%, and 90%. Their estimates of the incidence of waiver of counsel among these accused were generally low, ranging from zero to less than 10%, although one indicated "quite a few" and that it depended on who the judge is.

Most of the district attorneys did not comment on whether lawyers who represent indigents should be compensated. The two who did reply said "yes." Four commented on present rates of compensation: two deemed them inadequate; one, adequate; and the fourth replied that in capital cases the $1000 fee is enough except in cases involving a long trial and an appeal.

Questions concerning cooperation with the defense elicited varied responses. Since subpoenas for defense witnesses are issued by the court there can be no assessment of district attorney cooperation in this aspect of defense preparation. Disclosure of the state's case to defense counsel is another matter, however. Two prosecutors replied unqualifiedly that they turn over their whole file if defense counsel requests it. Two indicated that this is their usual practice although there were some cases in which some or all of the file would be withheld. The fifth said he has a policy of never giving up a confession, while the sixth said he discloses nothing without being ordered to do so by the court. He did indicate, however, that if a reputable attorney assures him that the accused will plead guilty then he can see anything "within reason."

Three out of four prosecutors said their cooperation with the defense is the same, regardless of whether the accused is indigent or who represents him. The fourth said he cooperates more with the defender than he does with others because the former usually lacks experience.

All of the district attorneys felt that the fact that the Massachusetts Defender is paid from public funds in no way affects his zeal or independence. A question suggesting such an effect was, for example, termed "one hundred per cent wrong" or evoked "It doesn't work that way at all." Another reply was, "The Public Defender in this county does an excellent job."

In regard to the problem of the accused who can pay a moderate fee, the tenor of comment was to the effect that such a person can find a good lawyer on his own and that it is not necessary to retain a specialist in order to be well represented.

All of the prosecutors who replied to a question about trying a case against an unrepresented person provided negative responses such as "worst thing" or "hate to do that." Two prosecutors waive their right to closing argument in such cases.

Two comments made for improving the system for providing counsel to indigent defendants agreed on a need for more lawyers but differed as to the source of additional help. One prosecutor expressed a need for more defenders in his county. The other favored obtaining more counsel by appointing experienced members of the bar who would be paid their expenses and a reasonable fee. A third comment suggested that persons who expend money for bail ought not to be supplied with counsel.

E. OPINIONS OF THE MASSACHUSETTS DEFENDERS

This section relates to interviews with the chairman of the Massachusetts Defenders Committee and with its chief counsel. Both were satisfied completely that the system of privately hired and publicly financed attorneys is the best means of assuring qualified representation of indigents. It is also their opinion, however, that more public funds are needed to do the job properly. Each stressed the need to hire more lawyers and to establish investigative resources for the defenders.

They further emphasized the need to reach indigents at the district court level. This is now partly done in the Boston area with the assistance of the Harvard and Boston University Voluntary Defenders. It could be done in all areas, it was suggested, by having a defender come to each court on a given day of the week so that those jailed persons who wanted to see the defender could do so by agreeing to their district court appearance being postponed to that day. Another suggestion was to explore the possibility of changing the venue law so as to permit trial of indigent cases in a district court centrally located in a county to which a defender might be assigned.

F. COMPARISONS AMONG JUDGES, PROSECUTORS, AND DEFENDERS

The survey revealed several points of strong agreement among judges, prosecutors, and the Massachusetts Defenders, as shown in Table 2.

What appears most clearly from the tabulation below is that the great majority of those responding entertain a broad conception of the role of counsel for indigents. Twenty-five out of 30 responses (83%) favored provision of counsel at or before the district court hearing. Except for misdemeanors, a majority, up to 77% in two cases, thought it desirable to have counsel in each type of proceeding mentioned. Among those replying to the question of financial support of the Massachusetts Defenders, 87% thought it inadequate. Not one of the prosecutors felt the support was adequate. The judges were four to one for more money.

G. DOCKET STUDIES

Docket studies were conducted in three of the sample counties, Suffolk, Norfolk, and Worcester. (For details of methods used see volume 1, pages 178-179.) Results are shown in Tables 3 to 8.

Table 3 shows that 95% of the defendants in Suffolk County (Boston) had counsel. For Norfolk the figure was 82%, and for Worcester, 76%. These figures were projected to the state as a whole by using a weighted average. The state-wide estimate was 85%. This table also indicates that for the state as a whole about 57% of the defendants retained their own counsel and about 22% were represented by the defender or assigned counsel.

The percentage of defendants officially determined to be indigent varied from 43% in Suffolk County downward to 7% in Worcester, as shown in Table 4. Perhaps a better measure of indigency is whether the defendant was able to obtain his release on bail. Table 5 indicates that the proportion of defendants who were not released varied from 56% in Suffolk County to 31% in Worcester, with a state-wide projection of 42%.

Table 6 shows the frequency of preliminary hearings for two of the counties. They were held in about three-fourths of the cases in each county, and most of the other cases were of a kind where such hearings are not used. Very few waivers were reported. In Suffolk County hearings were held in at least half the cases (data unavailable for almost all the other half).

TABLE 2
Comparison of Views

	Judges	Prosecutors	Public defender	Total
Total responding	22	6	2	30
Ideal stage for first appointment of counsel:				
Between arrest and first appearance	7	4	2	13
At preliminary hearing or first appearance	11	1	0	12
After preliminary hearing but before indictment	0	0	0	0
At arraignment	1	0	0	1
After arraignment	2	0	0	2
At trial	1	0	0	1
When in court that can dispose of case	0	1	0	1
Does Massachusetts Defender have adequate financial support?				
Yes	2	0	0	2
No	8	3	2	13
No answer	12	3	0	15
A lawyer should be provided for:				
Sentencing of a defendant who pleaded guilty	11	3	2	16
Sentencing of a defendant convicted by trial	15	3	2	20
Habeas corpus or other postconviction remedy	17	4	2	23
Hearing on revocation of probation	11	3	2	16
Sexually dangerous person hearing	16	5	2	23
Misdemeanors	10	2	2	14
Civil commitment	10	4	2	16

Dispositions of cases are reported in Table 7. For the state as a whole, an estimated 61% of the defendants pleaded guilty, including 2% who pleaded to lesser offenses (all in Suffolk County). Of the 25% of the cases that went to trial, about half resulted in convictions and half in acquittals.

Table 8 shows the sentences, if any, imposed on the various defendants. For the state as a whole, 30% of the defendants were sentenced to prison (including county jails), 35% were placed on probation, and 8% were fined. In Worcester County probation was most frequently granted in relation to prison sentences. Fines were also common in Worcester.

TABLE 3
Retained and Assigned Counsel in Felonies
Massachusetts, 1962

County	Total sample	Did defendant have counsel? yes No.	%	no No.	%	Re-tained No.	%	As-signed No.	%	Public de-fender No.	%	Combi-nation or type un-known No.	%	No data[*] No.	%
Suffolk	96	90	95	5	5	51	54	4	4	22	23	13	10	1	1
Norfolk	75	57	82	13	19	38	54	0	0	18	26	1	1	5	7
Worcester	46	34	76	11	24	30	67	1	2	2	4	1	2	1	2
Weighted total percentages		85		16		57		1		21		3		4	

[*] % of no data refers to total sample; % in other columns refers to cases where data were available.

TABLE 4
Was Felony Defendant Determined Indigent?
Massachusetts, 1962

County	Total sample	Yes No.	%	No No.	%	No data[*] No.	%
Suffolk	96	36	43	47	57	13	14
Norfolk	75	22	31	50	69	3	4
Worcester	46	3	7	42	93	1	2
Weighted total percentages		29		71		7	

[*] % of no data refers to total sample; % in other columns refers to cases where data were available.

TABLE 5
Frequency of Release on Bail of Felony Defendants
Massachusetts, 1962

County	Total sample	Yes No.	%	No No.	%	No data[*] No.	%
Suffolk	96	34	44	44	56	18	19
Norfolk	75	41	60	27	40	7	9
Worcester	46	31	69	14	31	1	2
Weighted total percentages		58		42		10	

[*] % of no data refers to total sample; % in other columns refers to cases where data were available.

TABLE 6
Frequency of Preliminary Hearings in Felonies
Massachusetts, 1962

County	Total sample	Yes No.	Yes %	No, waiver No.	No, waiver %	No, not used in this kind of case No.	No, not used in this kind of case %	No, reason unknown No.	No, reason unknown %	No data* No.	No data* %
Norfolk	75	52	76	2	3	6	11	1	2	7	9
Worcester	46	30	70	0	0	13	19	1	1	3	7
Weighted total percentages			77		2		20		1		19

* % of no data refers to total sample; % in other columns refers to cases where data were available.

TABLE 7
Disposition in Felony Cases
Massachusetts, 1962

County	Total sample	Plea guilty	Plea lesser offense	Dis-missed	Found guilty	Ac-quitted	Mental com-mit-ment	Pend-ing	Stet*	Other
Suffolk	96	47	7	4	10	16	1	2	6	3†
Norfolk	75	50	0	0	7	7	0	4	4	3‡
Worcester	46	22	0	0	10	7	1	3	1	2
Weighted total percentages		59	2	1	12	13	1	5	5	3

* Held on inactive docket.
† Includes 2 no data cases.
‡ Includes 1 no data case.

TABLE 8
Sentencing in Felony Cases
Massachusetts, 1962*

County	Total sample	No sentence No.	No sentence %	Prison No.	Prison %	Pro-bation No.	Pro-bation %	Suspended sen-tence No.	Suspended sen-tence %	Fine No.	Fine %	Sentence pending No.	Sentence pending %
Suffolk	96	28	29	34	35	24	25	1	1	8	8	1	1
Norfolk	75	20	27	25	33	27	36	0	0	5	7	0	0
Worcester	46	13	28	5	11	22	48	0	0	6	13	0	0
Weighted total percentages			28		30		35		0		8		0

* If sentence was any combination of prison, probation, suspended sentence (without probation), and fine, it is recorded under each of these columns.

H. CONCLUSIONS AND RECOMMENDATIONS

[Editor's note: the following recommendations were written before the amendment to Rule 10 referred to in the text and quoted in Appendix 2, wherein counsel are to be offered to indigent defendants in any court for any charge punishable by a term of imprisonment. This amendment particularly affects recommendation no. 3. The original recommendation has been left intact because it has a discussion of the general problem of providing counsel for misdemeanors.]

1. Representation of indigents in the Superior Court is excellent according to the practically universal reputation for quality that the Massachusetts Defenders enjoy. Zeal, independence, and devotion are characteristic of their work in the minds of a large majority of persons with whom they have had professional relations. Most significantly, there was a complete absence of negative comment concerning politics interfering with the services provided. It is strongly recommended that the present system be continued and expanded.

The skill the defenders exert, however, on behalf of indigent defendants is handicapped by three factors: (1) a relative lack of experience, (2) lack of investigative resources sometimes necessary for a proper defense, and (3) a lack of man-hours that would generally permit reaching their clients at the district court level.

It is, therefore, further recommended that the appropriation for the Massachusetts Defenders be increased sufficiently to permit staff lawyers to remain in the organization for approximately five years, so as to make for a core of attorneys experienced in the trial of criminal cases. This is almost entirely a matter of adjusting salary scales. The observation made by many that the defenders do not have adequate financial support relates directly to the salaries of staff attorneys. While it is true that recruiting of this staff has been and must continue to be based on a policy of seeking those sincerely interested in performing a public service as well as enhancing their professional abilities, it does not undermine this policy to provide salaries at or near those available in private law firms or public prosecutors' offices. There is, to be sure, the danger that salaries may become sufficiently attractive to produce irresistible political pressure regarding staff appointments, and it takes no extensive argument to demonstrate that incorporation of the Massachusetts Defenders into a spoils system would tend to destroy the goals of skillful, zealous, and independent representation of indigents. It seems perfectly clear that those now holding responsibility for hiring decisions have exercised their authority completely outside the arena of politics and patronage. Two factors appear to be responsible for this, and these must be maintained regardless of any changes that may occur. The primary one is the outstanding personal integrity of the committee and its chief counsel. Secondly, the committee is appointed by the Supreme Judicial Court, whose members are appointed for life and thereby maximally insulated from pressures to do political favors. The preservation of these two values is extremely important. The point emphasized here is that the values of integrity and independence are not diminished by adjustments in staff salaries. A system firmly based on these values, as ours presently is, can withstand demands for a $6000 job as well as it can demands for a $3000 one.

2. An increased appropriation for the defenders is also needed for investigations. Two desiderata are relevant: (1) in some cases the defense cannot be adequately conducted without great effort being spent on investigation, and (2) the fact that the commonwealth in every case has police resources available for this function reveals an unfairness that no system of equal justice can knowingly retain.

3. There are two aspects to the need for providing defenders in district courts. The one considered here relates to indigent accused persons who appear in these courts on their way to the Superior Court—those who are bound over for the grand jury and those who are tried and take an appeal to the Superior Court. The other aspect, relating to indigents whose cases come to rest in the district courts, is discussed below.

In cases on their way to the Superior Court, there is the danger of the defendant prejudicing his case by what he says and does in the district court. All of his admissions, for example, may be used against him in the Superior Court. If counsel is deemed necessary in the Superior Court for such felony defendants, as Massachusetts law now declares, it is entirely illogical and unfair to permit an uncounseled person to vitiate in the district court the value of his later representation. It would appear appropriate that the staff of the Massachusetts Defenders be increased so that they may appear for these indigents in the district court.

Counsel cannot be provided solely for those who are going to be bound over and those who are going to appeal without providing counsel for everyone charged with an offense in the district court. This is because at the outset there is no certain way of segregating such accused from those charged with like offenses but whose cases will be neither bound over nor appealed.

Apart from this practical problem of identifying incipient Superior Court noncapital felony indigents it should be recalled that *Gideon v. Wainwright*, 372 U.S. 335 (1963), involved a felony with a five-year penalty. The district courts in Massachusetts do have jurisdiction to try such felonies and a minimal compliance with *Gideon* would seem to be the assignment of counsel in the district court to indigents charged with such felonies.

It is true that Massachusetts felonies involve offenses with a two-and-one-half-year penalty, not the five-year penalty of *Gideon*. But there is no reason to engage in such a narrow reading of that case and every reason to guarantee fairness to one facing any term of imprisonment.

It is, therefore, recommended that Rule 10 be enlarged so as to require appointment of counsel for an indigent person accused of an offense for which the penalty may be any loss of liberty, and that this be done upon his first appearance in any court. Felony and misdemeanor distinctions become quite unimportant for these purposes. If it appears that some misdemeanor offenses carry an incarceration penalty but are so bereft of moral turpitude that provision of counsel appears unnecessary, it is strongly suggested that the absence of moral turpitude is reason for eliminating the imprisonment penalty, but not for doing without counsel.

4. In regard to the determination of indigency, it is recommended that a more

uniform system be used than is presently employed. Two defects appear in the current practice. One is that it is very unclear where responsibility for determination of indigency lies. Secondly, to the extent that the decision is now controlled by the judge sitting in each case, the standards vary too widely. The diversity of standards is highly undesirable, since it produces an unequal application of the law. It is inherently unfair when two men accused of crime and similarly lacking in financial resources are treated differently in having counsel assigned to them. This inequality ought to be eliminated as much as possible.

Responsibility for formulating state-wide standards can best be lodged with the Massachusetts Defenders, subject to approval by a committee of Superior Court judges. Although this ought not and cannot preclude a judge in any case from appointing counsel for a person not found indigent by committee criteria, the over-all result would be greater uniformity than now apparently obtains.

5. It is recommended that, as soon as the appropriation of the defenders has been sufficiently enlarged to insure a core of experienced counsel and investigative resources and it further appears that these counsel do in fact remain on the staff for at least five years, the law be changed so as to lodge responsibility for defense of capital cases with the defenders. This would provide experienced, independent, and zealous representation for cases which many in positions to know feel are now receiving less than competent defense.

(Grateful appreciation is expressed to all who helped in the conduct of this study. The judges, prosecutors, and others who took time to discuss these questions with the reporter or to fill out a detailed questionnaire made the research possible. The clerks of courts in which the docket studies were made also gave generously of their assistance. Although not tabulated anywhere, the discussions with Chief Justice Wilkins, Justice Reardon, and Livingston Hall, President of the Massachusetts Bar Association, provided valuable perspectives.)

APPENDIX 1

"If a prisoner, under indictment for a capital crime, pleads guilty, upon being arraigned, the court shall award sentence against him; if he does not plead guilty, the court may assign him counsel and take all other measures preparatory to a trial. . . ." Mass. Gen. Laws Ann. ch. 277, § 47.

"A justice of the court, sitting at the trial or other proceedings upon an indictment for murder, may allow reasonable compensation for the services of counsel assigned to defend the prisoner if he is otherwise unable to procure counsel, and such compensation shall be paid by the county where the indictment is found." Mass. Gen. Laws Ann. ch. 277, § 55.

"The reasonable expenses incurred and paid by counsel assigned by the court for the defense of a person indicted for murder, who is otherwise unable to procure counsel, shall be paid by the county where the indictment is found after approval by a justice sitting at the trial or other proceedings of the case." Mass. Gen. Laws Ann. ch. 277, § 56.

"If a person is brought before a district court or trial justice for examination upon charge of a capital crime and does not waive examination, the Superior Court may assign counsel upon his petition and upon certification of the charge to the Superior Court by the clerk of the district court or by the trial justice. The examination shall thereupon be continued until the assignment of counsel has been made, and certification thereof received by the clerk of the district court or by the trial justice, or until the petition for assignment of counsel has been otherwise disposed of. The Superior Court may allow reasonable compensation for the services at the examination in the district court, or before the trial justice, of counsel assigned to appear for the accused, if he is otherwise unable to procure counsel, and such compensation shall be paid by the county where the crime was alleged to have been committed." Mass. Gen. Laws Ann. ch. 276, § 37A.

Superior Court Rules

Rule 95

Counsel in Capital Cases

The court may assign counsel for a defendant charged with murder, who is unable to procure counsel, but will not allow compensation for the services of counsel if the charge in the indictment is limited to murder in the second degree or if such services were performed after it appeared that a conviction in the first degree will not be asked.

Before assigning counsel, the court shall interrogate such defendant in open court and shall satisfy itself that he is unable to procure counsel.

No person shall be assigned as counsel in a murder case unless he has been a member of the Bar for more than ten years, and the court has satisfied itself that he is fully qualified by training, experience, reputation and character to discharge the responsibility imposed upon him. No person shall be assigned as such counsel unless he has filed with the clerk of the court an affidavit stating that neither he nor any person in his behalf has directly or indirectly solicited employment as counsel for the accused, that he has not received or requested or been promised any compensation for his services, and that he does not expect and will not accept any compensation for his services from any source other than that which may be allowed by the Court.

Counsel shall be allowed no more than one hundred dollars for services in a district court or before a trial justice, and no more than one thousand dollars for all other services and no more than one hundred dollars for expenses, when there is not more than one trial, and when there is more than one trial, no more than one thousand dollars for services and no more than one hundred dollars for expenses for each retrial, unless an order of court authorizing further expenses and limiting the amount thereof is made before the expenses are incurred.

A bill for services and expenses shall state the items of expense in detail.

APPENDIX 2

Supreme Judicial Court Rules

Rule 10

Assignment of Counsel in Noncapital Cases

If a defendant charged with a crime, for which a sentence of imprisonment may be imposed, appears in any court without counsel, the judge shall advise him of his right to counsel and assign counsel to represent him at every stage of the proceeding unless he elects to proceed without counsel or is unable to obtain counsel. Before assigning counsel, the judge shall interrogate the defendant and shall satisfy himself that the defendant is unable to procure counsel. If the judge finds that the defendant is able to procure counsel, he shall make a finding to that effect which shall be filed with the papers in the case. If the defendant elects to proceed without counsel, a waiver and a certificate of the judge on a form herein established shall be signed, respectively, by the defendant and the judge and filed with the papers in the case. If the defendant elects to proceed without counsel and refuses to sign the waiver, the judge shall so certify on a form herein established, which shall be filed with the papers in the case.

MASSACHUSETTS

The forms established by this rule shall be as follows:

Commonwealth of Massachusetts

. . . . SS   . . . . Court

No. . . . .

Commonwealth

. . . . v. . . . .

Waiver of Counsel

I, ... , have been informed of my right pursuant to General Rule 10
Name of Defendant
of the Rules of the Supreme Judicial Court, to have counsel appointed by the court to represent me at every stage of the proceedings in this case. I elect to proceed without counsel and
waive my right to such appointment.

. . . .
Signature of Defendant

. . . . 19 . .

Certificate of Judge

I, ... , hereby certify that . . . . has been informed of his right
Name of Judge   Name of Defendant
to have counsel appointed by the court to represent him at every stage of the proceedings
in this case; that he has elected to proceed without counsel; and that he has executed the
above waiver in my presence.

. . . .
Signature of Judge

Commonwealth of Massachusetts

. . . . SS

No. . . . .

. . . . Court

Certificate of Judge

I, ... , hereby certify that . . . . has been informed of his right
Name of Judge   Name of Defendant
to have counsel appointed by the court to represent him at every stage of the proceedings
in this case; that he has elected to proceed without counsel; and that he has refused to
sign a waiver.

. . . .
Signature of Judge

. . . . 19 . . . .

APPENDIX 3

Harvard Voluntary Defenders
Annual Report
1962-1963

Organization and Purpose

The Harvard Voluntary Defenders was organized in 1949 to render free legal assistance
to indigent persons accused of crime. Membership, selected primarily on the basis of interest,
consists of thirty-three students from the second and third year classes of the Harvard Law
School. The activities of the organization provide an invaluable range of practical experience
for the membership, and at the same time serve a vital community need in the Boston area.

Special Legislation

Rule 11 of the Massachusetts Supreme Judicial Court permits third year law students
to appear on behalf of indigent defendants in all District Court actions, provided that the
conduct of the case is under the general supervision of a member of the bar employed by
a recognized voluntary defender committee. Under the Rule students are permitted to appear
alone in the actual trial or probable cause hearing.

The court appearances are supervised by Messrs. Samuel A. Wilkinson and James P. Lynch,

DEFENSE OF THE POOR

Jr., who are employed for this purpose by the Boston Voluntary Defenders. Professor Livingston Hall oversees the entire operation, which is closely integrated with the work of the Massachusetts Defenders Committee, a state financed agency which represents indigents in non-capital felony cases in Superior Court and when appointed, in District Court.

The Nature of the Work

The major portion of the work carried on by the Harvard Voluntary Defenders is the interviewing of those needing defense assistance. Memoranda of the interviews are forwarded to the Massachusetts Defenders Committee, Wilbur G. Hollingsworth, Esq., Chief Counsel. These reports form a part of the material utilized by that office in its conduct of trials. During the past year over 500 persons were interviewed at the jails, prisons, mental hospitals and other state institutions.

The District Court appearances represent the "internship" at its best. The fact that the appearances this year were more than double those of last year demonstrates an increasing and favorable recognition of student counsel by the courts.

In addition, the Harvard Voluntary Defenders conducted research in answer to inquiries from persons incarcerated within and without the Commonwealth. While this year the research served only to satisfy persons that their convictions were legal, last year appellate briefs were drawn up to assist local counsel representing an ultimately successful Indiana prisoner.

The practical value of the work, involving a participation in the operation of the criminal law, with the resulting contact with clients and courts is obvious. It has been made the more so by the splendid supervision of Messrs. Hall, Hollingsworth, Wilkinson, and Lynch. But equally important to the training of the lawyer, as remarked by Mr. Justice Brennan at the Harvard Legal Aid Banquet in February of this year, is that voluntary defender work clearly teaches that "contributing one's legal services to an unpopular or unremunerative cause need not be dirty, or nasty, or opprobrious."

Evaluation of District Court Work

The Harvard Voluntary Defenders represented 114 defendants in District Court, compared to 45 defendants in 1961-1962. In twelve cases there were acquittals or dismissals of the complaint. Ten cases were filed. Twenty-seven cases resulted in suspended sentences and/or probation or fines. Seven juveniles were committed to the Youth Service Board. Eighteen defendants received sentences and in thirty-three cases probable cause was found. Two juveniles were held for criminal court, and five cases are now pending.

Of the thirty-three defendants bound over, seventeen have since been tried. Only five received sentences; two were ultimately acquitted and four were placed on Probation in Superior Court. One case received a No Bill from the Grand Jury, and five defendants obtained other counsel.

Thus, in 114 cases, twenty-three defendants received jail sentences, and 15 cases resulted in complete exoneration for the defendants. A total of 23 cases are still pending.

The following cases are illustrative of those handled by members. In one instance a charge of abduction was dismissed; in another case charges of forgery and desertion were reduced to a charge of non-support.

A comparison of this record with the highly successful program of last year suggests that the 150% increase in District Court clients did not impair the quality of representation.

Outlook

As the organization enters its fifteenth year, there is every indication that the increased demand for our services will continue. Especially in the area of District Court appearances, the favorable reception given counsel by the courts, and the increasing awareness of the service among the indigent point to increased participation. Also, in the field of post-conviction research there is a steady increase in requests for our investigation of possible grounds for appeal.

In order to meet these demands and to adapt to any new demand, the authorized membership has been increased from thirty-three to forty, to be equally divided among the second and third year classes; also, a fourth officer has been elected.

MASSACHUSETTS

Believing there is a need for a 'law internship' of this sort in the training of lawyers, this organization would be glad to share its experience with other interested student groups or law schools.

Budget

The expenditures for office maintenance and office staff salary totaled $1,646. This sum is donated by the Harvard Law School. In addition, the Permanent Charities Fund made a grant to the Boston Voluntary Defenders Committee, to finance supervision of District Court appearances. During 1963-1964 this supervision will be financed by the Boston Voluntary Defender Committee. Traveling expenses, which amounted to $141, were met by a gift from the Ames Fund and by the Law School. Costs of a social nature, such as the annual banquet, are paid for from the annual dues of the individual members.

District Court Appearances			
Appearances made under Rule 11			136
District Court		119	
Juvenile Court		17	
Boston Municipal Court	22		
Chelsea	2		
Dedham	2		
Dorchester	13		
East Cambridge	29		
East Cambridge Juvenile	4		
Framingham	1		
Lowell	3		
Malden	4		
Newton	2		
Quincy Juvenile Court	2		
Roxbury	15		
Roxbury Juvenile Court	5		
Somerville	7		
Somerville Juvenile Court	1		
South Boston	11		
Waltham	3		
Waltham Juvenile Court	2		
West Roxbury	3		
West Roxbury Juvenile Court	3		
Wrentham	2		

(Note: This table represents the total number of appearances on behalf of 114 clients. Some cases required multiple appearances. During the previous academic years, 1961-1962, the Harvard Voluntary Defenders appeared in the District Courts on 60 occasions.)

APPENDIX 4

Boston Municipal Court
"Misdemeanors"

I certify that I have no money or other financial assets with which to retain a practicing member of the Bar of the Commonwealth of Massachusetts.

I hereby request the services of a certified member of the Voluntary Defenders of Boston University to act as my attorney for the case now pending at Boston Municipal Court criminal division.

Date: _____

_____
(Signed under pains and penalties of perjury)

Trial Date: _____

_____
(Witnessed by)

APPENDIX 5

You Must Sign This Affidavit Yourself

To the Massachusetts Defenders Committee:

I am in the .... Jail waiting trial or disposition
on a charge of

I hereby certify that I have no money nor means of obtaining money to hire a private lawyer and therefore request the services of a lawyer furnished by the Massachusetts Defenders Committee.

Signed under the pains and penalty of perjury.

Cell No. ....   Signature ....

Date ....

Attorney's comments on financial condition:

MICHIGAN

Prof. Harold Norris, Detroit, and John T. Hammond, Benton Harbor

We wish to acknowledge the advice, cooperation and assistance of the A.B.A. Associate State Committee. The committee consisted of Edmond F. DeVine, Ann Arbor, chairman; George E. Bushnell, Jr., Detroit; Robert E. DeMascio, Detroit; George Cronewald, Jr., Battle Creek; John T. Hammond, Benton Harbor; Joseph C. Hooper, Jr., Ann Arbor; Sam Ford Massie, Jr., Grand Rapids; William T. Myers, Detroit; Alexander C. Perlos, Jackson; and Cassius E. Street, Jr., Lansing. We wish also to thank the judges, attorneys, and clerks who gave generously of their time in submitting to interviews or answering questionnaires. We note also our acknowledgment of gratitude to Mr. Edwin Johnson, a student at the Detroit College of Law, for his work on the docket study.

A. INTRODUCTION

It is the purpose of this audit "to study the present practices" in Michigan and to help further the effort "to assure the adequacy of defense provided indigent persons accused of crime."[1]

The 7 counties selected out of Michigan's 83 counties for this audit are situated in the western, central, and southeastern sections of the state. They contain about one-half of the 8,000,000 people in the state, an even larger percentage of the state's lawyers, judges, and prosecuting attorneys, and also a large percentage of the felonies (see Tables 1 and 2). Wayne, Kent, Ingham, and Saginaw Counties are large counties, each dominated by a single city. Monroe County lies between Wayne County and Lucas County, Ohio, where Toledo is located; Livingston County is a rural county midway between Lansing and Detroit; Macomb County adjoins Wayne County to the north-northeast and is the third most populated county in the state. Many Macomb and Monroe residents work in Detroit.

The reporters conducted interviews with judges, prosecuting attorneys, and clerks in the sample counties on the basis of comprehensive questionnaires prepared by the American Bar Foundation. What follows is a composite, relatively representative montage or audit of practices and opinions in this state regarding providing counsel for indigent defendants in criminal cases. Although there have been limitations in the availability and authoritativeness of data, some useful information has been obtained upon which appropriate recommendations can be offered and further studies undertaken.

Under the newly ratified constitution, effective January 1, 1963, "the judicial power of the state is vested exclusively in one court of justice which shall be divided into one supreme court, one court of appeals, one trial court of general jurisdiction known as the circuit court, one probate court and courts of limited jurisdiction that the legislature may establish."[2] It will be seen that a four-tier court structure is envisioned. During the period of this study, however, Michigan had a three-tier judicial structure. The Supreme Court, with its powers of general superintending control, represents the first tier. The circuit court, with its superintending power over all inferior courts, represents the second. There

TABLE 1
Data Regarding the Sample

County	Population, 1960	Largest city	Population of largest city	No. of judges with general jurisdiction	Size of staff of prosecuting attorney	No. of lawyers in county*
Wayne	2,666,297	Detroit	1,670,144	28†	55	5013
Macomb	405,804	Warren	89,246	4	12	182
Monroe	101,120	Monroe	22,968	1	3¶	33
Livingston	38,233	Howell	4861	1‡	1	23
Saginaw	190,752	Saginaw	98,256	3	4	182
Ingham	211,296	Lansing	113,058	3	6	316
Kent	363,187	Grand Rapids	197,198	4§	6	368

* The numbers here, obtained from the State Bar of Michigan, indicate the number of lawyers admitted to practice in the state. There are 9307 lawyers so admitted in Michigan. However, it must be noted that many do not practice law, or are employed otherwise than in private practice, e.g., government or bank trust officers.
† The figure includes 18 circuit judges, and 10 Recorder's Court judges.
‡ The circuit judge here is shared with another county.
§ One of these is from the Superior Court in Grand Rapids.
¶ The prosecutors in Monroe are all part-time.

TABLE 2
Data Regarding Appointment of Counsel, 1962

City or county	No. of felony defendants charged	No. of felony defendants guilty	No. of appointments of counsel	No. of lawyers who served	Total payments to assigned counsel	Average payment to assigned counsel	No. of counsel appointed as % of felony cases*	% accused in felony cases thought to be indigent By judges	% accused in felony cases thought to be indigent By prosecutors
Wayne	982	681	224	166	$ 27,015	$121	23	25	NE¶
Detroit	6196†	4637	2674	ND‡	268,567	100	39	60	NE¶
Macomb	617	433	59	44	9044	151	10	60	30
Monroe	164	ND‡	30	11	3545	118	18	20	NE¶
Kent	210	130	98	52	7345	75	12	50	66
Grand Rapids	619	478	§	§	§	§	§	50	66
Saginaw	391	229	19	12	3575	188	5	55	60
Ingham	805	203	55	22	7980	145	8	55	NE¶
Livingston	35	23	16	7	1710	106	41	20	75

* Relating the number of counsel appointed to the number of felony cases is the only rough arithmetic measure we have of the percentage of felony cases actually deemed to be indigent by the courts.
† Includes gross misdemeanors.
‡ No data.
§ Grand Rapids included in Kent data.
¶ No estimate.

are 41 judicial circuits in Michigan, ranging from a bench of 18 judges in the 3rd judicial circuit for one county, Wayne, to one judge for six counties in the 34th circuit. There are a total of 85 circuit judges. The court administrator may assign a circuit judge temporarily to another circuit, or to the Recorder's Court or the superior court. The magistrates' courts are in the third or bottom tier of the structure.

Each county has its own elected prosecuting attorney. Most prosecutors are part-time, but it is reported that they work almost full time.

The superior court for the city of Grand Rapids exercises general jurisdiction within the city, including exclusive criminal jurisdiction for cases arising in the city.[3] The Recorder's Court for the city of Detroit has general criminal jurisdiction within the city[4] and very limited civil jurisdiction.

A variety of courts function as magistrates, with jurisdiction to hear and determine misdemeanors and to act as examining magistrates in felonies.[5] The magistrates include justices of the peace in townships and smaller cities;[6] municipal courts, established under a number of different and overlapping statutes;[7] the police court of Grand Rapids;[8] the Recorder's Court of Detroit; and circuit court commissioners.[9] All magistrates have county-wide jurisdiction except in Grand Rapids and Detroit.

Although grand juries, either of the common law variety or of the "one-man" variety, in which the grand juror is a circuit judge, are provided for by statute,[10] they are very rare in Michigan, averaging less than one per year for the state.

B. CRIMINAL PROCEDURE AS IT AFFECTS INDIGENT PERSONS

The criminal procedure in felony cases involves the following elements, not all of which will appear in every case:

1. Arrest for the commission of a felony is typically made without warrant. This is one of two stages (the other being arraignment on the complaint and warrant) in which the procedure has materially changed in recent years. The Michigan Supreme Court has adopted the McNabb-Mallory rule[11] in *People v. Hamilton*,[12] and has ruled that failure to bring an accused before a magistrate "without unnecessary delay" constitutes a denial of due process.[13] An officer may arrest for a felony without a warrant whenever he has reasonable grounds to believe that a felony has been committed and that the person to be arrested has committed it.[14]

2. Before taking a complaint and issuing a warrant, a magistrate must obtain the authorization of the prosecuting attorney or security for the payment of costs.[15]

3. The complaint and warrant, though theoretically drawn by the magistrate, are usually prepared by the prosecuting attorney's office, at least in the larger counties.

4. Arrest with a warrant, which may be either a warrant issued by a magistrate or a bench warrant issued on the basis of a grand jury true bill, though theoretically the usual procedure, occurs in only a small minority of the cases.

5. Arraignment on the complaint and warrant (the "first appearance"):

a. In Recorder's Court in Detroit the presiding judge handles the complaint and warrant. He sets the amount of bail and the date of the preliminary examination, if one is demanded. In addition, if the accused is indigent and has not waived preliminary examination, the judge appoints counsel for him.[16] Even if preliminary examination is waived, the judge will appoint counsel at this stage, where this is indicated. The court uses an application form for assigned counsel which must be signed and sworn to by the accused.

b. In magistrates' courts throughout the state, exclusive of the city of Detroit, the accused, on arraignment on the complaint and warrant, is not permitted to plead, but may merely demand or waive preliminary examination. In either event the court sets the amount of the bond at this time. If a preliminary examination is asked for, it is set at this time for a day certain within 10 days. If the accused demands a preliminary examination, and is without counsel at that time, the magistrate must proceed according to the following statute:[17]

> Whenever any person charged with having committed any felony or misdemeanor not cognizable by a justice of the peace or magistrate and who appears before such justice of the peace or magistrate without counsel, and who shall not have waived examination upon the charge upon which he appears, such person shall be advised of his right to have counsel appointed for such examination, and if such person states that he is unable to procure counsel the justice or magistrate shall notify the presiding judge of the circuit court in the jurisdiction of which the offense is alleged to have occurred, and upon proper showing the presiding judge shall appoint some attorney to conduct the accused's examination before a justice court or examining magistrate and to conduct the defense, and the attorney so appointed shall be entitled to receive from the county treasurer on the certificate of the presiding judge that such services have been duly rendered, such an amount as the presiding judge shall in his discretion deem reasonable compensation for the services performed.

This procedure is new to Michigan. Prior to Public Act No. 132, of 1963, there was no way for a case to be brought before the presiding circuit judge for appointment of counsel prior to the preliminary examination. Except in Recorder's Court in Detroit, the examining magistrate has no authority to appoint counsel. Although the actual mechanism used in the various counties has not yet been fully developed, the circuit court for Wayne County has directed magistrates to contact a particular person in the office of the prosecuting attorney. This person makes the arrangements to bring the accused before the court for determination of indigency and appointment of counsel. In other counties the presiding circuit judge is notified directly or through the assignment clerk, prosecuting attorney, or county clerk.

6. Preliminary examination:

a. In Recorder's Court in Detroit a preliminary examination is held before the examining judge. The judges rotate their positions monthly: one acts as presiding judge, one as examining judge, and the other eight as trial judges. There is also the traffic court division, with two judges. This is, for all practical purposes, a separate court.

b. Outside of Detroit, preliminary examinations are heard by the magistrate who issued the warrant. Theoretically, the purpose of the preliminary examination is to save innocent defendants the expense and risks of a trial in circuit court by screening the accusation. It also affords the defense quasi-discovery of the prosecution's case. This may constitute a possible risk, since the transcript of a witness's testimony on a preliminary examination may be employed for impeachment or may be admitted in evidence at the trial where the witness has become unavailable.[18] Since the prosecution need only show that there is probable cause to believe that the felony has been committed, and that the accused has committed it, the prosecution may have the defendant bound over practically as a matter of course.

7. When the accused has been bound over for trial, an information is filed which constitutes the formal charge against the defendant in a felony case. If the accused has waived preliminary examination and has been bound over for trial without having counsel appointed, Supreme Court Rule 785.3 applies. It provides as follows:

3. Arraignment and Sentencing. In every prosecution wherein the accused is charged with a felony, the trial court shall conform to the following practice:

(1) Arraignment. If the accused is not represented by counsel upon arraignment, before he is required to plead, the court shall advise the accused that he is entitled to a trial by jury and to have counsel, and that in case he is financially unable to provide counsel the court will, if accused so requests, appoint counsel for him. If the accused states he will procure counsel or requests that counsel be appointed, a reasonable time thereafter shall be allowed for counsel to consult with the accused before his plea shall be taken.

(2) Imposing Sentence. If the accused pleads guilty, after such plea and before sentence the court shall inform the accused of the nature of the accusation and the consequences of his plea; and regardless of whether he is represented by counsel, the court shall examine the accused, not necessarily under oath, and as a condition of accepting the plea of guilty and imposing sentence shall ascertain that the plea was freely, understandingly, and voluntarily made, without undue influence, compulsion, or duress, and without promise of leniency. Unless the court determines that the plea of guilty was so made, it shall not be accepted.

(3) Record. The trial court shall cause a stenographic record to be made and promptly transcribed of the proceedings had under (1) and (2) above, and shall certify over his signature thereto that the same is a true record of the proceedings had. Thereupon the record so made shall be filed with the clerk of the court and become and be kept as a part of the record in the case. In any subsequent proceedings such record shall be competent evidence of the facts and circumstances therein recorded.

(4) This rule is mandatory but failure to comply therewith shall not be considered jurisdictional.

The making of a plea of either guilty or not guilty to the information constitutes a waiver of all non-jurisdictional defects theretofore. For this reason an accused represented by counsel will usually stand mute to the charge. The same process is followed even if the accused has been represented by counsel at a preliminary examination, though sometimes the court's interrogation of an accused person who wishes to plead guilty is shorter where he has been advised by counsel. Assigned counsel represent the accused through and including appearance for sentence.

8. Jury trial is required unless expressly waived. For felony cases that went to trial in 1962 the average interval between the commencement of the case and disposition by trial was 3.8 months. Non-jury cases took slightly longer than jury cases.[19] In over 40% of the felony trials in circuit courts, the accused waived trial by a jury. In the Detroit Recorder's Court over 75% of those tried waive a jury trial.[20]

9. A pre-sentence report from the probation department must be obtained before sentence can be imposed, regardless of whether the accused has been convicted by plea or by trial. Where the probation report discloses misunderstanding or involuntariness of the plea or that the accused is not guilty of the offense, the accused will be brought back before the presiding circuit judge by the probation officer and asked if he wishes to withdraw his plea of guilty and enter a plea of not guilty. A plea of guilty may be withdrawn at any time prior to sentence.

10. If a motion for new trial is indicated, this is ordinarily the responsibility of the trial counsel, particularly where the accused has been supplied with assigned counsel. As a practical matter, the time limit for the filing of a motion for a new trial generally is equal to the period between verdict and sentence.

11. Since the defendant in every criminal case is entitled to one appeal as a matter of right,[21] this area of the law will receive much more attention than previously. If *Douglas v. California*[22] and *Draper v. Washington*[23] are to be given their full effect in Michigan, it is likely that additional expense will have to be borne by the county, as the county usually pays this cost, or by the state. The statutes do not presently provide for the payment of expenses or costs for an indigent accused person, except for witness and attorney fees. Procedures will have to be amended to make it possible for the transcripts or their equivalent, required by the *Draper* rule, to be supplied to the accused at public expense.

C. OPINIONS OF THE JUDGES

Fourteen circuit judges, one superior court judge, and one Recorder's Court judge were interviewed in this audit. For Wayne County, the presiding judge spoke for his bench of 18 circuit judges. The executive judge of the Recorder's Court spoke for his bench of 10 judges. Three of the four circuit judges of Macomb County met *en banc* with one of the state reporters. Nine circuit judges were interviewed for Kent, Ingham, Saginaw, and Livingston Counties. A mail ballot was sent to 38 circuit judges in the nonsample counties. This yielded replies from 27 judges, each in a different circuit. In short, the opinions herein approximately reflect the views of judges from 34 of the state's 41 circuits.

Generally, the judges favored appointment of counsel at a stage earlier than preliminary hearing (Table 3). The judges were divided on the question whether it would be unfair if counsel were not so provided. Opinions were expressed that some administrative problems might be present with earlier appointment. It is pertinent to note that the statute providing for the appointment of counsel between the time of first appearance before a magistrate and the time of preliminary examination, though already passed by the legislature, had not yet gone into effect at the time of the interviews. The presiding judge of the Wayne circuit bench has called attention to the observation that the need for counsel exists at the time of arrest, and before first appearance when the defendant's statements can be used against him. Recent United States Supreme Court cases involving the constitutional vulnerability of confessions taken when counsel was not present or when the rights of the accused were not explained reinforce the judge's observation. Several judges ventured the opinion that the nearer the time of arrest counsel is provided, the greater the cost might be to provide such services.

Of the 27 circuit judges responding by mail to the "ideal stage" question, 9 thought counsel should first be provided between arrest and first appearance before a magistrate, 5 at first appearance, 4 between first appearance and preliminary hearing, 3 at preliminary hearing, 2 after the filing of an information but before arraignment, and 4 at arraignment. Six of the 9 judges who favored appointment between arrest and first appearance were from multiple-county circuits. On the question of unfairness, 10 said "yes," 10 said "no," and 7 did not answer. As to whether the ideal system could be financed, 11 said "yes," 3 said "no," and 13 did not answer.

TABLE 3
Judges' Views Regarding the Appropriate Stage for Appointment of Counsel for Indigent Accused

County, city, or court	Appointment under an ideal sytem	Unfair if not so appointed	Stage at which counsel is in fact appointed
Wayne	Between arrest and first appearance or at preliminary hearing*	Yes	Between first appearance and preliminary hearing
Detroit	First appearance	Yes	Same as Wayne
Macomb	Between first appearance and preliminary hearing	Yes	Same as Wayne
Monroe	Between first appearance and preliminary hearing	Yes	Same as Wayne
Ingham	Between first appearance and preliminary hearing	No	Same as Wayne
Kent	Between first appearance and preliminary hearing	No	Same as Wayne
Superior Court	After filing information but before arraignment	Yes	Same as Wayne†
Livingston	At arraignment on information	Yes	After filing information and prior to arraignment†,‡
Saginaw	At first appearance	No	Between first appearance and preliminary hearing

* The presiding judge stated: "In serious crimes counsel should be provided between arrest and first appearance if defendant's statement can be used against him, if not counsel should be provided at preliminary hearings. By serious crimes I mean felonies, or misdemeanors carrying a penalty of over 90 days confinement."

† Counsel is actually provided prior to the stage that, in the opinion of the judges, represented an ideal standard.

‡ At the time that this county was audited, Act 132 of P.A. 1963 had not yet gone into effect, and the judge's response reflects the prior law.

The judges generally thought that an ideal system would include the appointment of counsel for indigents in cases or proceedings involving a hearing to determine whether a party was a criminal sexual psychopath, whether a person was sufficiently mentally ill to be committed, and in habeas corpus proceedings (see Table 4). It was generally not thought that an ideal system included the appointment of counsel in misdemeanors or hearings on revocation of probation. All of the judges stated that counsel were already appointed in sexual psychopath hearings, though the authority for such appointments is open to question. To a varying degree counsel are not generally made available for sentencing alone, or for civil commitment of the mentally ill, though an ideal system would provide counsel for the latter. The criminal sexual psychopath proceeding is, technically, not a criminal proceeding; therefore, the usual procedures for the appointment of counsel are not available. This is a matter of some concern to all of the judges, but many felt that they had been able to appoint with strained authority. A person found to be a criminal sexual psychopath could be given an indeterminate sentence of one day to life, "until he recovers," and is no longer a danger to himself or others.

In regard to sentencing, the Macomb judges observed that "a defendant ought to have counsel appointed at any stage." The circuit judge of Monroe thought that the expertise of the pre-sentence report prepared by the probation department in his county obviated the need for the appointment of counsel at the sentencing stage. The Detroit Recorder's Court executive judge stated: "Even if he wants to plead guilty, we assign counsel . . . we believe that both assigned and retained counsel, should appear on sentencing, all sentencing, whether by conviction by trial or by plea." Appearance on sentencing, by both retained and assigned counsel, could be the subject of greater court insistence, however, and steps have been taken in recent months in this direction. The executive judge estimated that both assigned and retained counsel appear in about 50% of the sentences.

As to furnishing counsel for appeals and delayed appeals, the executive judges of both the Detroit Recorder's Court and the Wayne circuit court thought "this should be discretionary with the court, as it now is in our court," though most of the circuits usually do not provide counsel for this proceeding.

Very few of the judges provide counsel for hearings on revocation of probation. Both the Macomb and Wayne circuit judges interviewed noted that if questions of fact become important (in Detroit the question of "association" is frequently controverted) and cross-examination would serve a useful purpose, counsel might very well be appointed in such cases, though this has rarely been done anywhere in the state. The Wayne judge concluded that:

> [I]n nine out of ten of these matters of revocation, the defendant admits his guilt. The violation of probation has to be substantial however. A single instance of intoxication or being out after 12 at night is not substantial. But if these events occur continuously, and are associated with other acts or crimes—felonies or misdemeanors—we find a substantial violation of probation.

Most of the judges have been appointing counsel for high misdemeanors even before the *Gideon* case, but reservations are expressed as to whether this is constitutionally required or whether it is wise in policy, administration, or finance

361

TABLE 4
Opinions of Judges Re Counsel in Miscellaneous Cases*

Type of case or proceeding	Judges personally interviewed		Judges interrogated by mail who favored such appointments		Total in favor
	Favored such appointments	Now make such appointments	Single-county judicial circuits	Multiple-county judicial circuits	
Sentencing of defendant who has pleaded guilty	5	1	4	4	13
Sentencing of defendant convicted by trial	5	1	5	3	13
Habeas corpus or other postconviction remedy†	10	1	7	13	30
Hearing on revocation of probation	5	0	5	7	17
Sexual psychopath hearing	16	15	11	12	39
Misdemeanors‡	1	0	4	5	10
Civil commitment of the mentally ill§	16	4	8	10	34

* 16 judges were personally interviewed; 13 replied by mail from single-county judicial circuits and 14 from multiple-county circuits.
† Habeas corpus is not a postconviction remedy in Michigan (Mich. Stat. Ann. § 27A.4310). After the time for appeal has run (GCR 803.1), the postconviction remedy is an application for delayed appeal (GCR 806.4).
‡ Throughout this report, the unqualified word "misdemeanor" refers to misdemeanors punishable by not more than 90 days and/or $100 fine. "High" misdemeanors are, for purposes of this audit, treated as felonies.
§ This is a probate court proceeding.

to appoint counsel in less than high misdemeanor cases. Several judges expressed precise concern about the effect of a misdemeanor conviction on future employment by both government and private enterprise. A simple assault or larceny by an 18- or 19-year-old can have, they observed, a great bearing on his future. Several judges noted that a drunk motor law conviction, especially under the Michigan traffic-point system, with its impact on the driving privilege and livelihood, might constitute a crime "serious" enough under *Gideon* to merit appointment of counsel for an indigent defendant.

Of the judges interviewed, eight estimated that 60% of those who came before them in criminal cases were indigent, three estimated 50%, two 30%, one 25%, and two 20%. The percentage estimates of the judges did not correspond to the ratio of the number of counsel appointed to the number of felonies in their respective jurisdictions. The wide variance, however, in the number of accused felons who are deemed sufficiently indigent to qualify for appointed counsel does suggest that the criterion for the determination of indigency varies, or is disparately applied, or that the financial position of those who are accused in the counties audited differs widely. As shown in Table 2, the proportion of accused indigent felons who are accorded counsel varies from 39% in Detroit to 5% in Saginaw County. That this is not necessarily an urban-rural discrepancy is established by the fact that counsel are appointed in 39% of the cases in Detroit and in only 23% in Wayne County outside of Detroit, both areas being urban. In any event, the data elicited suggest that to provide equal justice further study is needed to ascertain whether (1) there are not in fact a larger number actually indigent for whom counsel ought to be appointed; (2) the number actually indigent is less variable between counties than suggested by this audit; and (3) the criteria or the application of criteria for determining indigency are as adequate and uniform as required by the equal protection clause. In this connection, the reader should consult Tables 12 to 14 below, reporting on the docket studies. These also show considerable variation among the counties in matters relating to indigency.

Considerable variance exists in the judges' estimates of the number of indigents who waive their right to appointed counsel, but it may be concluded that a large number waive their right. Two judges estimated 90% of those indigent waived their right to counsel, four stated 80%, two 75%, and one 60%. In sharp contrast, in the Detroit Recorder's Court, the executive judge stated: "It is very rare to have counsel waived. We think he is a crank if he does so." It has already been noted that counsel is appointed before felony pleas are accepted in Detroit, where felony is punishable by life imprisonment. In the Wayne circuit the executive judge stated:

> We inform the defendant as to his rights. If we accept the plea, counsel is waived. We do not have a breakdown of those who plead guilty who are indigent. Inquiry as to accepting the plea is thorough-going. If defendant has no record and pleads guilty to robbery armed, we do not accept his plea. This court will permit the withdrawal of a plea of guilty any time before sentence, and the plea or withdrawal of the plea cannot be commented upon. Also if the probationary report reflects lack of voluntariness of the plea, the court will set aside the plea of guilty upon its own motion.

In view of the presumption against the waiver of a constitutional right, unless there is a clear and unambiguous intent to waive, it would seem from the wide variation in the estimated percentages that there is some ambivalence in the matter of waiver that suggests the need for clarification.

Although most of the judges in the sample counties assigned counsel in accordance with an informal local court rule with discretion and with some recognition for out-of-pocket costs, a number do not proceed by court rule or fee schedule. In Saginaw County, the fees paid to assigned counsel are the recommended minimum fees of the county bar association for non-appointive counsel. The counties with a formal rule provide for a petition for extraordinary fees. Half of the judges, who use a fee schedule for appointed counsel that is less than the minimum fee schedule for private counsel, reported that they reimbursed counsel for reasonable and necessary out-of-pocket expenses. Typically, in Macomb County, Rule 10 provides: "$50 per day or fraction thereof for all court appearances and $35 per day, or fraction thereof, for all other services . . . A trial on the merits shall be compensated for at the rate of $100 per day in court for the first day and $50 per day for each day thereafter but not to exceed the total sum of $300." In Detroit, the executive judge described the local system: "$25 for the examination, $75 for a non-capital case; $150 for a capital case. Provision is likewise made for a petition for extraordinary fees, which petition is considered at our regular judges' meeting by the entire bench. In considering such petition, involving trials running into several days, a rule of thumb of $100 a day is used as a guide."

In counties that have a formal court rule, petitions for extraordinary fees are commonly granted. Wayne County requires a resumé of services performed filed in affidavit form, with the sworn statement, required by statute, that counsel "has not received or been promised from or by any source payment of any kind therefor."

Several sample counties reported that the matter of fees is within the discretion of the judge without the immediate aid of a formal court rule or minimum fee schedule.

Compensation of assigned counsel is further discussed in Section F below.

About half of the judges interviewed thought that appointed counsel had more experience and ability than retained counsel and about half thought the performance was equal. Almost the same ratio thought that the performance of assigned counsel compared favorably with that of prosecuting attorneys. A few judges noted, however, that assigned counsel were "less experienced as a rule." It was also remarked that "the prosecutor has considerable in his favor to begin with—investigations, experience, etc.; the appointed lawyer is handicapped by suspicion of his client, out-of-pocket costs, etc." Most seem to agree with the Wayne circuit judge's observations that "just as there are relatively less experienced criminal law counsel, there are relatively less experienced prosecutors. It boils down to the individual, his ability and his conscientiousness."

Among the 27 judges contacted by mail, 18 thought appointed lawyers were equal to retained lawyers, 4 thought appointed lawyers were better, 3 thought retained lawyers were better, and 2 did not answer. In comparing appointed counsel and the prosecuting attorney, 17 judges said they were equal, 8 said appointed counsel were better, and 2 said they were not as good. Most of the judges concurred that relatively few counsel ask to be excused, and that they generally do not call on those unavailable or not interested. Estimates of the percentage of declinations ranged from less than 1% to almost 10%. It would appear that some consideration should be given to the duty of the bar in this connection, though the urgency of this concern is small in view of the large number of lawyers willing to serve.

The judges appeared to be about equally divided between those who use the system of a roster of all attorneys admitted to practice and the judge's own list of names as the means of finding lawyers to appoint in criminal cases. Macomb County was typical of those using the roster method. Local rules state that "appointments shall be made in rotation from any alphabetical list of Macomb County Bar Association active members in good standing" and "any active member . . . may have his name placed upon this list upon making such request in writing to the presiding judge." Exceptions in the alphabetical rotation may be made for "reasons of expediency in trial" and "inexperienced counsel should not be assigned to cases carrying a life sentence." (Michigan has no capital punishment.)

The Detroit Recorder's Court executive judge's view summarizes the approach in Wayne County and Detroit:

> A bar association list of names was used some years back but this method is not used at present. It didn't work out during the war. Today, a judge's list is prepared from those names which counsel submit either by correspondence or by leaving their office cards with the clerk of that particular judge. Each judge compiles a list from names thus submitted and follows a rotation order in assignment. However, in unusual cases and in cases involving public interest, assignments are made after consultation among the several judges. The court tries to appoint more experienced counsel for the more serious cases.

The judges also universally depart from a strict rotation system not only because of inexperience, but also for reasons of age, infirmity, availability, and conflict of interest. In actual practice, however, many assignments have gone to the younger lawyers, though this practice has been altered somewhat; recently courts have been appointing leading civil lawyers to represent indigents in serious criminal cases. In several of the circuits, for example, the president of the local bar association has been appointed in capital cases. However, judges frequently noted that the zeal, energy, and time devoted by younger counsel in part compensated for lack of experience in redressing the inherent imbalance between the state and the accused. In most counties it is quite difficult to obtain information about cases in which counsel has been assigned since the counties keep no records of the docket numbers of such cases.

The judges employ a number of criteria in determining eligibility for the appointment of counsel, though there is a noticeable reluctance on the part of some to appoint counsel if the accused is out on bond. The most important criteria, in the order of importance, are: (1) salary or wages of the accused; (2) ownership of real property; (3) ownership of stocks, bonds, and bank accounts; (4) ownership of an automobile; and (5) pensions, social security, and unemployment compensation. The judges were almost evenly divided on the question of taking into account the financial resources of parents, spouse, or other relatives; in the mail poll of 27 circuits, the judges of 4 circuits would refuse to appoint counsel if the financial resources of such relatives were adequate. Eight would not appoint if the accused was out on bail, and six if he owned an automobile. In the Wayne circuit "it depends on the market value of the auto, whether it is needed for work, whether the equity is sufficient. We do not use a specific standard for determining indigency. It depends on take-home pay, dependents, obligations. This court employs a rule of fairness or equity rather than a mechanical arithmetic rule." In Detroit and Wayne County, and in the majority of circuits, the fact that the accused is out on bail is one and not the dispositive factor to be taken into account in determining eligibility for the appointment of counsel. The estimated incidence of defendents on bail being provided with counsel per year ranges from "none" or "very rare" to "20 to 25%." The Detroit Recorder's Court executive judge stated: "Suppose the defendant makes bail to keep his job. The court may still appoint counsel. The main question is—does defendant have the resources to finance private counsel?"

Most judges seemed indisposed toward requiring a moderate fee to be paid by defendants to whom counsel had been assigned. The reason most frequently given for this was that such a requirement would place an additional administrative burden on the court without commensurate advantage to the taxpayer. At present, a guilty defendant is normally required to pay, as one component of his sentence even when probation is ordered, a sum described as "court costs," which includes the cost of providing counsel and goes into the general fund of the county. Moreover, when it is ascertained that the defendant does have the requisite funds to pay retained counsel, the court will cause the defendant to pay that sum to the county or to his assigned counsel and thus eliminate the expense to the county. In no case may assigned counsel receive pay from both the county and the accused. Many judges asked: "What is the capacity to pay a moderate fee? What is 'moderate' in relation to indigency?"

D. OPINIONS OF THE PROSECUTING ATTORNEYS

Interviews were held with prosecuting attorneys in the seven sample counties. In addition, mail questionnaires were sent to the other 76 prosecutors in the state, and 51 responded (67%).

The prosecutors were asked the following questions: (a) "Under an ideal system, at what stage in a criminal case do you think a lawyer should first be made available to the indigent person?" (b) "Do you think it is unfair to the indigent person if he does not get a lawyer at this stage?" (c) "Do you think that such a system could be financed?" Answers of those responding by mail are reflected in Table 5.

Of the 51 respondents, 26 felt that ideally counsel should be made available at least as early as the first appearance before a magistrate, and only 9 (18%) felt that a lawyer should first be made available after the filing of an information. One would probably expect that a large percentage of those who believed counsel should be provided at later stages would feel it was unfair if counsel was not

TABLE 5
Opinions of Prosecutors as to First Appointment of Counsel

Stage counsel should be provided	No. of replies	Unfair if not provided at that stage?				Could such a system be financed?			
		Yes	No	Depends or maybe	No answer	Yes	No*	Depends or maybe	No answer
1. Between arrest and first appearance before a magistrate	14	10	4	0	0	10	2	2	0
2. At first appearance before a magistrate	12	5	5	1	1	7	1	2†	2
3. Between first appearance and preliminary hearing	10	2	6	1	1	6	4	0	0
4. At preliminary hearing	6	3	2	1	0	5	0	1	0
5. After preliminary hearing but before filing of information	0	0	0	0	0	0	0	0	0
6. After filing of an information but before arraignment thereon	2	1	0	1	0	0	0	2†	0
7. At arraignment on information	3	0	2	1	0	2	0	0	1
8. After arraignment on information	1	0	1	0	0	0	0	0	1
9. At trial	0	0	0	0	0	0	0	0	0
10. Other	3	1	2	0	0	1	0	1†	1

* With the exception of two replies indicating an unqualified "no" answer to stage 3, all responses indicated a possibility of financing with a change in county support or a change in the present financial set-up.
† One respondent said it could be done, but at tremendous cost to the taxpayer.

provided at the stage selected; however, the table shows the opposite result. In any event, 20 of the 51 prosecutors believed it would be unfair if the defendant did not get a lawyer by the preliminary hearing or earlier; and 10 felt it would be unfair if he did not obtain a lawyer at the first appearance.

Substantially the same question was asked prosecutors who were interviewed. They chose five different stages. Three selected stage 3 (between first appearance and preliminary hearing); one selected stage 1 (between arrest and first appearance before a magistrate); one stage 2 (at first appearance before a magistrate); one stage 4 (at preliminary hearing); and one stage 7 (at arraignment on indictment or information).

The mail questionnaires also contained a question asking whether, under an ideal system, a lawyer should be provided for an indigent person in certain kinds of cases and proceedings. Answers of those responding are presented in the following table:

TABLE 6
Opinions of Prosecutors as to Miscellaneous Cases

Case or proceeding	Under an ideal system do you think a lawyer should be made available to the indigent person in the following kinds of cases and proceedings?				Do you think it is unfair to the indigent person if he does not have a lawyer for such cases and proceedings?			
	Yes	No	"Depends," "on request," etc.	No answer	Yes	No	"Depends," "on request," etc.	No answer
Sentencing of a defendant who pleaded guilty	13	32	2	4	9	31	6	5
Sentencing of a defendant convicted by trial	16	28	1	6	9	28	5	9
Habeas corpus, coram nobis, or other postconviction remedy	31	13	3	4	23	13	6	9
Hearing on revocation of probation	20	25	2	4	13	23	5	10
Sexual psychopath hearing	41	7	1	2	32	7	5	7
Misdemeanors	14*	28	2	7	9*	23	7†	12
Civil commitment of the mentally ill, including alcoholics and narcotics addicts	30	15	5	1	25	15	5	6

* One prosecutor said "High misdemeanor only."
† One prosecutor said "Yes, excluding traffic offenses."

The table reveals that there were large numbers of prosecutors who felt that it was unfair if an indigent did not obtain counsel at a sexual psychopath hearing. Some of them mentioned the gravity of the sentence, as referred to above in Section C. It was also the consensus that it would be unfair to an indigent if he did not have a lawyer for civil commitment of the mentally ill, including alcoholics and narcotics addicts, and for postconviction relief.

In response to a question about whether they thought it possible to finance a system to provide counsel in these kinds of cases and proceedings, approximately 49% said "yes"; 15% said "no"; 22% gave answers such as "yes, but at tremendous cost to the taxpayer," "maybe," "depends," "very difficult," or "doubtful"; and 14% gave no answer or did not know. A number recommended using proceeds from fines to finance such a system.

The prosecutors who were interviewed were also asked the same questions. All seven said that under an ideal system counsel should be provided for a sexual psychopath hearing, but they were split on whether counsel should be provided for other types of proceedings. They voted five to one for providing counsel in civil commitment proceedings, but four to three against providing counsel in misdemeanors and five to two against providing counsel in all other proceedings.

The prosecutors were asked what percentage of felony defendants in their jurisdiction were indigent. Their estimates ranged from 3% to 85%. Almost half estimated from 5% to 30%, but as many as a fifth estimated 60% or over. Another question was: "Of those felony defendants who are indigent, what percentage waive appointment of a lawyer to represent them?" Here the variance in answers was even more striking—from none in some counties to 99% in others. Over half of those responding by mail estimated that over 50% waived counsel. One outstate prosecutor replying by mail made this observation:

> I am amazed at how many accused refuse a lawyer's services when they are practically pressed on them free of charge. I conclude that the setting for the inquiry, which is at arraignment in circuit court, must be responsible for this bizarre performance. I believe that the probation officer or some such neutral figure should have the job of contacting each felony defendant and person lodged in jail awaiting trial or preliminary hearing to find out whether the man can afford counsel and whether he wishes counsel. His report should dispose of the present doubts.

In some jurisdictions, counsel is provided at certain stages of the proceedings if the defendant asks for one, but waived if he does not. It is apparent that more attention has to be directed to how, by whom, and under what circumstances the right to counsel is brought to the attention of these defendants.

Prosecutors were also asked their opinion concerning the tests the courts use in determining whether a defendant is indigent. Six out of the 7 prosecutors interviewed and 34 of the 51 returning mail questionnaires believed the present system was "about right." Twelve of those responding by mail thought the system was "too lenient," one thought it was "too strict," one said "it depends upon the judge," and three did not answer the question. The Wayne prosecutor made the following comment:

> I have heard some criticism that courts are too lenient in the determination of indigency, and will assign counsel upon a defendant's bare representation without making further

inquiry. I do not know whether this is fact. However, I would prefer that the courts give the defendant the benefit of any doubt, and it is perhaps preferable to allow the courts to be as lenient as they feel inclined to be. The presence of counsel facilitates the work of the prosecuting attorney. It prevents doing the same thing twice and the record is more sound for appeal purposes.

One prosecutor thought that juries are more sympathetic to accused who try their cases in pro per. Many, however, underscored their belief that fairness and finality are desirably advanced with the presence of counsel.

Equally noteworthy is the disposition of the prosecuting attorneys to the notion that discovery procedures promote the administration of justice. The Monroe prosecuting attorney was of the view that "the law gives the defendant the right to the entire file of the prosecutor and we do what the law says." Like the majority of the prosecutors interviewed, he felt that such permitted discovery resulted in a larger number of soundly based guilty pleas and a much smaller number of trials, thereby reducing costs to the taxpayer. One prosecutor, however, stated: "I tell defense counsel absolutely nothing unless and only to the extent that, I am required to tell him anything. The only exception is where I am trying to encourage a plea by showing that the case is absolutely hopeless from a defense standpoint." Midway between the two views is the Wayne prosecutor who concluded:

> I have promulgated a liberal policy in keeping with the opinions of the appellate courts, which gives defense counsel access to much of the prosecution's evidence. There is no hard and fast distinction as between those matters which are disclosed and those which are not. The distinction is based upon the individual case. Considerations of public policy and safety of witnesses sometimes requires that matters be not fully disclosed, when the danger of disclosure is considerably greater than the questionable benefit to be derived by the defense. It is my feeling that a liberal policy will obviate the necessity of trying many criminal cases, for the reason that when the facts supported by the disclosure of the formal statement are fully disclosed to the defense counsel, he may try to effect a plea without the necessity of trial.

A substantial number of all prosecutors surveyed believed that the present rates of compensation to lawyers for their services to indigent persons were inadequate. Although 5 of the 7 interviewees felt that the rates were adequate, of those giving unqualified "yes" and "no" answers to the mail questionnaires, a 24 to 19 majority indicated they were inadequate. A clear majority of those answering felt that counsel should be reimbursed for out-of-pocket expenses for investigation and preparation.

The prosecutors were also asked how they thought assigned counsel compared in experience and ability with retained counsel. Their answers are reflected in Table 7.

The prosecutors were asked to offer suggestions on how, in their judgment, the present system for providing counsel to indigent defendants might be improved. Among the answers were the following:

1. Pay assigned counsel more or they are likely to plead the defendant guilty.

2. The defendant should be given his choice of counsel and the state should pay adequate expenses so that the best lawyers will defend him.

3. All lawyers who have ever handled criminal cases should be appointed, not just young lawyers.

TABLE 7
Prosecutors' Opinions About Assigned and Retained Counsel

	Those responding by mail	Those interviewed
They are the same, just as good, or compare favorably	30	4
Retained counsel are better	7	0
Assigned counsel are better	2	0
Assigned counsel are as good, and sometimes better	3	2
Assigned counsel are as energetic or as good, but less experienced	3	0
Assigned counsel do their best, but devote less time	3	0
It depends upon the person	1	1
No answer	2	0
Total	51	7

4. Make sure the judge appoints qualified counsel instead of his favorites. Have the bar association provide him with an approved list.

5. If there were less vigor in defending persons obviously guilty, then I believe those who really needed counsel would be more adequately represented.

6. No person should arbitrarily be assigned a lawyer. After being instructed as to his right by the judge, a defendant should be allowed to accept or reject counsel.

7. If counsel are not provided for misdemeanors, then a statute should be enacted expunging the record.

A number of prosecutors recommended instituting the public defender system, although others explicitly stated that the public defender is not the answer.

E. OPINIONS OF THE DEFENSE ATTORNEYS

This portion of the survey report is based upon interviews in the four outstate Michigan counties with individual defense counsel, either known to the reporters for their abilities and accuracy, or recommended by the prosecuting attorney or one of the circuit judges, together with responses to mail questionnaires to attorneys in 1962 in Kent, Livingston, Saginaw, and Wayne Counties. In the outstate counties, 18 out of 32 attorneys responded, in Wayne, 24 out of 51.

Tables 8 and 9 show fees paid to assigned and retained counsel.

Ingham County paid $7980 for assigned counsel fees in 1962, which was estimated to be the equivalent of $20,000 paid to retained counsel. For the other counties, the corresponding figures are: Kent, $7345 and $20,000; Livingston, $1710 estimated and $3500; Saginaw, $2945 and $4500.

One of the reporters had previously made other surveys in this state covering the compensation of assigned counsel,[24] with the results shown in Table 10 (using the same classifications as above).

TABLE 8
Fees Paid to Assigned Counsel

County	1. Consultation and plea of guilty to crime charged	2. Consultation and representation at preliminary examination, etc., ending in disposal without trial	3. Same as 2 and trial lasting one day or less	4. Same as 2 and trial lasting two days or more
Ingham	$50	$75	$125	$225
Kent	35	75	125	200
Livingston	50	75	150	225
Saginaw	100	150	250	400
Average	$59	$94	$162	$262

TABLE 9
Normal Fee to Retained Counsel

County	1. Consultation and plea of guilty to crime charged	2. Consultation and representation at preliminary examination, etc., ending in disposal without trial	3. Same as 2 and trial lasting one day or less	4. Same as 2 and trial lasting two days or more
Ingham	$100	$250	$350	$500
Kent	100	200	350	500
Livingston	100	200	300	400
Saginaw	150	250	400	550
Average	$112	$225	$350	$488

TABLE 10
Compensation for Assigned Counsel, Single County Judicial Circuits, 1961

	1.	2.	3.	4.
High	$50	$100	$125	$500
Low	25	50	50	100
Median	50	75	100	150

These are standard fees in the various counties. The high figure is the maximum standard fee in any county, and the low figure is the minimum standard fee. In multiple-county judicial circuits, the corresponding medians were $35, $50, $100, and $100, for situations 1 through 4.

For 1962, the comparable figures were:

TABLE 11

Compensation for Assigned Counsel, Single County Judicial Circuits, 1962

	1.	2.	3.	4.
High	$100	$100	$300	$300
Low	25	35	60	100
Median	50	75	125	175

Figures for multiple-county judicial circuits in the year 1962 are not yet available. The single largest fee allowed in 1962 was $2500, and the next largest were $2206, $800, $750, $700, and $661. Thereafter no fees exceeded $500. If all counties are ranked according to the average fee paid in each county, the median county paid $118 in 1962, up from $99 in 1961. The Recorder's Court of Detroit pays more per year in assigned counsel fees than all of the outstate circuit courts combined. The average fee paid by the Recorder's Court in 1961 was $99, which was the same as the median outstate county.

Of the 42 attorneys responding to the mail questionnaire, all but one had been appointed to serve as counsel for an indigent person in a trial court in 1962. None of the lawyers represented indigents for appeals or postconviction remedies such as a delayed motion for new trial. The majority of the Wayne County attorneys had considerable experience, while those outstate had less. Of the 24 lawyers reporting from Wayne, 18 had handled 50 or more criminal cases before their first case in 1962, and only 2 lawyers had handled less than 5 cases. Outstate, however, 2 lawyers had had no previous criminal experience, 4 had handled 1 to 4 cases, 3 had handled 5 to 9 cases, and only one had handled 50 cases or more. Of the Wayne County lawyers, 9 had been admitted to practice for 6 to 14 years and 11 for 15 years or longer; only 3 had been admitted for 5 years or less. Of the 18 outstate lawyers, 7 had been admitted for 6 to 14 years, 2 for 15 years or longer, and 9 for 5 years or less.

Although all the lawyers received compensation for their services, or expected to, 18 of them reported that they were not repaid for out-of-pocket expenses, 3 said they were paid in part, and only 12 said they were paid in full.

The lawyers were asked: "Is the system fair to the indigent persons?" In reply, 25 said "yes," 13 said "no," and 2 said "usually" or gave a similar qualified answer. On this question, the outstate lawyers voted "yes" by 16 to 1, while the Wayne lawyers voted "no" or gave a qualified answer by 14 to 9. The next question was: "Is the system fair to the lawyers?" On this 16 lawyers said "yes," 19 said "no," and 2 gave a qualified "yes." Again, the outstate lawyers voted "yes" by 10 to 7, while the Wayne lawyers voted "no" or gave a qualified "yes" by 14 to 6.

On the question of what changes, if any, they would recommend, the most popular recommendations were to pay lawyers more for their services (23 votes), pay out-of-pocket expenses (20 votes), provide counsel in additional kinds of cases, such as serious misdemeanors (20 votes), and improve the system for selecting assigned counsel (13 votes). On the last point, it seems generally agreed that a slightly more formalized, and certainly more uniform, system of selecting counsel could be used advantageously, except, of course, in the smallest counties. Six lawyers from Wayne County and one from Saginaw complained specifically of favoritism in appointments. On the matter of fees, it appears to be generally agreed that not only should the fees be raised, but there should be some well-understood minimum fee paid in each case.

F. COMPARISONS AMONG JUDGES, PROSECUTING ATTORNEYS, AND DEFENSE COUNSEL

Perhaps the most remarkable thing is that prosecuting attorneys, defense counsel, and the judges are all in general agreement about the operation of the assigned counsel system. The judges and the prosecuting attorneys were not in disagreement with any of the recommendations of assigned counsel, though, as noted previously, some of the judges do not feel that they can reimburse counsel for out-of-pocket expenses, however reasonable or necessary. Though the estimates with regard to percentage of indigency vary as between judges and prosecutors, they also vary within each group. The judges were generally more inclined to favor earlier appointment of counsel. Those who were, however, were unanimous in the viewpoint that failure to follow such an ideal standard would not constitute unfairness. Much of the discussion about the point in time at which counsel should be appointed under an ideal system was rendered moot by Act. No. 132 of the Public Act No. 132 of 1963, quoted in Section B above. This act provided, for the first time, for the appointment of counsel prior to arraignment on the information. The act was drafted by a prosecuting attorney and introduced in the legislature at his behest.

G. DOCKET STUDIES

Docket studies were made for the year 1962 in four counties: Kent, Livingston, Macomb, and Wayne. In Kent the results were tabulated separately for the circuit court and the Superior Court of Grand Rapids. In Wayne the same applies for the circuit court and the Recorder's Court. Results of the study are shown in the following tables. If data were unobtainable for more than 20% of the cases in the sample for a county, it is omitted. In tables where both a number and a percentage are given, the percentage refers to the number of cases for which data were available. The last column to the right shows the number of cases for which no data were available, and the percentage here refers to the total sample.

Table 12 shows that the proportion of defendants who had counsel ranged from 33% in the Superior Court of Grand Rapids to 98% in the Recorder's Court of Detroit. The proportion of defendants who had retained counsel varied from 11% in Livingston County to 50% in Wayne circuit court.

The proportion of the defendants found to be indigent is shown in Table 13. This proportion ranged from 15% in the Superior Court of Grand Rapids to 58% in the Recorder's Court of Detroit. Table 14 shows that the proportion of defendants not released on bail varied from 36% in Macomb County to 68% in Livingston.

TABLE 12
Retained and Assigned Counsel in Felonies
Michigan, 1962

County	Total sample	Did defendant have counsel?				Retained		Assigned		Combination or type unknown		No data*	
		Yes No.	%	No No.	%	No.	%	No.	%	No.	%	No.	%
Livingston	19	11	58	8	42	2	11	8	42	1	5	0	0
Kent (C)	20	11	55	9	45	7	35	4	20	0	0	0	0
Kent (S)	60	20	33	40	67	9	15	10	17	1	2	0	0
Wayne (R)	188	183	98	3	2	83	45	76	41	24	7	2	1
Wayne (C)	43	29	77	9†	23	19	50	7	18	3	8	5	12
Macomb	74	53	72	21	28	35	47	14	19	4	5	0	0
Weighted total percentages			74		26		36		31		4		2

(C) means circuit court.
(S) means Superior Court of Grand Rapids.
(R) means Recorder's Court of Detroit.
* % of no data refers to total sample; % in other columns refers to cases for which data were available.
† One defendant waived counsel.

375

TABLE 13
Was Felony Defendant Determined Indigent?
Michigan, 1962

County	Total sample	Yes No.	%	No No.	%	No data* No.	%
Livingston	19	8	44	10	56	1	5
Kent (C)	20	4	20	16	80	0	0
Kent (S)	60	9	15	50	85	1	2
Wayne (R)	188	106	58	77	42	5	3
Weighted total percentages			40		60		8

(C) means circuit court.
(S) means Superior Court of Grand Rapids.
(R) means Recorder's Court of Detroit.
* % of no data refers to total sample; % in other columns refers to cases for which data were available.

TABLE 14
Frequency of Release on Bail of Felony Defendants
Michigan, 1962

County	Total sample	Yes No.	%	No No.	%	No data* No.	%
Livingston	19	6	31	13	68	0	0
Kent (C)	20	9	45	11	55	0	0
Kent (S)	60	29	49	30	51	1	2
Wayne (R)	188	97	52	91	48	0	0
Wayne (C)	43	25	64	14	36	4	9
Macomb	74	74	47	26	36	1	1
Weighted total percentages			51		49		1

(C) means circuit court.
(S) means Superior Court of Grand Rapids.
(R) means Recorder's Court of Detroit.
* % of no data refers to total sample; % in other columns refers to cases for which data were available.

Table 15 shows the frequency of preliminary hearings. They were held in relatively few cases, the lowest figure being 17% in the Superior Court of Grand Rapids and the highest 46% in Macomb County. Waivers ran from a high of 83% in Grand Rapids to a low of 48% in Wayne circuit court. In a few cases the preliminary hearing results in a dismissal without the filing of an information. Such cases were excluded from the docket survey; hence the figures in Table 15 slightly understate the incidence of preliminary hearings.

Table 16 shows the final dispositions of the cases in the docket study. Although the great majority of all defendants pleaded guilty, in Wayne County the

TABLE 15
Frequency of Preliminary Hearings in Felonies
Michigan, 1962

County	Total sample	Yes No.	%	No, waiver No.	%	No, not used in this kind of case No.	%	No, reason unknown No.	%	No data° No.	%
Livingston	19	5	26	13	68	1	5	0	0	0	0
Kent (C)	20	5	25	14	70	0	0	1	5	0	0
Kent (S)	60	10	17	48	83	0	0	0	0	2	3
Wayne (R)	188	42	22	146	78	0	0	0	0	0	0
Wayne (C)	43	7	18	19	48	12	30	2	5	3	7
Macomb	74	33	45	41	55	0	0	0	0	0	0
Weighted total percentages			25		70		4		1		1

(C) means circuit court.
(S) means Superior Court of Grand Rapids.
(R) means Recorder's Court of Detroit.
° % of no data refers to total sample; % in other columns refers to cases for which data were available.

TABLE 16
Dispositions in Felony Cases
Michigan, 1962

County	Total sample	Plea guilty	Plea lesser offense	Dis- missed	Found guilty	Found guilty lesser degree	Ac- quit- ted	Mental com- mit- ment	Pend- ing	Other
Livingston	19	11	2	4	2	0	0	0	0	0
Kent (C)	20	14	2	1	2	0	1	0	0	0
Kent (S)	60	42	7	6	1	1	0	1	2	0
Wayne (R)	188	19	113	19	15	9	9	2	0	2
Wayne (C)	43	9	19	5	1	0	1	0	4	4
Macomb	74	30	13	5	20	0	4	0	0	2
Weighted total percentages		36	35	11	9	2	3	0	2	1

(C) means circuit court.
(S) means Superior Court of Grand Rapids.
(R) means Recorder's Court of Detroit.

majority pleaded to a lesser offense while in the other counties they pleaded to the original offense. Macomb had the highest proportion of trials. Table 17 shows the sentence imposed on those who pleaded guilty or were convicted. The proportion sent to prison varied from 22% in Macomb County to 70% in Kent circuit court.

TABLE 17
Sentencing in Felony Cases
Michigan, 1962*

County	Total sample	No sentence No.	%	Prison No.	%	Pro- bation No.	%	Sus- pended sen- tence No.	%	Fine No.	%	Sen- tence pend- ing No.	%
Livingston	19	5	26	5	26	7	37	0	0	1	5	0	0
Kent (C)	20	2	10	14	70	3	15	0	0	4	20	1	5
Kent (S)	60	9	15	25	42	22	28	0	0	8	13	1	2
Wayne (R)	188	31	16	91	48	70	37	3	2	7	4	0	0
Wayne (C)	43	14	33	14	33	13	30	1	2	7	16	0	0
Macomb	74	23	32	16	22	37	50	0	0	2	3	0	0
Weighted total percentages			21		42		35		9		9		1

(C) means circuit court.
(S) means Superior Court of Grand Rapids.
(R) means Recorder's Court of Detroit.
* If a sentence was any combination of prison, probation, suspended sentence (without probation), and fine, it is recorded under each of these columns.

H. CONCLUSIONS AND RECOMMENDATIONS

On the basis of the field investigation and the foregoing report, the following conclusions and recommendations are submitted:

1. In the interest of equal justice under the law and equal protection of the law, the assigned counsel system should be strengthened at least in the following particulars:

a. General Court Rule 785 should be amended to provide for discovery in criminal cases, including but not limited to:

(i) all statements or confessions made by the defendant;

(ii) all reports and results of all tests or examinations of a scientific or technical nature, including all medical, mental, post-mortem, bacteriological, toxicological, chemical, ballistic, metallurgical, electronic, or radiological tests or examinations;

(iii) all statements or confessions made by res gestae witnesses relating facts, knowledge, intelligence, observations (or non-observations), acquired or obtained during the res gestae.

The terms "statement," "confession," "report," and "result" should apply equally to oral statements, written (signed or unsigned) statements, confessions, reports, and results, regardless of whether acknowledged or executed under oath, and all transcripts, recordings, or other accurate records thereof. Discovery to the extent here advocated is presently allowed in federal district courts and the trial courts of certain states, notably California. The rule would thus be changed to match the actual practice and procedure of most of the experienced prosecuting attorneys in the more populous counties.

b. Appropriate consideration should be given to providing adequate investigative assistance at public expense for the purpose of assisting assigned counsel in the preparation of an effective defense of indigent defendants.

c. The State Bar, the Institute for Continuing Legal Education, the attorney general, the Judicial Conference, the law schools, and any other appropriate agency should be encouraged to undertake and provide more adequate, precise, and regular training for defense counsel and prosecuting attorneys and prosecuting attorneys-elect in criminal law and procedure including trials.

d. The state and local bar associations, in the light of the expansion of the right to counsel and to equal protection, which will enlarge the responsibilities of the bar for equal justice under law, should reappraise the adequacy of court rules and minimum schedules as to fees for assigned counsel. The bar ought to study also whether the increased costs of representation ought to be borne wholly or in part by the practicing bar, or by some appropriate insurance structure as part of its proper contribution to the public good. The statute presently requires "reasonable compensation for services performed." (Mich. Stat. Ann. § 28.1253.) In view of the disparity between "reasonable compensation" as presently allowed to assigned counsel and the provisions of bar association recommended minimum fee schedules disclosed by this study, the need for reappraisal of the adequacy of fees for assigned counsel is underscored. Whatever is done about the adequacy of fees, more attention should certainly be accorded the reimbursement of counsel for out-of-pocket expenses over and above office overhead. The opportunity should be created for assigned counsel to petition the court in advance for expert witnesses and the hiring of investigative or expert assistance. Assigned counsel should be required to submit, at the time of application for his fee, an itemized statement of the time, date, and amount of services performed, and the expenses incurred, and such expenses should be paid in addition to the fee. In order to clearly provide the statutory authority for out-of-pocket expenses, the appropriate amendment should be made to the Code of Criminal Procedure. (Act 175 of 1927.)

e. In the more populated areas of the state, the Michigan Supreme Court should appoint one or more lawyers as assigned counsel administrative officers, who would assist the judges in making assignments, assist in maintaining the list of attorneys to be assigned, make any necessary investigations of indigency, assist in settling fees and expenses of assigned counsel, and make themselves available to advise and assist assigned counsel who are inexperienced in trying criminal cases.

2. General Court Rule 785 should be amended by placing an obligation upon the court in two respects: (1) to make clear to the accused that any appointment of counsel will be at public expense and not at his expense; and (2) to advise the accused of the nature of the accusation against him and of the consequence of his plea prior to permitting any plea to be taken. These recommendations would change the rules to conform to the actual practice in most of the circuits. More particularly, Rule 785.3 (1) should be amended to read as follows:

(1) Arraignment. lf the accused is not represented by counsel upon arraignment, before he is permitted to plead, the court shall *inform the accused of the nature of the accusation and of the maximum penalties possible upon conviction,* and shall advise the accused that he is entitled to a trial by jury and to have *the assistance of* counsel, and that in case he is financially unable to provide the counsel, the court will, if *the* accused so requests appoint counsel for him, *at public expense . . .*" (Additional and amending language is italicized.)

3. General Court Rule ᐧ785 should be amended to cover all felonies and all misdemeanors punishable by confinement or imprisonment for one year or more. This is in accord with the present practice of most of the circuits, particularly since the adoption of Public Act No. 132 of 1963, Mich. Stat. Ann. § 28.1253, C.L. of 1948, § 775.16.

4. The Supreme Court, in the exercise of its power of general superintending control, should promulgate a court rule substantially in accord with the provision of Rule 5 (a) of the Federal Rules of Criminal Procedure providing for prompt arraignment ("without unreasonable delay"). Such a rule would require no more than what the court has required, as a matter of due process, in *People v. Hamilton* and *People v. McCager.*[25] Prompt arraignment would bring about an earlier judicial recognition of the right and need for counsel.

5. In view of Article I, Section 20, of the Michigan Constitution of 1963 providing for an appeal in a criminal case as a matter of right, and such decisions as *Griffin v. Illinois,* 351 U.S. 12 (1955), and *Draper v. Washington,* 372 U.S. 487 (1963), requiring that the accused in an appeal as of right from a conviction in a state court be furnished with sufficient transcript to enable him to properly prosecute an appeal, the Michigan Code of Criminal Procedure should be amended to provide for the furnishing at public expense of a sufficient transcript to enable an indigent to properly prosecute his first appeal.

6. The Code of Criminal Procedure should be amended to provide for appointment of counsel for indigent persons accused of being criminal sexual psychopaths to the same extent and in the same manner as in the case of felonies. The lack of present clear authority to make such appointments is a matter of considerable concern to many circuit judges, and such an amendment would serve an immediate useful purpose.

7. The study has revealed a substantial disparity between the estimates of the extent of indigency among felony defendants and the actual number of counsel assigned to defend them. The fact that in some counties the ratio of estimated indigents to the number of actual appointments reaches eight to one should support the recommendation that further study be undertaken of the actual extent to which counsel are assigned for the defense of indigent persons accused of crime.

8. Quarterly reports made to the court administrator by the circuit and other courts should include more adequate data with which to appraise the operation of the assigned counsel system, including data on the number and name of counsel assigned, the docket number of cases or proceeding in which assignments are made, the compensation and expenses paid, and other pertinent data.

9. A suitable form of written exposition of the rights of an accused, including the right to counsel, should be prepared for distribution through magistrates and

other courts and local bar associations, as is presently done in a few municipal courts.

10. Consideration should be given to revising Canon 5 of the American Bar Association Canons of Professional Ethics to recognize a greater duty of the bar in criminal cases than heretofore.

I. SUPPLEMENTAL RECOMMENDATIONS

[Editor's note: the reporters later submitted the following supplemental recommendations, with an explanation that the associate state committee concurred in all except No. 2, from which one member of the committee dissented.]

1. The appointment of counsel for the defense of an indigent person accused of crime should constitute an appointment not only for proceedings in inferior courts and proceedings in the trial court but also for the preparation of post-trial motions in the trial court, including motions for a new trial and claims of appeal as a matter of right.[26]

The purpose of this recommendation is to insure that the attorney handling the appellate proceedings, in at least the initial stages of the appeal, be the attorney who has tried the case. The rule in the *Hardy, Griffin, Douglas, Draper,* and *Lane* cases would seem to require that a complete transcript of the entire case be furnished where the counsel preparing the motion for a new trial or claim of appeal is not the trial counsel. This is because counsel who did rot represent the defendant at the trial would have no way of knowing where there might be a substantial error in the proceedings. Trial counsel, however, would already know where any error is likely to be found and thus would only need to request transcripts of certain portions of the proceedings. This rule would therefore serve two simultaneous purposes: to provide effective counsel for appeal and to reasonably reduce transcript costs.

2. In every appeal from a criminal conviction in a court of record counsel for the appellant, as a condition of the filing of the appeal, should be required to certify, as an officer of the court, that in his best professional judgment, every portion of the trial transcript ordered is necessary for the effective preparation and prosecution of the appeal.

It is desirable to limit the transcripts in criminal cases to those portions which are actually necessary for the effective preparation and prosecution of the appeal. Such certifications would increase the consciousness of counsel as to the need for only those sections of the transcript material and relevant to the appeal.

3. Counsel for the defendant should be permitted to file his claim for services rendered and necessary expenses incurred in inferior courts and the trial court, and such claim should be allowed and paid prior to receipt of the transcript or the commencement of work on the brief and appendix.

Since the level of compensation paid for the services of assigned counsel is ordinarily far below the level of compensation which an attorney might ordinarily expect to receive from any other client, the attorney who files a claim of appeal should not have to wait for the completion of the appellate process before receiving his fee.

4. Where a claim of appeal as of right has been filed, the trial court should, at the same time that the fees and expenses are allowed for the services and expenses of counsel in inferior courts and the trial court, appoint counsel to continue the appeal. Unless the cause of justice requires otherwise, the court should ordinarily reappoint the trial counsel for the purpose of continuing the case on appeal.

The reason for this proposal is contained in the remarks following supplemental proposal No. 2.

5. Fees and expenses of counsel representing defendant on appeal should be allowed in the court to which the appeal is taken. (At present, this is the Supreme Court, but, upon implementation of the court of appeals provisions in the constitution of 1963, this will be the court of appeals or possibly the court of appeals and the Supreme Court.)

The principle inherent in this rule is that the court before whom the case is heard is best qualified to evaluate the fees and expenses for the services rendered.

6. The provisions of the Michigan Code of Criminal Procedure should be amended to make it clear that the defendant has a right to a transcript on appeal, and, at the same time, it should be made clear which government body is obliged to bear the expense of the transcript.

At present there is no statutory authority for the payment of this sum of money.

7. Fees of appointed counsel on appeals to the Supreme Court or to the court of appeals ought to be allowed and paid out of the treasury.

At present, this expense must be borne by the county. This proposal would leave the expense in the trial court, including all postconviction motions in the trial court, on the county, but would transfer the burden to the state as a whole as to the actual services of the attorney in the appellate court (including preparation of the briefs and appendix). At the present time, one or two appeals from a smaller county could more than wipe out the amount budgeted for the county for all cases for the year. At present, the state pays all of the attorney fees and expenses of appointed counsel in cases in which the accused is charged of the commission of a felony within a state prison. This includes not only the expenses at trial, but also the expense on appeal. This provision would not be changed.

8. In view of recent Supreme Court rulings, counsel should be encouraged, on every appeal taken as a matter of right, to include all possible allegations of error, subject to the limitations of the canons of ethics.

In view of recent decisions holding that a defendant may not be barred from repeated appeals, unless the ground for appeal alleged in a subsequent appeal is the same as one of the grounds alleged and argued in a previous appeal, it becomes necessary, if we are to have any finality to our judicial process, to require that all possible errors be urged or expressly waived at the time of the first appeal. The constitutional right is to *an* appeal and it should be as effective and complete as possible.

9. The Michigan Court Rules should be amended to require the judge, after imposition of sentence, to advise the respondent of his postconviction rights. The following form is suggested for use by the judge:

Appeal from this conviction is a right guaranteed you by the constitution of this state. As an incident of this right the state will supply you with counsel at public expense to prepare and prosecute the appeal if you are financially unable to employ such counsel. This right to appeal must be experienced within 60 days of this date, or the appeal of right may be lost. Do you understand this?

The transcript of the foregoing, including the defendant's answer, should be transcribed, the original made a part of the file, a copy furnished to the defendant, and a dated receipt taken from the defendant.

The foregoing or similar procedure is suggested to give vitality to the right and to encourage that appeals be taken as a matter of right and that a minimum number of appeals are taken as appeals by leave (delayed appeals). A delayed appeal may be a less effective appeal both for the defendant and for the state.

10. In order to prevent abuse of the appellate process, investigation should be made of the possibility and desirability of effective measures to prevent an

appeal that is wholly without color of merit being brought to the court of appeals or to the Supreme Court.

The constitution of 1963 provides for an appeal as a matter of right in every criminal case. While there would appear to be no need for any measures to restrict the taking of appeals from courts of limited criminal jurisdiction, the very real possibility exists, particularly in indgent cases, for appeals to be brought without any reasonable basis. While the true extent of this possible problem is not yet known, and therefore no specific recommendations are made, further study is recommended.

11. Where application is made for leave to appeal in a criminal case, either as a delayed appeal or otherwise, the appellant should, if he desires the assistance of appointed counsel on appeal, petition the court from which the appeal is to be taken for the appointment of counsel. The format of the petition should be provided by court rule.

In light of the fact that the petition is prepared without the assistance of counsel, the format of the petition should include specific questions to be answered by the petitioner, so that the court hearing the petition may have before it the facts necessary for a proper determination of the issues presented to the court. If a hearing is granted on such a petition, the court should appoint counsel to represent the accused for the purpose of the hearing. If the court should find the defendant to be an indigent person, unable to obtain the assistance of counsel, it should appoint counsel for the purpose of assisting the accused in the preparation of the application for delayed appeal, affidavit of facts, and brief in support thereof, unless it shall appear to the court that the petition does not set forth a meritorious case for an appeal, in which case the petition should be denied.

The appropriate place for the determination of indigency would appear to be in the trial court. The burden of proof, on the petition for the appointment of counsel, shifts to the prosecution once the defendant has been shown to be an indigent person unable to obtain the assistance of counsel. If other portions of these supplemental recommendations are adopted, a meritorious application for delayed appeal should be quite unusual.

NOTES — Michigan

[1]"Resolution of the A.B.A. House of Delegates," 87 A.B.A. Rep. 468 (August, 1962).

[2]Mich. Const. of 1963 art. VI, §1.

[3]Mich. Stat. Ann. §27.3263.

[4]Mich. Stat. Ann. §27.3561.

[5]Mich. Stat. Ann. §28.920.

[6]Mich. Stat. Ann. §28.1192.

[7]Mich. Stat. Ann. §27.3751 et seq., 27.3831 et seq., 27.3937 (1) et seq.

[8]Mich. Stat. Ann. §27.3711.

[9]Mich. Stat. Ann. §28.860.

[10]Mich. Stat. Ann. §§28.941,943.

[11]McNabb v. United States, 318 U.S. 332 (1943); Mallory v. United States, 354 U.S. 449 (1957).

[12]359 Mich. 410, 102 N.W. 2d 738 (1960).

[13]People v. McCager, 367 Mich. 116, 116 N.W. 2d 205 (1962).

[14]Mich. Stat. Ann. §28.774. There is a continuing problem in Detroit of a larger volume of investigative arrests, a phenomenon that is related to the needs of poor persons for counsel. From 1950 through 1959, there were approximately 60,000 arrests each year in Detroit, and one-third were "investigative arrests." In recent years, the situation has improved. The number of investigative arrests decreased to 15,000 in 1960, the last year

for which reporters have compiled accurate data. Many if not all of these arrests are illegal. In 1960 also, the writ of habeas corpus in Detroit was sustained, and the prisoner discharged, in 5733 cases. For a more complete resume of data on arrests in Detroit, see Norris, "Annual Survey of Michigan Criminal Law, 1961," 8 Wayne L. Rev. 58. See also U.S. Civil Rights Commission Hearings, Detroit, 1960 statement by Norris, pp. 480-490; Norris, "Arrests Without Warrant," Crisis Mag. (October, 1958).

[15]Mich. Stat. Ann. §28.860.

[16]See letter from E. Burke Montgomery, clerk, Recorder's Court, Aug. 21, 1963: Immediately after the warrant issues in a felony case the defendant is brought before the Examining Magistrate for Arraignment on the Warrant. If, in response to the Court's questioning, the defendant requests an Examination and states he is indigent the Examining Magistrate has him sign an Affidavit of Indigency, and the Presiding Judge, if satisfied, assigns counsel for Preliminary Examination. If Examination is waived, counsel is assigned at the time of Arraignment on the Information, after examination as to his indigency by the Presiding Judge's clerk, who lists all pertinent data on a questionnaire, takes the defendant's oath as to answers therein contained and has defendant sign it in addition to the affidavit of indigency. Assigned Counsel, on occasion, will ask that the case be sent back for Preliminary Examination even after waiver.

[17]Mich. Stat. Ann. §28.1253.

[18]See People v. Pickett, 399 Mich. 294, 63 N.W. 2d 681 (1954).

[19]Supreme Court of Michigan, Office of the Court Administrator, Annual Report and Judicial Statistics for 1962 20, 31.

[20]Annual Report for the Recorder's Court for the City of Detroit 8 (1962).

[21]Mich. Const. of 1963 art. I, §20, quoted in note 26 infra.

[22]372 U.S. 353 (1963).

[23]372 U.S. 487 (1963).

[24]Reported in Inter Alia 2-3 (February, 1963).

[25]See notes 12 and 13, supra.

[26]Mich. Const. of 1963 art. I, §20 reads: "In every criminal prosecution, the accused shall . . . have an appeal as a matter of right and in courts of record, when the trial court so orders to have such reasonable assistance as may be necessary to perfect and prosecute an appeal." Professor Norris, as a delegate to Michigan's Constitutional Convention, was the author of the provision creating a constitutional right to appeal.

MINNESOTA

Prof. Jesse Choper, formerly University of Minnesota, and
Prof. Yale Kamisar, University of Michigan,
formerly University of Minnesota

The members of the A.B.A. Associate State Committee were John S. Connolly, St. Paul, chairman; Frederic N. Brown, Rochester; John A. Cochrane, St. Paul; Irving Gotlieb, St. Paul; Harry L. Munger, Duluth; and Gerald M. Singer, Minneapolis. Of helpful assistance in gathering data for this report were Nathan G. Mandel, State Department of Corrections; Roy T. Noonan, State Bureau of Criminal Apprehension; and Michael Berman, James O'Connor, and William Bast, students at the University of Minnesota Law School.

A. INTRODUCTION

Minnesota had a population of 3,413,864 in 1960. It is estimated by the state department of health that the population in 1962 was 3,492,716. The state is divided into 87 counties, which are organized into 10 judicial districts. Each district has three or more district judges; each county has its own prosecuting attorney. The counties selected for survey are shown in the following table.

TABLE 1
Sample Counties

County	1960 population in thousands*	Location in state	Remarks
Chisago	13	East central	Rural, reformatory and prison in the judicial district
Dakota (D)	78	Southeast	Wealthy, suburban
Freeborn (D)	38	South central	Rural, some Indian population
Hennepin (D)	843	East central	Almost 50 political subdivisions, urban, commercial center
Ramsey (D)	423	East central	State capital, urban, commercial center
St. Louis (D)	232	Northeast	Declining economy, very large geographic area
Stearns	80	Central	Small college

(D) indicates that a docket study was made.

*These counties contain over half of the population of the entire state and, according to FBI arrest figures, have more than 80% of the state's crimes. (In the original sample, Beltrami and Faribault Counties were selected. St. Louis was substituted for Beltrami because, by wide margin, it was the state's largest county in area and third in terms of major prosecutions and population. St. Louis County is in a judicial district immediately adjacent to Beltrami's. Freeborn was substituted for Faribault, which it adjoins, because the latter had not had a single criminal trial in the last two years in which statistics were available.)

Table 2 gives additional information about the counties surveyed.

TABLE 2
Additional Data on Sample Counties

County	Felony and gross misdemeanor defendants, 1962	% indigent*	% of indigents who waived counsel*	Lawyers in private practice	No. of appointments of counsel in felonies and gross misdemeanors, 1962	No. of lawyers who served	Typical payment for guilty plea
Chisago	12	70	0	4	8	4	$ 50
Dakota	63	65	3	31	25	13	35-75
Freeborn	58	85	0	20	54	16	25-85
Hennepin	765	75	0	1450	600†	P.D.‡	P.D.‡
Ramsey	274	70	0	700	170†	P.D.‡	P.D.‡
St. Louis	111	70	0	210	92	34	no data
Stearns	55	70-75	3	39	23	11	25

*This figure is an average of estimates supplied by the judges, prosecuting attorneys, and public defenders in the county.
†Estimate.
‡Public defender.

B. CRIMINAL PROCEDURE AS IT AFFECTS INDIGENT PERSONS

Jurisdiction to return indictments and to try felony cases and gross misdemeanor cases (crimes carrying a sentence of 90 days to one year) is vested exclusively in the district court.

The great majority of these cases begin with the arrest of the suspect. He is required, by statute, to be taken promptly before a magistrate, but the amount of time that elapses between the formal charge and booking of a person by the arresting authorities and the accused's first appearance before a magistrate varies, on the average, in the counties surveyed from less than 12 hours to over three days.

In most counties, almost all first appearances in felony and gross misdemeanor cases are held before municipal judges. In the counties surveyed, these were always lawyers, but there are a number of lay municipal judges elsewhere in the state. In one county, Chisago, first appearances are held before a justice of the peace. Throughout the state these are mostly laymen.

At all first appearances, the accused is informed of the charges against him and bail is set, although some magistrates in one county do not even mention the matter of bail if it appears that the defendant will request appointed counsel. In six of the sample counties, the prosecutor's recommendation as to bail carries great weight, particularly when the defendant is unrepresented, although in one of the larger counties, Ramsey, some magistrates set it independently. In Stearns County, the municipal judge, a man of 28 years' experience, ignores the prosecutor's recommendation.

In all of the counties surveyed, the magistrates advise the accused of their right to appointed counsel, but in only two of the counties, Ramsey (a public defender county) and Dakota, is counsel regularly appointed at the first appearance stage. In a third, Hennepin, counsel is often appointed at this stage. In the remaining four, appointed counsel rarely appears until after the indigent has been bound over to district court. Evidently the basis for the diversity stems from the different attitudes of the judicial officers conducting first appearances.

Most magistrates inform the accused of his right to a preliminary hearing, although it was reported that, in one county, one municipal judge as a rule does not offer the preliminary hearing to indigents. When these hearings are held for indigents, counsel is almost always appointed. With the exception of Dakota County, however, they are not held very frequently. There is some evidence that preliminary hearings are held more frequently for indigent defendants in those counties in which counsel is regularly appointed at the first appearance stage.

Throughout Minnesota the formal charge against the defendant is usually made by information. Grand jury indictments are mandatory for offenses which carry a sentence of life imprisonment, the most severe penalty under state law. Occasionally, indictments are employed when the prosecutor wishes to shift responsibility for the decision of bringing an accused to trial. e.g., in sex offenses when the county attorney has some doubt about the complaint's credibility, in criminal negligence cases, and in cases involving the embezzlement of funds by a public official. In several rural counties, it was reported that the convening of a grand jury is extremely unusual.

Procedure for appointment of counsel does not differ significantly in the seven counties surveyed. As has been noted, counsel is usually appointed (and the determination of indigency is made) either at the first appearance stage by the magistrate or at the arraignment stage by the district judge. The only difference of any note is that some magistrates do not put the accused under oath.

Only district judges have statutory authority to appoint counsel but counsel may be appointed before the accused reaches district court pursuant to Minn. Stat. § 611.07, which provides that "when a defendant . . . shall request the magistrate to have counsel appointed . . . the county attorney shall immediately certify to the judge of the district court . . . that the defendant is without counsel and that he has shown, under oath, that he is financially unable to procure counsel. The district court shall then appoint counsel." In Hennepin County, the district court has signed a blanket order permitting the municipal judge to appoint counsel for indigents. In several rural counties, in the geographically large but sparsely populated judicial districts, a problem arises when the judge is not sitting in the county. In these counties, the meeting of attorney and client is expedited by an "informal" appointment of counsel, either by county attorney or clerk of court one or more days before arraignment. The district judge subsequently makes the formal appointment.

All judges, municipal and district, question the accused in open court—and that is about all. In one sample county, Stearns, law enforcement authorities and defense counsel (who may have already consulted with the defendant without formal appointment) also disclose any information they may have about the accused's financial status. The inquiry in open court concerns the defendant's assets—salary, real and personal property, wages due from last employer. Most judges inquire as to the financial resources of parents and relatives, but two judges made the point that, if these persons were to refuse to retain a lawyer for the defendant, counsel would be appointed. If the accused had sufficient equity in an automobile to cover an attorney's fee for this particular kind of case, he would probably be forced to sell it—but this is a rare case. Generally, if the assets of the accused are inadequate to retain counsel, counsel is appointed.

Various methods are used by the judges to select lawyers to be appointed, although generally they encounter no serious problem in getting lawyers to serve. Some judges make their selection from a list of almost every lawyer in the county; others generally appoint younger attorneys; still others, "willing lawyers." All judges stressed that an experienced lawyer is specially selected for more serious cases. One judge usually appoints from a list of lawyers with substantial criminal defense experience. Judges interviewed disagreed over whether the indigent's request for a specific attorney should be honored and whether another lawyer should be appointed if the defendant objects to the first appointee, although more were inclined to honor the latter request than the former.

Magistrates in some counties are much less insistent than those in others about encouraging the indigent defendant to accept counsel at the first appearance stage, but in every county studied it was plain that the district judges were painstakingly careful in providing counsel before accepting a plea. This scrupulousness is sometimes carried to the point of simply not permitting a defendant to waive the assistance of counsel at arraignment. As the Ramsey County prosecutor put it: "We don't let an indigent waive. He has nothing to say about it." Fear of reversal on appeal or of later collateral attack rather than concern for the rights of the accused, as such, seemed to be the dominant motivation in many cases.

Compensation for attorneys is provided by statute, "not exceeding $25 per day for each counsel for the number of days he is actually employed in the preparation of the case, and not exceeding $50 per day for each day in court, together with all necessary and reasonable costs and expenses incurred or paid in said defense." In practice, the amount varies quite widely among the sample counties using the appointed counsel system; indeed, sometimes within the same county according to the particular judge. One judge reported that he automatically gives the maximum statutory fee; another, that he awards between $35 and $75 for a guilty plea; still others "adjust" the statutory fees depending on the amount of time they feel was spent on the case. Expenses are reimbursed.

The Hennepin County public defender has an annual salary of $8000; he has four assistants, each earning $6000, and he has an additional general fund of $3100. The Ramsey County public defender has an annual salary of $7500 and one assistant at $3500.

With rare exceptions in Hennepin and Ramsey Counties, counsel is not provided for simple misdemeanors (offenses carrying sentences not in excess of 90 days) in any of the sample counties. This appears to be the practice throughout the state. On the other hand, apparently without exception throughout the state, indigent defendants are furnished free counsel for pleas, trials, and sentencing in all felony and gross misdemeanor cases.

In past years counsel has occasionally been appointed by some judges in probation revocation hearings, but not frequently. However, the new criminal code provides that a probationer facing revocation "is entitled to be heard and to be represented by counsel," and judges in Hennepin and Ramsey Counties have construed this statute as requiring the assignment of counsel for indigent probationers in revocation proceedings.

With few exceptions, counsel has not been appointed for indigents in respect to appeals in the past. However, in 1961, the Minnesota Supreme Court directed the trial courts to prepare sufficiently detailed synopses in all felony and gross misdemeanor cases so that it could "adequately determine whether there is any justification for . . . appointment . . . on appeal." And, shortly after Douglas, the legislature appropriated funds to compensate appointed counsel on appeal, on a finding by the state Supreme Court that review is "sought in good faith" and "upon reasonable grounds." To date, the Supreme Court has granted all requests for counsel on appeal to those unable to afford one. According to Chief Justice Oscar Knutson, travel expenses, funds for the preparation of the necessary portions of the trial transcript, and "anything else needed" will be supplied. To date, more attorneys have volunteered their services without charge than have been requested by indigent prisoners in appeals and post-conviction proceedings.

In Minnesota the postconviction remedies of habeas corpus and coram nobis are both used. In the past some judges in some counties appointed counsel if the claim appeared to have merit. The post-*Douglas* legislative appropriation, referred to above, also covers postconviction relief. The Supreme Court at first granted all indigents who have not had the assistance of counsel on appeal an absolute right to counsel in the first postconviction proceeding. However, the steady flow of applications, coupled with the realization that some were abusing this liberal practice, led the court to modify its approach: in late September, 1963, it appointed an attorney to "sift" these applications for merit.

[Editor's note: In May, 1965, the Minnesota Legislature enacted a bill creating the office of state public defender to represent indigent persons on appeals and postconviction remedies, and also to supervise the training of assistant state public defenders and district public defenders. A district public defender may be established by the judges of any judicial district, beginning January 1, 1966. The state public defender is to serve a four-year term beginning July 1, 1965. He is selected by the Judicial Council and may be removed only for cause. Another section provides that "In every criminal case or proceeding in which any person entitled by law to representation by counsel shall appear without counsel, the court shall advise such person that he has the right to be represented by counsel and that counsel will be appointed to represent him if he is financially unable to obtain counsel." Waiver of counsel must be in writing. A detailed financial affidavit is required for eligibility.

The National Legal Aid and Defender Association will help support the new office for a two-year period.

Financial tables prepared by the Judicial Council in connection with the legislative proposal are appended to this report.]

C. OPINIONS OF THE JUDGES

In each of the sample counties at least one of the presiding district judges was interviewed. In Hennepin, Ramsey, and St. Louis three judges were interviewed; in Freeborn, two judges. Personal interviews were also held with four municipal judges because of their expertise with misdemeanors and the early stages of felony and gross misdemeanor proceedings. In addition, the reporters spoke with Chief Justice Oscar R. Knutson and Associate Justice Robert J. Sheran of the Minnesota Supreme Court. Finally, mail questionnaires were sent to 27 additional district judges throughout the state. Replies were received from 15 of these (55%).

On question 7 of the judge interview—"Under an ideal system, at what stage in a criminal case do you think the indigent person should first be provided with a lawyer if he wants one?"—6 of the 14 judges interviewed felt that counsel should be provided shortly after arrest and 6 believed counsel should be appointed at the first appearance before a magistrate. One thought that the preliminary hearing was the proper stage at which to appoint and one judge, the arraignment. Of those judges responding to this question on the mail questionnaire, 5 designated between arrest and first appearance before a magistrate, 4 at first appearance before a magistrate, 3 between first appearance and preliminary hearing, one at preliminary hearing, and one after the filing of an indictment or information but before arraignment thereon.

On the question of unfairness to the indigent person if he does not get a lawyer at the stage designated by the judge, approximately half of both groups of judges, those interviewed and those questioned by mail, agreed that it would be unfair. Most of the others felt that "it may be," or they replied "no" or "not necessarily." On the question of financing such a system, 75% found little or no problem, while 20% recognized that it could be fairly expensive, but that the cost would not be insuperable. Only one judge felt that his ideal system could not be financed.

On question 8—"Under an ideal system do you think a lawyer should be provided for the indigent person in the following kinds of cases and proceedings?"— the following answers were given. As to postconviction relief, one of the judges interviewed favored appointment as of right, at least in the first postconviction proceeding. Four felt that counsel should be appointed whenever there is "substance" or "merit" to the claim. Three were inclined to deny counsel in all postconviction proceedings. The remaining judges interviewed "hadn't thought it out yet" or had no comment. Eleven of the judges who responded to the mail questionnaire felt that counsel should be provided in postconviction proceedings; three replied "sometimes"; one, "no."

As to probation revocation, 7 of the 12 judges interviewed who took a position on the issue favored the appointment of counsel in all probation revocation hearings. Six of the 14 judges responding by mail agreed.

As to misdemeanors, only 2 of the 16 district and municipal judges interviewed who replied thought that no misdemeanant should be provided with counsel. On the other hand, no judge took the position that counsel should be appointed in every misdemeanor case. The core of the ideas expressed by the majority was that the test should turn in large measure on the nature and consequences of the offense, and on the way in which friends, neighbors, employers, and the general public viewed the matter. Petty larceny, simple assault, "driving under the influence," and issuance of "bad checks" were the misdemeanors most frequently mentioned as warranting the appointment of counsel. Only one of the judges replying by mail felt that counsel should be provided in misdemeanor cases; 12 replied in the negative; one said "sometimes"; another, "almost always."

There seemed to be no differences of any great significance between the rural and urban judges interviewed, except for the greater concern with the financial burden of providing counsel expressed by the rural judges.

For purposes of comparison, in the following table the judges interviewed and the judges responding by mail are each divided into two groups of equal size according to years of service on their present courts. The half with the longest periods of service are called senior judges and the remainder are called junior judges. Their answers to most of the questions are found in Table 3.

The six district judges interviewed in the public defender counties were all very enthusiastic about the public defender system. Also, a large majority of those judges interviewed in the appointed counsel counties who addressed

TABLE 3
Opinions of Judges

	Judges interviewed		Judges responding by mail		
	Senior	Junior	Senior	Junior	Total
Total responding	6	7	8	7	28
Ideal stage for first appointment of counsel:					
Between arrest and first appearance	4	2	3	2	11
At first appearance before a magistrate	2	4	2	2	10
Between first appearance and preliminary hearing	0	0	1	2	3
At preliminary hearing	0	1	1	0	2
After information but before arraignment	0	0	0	1	1
At arraignment	0	0	0	0	0
No answer	0	0	1	0	1
Is present compensation adequate?					
Yes	2	0	6	1	9
Depends on kind of case	1	1	0	4	6
No	0	3	2	1	6
No answer because public defender county	3	3	0	0	6
No answer	0	0	0	1	1
Appointed counsel counties:					
How do apointed lawyers compare with retained?					
Well	2	1	5	5	13
Less experienced	1	1	0	0	2
Poorly	0	2	3	2	7
Public defender counties:					
How does public defender compare with retained lawyers?					
Better than most	2	3	0	0	5
As good as most	1	0	0	0	1
Appointed counsel counties:					
How do appointed lawyers compare with county attorney?					
Well	2	2	6	4	14
Less experienced	1	2	1	3	7
Poorly	0	0	1	0	1
Public defender counties:					
How does public defender compare with county attorney?					
Better	2	2	0	0	4
As good	1	1	0	0	2

themselves to the issue, including a number who were pleased with the present system, favored the establishment of some sort of public defender system.

D. OPINIONS OF THE PROSECUTING ATTORNEYS

The county attorney in each of the sample counties was interviewed and in three of these counties the views of several assistant prosecutors were also recorded. Finally, mail questionnaires were sent to 80 additional county prosecutors. Replies were received from 56 of these (70%). Thus over two-thirds of the prosecuting attorneys in the state were included in the survey.

The prosecutors were asked whether, under an ideal system, a lawyer should be provided for indigents in various types of proceedings. As to postconviction remedies, three of the prosecutors interviewed favored appointment as of right at least in the first postconviction proceeding; one felt that counsel should not be provided; those remaining had no comment. Half of those responding by mail answered "yes"; 10% believed "sometimes"; the remaining 40% said "no."

As to probation revocation, only one prosecutor interviewed (the same lone prosecutor inclined to assign counsel in some misdemeanor cases) favored the appointment of counsel in all probation revocation hearings; one had no comment; the other five were flatly opposed. Those responding to the mail questionnaire split two-thirds to one-third, the larger group being opposed.

As to misdemeanors, six of the seven county attorneys interviewed thought that counsel should not be provided in any misdemeanor case (although one added: "with the possible exception of driving while intoxicated"); one prosecutor joined the majority of the judges interviewed on this point. Of those prosecuting attorneys responding by mail, 52 out of 56 answered "no"; three replied "yes"; one thought "sometimes."

To save space and to facilitate comparison, the remaining significant information obtained from the county attorneys is presented in Table 4.

The answers of the prosecutors varied considerably concerning their policy of disclosing information to defense counsel. However, no county attorney stated that his policy in regard to appointed counsel was any different than it was in respect to retained counsel. Finally, both prosecutors from the public defender counties agreed that the defenders were extremely zealous.

E. OPINIONS OF DEFENSE ATTORNEYS

The public defenders of Hennepin and Ramsey Counties were interviewed. Furthermore, mail questionnaires were sent to 53 lawyers who had acted as assigned counsel in the other sample counties and 29 responded (55%).

Both public defenders are permitted to engage in a private civil practice, but both estimated that they spent 30 hours a week or more on their public duties. They split on the question of whether they had adequate funds to run their offices. Both felt that the present system for determining indigency was about right. One reported that he received much greater cooperation from the county attorney's office than the other did. Both rejected the notion that a public defender could not be completely independent and zealous. On the question at what stage in a criminal proceeding the indigent person should first

TABLE 4
Opinions of Prosecutors

| | Prosecutors interviewed | | Prosecutors responding by mail | | |
	Senior	Junior	Senior	Junior	Total
Total responding	4	3	28	28	63
Ideal stage for first appointment of counsel:					
Between arrest and first appearance	1	1	8	11	21
At first appearance before a magistrate	2	1	5	4	12
Between first appearance and preliminary hearing	0	0	4	9	13
At preliminary hearing	0	0	2	1	3
After preliminary hearing but before information is filed	0	0	5	1	6
After information is filed but before arraignment	0	0	2	2	4
At arraignment	1	1	2	0	4
Are funds you have adequate to run your office?					
Yes	2	2	20	14	38
No	2	1	8	14	25
Appointed counsel counties:					
How do appointed lawyers compare with retained?					
Well	0	3	18	21	42
Less experienced	1	0	2	1	4
Poorly	1	0	4	4	9
No answer	0	0	4	2	6
Public defender counties:					
How does public defender compare with retained lawyers?					
Better than most	1	0	0	0	1
As good as most	1	0	0	0	1
How do you feel about present system for determining indigency?					
Too lenient	1	2	10	6	19
Too strict	0	0	1	0	1
About right	3	1	15	21	40
No answer	0	0	2	1	3
Is present compensation adequate?					
Yes	2	0	17	14	33
Depends on kind of case	0	2	1	2	5
No	0	1	7	11	19
No answer because public defender county	2	0	0	0	2
No answer	0	0	3	1	4

be provided with a lawyer, one believed that "counsel should be provided as soon as a man is arrested"; the other: "at first appearance before the magistrate, *if* there is a *prompt* arraignment." The former believed that it was unfair to the defendant if he was not afforded counsel at the stage suggested by him; the latter did not. Neither thought that the financial burden would be too great. One believed that counsel should be provided to assist in meritorious postconviction proceedings; the other had no comment on this. Neither felt that a lawyer would be very helpful in probation revocation proceedings, but one favored appointment to "keep the probation officer honest." Both approved of the appointment of counsel in some misdemeanor cases.

About 70% of those appointed lawyers who responded to the mail questionnaire felt that they were appointed in time to represent the accused adequately. Only four responded "no" to this question and two others expressed some doubts. Nonetheless, 15 of the lawyers responding recommended that counsel be appointed at an earlier stage in the case. Fourteen felt that the present system was fair to indigent persons; eight did not; four believed that it sometimes was. Thirteen appointed lawyers reported that the system was fair to the lawyers; 14 did not; 18 felt that lawyers should be paid more for their services. Nine of those responding thought that counsel should be provided in additional kinds of cases, such as serious misdemeanors. Nine believed that the system of selecting lawyers used by the judge should be improved. Five volunteered the suggestion that some sort of public defender system be established.

F. DOCKET STUDIES

Docket studies were conducted in five of the sample counties, as indicated in Table 1. Results of the docket study appear in Tables 5 to 10. Each table has not only the figures for the five counties but also a projected average for the state as a whole, based on the weighted total of the five counties. (The method used in making the study is explained in volume 1, pages 178-179.)

Table 5 shows that virtually all defendants in the five counties had counsel. The percentage who retained their own counsel was fairly uniform throughout the state, averaging 34%, while at least 58% of the defendants were represented either by assigned counsel or a public defender.

As shown in Table 6, a state-wide average of 64% of the defendants were officially determined to be indigent. The highest rate of indigency was in Freeborn County, the lowest in Dakota. Similarly, as indicated in Table 7, 64% of the defendants were not released on bail, which is another test of indigency. For the individual counties the range was considerably wider, however, from a high of 74% in Ramsey County to a low of 53% in St. Louis County.

Data on race, available for Hennepin County only, showed that 75% of the defendants were white and 25% were Negro.

Table 8 shows that preliminary hearings are relatively uncommon throughout the five counties, although they are considerably more frequent in Freeborn and Dakota Counties than elsewhere.

Dispositions of the sample cases are shown in Table 9. For the state as a whole, 79% of the defendants pleaded guilty, including 19% who pleaded to lesser

TABLE 5
Retained and Assigned Counsel in Felonies
Minnesota, 1962

County	Total sample	Did defendant have counsel? Yes No.		No No.		Re-tained No.		As-signed No.		Public defender No.		Combination or type unknown No.		No data° No.	
		No.	%	No.	%	No.	%	No.	%	No.	%	No.	%	No.	%
Ramsey	47	41	98	1	2	12	29	1	2	23	55	5	5	5	11
Dakota	19	19	100	0	0	8	42	8	42	0	0	1	5	0	0
Freeborn	20	19	100	0	0	7	37	12	63	0	0	0	0	1	5
St. Louis	46	44	96	2	4	15	33	25	53	0	0	3	6	0	0
Hennepin	80	76	98	2	3	25	32	0	0	50	64	1	1	2	3
Weighted total percentages		98		2		34		25		33		4		3	

° % of no data refers to total sample; % in other columns refers to cases for which data were available.

TABLE 6
Was Felony Defendant Determined Indigent?
Minnesota, 1962

County	Total sample	Yes No.	%	No No.	%	No data° No.	%
Ramsey	47	29	67	14	33	4	9
Dakota	19	11	58	8	42	0	0
Freeborn	20	13	68	6	32	1	5
St. Louis	46	28	61	18	40	0	0
Hennepin	80	49	64	28	36	3	4
Weighted total percentages			64		37		4

° % of no data refers to total sample; % in other columns refers to cases for which data were available.

TABLE 7
Frequency of Release on Bail of Felony Defendants
Minnesota, 1962

County	Total sample	Yes No.	%	No No.	%	No data° No.	%
Ramsey	47	11	26	32	74	4	12
Dakota	19	8	44	10	56	1	6
Freeborn	20	8	42	11	58	1	5
St. Louis	46	20	47	23	53	3	7
Hennepin	80	23	29	56	71	1	1
Weighted total percentages			36		64		3

° % of no data refers to total sample; % in other columns refers to cases for which data were available.

TABLE 8
Frequency of Preliminary Hearings in Felonies
Minnesota, 1962

County	Total sample	Yes No.	%	No, waiver No.	%	No, not used in this kind of case No.	%	No data° No.	%
Ramsey	47	4	9	38	86	2	5	3	6
Dakota	19	4	21	15	79	0	0	0	0
Freeborn	20	7	37	12	63	0	0	1	5
St. Louis	46	5	11	40	89	0	0	1	2
Hennepin	80	7	10	58	87	2	3	13	16
Weighted total percentages			16		82		2		8

° % of no data refers to total sample; % in other columns refers to cases for which data were available.

TABLE 9
Disposition in Felony Cases
Minnesota, 1962

County	Total sample	Plea guilty	Plea lesser offense	Dis-missed	Found guilty	Found guilty lesser degree	Ac-quitted	Mental com-mit-ment	Pend-ing	Other
Ramsey	47	31	9	2	1	0	1	1	1	1
Dakota	19	11	6	0	0	0	0	0	0	2
Freeborn	20	9	5	6	0	0	0	0	0	0
St. Louis	46	23	5	11	1	1	3	0	2	0
Hennepin	80	53	12	3	5	1	3	0	2	1
Weighted total percentages		60	19	10	3	1	3	0	2	0

offenses, a relatively high proportion compared to other states. Only 7% of the cases went to trial, and about half of these resulted in convictions and half in acquittals. The highest rate of guilty pleas was in Dakota County (89%) and the lowest rate in St. Louis (61%).

Table 10 shows the sentences, if any, imposed in the sample cases. For the state as a whole, 41% of the defendants were sentenced to prison and 41% placed on probation. Although the variations among the five counties were not great, Dakota had the most frequent and St. Louis County had the least frequent use of probation vis-à-vis imprisonment.

TABLE 10
Sentencing in Felony Cases
Minnesota, 1962*

County	Total sample No.	No sentence No.	%	Prison No.	%	Pro-bation No.	%	Suspended sentence No.	%	Fine No.	%	Sentence pending No.	%	No data† No.	%
Ramsey	47	6	13	23	49	25	53	0	0	0	0	0	0	0	0
Dakota	19	0	0	6	32	9	47	0	0	0	0	2	11	0	0
Freeborn	20	6	32	6	32	7	37	0	0	0	0	0	0	1	5
St. Louis	46	16	36	19	42	14	31	0	0	0	0	1	2	1	2
Hennepin	80	11	14	36	45	32	40	1	1	1	1	1	1	0	0
Weighted total percentages			17		41		41		1		1		2		1

* If a defendant had a combination sentence, such as a term of imprisonment followed by probation, he is counted under both columns. Hence the totals may be more than 100%.

† % of no data refers to total sample; % in other columns refers to cases for which data were available.

(For further discussion of certain aspects of the docket study, see Kamisar and Choper, "The Right to Counsel in Minnesota: Some Field Findings and Legal-Policy Observations," 48 Minn. L. Rev. 1 [1963].)

G. CONCLUSIONS AND RECOMMENDATIONS

On the basis of the foregoing report the following conclusions and recommendations are submitted:

1. A much more liberal use should be made of releases on personal recognizance than is presently the case. In the meantime, the ability to raise bail should not automatically take a defendant out of the "indigency" category, as it now does in some counties. A better approach in this area would seem to be a case-by-case judgment as to how much each defendant can reasonably afford for counsel, taking into account such matters as his family obligations and need for investigation funds. If the defendant is unable to retain counsel, the state should provide an attorney and the defendant should be required to partly reimburse the county by the amount it is determined he can afford. Such an approach would be likely to significantly reduce the possibility that the borderline indigent, who may be forced to retain sub-par counsel, will receive less adequate representation than the total pauper.

2. There is mixed feeling about the court-appointed system, but widespread approval of the operation of the public defender's office in the state's two largest counties. There is a strong consensus in the state that the defender's office usually provides a defense superior to that of appointed counsel. Moreover, if it is assumed that counsel may be provided, for example, in serious misdemeanor cases and at probation revocation hearings, in addition to all appeals, time,

money, and effort may well be economized by specialist-defenders rather than by attorneys appointed on a case-by-case basis. This suggests that serious consideration should be given to the establishment of public defender offices throughout the state—either a full-time public defender for several counties where this is feasible geographically, or a part-time defender in each of the counties presently without one. (In 82 of the state's 87 counties, the prosecutor operates on a part-time basis.) [See editor's note at end of Section B above.]

3. Counsel should be assigned early enough so that the poor man enjoys the assistance of counsel as soon as the rich man does. Since judicial determination of indigency is a rather perfunctory procedure, any person who claims indigency could be provided counsel from a special list of lawyers or by the utilization of a member of the public defender's staff. (If it later develops that the defendant is not in fact "indigent," the lawyer, or, in the case of the public defender, the county, would be reimbursed.) Nor, when an arrestee is not informed by law enforcement officials of his right to assigned counsel—and he is not now—should any significance attach to whether he requests counsel. If the right is deemed sufficiently important to "begin" when an arrested person asks for his own lawyer or for the public defender or appointed counsel, it is sufficiently important to be made available to the unwary, ignorant, and inexperienced, as well as to the informed, sophisticated, and professional.

4. In the two largest counties of the state, Hennepin and Ramsey, counsel is now being assigned at all probation revocation hearings as a matter of statutory interpretation of a provision of the new criminal code. There is much to be said for following this practice throughout the state. At the very least, a year or so from now the legislature should intensively examine the experience and attitudes in the two counties where counsel is presently being appointed at this stage, with an eye to making the procedure state-wide.

5. Most of the judges interviewed about the matter favored the appointment of counsel in "serious" misdemeanors, or those involving "moral turpitude," e.g., petty larceny, simple assault, issuance of "bad checks." We believe such proposals merit serious consideration by the legislature. Prospective employers, neighbors, and the public generally, regard these offenses as crimes. It is true that persistence in the principle of appointing counsel in serious misdemeanor cases might result in appointment in the most trivial cases—something no person interviewed suggested—but this "wedge" argument does not render less appropriate the appointment of counsel in serious misdemeanor cases.

APPENDIX

Expenditures for Indigent Defendants
Minnesota, 1963

District	No. of felony and gross misdemeanor cases in district court	No. of cases in district court with assigned counsel	No. of attorneys appointed as assigned counsel in district court	Total amount counties paid to attorneys for indigents	Total amount counties paid for transcripts for indigents	Total amount counties paid for investigation for indigents
First	177	100	55	$ 7390.29	$1454.75	$ —
Second*	353	179	5	9670.65	—	—
Third	215	126	140	17,497.67	1029.72	237.47
Fourth*	672	373	5	29,737.96	450.00	2223.00
Fifth	139	94	97	8375.42	1308.75	302.00
Sixth	258	152	156	14,673.01	353.34	75.00
Seventh	214	76	80	7869.67	724.80	89.15
Eighth	89	55	43	4280.26	178.30	176.11
Ninth	312	169	152	19,868.85	2199.52	357.33
Tenth	126	91	64	8906.00	41.70	—
Totals	2555	1415	797	$128,269.78	$7704.88	$3460.07

Source: Minnesota Judicial Council and National Legal Aid and Defender Association.
* These judicial districts employ a public defender system.

*Expenditures for Indigent Defendants
Minnesota, 1964*

District	No. of felony and gross misdemeanor cases in district court	No. of cases in district court with assigned counsel	No. of attorneys appointed as assigned counsel in district court	Total amount counties paid to attorneys for indigents	Total amount counties paid for transcripts for indigents	Total amount counties paid for investigation for indigents
First	193	120	65	$ 15,620.04	$ 1673.87	$ —
Second†	467	232	7	14,635.07	1701.93	2097.67
Third	209	143	135	17,807.34	440.73	420.00
Fourth†	734	441	7	34,237.20	408.72	2666.67
Fifth	150	107	104	9684.26	1969.59	676.96
Sixth	315	176	191	16,847.10	—	26.67
Seventh	168	99	92	11,505.08	1453.86	392.03
Eighth	67	49	43	4033.33	258.84	303.81
Ninth	297	176	101	23,113.98	1256.45	415.49
Tenth	168	127	59	12,271.55	888.47	—
Totals	2768	1675	803	$159,754.95	$10,052.46	$6999.29

Source: Minnesota Judicial Council and National Legal Aid and Defender Association.
* These are projected figures based on reports for the first nine months of 1964.
† These judicial districts employ a public defender system.

401

MISSISSIPPI

Merrimen M. Watkins, Crystal Springs

The A.B.A. Associate State Committee consisted of Howard A. McDonnell, Biloxi, chairman; Gerald C. Gex, Louis; Ralph L. Peeples, Brookhaven; James H. Ray, Tupelo; and Tom T. Ross, Clarksdale.

A. INTRODUCTION

Mississippi had a population of 2,178,141 in 1960. The state is divided into 82 counties, which are organized into 18 circuit court districts. Each circuit has at least one circuit judge elected for a four-year term. The circuit judge holds court in his district as required by state statute and many hold terms of court in any other district when public interest so requires. Each circuit has a district attorney elected for four years. In any circuit court district that has a population of not less than 210,000 persons according to the latest federal census and has more than one circuit judge, or in any district that borders on the Gulf of Mexico and has a county with a population in excess of 80,000 in which county there are two cities each with a population in excess of 20,000, an assistant district attorney is permitted, who is appointed by the district attorney with the approval of the circuit judges in the district. The counties selected for detailed survey are shown in the following table:

County (city)	Population, 1960	Section of state	Remarks	Felony defendants, 1962	No. of lawyers in private practice
Pontotoc	17,232	North central	Rural, farming	21	10
DeSoto	23,891	Northwest	Industrial, farming	35	9
Sunflower (Indianola)	45,750	West central	State penitentiary, farming	51	19
Loundes (Columbus)	46,639	East central	Industrial, farming	110	26
Hinds (Jackson)	187,045	Central	Industrial, farming, state capital	190	546
Lauderdale (Meridian)	67,119	East central	Industrial, farming, Navy airbase	63	97
Hancock	14,039	South	Resort, industrial	22	15

B. CRIMINAL PROCEDURE AS IT AFFECTS INDIGENT PERSONS

Jurisdiction to return indictments and try offenses punishable by a fine and/or imprisonment other than in the county farm is vested in the circuit court.

Most felony cases, i.e., crimes punishable by one year of imprisonment or more, begin with the arrest of the suspect. In this type of case, unless the accused waives the preliminary hearing, the accused is given a preliminary hearing within 24 to 48 hours after the arrest. The preliminary hearing is usually conducted by the justice of the peace. He is not required to be an attorney or to have any legal training, and very few are attorneys. At the preliminary hearing, the arrested person is informed of the charge against him, and, if he pleads not guilty, evidence is presented and the justice of the peace decides if there is probable cause to believe that the accused committed the crime. The accused has the opportunity to present witnesses on his behalf and to cross-examine the witnesses of the state. A court reporter is available to make a record of the proceedings at the expense of the accused. If probable cause exists, the accused is bound over to the next term of the county grand jury. The accused may make bond as required by the justice of the peace if the offense is bondable. There is no set amount for each criminal offense. The arrested person may waive the preliminary hearing.

Until *Gideon v. Wainwright,* 372 U.S. 335 (1963), counsel compensated by the state were furnished to indigents only in capital felony cases. There is still no provision for compensation for appointed counsel for their out-of-pocket expenses. Except for some local legal aid groups, the appointed counsel system is the only method of furnishing indigents with counsel in Mississippi. One county made a change after the *Gideon* decision wherein the court would appoint counsel for the indigent person in other than capital felony cases: the circuit judge would enter a court order directing the board of supervisors of the county to pay the attorney a stated amount. This change was made without statutory authority. In two of the other counties, the local bar association would offer its services free for defending indigent accused.

The usual stage at which counsel is made available for an indigent is when the indictment has been returned by the county grand jury and filed but before the arraignment on the indictment. If the criminal offense is a capital felony case, the judge informs the accused that he has the right of counsel at no expense to him, provided he is indigent. The question of indigency is determined by the circuit judge after he has questioned the accused and also the officers of court as to the indigency of the accused. (In one of the sample counties, the circuit judge placed the accused under oath while asking him questions as to his indigency.) If the accused is determined by the circuit judge to be indigent, counsel is appointed, unless the accused waives this right of counsel. Usually counsel is appointed from a list of the local bar association or from attorneys that are present in the courtroom at the time. No set pattern was revealed by this survey. When the accused has counsel appointed, the court allows the appointed counsel ample time to prepare a defense. The courts are usually liberal in granting time for the preparation of the defense.

It is generally the practice that the same counsel that is appointed for the trial of the case conducts the case on appeal. Counsel is not compensated for out-of-pocket expenses either for the trial or on the appeal. A stated sum is provided for the trial of the case and an additional sum is allowed if the case is appealed.

C. OPINIONS OF THE JUDGES

The study included an interview with six circuit judges from the counties personally surveyed. The remaining 11 circuit judges were mailed questionnaires, six of which were returned. Four of the circuit judges felt that under an ideal system counsel should be appointed between arrest and first appearance before a magistrate; two, at first appearance before a magistrate; five, after the filing of an indictment but before arraignment; and one, at arraignment on indictment. All the judges but one felt that it would be unfair to the indigent person if he did not get a lawyer at the stage chosen. One thought that it would "possibly" be unfair.

The circuit judges had varied opinions as to whether, in an ideal system, a lawyer should be provided for the indigent person in sentencing of a defendant who pleaded guilty; sentencing of a defendant convicted by trial; habeas corpus or other postconviction remedy; hearing on revocation of probation; sexual psychopath hearing; and civil commitment of the mentally ill, including alcoholics and narcotics addicts. (See second table in Section F.) None of the judges felt that under an ideal system a lawyer should be appointed for the indigent person charged with a misdemeanor.

A list of the local bar association is the most common system used in selecting a lawyer to represent the indigent defendant, but this is not a uniform practice throughout the state. In one of the districts the local bar association appoints a committee that has the duty of making up a list of lawyers who will defend indigent defendants. This list is made available to the circuit judge. The circuit judge then uses this list and rotates the lawyers on it. One circuit judge appoints an experienced criminal lawyer and a young lawyer to defend the indigent defendant. However, at the time of the survey, this district appointed a lawyer only for the indigent defendant accused of a capital felony. It was generally the practice in the remaining jurisdictions to appoint lawyers for the indigent accused defendant from members of the local bar association who were engaged in the active practice of law.

Until the 1964 session of the state legislature, the state statute provided that an attorney appointed to defend an indigent defendant could be appointed with pay only in capital felony cases. In these cases, the maximum that could be paid was $75 if the defendant pleaded guilty without a trial and $150 if a trial was instituted. If the case was appealed, another $100 could be allowed for the appeal. Under the 1964 amendment, compensation is allowed in non-capital cases at corresponding maximum amounts of $50, $100, and $100. The circuit judge will sometimes appoint two attorneys to represent the indigent defendant. In these cases, the fee is divided between the two lawyers. No additional money is provided by the state for appointing two lawyers.

Among judges who were interviewed, the estimates of the percentage of indigent defendants who waive appointment of counsel ranged from none to 70%. (For district attorneys the range was from none to 80%.)

It seemed to be the general opinion of the circuit judges that the system could be improved by a public defender-type system. One judge felt that the public defender should be elected for each district as the circuit judge is elected. The main concern expressed in regard to this system was that the defendant might take advantage of it and thus take away some of the income of the local lawyers.

D. OPINIONS OF THE DISTRICT ATTORNEYS

Personal interviews were held with 7 district attorneys, and questionnaires were mailed to the remaining 11. Seven of the latter responded. All but two of the district attorneys serve on a part-time basis. The district attorney has the option under state law to conduct his office on a part-time basis at a certain pay or to conduct it on a full-time basis and receive a larger salary. When the district attorney selects the part-time basis, he can conduct civil practice of law. When this option is selected, his firm is prohibited under state law from accepting the defense of criminal cases. Seven of the district attorneys stated that they devoted more than 30 hours per week in their capacity as district attorney, and two devoted between 20 and 29 hours a week. All but one of the district attorneys felt that the funds provided for their office were not adequate. The district attorney who felt that the funds were adequate served the office on a full-time basis. One of the other district attorneys said: "No funds for investigation. No assistant District Attorneys. No public funds for secretarial or office expense. Limited travel allowance."

Most of the district attorneys felt that appointed lawyers either compared favorably or were just as diligent as lawyers retained by the defendant. One district attorney felt that if a lawyer was appointed by the court rather than retained by the defendant, he generally did not handle the job as thoroughly and he was more inclined to speed up the process.

One district attorney stated that he did not disclose any of the contents of the investigative file on the defendant before trial, unless ordered to do so by the court. Most of the other district attorneys, however, said they made their investigative file available to the defendant's attorney when asked.

The district attorneys felt that the lawyers should be compensated for their services for the indigent defendant. The amount suggested for such compensation varied from a nominal amount to a sum equal to the minimum suggested by the state bar association for the defense of such a criminal action.

Most of the district attorneys expressed concern as to a proper method for determining indigency. (For other responses from the district attorneys see Section F.)

E. OPINIONS OF DEFENSE ATTORNEYS

Only two of the questionnaires mailed to defense attorneys were answered. It was the opinion of one of the lawyers that, in view of the ruling of the U.S. Supreme Court, Mississippi should enact a public defender system for the defense of the indigent accused person. It is the opinion of this reporter from talking with lawyers in the state concerning the problem of providing counsel for the indigent that they favored the public defender system.

F. COMPARISONS BETWEEN JUDGES AND DISTRICT ATTORNEYS

The following table summarizes and compares the opinions of judges and district attorneys as to when counsel should first be provided under an ideal system. About half of each group would provide counsel earlier than under the present practice.

	Judges	District attorneys
Total responding	12	9
Ideal stage:		
Between arrest and first appearance	4	1
At first appearance	2	1
At preliminary hearing	0	2
After filing of indictment but before arraignment	5	6*
At arraignment on indictment	1	0

*Includes one district attorney who said this stage or the next one, depending on the circumstances.

The next table shows a comparison of views on providing counsel, under an ideal system, in miscellaneous cases and proceedings. Virtually no one said they would provide counsel for misdemeanors, but opinion was divided on the other proceedings. A higher proportion of judges would provide counsel for sentencing after trial, habeas corpus, hearings on revocation of probation, and civil commitment proceedings.

	Judges			District attorneys		
	Yes	No	Some-times*	Yes	No	Some-times*
Sentencing on a guilty plea	3	6	2	3	6	0
Sentencing after trial	5	2	3	4	4	0
Habeas corpus or other postconviction remedy	6	1	2	4	4	1
Hearing on revocation of probation	4	3	2	1	6	0
Sexual psychopath hearing	6	1	2	5	3	0
Misdemeanors	0	8	1	0	8	0
Civil commitment of mentally ill	5	2	2	2	6	0

* Includes such answers as "only in exceptional cases," "depends on circumstances."

Disposition in Felony Cases
Mississippi, 1962

County	Total sample	Plea guilty	Plea lesser offense	Dismissed	Found guilty	Found guilty lesser degree	Acquitted	Pending	Stet*	Other
Hinds	30	17	7	2	0	0	0	1	2	1
Sunflower	19	12	4	0	1	1	0	1	0	0
Pontotoc	13	7	1	0	1	0	0	4	0	0
Hancock	12	8	1	0	0	1	0	2	0	0
Weighted total percentages		61	15	2	3	3	0	14	1	0

*Held on inactive docket.

Sentencing in Felony Cases
*Mississippi, 1962**

County	Total sample	No sentence		Prison		Probation		Suspended sentence		Fine	
		No.	%	No.	%	No.	%	No.	%	No.	%
Hinds	30	5	17	16	53	3	10	7	23	2	7
Sunflower	19	1	5	17	89	0	0	0	0	2	11
Pontotoc	13	5	38	1	8	4	31	3	23	2	15
Hancock	12	2	17	10	83	0	0	0	0	0	0
Weighted total percentages			19		59		10		12		8

*A combination sentence, such as fine and imprisonment, is recorded under both columns; hence the total is more than 100%.

G. DOCKET STUDY

The docket study, conducted in four of the sample counties, revealed that the most common felonies charged are burglary, forgery, grand larceny, and embezzlement. The records in the circuit clerk's offices were not complete enough to determine whether the various defendants were released on bail, whether they were found to be indigent, or whether they had counsel. The records did show, however, the dispositions of cases, as reported in the two tables opposite. When the figures are projected for the state as a whole, based on the four sample counties, they show that 76% of the defendants pleaded guilty, including 61% who pleaded to the principal offense charged. All of the sample cases that went to trial resulted in convictions, at least of a lesser offense. A very large proportion of those who were convicted, either by plea or trial, were sentenced to terms in prison, including county farm, rather than getting probation or a suspended sentence.

H. CONCLUSIONS AND RECOMMENDATIONS

1. Under the present system of appointed counsel, the counsel is not compensated for out-of-pocket expenses but allowed only a maximum amount for defending a felony case. It is recommended that, if this type of system is to continue, the maximum fee should be increased to meet the standard set by the Mississippi State Bar Association for the defense of the criminal case. It is suggested that the circuit judge should have the authority to allow up to the maximum amount depending on the factual situation of each case.

2. If, due to the decision of *Gideon v. Wainwright*, the state legislature changes the present system of providing attorneys for indigent defendants, it is suggested that a public defender system be considered with a public defender elected for each circuit court district.

140